20 MAY 2014

Ensign Cayaban

Congratulations!

Commander Stinnella

Naval Ceremonies, Customs, and Traditions

SIXTH EDITION

NAVAL CEREMONIES, CUSTOMS, and TRADITIONS

Cdr. Royal W. Connell, USN (Ret.), and
Vice Adm. William P. Mack, USN (Ret.)

NAVAL INSTITUTE PRESS ★ ANNAPOLIS, MARYLAND

Naval Institute Press
291 Wood Road
Annapolis, MD 21402

ISBN-13: 978-1-55750-330-5
Library of Congress Cataloging-in-Publication Data
Connell, Royal W., 1948–
    Naval ceremonies, customs, and traditions / Royal W. Connell and William P.
Mack.—6th ed.
    p. cm.
    Rev. ed. of: Naval ceremonies, and traditions / by William P. Mack and Royal W.
Connell.
    Includes bibliographical references and index.
    ISBN 1-55750-330-3 (alk. paper)
    1. Naval ceremonies, honors, and salutes—United States. 2. Naval art and science—
Terminology. I. Mack, William P., 1915– II. Mack, William P., 1915– Naval ceremonies,
customs, and traditions. III. Title.
    V310.C65 2004
    359.1'336'0973—dc22

                                                                    2003023317

Printed in the United States of America on acid-free paper ⊗
11 10   9 8 7 6 5 4 3

My father, Col. Royal W. Connell, USAF, has been the standard against which I have measured my life. My coauthor for the fifth edition, Vice Adm. William P. Mack, USN, allowed me a brief insight to one of the brilliant military minds of our age. I am deeply sorry his influence in this work could not have been larger. I dedicate my efforts to both of these outstanding men.

Contents

Preface to the Sixth Edition

The fifth edition was written while great changes were occurring in the naval service. Those changes have defined themselves into a trend, and we can see the proposed track laid out for the Navy of the twenty-first century. Therefore, the scope and tenor of the previous edition was sadly out of date and in need of review. Before, we had been content to bring Vice Admiral Lovette's original work up to date. This time, while we have attempted to keep the concept of the original work in mind, the overall product was reviewed and in many instances completely revamped.

Vice Admiral Mack and I conferred before beginning this edition and set our course with certain goals in mind. For instance, we believed that the emphasis on the War of 1812 in previous editions gave short shrift to other deserving eras of U.S. naval history. Likewise, we believed that the section on the Marine Corps was inadequate, and that the Coast Guard had been essentially ignored. For a book covering naval ceremonies, we thought the coverage extended to certain of those ceremonies was insufficient, as was the discussion of formal dining in/out. Both of these areas now have their own chapters. We have excised the section on West Point traditions, partly because of space, and partly because the traditions specific to the Military Academy are worthy of their own work. The Army's traditions in general lie outside the scope of this effort. For similar reasons, we have either omitted or incorporated previous sections on Royal Navy traditions and usage.

Tradition is an ethereal subject to report upon. It is constantly in a state of flux. Today's traditions can easily be forgotten tomorrow, and something we view as simple happenstance might well be tomorrow's long-held tradition. While we have no desire to live in the past, we hold fast to the premise that in order to understand and appreciate who you are and where you are, you must first understand where you came from and from where you draw your legacy.

Additionally, traditions and customs are easier to follow if one has a basic understanding of how they arose. Today's sailors may never go "a-skippin' through the tops," but with this as background, they might appreciate more fully why the boatswain's pipe and the ship's bells are part of the nautical life they now live.

Vice Admiral Mack's passing is a great loss to this work. I pray that this effort is worthy of his approval.

Acknowledgments

To the late Vice Admiral Lovette, USN (Ret.), for leaving us a work of joy and a plethora of material to work from. To the late Vice Admiral Mack USN (Ret.), for his guidance and inspiration. To Vice Adm. Sir Paul Haddacks, Royal Navy, for keeping this "Yank" straight on how our traditional forbears act today. To Col. James W. "Wes" Hammond, USMC (Ret.), for his complete rewrite of the chapter on the U.S. Marine Corps and for allowing me to generously cut and slash his final product. To Capt. Don Van Liew, U.S. Coast Guard (Ret.), for helping me with both research and insight into our sister sea-service.

To Lt. Cdr. Christopher Barnes, USN, for helping me with the role of an aide in today's modern Navy. To Sally Johnston of the Star Spangled Banner Flaghouse, for reviewing my draft of the material on the flag. To Jim Cheevers of the Naval Academy Museum, the staff of the USNA Nimitz Library, and various other officers and staff members for answering myriad off-the-wall questions. To the editors and staff of the Naval Institute for carrying on in the grand tradition of commentary upon things maritime and naval.

And to my wife and family, for indulging me, for without them, I am nothing.

I thank you all.

Naval Ceremonies, Customs, and Traditions

1

CUSTOMS, CEREMONIES, TRADITIONS, AND USAGE

★

1

The Interrelationship of Customs, Ceremonies, Traditions, and Usage

May we not who are of their brotherhood claim that in a small way at least we are partakers of their glory? Certainly it is our duty to keep these traditions alive and in our memory, and to pass them on untarnished to those who come after us.

Rear Adm. Albert Gleaves, USN

The United States Navy has a tradition and a future. We look with pride and confidence in both directions.

Adm. Chester Nimitz, USN

Throughout life, traditions, ceremonies, customs, and usage exert a profound influence upon human behavior. The effect is particularly marked in such professions as the military. Organizations that impose discipline lend themselves to passing on and perpetuating venerated customs, heroic traditions, and dignified ceremonies. Such stimuli, when appreciated and properly applied, inculcate ideals and esprit de corps of incalculable value.

Throughout our society, however, ceremonies are diminishing. Not so long ago, religious, fraternal, and other organizations provided a constant stream of ceremonial punctuation to our lives. Weddings and funerals, anniversary and memorial meetings, speeches and parties, parades and wreath layings have dwindled in popularity. The trend in the hurry-up world we live in is to tone down any recognition of the milestones in life, for a wide variety of reasons: not enough time, too much bother, it seems an imposition on others, and on, and on, and on. But the end result is that we have cheapened the milestones themselves in the process.

The military today, like that of the past, is made up of young people doing an exceptional job under difficult circumstances. Here young sailors stand a terrorist watch on the quarterdeck of USS *Enterprise*.
U.S. Navy (Alisha M. Clay)

Pride in a great tradition serves well in chaotic times. Pride in the "outfit" and knowledge of the exploits of heroic soldiers, sailors, and airmen who have gone before are the warp and weft of tradition; these are the things that impel Americans today to go forth and do likewise. As the English statesman Disraeli said: "Nurture your minds with great thoughts. To believe in the heroic makes heroes."

The naval officer of the twenty-first century is required to devote more and more time to keeping abreast of a profession that becomes increasingly complex with the advance of technology. The personal factor remains strong, however. Human beings still drop bombs and fire missiles, and men and women still must sail on, and under, the seas and fly today's aircraft.

The Navy emphasizes its customs and traditions in times of peace, because the memory of them inspires men and women in times of stress and in battle. The effect that old customs had on the formulation of naval regulations is a marked example of the influence of tested usage. The courtesy of the sea and the worth of ceremony rest mainly on how they bind us to the past and at the same time lend an air of dignity and respect in official relations, whether at home or abroad. There are no greater "goodwill ambassa-dors" than the visits of U.S. ships to foreign ports. Here is where dignified and time-honored nautical ceremonies play their part, because ceremony is to a marked degree the cement of discipline, and upon discipline the service rests. Tradition, when coupled with courage and pride, gives to the officer corps its highest incentive to carry on both in peace and in war. It is good for us to ask ourselves: "Am I living up to the best traditions of those who have gone before?"

The finer traditions of other years provide support and inspiration for the carrying out of the Navy's high mission. An examination, however cursory, of the loyalty and devotion, both individual and collective, to the brother-hood that has passed on gives striking evidence of the tremendous worth of the traditional ethics of the naval code. President Theodore Roosevelt once said: "Every officer in the Navy should feel in each fibre of his being an eager desire to emulate the energy, the professional capacity, the indomitable de-termination, and dauntless scorn of death which marked John Paul Jones above all his fellows." Those who wear the Navy blue will find much that puts iron in character and enhances professional value if they take time to look closely at the brilliant tapestry of naval tradition.

Tradition is especially important in this age when awesome responsibility can be placed on the very young. Young Marines have been required to exe-cute national tasking in situations unique in American experience. In con-flicts such as Desert Storm and Iraqi Freedom, junior officers were launched in aircraft loaded with powerful weapons, and charged with making accurate delivery on military targets. In the uncertain world of fighting an enemy that is no longer identifiable by nationality, but is a faceless terrorist, only a strong grounding in the ways of those who have preceded us will carry us through. Only strong tradition firmly based on a code of ethics and morals can bring military professionals through safely.

Because this work treats custom, ceremonies, tradition, and usage, both in a general sense and in detail, it may be helpful to define the terms. To begin with, *custom* is defined as "repetition of the same act or procedure, established manner or way." Customs are to a major degree authoritative and often stand in the place of law and regulations for the conduct of groups of people. Cus-toms may change, however, as do fashions and manners, either for better or for worse. Custom has an important role in all systems of jurisprudence. An ancient legal maxim states that "custom is the best interpreter of the law."

Usage is best defined in comparison with custom. In its simplest sense, *usage* means an accepted way of acting—hence the English phrase, "ancient

Junior officers are given extremely important responsibilities. An error in judgment could kill countless numbers of innocents. Only professionalism and the sea anchor of traditions such as integrity and honor can stand in the way of disaster.
U.S. Navy (Steve Lightstone)

usages of Parliament." In our present context it is applicable to procedures or ceremonies. Under English law, usage, unlike custom, does not imply immemorial existence or general prevalence. Usage is sometimes considered as the habits of individuals or classes, such as those engaged in a particular trade or business, while custom is seen as the habit of communities or localities. One could therefore say, "The naval *usage* of playing the national anthem at the end of receptions became a *custom* in the community." However, the Navy would say, "It has always been our *custom*."

Usage in the Navy usually refers to matters of general etiquette, social procedures, or correctness in matters of correspondence, generally with the intent of determining the best accepted practice. "Try to do it right," Madame Celnart, an expert on manners, once said. "The grand secret of never-failing propriety of deportment is to have an intention of always doing right." This implies a sincere effort to conform to the best usage at home and abroad, and requires observation and application.

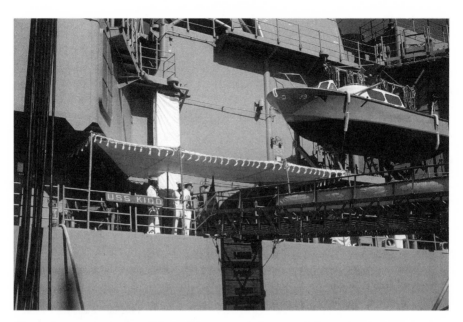

The ancient customs and traditions of the quarterdeck are carried on today.
U.S. Navy (Don S. Montgomery)

Tradition comes from the Latin *tradere*, "to hand down." In the context of the Navy, therefore, we assume that traditions are accumulated experiences and deeds passed on from sailor to sailor "both in memory and reality." Some cynically view tradition as "whatever was being done the day before I entered the service"; it is sometimes said that "it only takes three years to be a tradition at the Naval Academy." But tradition is more than whatever a personal memory can cover.

A secondary definition of tradition, applicable to "members of professions" and others, is "the accumulated experience, advance, or achievement of the past." For the Navy, this accumulated experience, some of which will be shown to date back to man's earliest adventures on the sea, constitutes a huge reservoir of fact and fancy from which has flowed the stream of deeds, ceremonies, and sea language that is our naval heritage. A not altogether regrettable conservatism, typical of all navies, has enabled ours to pass on to future generations our established customs and traditions. For the Navy, they constitute the essence of heroic enterprise, moral fiber, pride in the service, and correct deportment.

Apart from the spiritual value of this legacy, there is one of everyday practicality. Customs of the service have the full effect of law when they fulfill the

The custom of morning and evening colors aboard ship has spread ashore and has become part of the tradition of the nation.

naval legal definition. The *Manual for Courts-Martial* (2000 edition, art. 134) includes this statement in the article "Breach of Custom of the Service": "In its legal sense, 'custom' means more than a method of procedure or a mode of conduct which is merely of frequent or usual occurrence. Custom arises out of long established practices which by common usage have attained the force of law in the military or other community affected by them."

Ceremonies that originated in fear and awe are accepted today in military organizations as dignified gestures of respect to the symbols of the state and the state's officials. Ceremonies are a function of discipline. Definitive regulations exist for important ceremonial occasions and are tributes to worthy tradition. It follows that if the respect for lawful authority and the symbolism of the flag are worthy of preservation, they must be revered by their defenders: half-measures will not do.

A worthy member of the armed forces has pride in uniform, pride in service, and pride in his or her respect for the flag. Of the eighteenth-century British Admiral Lord Jervis, the Earl of St. Vincent, master seaman and classic disciplinarian, Capt. A. T. Mahan writes:

He wisely believed in the value of forms, and was careful to employ them, in this crisis of the mutinies, to enforce the habit of reverence for the insignia of the state and the emblems of military authority. The discipline of the cabin and wardroom officer is the discipline of the fleet, said the admiral [St. Vincent]; and savage almost were the punishments that fell upon officers who disgraced their cloth. The hoisting of the colors, the symbol of power of the nation, from which depended his own and that of all the naval hierarchy, was made an august and imposing ceremony. . . . Lord St. Vincent made a point of attending always, and in full uniform; a detail he did not require of other officers . . . the very atmosphere the seamen breathed was saturated with reverence.

Mahan again relates how Jervis adhered strictly to custom and ceremony:

To pay outward reverence to the national flag, to salute the quarterdeck as the seat of authority, were no vain show under him. "Discipline," he was fond of quoting, "is summed up in the one word, obedience," and these customs were charged with the observance which is obedience in spirit. They conduce to discipline as conventional good manners, by rendering the due of each to each, knit together the social fabric and maintain the regularity and efficiency of common life; removing friction, suppressing jars, and ministering constantly to the smooth and even working of the social machinery.

Ceremonies are sometimes mistakenly neglected, often as the result of personal humility. Particularly in recent years, the sentiments of "I don't want my shipmates to go to any trouble over me" or "I don't want any big ceremony" are heard more and more often. This attitude can actually be quite selfish, as we see when we realize that a ceremony is often not so much for the honoree as it is for the observers. For instance, older relatives facing impending death, in an effort to spare their survivors pain, sometimes will state that they do not want a funeral to be held, thinking that a funeral means much crying and mourning the loss of the loved one. In fact, such a funerary ceremony can provide a comforting sense of closure to those left behind, a reassurance of either a resurrection or other reuniting that brings peace to those who mourn. An individual receiving a promotion or a medal for his or her actions serves as an example to others in addition to being recognized for individual performance. To cheat those shipmates out of seeing the ceremonial recognition is to be very self-serving. While it may be human nature or the "aw shucks, ma'am" aspect of American culture not to want to be paraded in front of one's family and friends, such refusal also denies them

Three former prisoners of war (POWs) are decorated in ceremonies to honor their actions and contributions during Desert Storm.
U.S. Navy (Jeff Elliott)

the chance to pay well-deserved homage and therefore lessens in their minds the importance of the action or service being recognized.

There is also a practical justification for the fostering of traditional customs. Think of the difficulty should the officer of the deck be left to decide on each occasion whether the starboard or port side should be the ceremonial side, whether or not to "sound taps" at a funeral, or what side of the quarterdeck should be cleared for the captain. Early customs became established traditions and exact regulations.

When should we change custom and usage? Whenever such change is necessary. A reactionary spirit is only to be commended when it clings to an old tradition, custom, or usage, in certainty that a change will bring about neither enlightenment nor improvement.

Capt. Mahan in his essay *Military Rule of Obedience* wrote that "the value of tradition to the social body is immense. The veneration for practices, or for authority, consecrated by long acceptance, has a reserve of strength which cannot be obtained by any novel device. Respect for the old customs is planted deep in the hearts, as well as in the intelligence, of all inheritors of English-speaking polity."

A modern sailor pays tribute to a venerable part of today's Navy, the USS *Constitution* under sail celebrating the two-hundredth anniversary of her commissioning. U.S. Navy (John E. Gay)

The "reserve of strength" pointed out by Mahan should be pondered by the commissioned personnel of each generation. The outstanding officers of the service, from the days of the infant Navy, have never failed to recognize the power of tradition. In a desire to emulate the progenitors of tradition, they become imbued with some of the spirit that prompted the original words and deeds: an imponderable but vital factor that so influences morale that people often die without complaint when they have full knowledge that they have done their duty for country and organization, like those who went before. "Fight her till she sinks and don't give up the ship"; "Damn the torpedoes, full speed ahead"; "I have not yet begun to fight"; "We are ready now"; "Take her down"; and "Attack! Attack!" are not mere words of sound and fury but rather expressions that carry lofty overtones of valor, self-sacrifice, and proud glory. They are the essence of priceless tradition.

Worthy traditions also cause the voice of conscience to whisper to the patriot: "Can you go and do likewise?" Fate may decide for someone on active service whether the ordeal of decision comes early or late. There may be no

A ceremonial guard seaman renders honors during a retirement ceremony.
U.S. Navy (Johnny Bivera)

fame or glory, for the decision may result only in deeds and actions that will bring fame and glory to others. There may be painful personal decisions that involve friends, loved ones, and shipmates, yet whether those decisions are made in the face of death or in a time of peace, the remembrance of the traditions of honor and duty that have ever characterized the service will bring to mind the principle that should prevail: *Is what I am about to do in keeping with the "highest traditions of the United States naval service"?*

The highest praise that can be paid to officers or enlisted at retirement or death is the recognition that they lived and worked according to the best traditions of the service. Those who would live squarely up to this superlative code should early in their careers know something of its most distinguished exemplars—particularly, their contributions to the defense of the Republic, and the heritage they have bequeathed to the successive generations who will wear the uniform.

The Development of Tradition
in the Early Navy, 1775–1915

What you from your fathers have inherited,
Earn it, in order to possess it.

Johann Wolfgang von Goethe

The American Navy was born in 1775 at the start of the Revolutionary War. It was originally a collection of private ship owners fighting directly for General Washington. They met with some success, capturing a total of thirty-three British prizes before being incorporated into the Continental Navy. Congress established its Marine Committee in October 1775 and the committee, in turn, appropriated money to purchase several ships. However, most of the success of the early maritime service was due to private efforts. The building of privateers by private shipyards along the Chesapeake Bay shore began immediately, and by the time the war ended, some two thousand ships had been built and manned by private citizens. They ranged in size from pulling barges to good-sized schooners and throughout the war continued to harass the British naval vessels with great success. They were fast and rugged, and manned by experienced and seagoing sailors, mostly from the fishing fleets.

The birth of the Navy was at once exciting and traumatic. While our "Yankee" sailors had beaten the most vaunted navy of the world, the Americans had by no means established themselves in its place. England had other political dangers and military and naval threats to look toward, and the loss of an upstart bunch of colonies was of little import in the then-current world view. Besides, the reacquisition of the colonies was deemed to be not only inevitable, but simply a matter of concentration of will toward that goal.

John Paul Jones's ship the *Bon Homme Richard*
Naval Institute Photo Archive

From the fledgling American Navy's point of view, its ship-building and -handling skills were vindicated in the court of world affairs, and it was justifiably proud of its first major victory. America's own political process, however, interfered with the celebratory mood. With the end of the war and the responsibility of building a new government from scratch with no ability to levy taxes, quickly came the realization that a standing navy was expensive to operate. Coupled with the recognition that the country had not fought the war to become a world power but to relieve the oppression of the injustices of the British crown, the Navy became a perceived luxury. Simple existence was the national goal, and the Navy was discarded as superfluous.

From the parental Royal Navy, the nascent American Navy learned the organization and ways and means of operations, including the naval traditions and customs. It remained to the sailors and officers of this new force to develop this legacy in their own way. Captains, officers, and enlisted men established traditions by their performance. These could be seen by others and emulated in subsequent actions. With the passage of time a body of traditions evolved. The revolutionary birth of the Navy was replete with examples of heroic tradition. John Paul Jones led the popular list. We shall not here recount a history of battles and accomplishments; suffice it to state

Action between the *Constitution* and the *Guerriere*, War of 1812

that once separated from the "mother country," Americans did as all youth do and followed their own path.

The new country quickly learned that it could not remain apart from the world's intervention. Under British protection, American merchants had plied the seas and traded in the world's markets. Without that overarching shield, they were prey to all manner of restrictions. National and individual irritants intervened, and Americans were forced to find means of dealing with them. The realities of such confrontations as the quasi-war with France, the Barbary pirates, and the pirates about America's own southern coasts caused the young nation to reinvent the Navy.

The Navy Act of 1794 appropriated a substantial mount of money for the building of six large frigates—in essence, authorizing a navy for the first time in over a decade. Joshua Humphreys, a Philadelphia shipyard owner, was appointed supervisor of shipbuilding for the Navy. He designed a vessel that was larger and carried more guns than any of the British frigates. It was designed with a very large and heavy hull made of 12-inch oak ribs and lon-gitudinals and fitted with a new system of diagonal scantlings placed be-tween the ribs. The outside planking and decking were also unusually strong. The ships were long and low, and still maintained more speed than

Perry's victory on Lake Erie: Perry's
battle flag and a copy of his dispatch
to Gen. William Henry Harrison

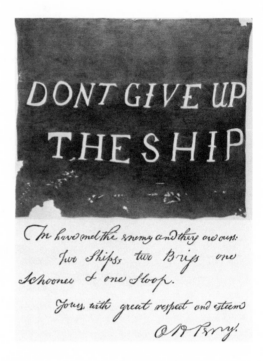

the British ships. The result was a strong-hulled ship that could resist all of
the British guns.

The first of these so-called Humphreys frigates, the *United States,* was
called "Old Ironsides" by the British when she turned away all the British
frigate guns. The *Constitution* was later given the same sobriquet. The British
were so exasperated that they eventually refused to send their ships of the
line to sea against the six American large frigates. These ships ruled the seas
throughout three wars, and the *Constitution* exists today as a living tradition.

Over and above troubles with the Barbary pirates, relations with other
European navies, and the establishment of a trans-Pacific trade, the American merchant marine began to flourish, requiring more naval protection.
The British forays into U.S. trade with the Orders in Council of 1793 and
onto the American continent in 1812 were impossible for the young nation to
ignore, and by the first quarter of the nineteenth century, the United States
was fully engaged in maintaining its Navy.

World trade further opened up the country to international intervention,
requiring naval power. As the United States became a trade destination and
origin, it was faced with the need for defense of its sailing merchants. The
development of the clipper trade and, later, oceanic steamships brought with

it more need for the Navy to grow and mature. The U.S. Navy slowly began to flex its muscle and widen its horizons. From a beginning as sailors serving with sea-going soldiers whose role was primarily security and close-order defense, the Navy–Marine Corps relationship became more equal with the beginnings of the amphibious warfare doctrine first on the "shores of Tripoli" and later at the "halls of Montezuma." U.S. ships ranged the world and were instrumental in diplomatic as well as tactical confrontations. America established its presence in the Orient with Perry's opening of Japan and with negotiations with China and Korea over the treatment of American merchants and sailors.

By the time the Civil War broke out in 1861, the U.S. Navy was starting to shut down the slave trade from Africa and to become accepted as an ally, if not an equal, by the major navies of the world. The U.S. Navy operated in conjunction with the Royal Navy off Africa and India, and with the French and Italians in the Mediterranean.

As America was the world's first democratic republic, it was also the first to have that government placed on trial by its own people. The rest of the world watched the American Civil War with interest to see not only the military and technological developments but the political outcome as well. The nation did not disappoint on either count. The experiment in democracy stood the test, and Americans were reunited. And the technological growth was stupendous, from such creature comforts as the development of foods packed in tin cans to medical breakthroughs in the treatment of wounds and disease. The Civil War was a war of firsts. In the area of naval warfare, particularly, America was the world's tutor. In the first battles between the new iron-clad ships, as in the improvements in naval weapons from the Dahlgren gun to rifled barrels, from turrets to underwater mines, and from submersibles to spar-torpedoes, America provided grist for the mill of world military study.

The Civil War was first in another area: it was the first major war to be fought with what we now refer to as "modern" warfare techniques. No longer was a military force content to defeat the enemy, he must now be destroyed. No longer would a vanquished foe admit defeat, as in earlier eras, but he would keep fighting at another time, in another place, and with renewed vigor. War became a condition where multitudes of men died in long-drawn-out conflicts of all-out war without the tempering of Marquis of Queensberry rules. Tactics ashore included the scorched earth of Sherman marching through Georgia, while at sea the Navy honed skills in blockade, amphibious support of the Army, and the hunting down of commerce

Though not the first iron-clads, the *Monitor* and the *Virginia* (ex-*Merrimac*) at the Battle of Hampton Roads were the first iron-clads to fight each other. The significance of the engagement was not only the tactical draw, but the innovations in naval warfare.
Naval Institute Photo Archive

raiders, such as the CSS *Alabama*. War has never been a civilized affair, but the Civil War was incrementally uncivil.

Following that war, the United States again learned that major war was expensive and that short-term savings could be realized by eliminating the bulk of the Navy. The rest of the watching world had learned vicariously that warfare had changed, and they set about to gain preeminence in that endeavor. So while the U.S. Navy decommissioned its most modern warships, other countries began to build newer and better models. Battleships became the capital ships of the fleet. Breech-loading guns, screw-driven ships, oil-fired boilers, new hull designs, and innovations like compartmentation all made their mark.

The U.S. Navy's fate was not without bright spots, however. Naval thought and education became the watchword in the new, smaller Navy. Innovators such as Adm. David Dixon Porter, Commodore Stephen B. Luce, and Captain Mahan began to stress upgraded education for officers and sailors. In response to the world's new path of naval development and tactics, the Naval Academy offered more of a technical education than the simple prewar school of seamanship and associated skills. The Naval Institute began its long

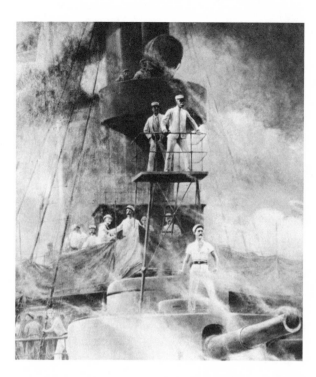

Dewey at Manila Bay

run of exploration of naval thought; the Naval War College was created and began to broaden senior officers' thoughts beyond the tactical to strategic thinking; and enlisted men, for the first time, were given standardized training before going to sea. Mahanian doctrine was debated in wardrooms around the world, and much of world and naval history of the first half of the twentieth century was an outgrowth of this renaissance of maritime discussion.

The newly renovated and well-trained and -led American fleet shocked the world by defeating the Spanish and leaping into prominence. Theodore Roosevelt's Great White Fleet signaled a new attitude in U.S. foreign policy, and the future of the Navy was now dawning brightly. New inventions kept expanding the world of naval warfare. From submarines to airplanes, the turn of the twentieth century promised amazing growth of technology and the demand for leaders to be equal to the tools they now had at their disposal. With each new technological innovation came the requirement to develop its counterweapon. Submarines therefore led to destroyers, mines to minesweeping, and aircraft to proximity fuses. These new technologies became their own sources of traditions. Actions in individual ships were replaced by actions of fleet commanders. Nevertheless, the customs and traditions of the old days were still followed and revered by those who came along.

Throughout the course of our nation's history, the Navy has been a sentry against world intervention. That experience has caused the Navy to develop into a modern fighting force, existing only because of its own success. Indeed, if the Navy had failed at any time during our history, the nation would have had a hard time standing. That lesson must not be forgotten in good times or ignored during times of threat.

Likewise, the timeline of naval custom and tradition continues and constantly grows. We can, and sometimes do, these days, say that there is no need to follow tradition. We have all heard the complaints that custom is restricting, difficult to maintain, and sometimes expensive. The problem is one of perspective. Customs and traditions are the comfortable clothes in which we honor the legacy of our forebears and the ways of the sea. They provide the color and texture of our lives, without which we would exist in a sterile and joyless state. More important, they become the means of educating our followers as to their heritage. Finally, they are the routines we fall back on in times of challenge. In the aftermath of the attacks on Pearl Harbor, on the Marine barracks in Beirut, on the USS *Cole,* or on the World Trade Center and the Pentagon, traditions and customs give us a daily framework to hang our grief upon while we go about the business of rebuilding and renewing our resolve to overcome all obstacles.

In recent times officers and enlisted personnel in the armed forces have been individually and collectively tested in the crucible of the prisoner-of-war atmosphere. Beginning in World War II with the Japanese, and continuing with the North Koreans during the Korean War, torture, harsh illegal treatment, and political abuse of prisoners reached a new high. The majority of prisoners in those days were young, ill-prepared Army infantrymen. It was to be expected that they would offer little resistance to torture. After the Korean War, the Defense Department was unable to document a single case of successful resistance to torture.

Given the relative lack of awareness and understanding of the requirements of the Geneva Convention on the treatment and requirements of prisoners of war in the Korean War, President Eisenhower established the Code of Conduct for the military. Although it nominally allowed more than the "Big Four and nothing more," it implied that to stray beyond that was disloyalty to the country and a breaking of faith with one's comrades.

In the Vietnam War a large percentage of prisoners held by the enemy were Navy and Air Force pilots of middle rank. Most had college educations, and many were products of the service academies. In spite of the severity and bestiality of North Vietnamese torture for periods as long as seven years,

Naval personnel who become prisoners of war must be prepared to resist their captors in the traditional ways established by those who were captives of the North Vietnamese.

many officers were able to resist successfully. The rigidity of the Code of Conduct gave way to a more reasoned resistance, based upon the reality of being treated as common criminals rather than being respected as prisoners of war. The evolved interpretation asked that the POWs make their captors work for every scrap of knowledge and that they bounce back as soon as they could after such admission. Men such as James Stockdale, Jeremiah Denton, William Lawrence, and John McCain took the worst the enemy could offer and at the same time offered outstanding leadership to their more junior campmates. At the end of long confinement they came home to heroes' welcomes and continued their careers in public service. Vice Admiral Stockdale publicly credited his ability to resist and to perform far beyond the call of duty to his Naval Academy training. For him, tradition provided strong moral guidance in an atmosphere of uncertainty. Others reported similar reactions.

Naval traditions have even reached into space. With the large numbers of naval officers involved in the astronaut program, it would seem inevitable that their background would come out. And indeed it did. When the International Space Station was placed in orbit, the first commander, William Shephard, began a custom of rendering arrival and departure honors, complete with a ship's bell, to space shuttle commanders bringing relief crews

A Marine flag appears in the wreckage of the Pentagon on September 11, 2001, after a terrorist attack that left 189 dead. Among the horrors of that day and the mourning for those lost, the recovery of these "colors" provided a welcome emotional anchor. U.S. Navy (Michael W. Pendergrass)

and supplies. He also started a "ship's log" called the Alpha Log as a record of conditions and happenings aboard the ISS.

For the newest ensign taking the ship's conn for the first time or the chief of naval operations trying to rally the morale of forces in the face of more and more horrible and unimaginable assaults on our brothers and sisters, customs and traditions bring comfort in the daily routine and allow us to go on in the face of extreme adversity. They are at once old and familiar and new and evolving, and they help define our identity and our character.

3

The Development of the Laws of the Service

Herein are the good ordinances of the sea, which wise men, who voyaged round the world, gave to our ancestors, and which constitute the books of the science of good customs.

The Consulate of the Sea

Let the law never be contradictory to custom: for if the custom is good, the law is worthless.

Voltaire, *Philosophical Dictionary*

Ever since the beginning of navies, there have been laws peculiarly applicable to the sea and seafaring people.

Rear Adm. Albert E. Jarrell, USN

The very first American naval articles of discipline were adopted by the Continental Congress on 28 November 1775. The infant Navy was administered by a committee of Congress, called the Marine Committee, and to John Adams of this committee was given the task of drafting the first rules of the Navy. He modeled these rules after existing British regulations. Although John Paul Jones considered them inadequate, they served for the period of the Revolutionary War. On 2 March 1779 a code of fifty articles was made effective.

Eleven of the original thirteen states fitted out one or more armed vessels. New Jersey and Delaware were the two exceptions. Various state laws were enacted relative to discipline, prizes, and general administration. The largest forces were maintained by Massachusetts, Connecticut, Pennsylvania, Maryland, Virginia, and South Carolina. New Hampshire had only one ship, and Georgia commissioned four galleys. No state navy was as large as that of the Navy authorized by Congress, but their work was in most cases effective, and their deeds belong to the common naval tradition.

Despite the excellent performance of the American Navy in the Revolutionary War, public interest and congressional sympathy grew cold to the needs of a naval service, and by 1785 the last ship of the fleet had been disposed of. In the establishment of the new federal government, no provisions in the way of laws or regulations were made for the Navy. It was not until 1798 that a Naval Department was formed, and we may consider that this year marks the beginning of the permanent service that has been maintained ever since. In the same year were drafted the *Articles for the Government of the Navy.* All the discipline and justice of the Navy until 1951 derived from these *Articles,* called "Rocks and Shoals" by generations of sailors.

To establish the historic background for our naval law, we must first examine the development of ancient customs and laws of the sea that had merged with the British naval regulations, such as those in force at the time of the American Revolution.

Although no definite organization that could properly be called an English Navy existed until the late Middle Ages, an organization did exist known as the "King's Ships." The quaint title "Keeper of the King's Ships" appears upon an appointment made by King John of England. In time, Lords of the Admiralty were created to carry on the duties of the Keeper. The titles "Keeper and Governor of the King's Ships" and "Clerk of the King's Ships" survived until the late sixteenth century. Early English sea power was, in reality, a fleet of private donations. The King owned a few ships, but the towns of the Cinque Ports (Hythe, Romney, Hastings, Dover, and Sandwich) were obliged, in return for royal favors, to furnish the King with fifty-seven vessels upon request.

This maritime power of England was governed for many years by the general tenets of the Code of Oleron. The Laws of Oleron were based upon the sea law of the republic of Rhodes, derived from old Roman law and codified previously by other Mediterranean cities and states. This code was one of five or six existing codes of the time. It is recorded that Richard Coeur de Lion used it at Marseilles in 1190 while awaiting transport for his Crusade to the Holy Land. William de Forz of Oleron, who was one of the five commanders of Richard I on this expedition and afterward became one of the justiciaries of the English Navy, was probably instrumental in urging its adoption. Alphonso X introduced and adopted the same code in Castile in the thirteenth century. It was Richard I, after his return from the Crusades, who introduced the Code of Oleron (with additions) to England. The Code of Oleron was originally compiled and promulgated by Eleanor of Aquitaine, mother of Richard I of England. Parts of the Code were embraced in manuscripts of the fifteenth century, collectively called the *Black Book of the Admiralty*.

The original *Black Book*, a most valuable legal codification, was lost at the end of the eighteenth century but fortunately was found in 1874 in an old chest. Inasmuch as it was the basis of British sea law, a brief description of this rare book may be of interest. It was written in Norman French, which at that time was the language of court as well as of judicial and legal proceedings. The first part of the book dates from the reign of Edward III; the latter belongs to the reigns of Henry IV, Henry V, and Henry VI. E. Keble Chatterton, in his book *Sailing the Seas*, writes in regard to the *Black Book*, "What immediately interests us is that we see order emerging out of chaos."

A few of the laws of the Code of Oleron illustrate the punishments of that day:

> Anyone that should kill another on board ship should be tied to the dead body and thrown into the sea.
> Anyone that should kill another on land should be tied to the dead body and buried with it in the earth.
> Anyone lawfully convicted of drawing a knife or other weapon with intent to strike another, or of striking another so as to draw blood, should lose his hand.
> Anyone lawfully convicted of theft should have his head shaved and boiling pitch poured upon it and feathers or down should then be strewn upon it for the distinguishing of the offender; and upon the first occasion he should be put ashore.

The duties of an admiral in the fifteenth century were manifold, and he exercised autocratic authority. The very power of creating a navy was delegated to him, as well as the power to appoint lieutenants, to impress ships and men of the kingdom, and to administer justice "according to the law and ancient customs of the sea."

These beginnings of definitive rules and punishments led to "orders for war." They in time were merged with maritime law, such as was embraced in the Code of Oleron and Laws of Wisby. (The Laws of Wisby were the sea law of the northern maritime countries of Europe as adopted in the island of Gotland in the Baltic. Some writers claim these laws antedate the Code of Oleron.)

Although British authorities trace the descent of English men-o'-war and men-o'-war's men from the "buscarles" or sea police of nine centuries ago, it was not until the time of Henry VIII and his daughter Queen Elizabeth that the Royal Navy was shaped as an administrative entity with a book of *Orders for War*. Sir Thomas Dudley, an aide to Henry VIII, framed the first book of *Orders of War* to be used on land and sea. One of the instructions was: "First, the laws which be written what every man ought to do in the ship towards his Captain to be set in the main mast in parchment to be read as occasion shall serve." On the fourth offense of a man sleeping on watch the following "mild" punishment was ordered: "Being taken asleep he shall be hanged to the bowsprit end of the ship in a basket, with a can of beer, a loaf of bread, and a sharp knife, and choose to hang there until he starve or cut himself into the sea."

There are to be found during this period certain special instructions, such as those issued by the Earl of Essex and by Lord Howard of Effingham during the Cadiz Expedition. These instructions consisted of twenty-nine articles. They were to be "openly read" twice each week. The first article ordered that religious exercises take place twice each day. Another article said that the watch was "to be set every night by eight of the clock, either by trumpets or drum and singing the Lord's Prayer, some of the Psalms of David, or clearing the glass."

Punishments have been anything but uniform throughout the years. The punishments of the early years were often cruel and drastic, and as late as 1750 more death sentence offenses were added, while the practice of flogging was exercised on the slightest pretext. For example, for blasphemy, by the Code of Oleron, the offender was fined in silver. In the early seventeenth century, the offender was gagged and his tongue scraped; in 1644, an order stated that blasphemy was to be punished by burning the tongue of the offender with a red-hot iron. The strong religious instinct may be clearly followed through the Elizabethan and post-Elizabethan age in the reverence shown for the Scriptures, and in the severe sentences for impiety and blasphemy. But in the seventeenth and eighteenth centuries the religious fever of former days was disappearing.

The Elizabethan period of maritime history gives the first inkling of some system of standardized discipline. The court-martial is the present-day heir of the Curia Militaris, or Court of Chivalry, called also the Marshal's Court. This was originally the only military court that was established by the laws of England.

There is no etymological connection between the words *martial* and *marshal*. The former is derived from the Latin adjective *martialis* meaning "sacred

A court-martial on deck
Heck's Iconographic Encyclopedia

to Mars or pertaining to him." The latter comes from the Old English *mearh scalc,* which meant literally "horse boy," but was the title of a high officer at the Saxon court.

Originally the Marshal's Court was held before the Lord High Constable and the Earl Marshal jointly. In the reign of Henry VIII, the office of Lord High Constable was eliminated, and all cases regarding civil matters of the military were held before the Earl Marshal.

The court by statute (13 Richard II, c. 5) had jurisdiction over "contracts and other matters touching deeds of arms and war" both within the kingdom and without. Originally it was purely a military court, or court of honor, when held before the Earl Marshal, and a criminal court when held before the Lord High Constable. Because of their weak jurisdiction and lack of power to enjoin their judgments, and because they were not courts of record, both courts fell into disuse.

The constitution of military courts as we know them was adopted by ordinance in the reign of Charles I, and was in a great measure borrowed from the *Articles of War* of Gustavus Adolphus. Their adoption was expedited by

the mutiny of a number of English and Scottish dragoons that had been ordered to Holland to replace certain Dutch troops ordered to England.

The first statutes setting forth the courts-martial are found in the original Mutiny Act of 1689 (I William and Mary, c. 5). This act was annually renewed "for the regulation of the Army." (The reason for the annual passing
of the Army Act or Mutiny Act is that the existence of a standing army in
Britain is prohibited. The existence of the army is authorized by the act. If
the King fails to call Parliament one year, the act lapses and the army discipline is void, so that the army cannot be used for oppressing the people in
the absence of Parliament.) By this act the sovereign was authorized to
grant, when he desired, "commission, under his royal sign manual," giving
to any officer not under the rank of a field-officer authorization for holding
a general court-martial. It further provided that he could by warrant give the
Lord Lieutenant of Ireland, the governor of Gibraltar, or governors of "any
of the dominions beyond the sea" necessary authority to appoint courts-
martial.

Although it has been over three hundred years since those statutes were
enacted, they are still the source of military law of the English-speaking
peoples. They exist in modified form in the United States, and many striking similarities will be found in a comparison of these statutes of 1689 and
our own courts-martial system of precepts and jurisdiction.

Naval law and military law in England originally had many wide diver-
gences. In the early days, the Lord High Admiral issued the instructions and
regulations of both the Royal and the Merchant Navy. Commanders administered at their discretion naval law under the general instructions of the Lord
High Admiral. Sentences at times were excessive: death sentences were even
given in peacetime at the discretion of the commanders. Blackstone says, "If
anyone that hath commission of martial authority doth, in time of peace,
hang, or otherwise execute any man by colour of martial law, this is murder;
for it is against Magna Charta."

The first regular naval tribunal was instituted by the leaders of the Long
Parliament in 1645. They passed a measure called "An Ordinance and Article of Martial Law for the Government of the Navy." This act for the first
time authorized "general and ships' courts-martial with written records,"
the former for captains and commanders, and the latter for subordinate
officers and men. It was in a later law (Art. 13, Charles II, c. 9) that the Lord
High Admiral was given the power to issue commissions (precepts) to officers to hold courts-martial. The first *Articles of War* for the Royal Navy were
promulgated in the rule of Cromwell; these were gathered from a collation

The brig. The two men are secured to the iron rod by leg irons.
Heck's Iconographic Encyclopedia

of pertinent instructions issued by admirals in command, and were approved about 1661 during the reign of Charles II. In 1749 Parliament enacted new *Articles of War,* mainly through the efforts of Lord Anson. These articles incorporated many death penalties, and without doubt this accounts for the numerous death penalties in our own *Articles for the Government of the Navy.*

The Cromwellian *Articles of War* were not sufficient for naval administration. Commanders of the fleet and their immediate subordinates found it necessary from time to time to issue instructions and "details of service and discipline." With these instructions as a foundation, and guided by the best usage and customs of the sea, there appeared in 1731 the first issue of the *King's Regulations and Admiralty Instructions.*

British naval law, maritime history, and general sea traditions were common knowledge to the educated and well informed in the American seaboard colonies. British maritime law as well as common law was the existing law of the Colonies; furthermore, colonials, both officers and men, had served in the Royal Navy.

One of the staunchest supporters of the newborn Navy in the Continental Congress was John Adams who compiled the *Rules for the Regulation of the Navy of the United Colonies,* adopted by the Continental Congress on 28 November 1775. These *Rules* formed the basic articles of the government of the Navy, and inadequate as they were, they served during the period of the

Flogging a seaman. The seaman to be flogged is lashed to a grating, while the petty officer with the cat-o'-nine-tails stands ready to administer the punishment. By George Cruikshank, 1825, from *Old Ship Prints* by E. Keble Chatterton

Revolution. Adams always showed a keen interest in matters maritime, and although he had no experience as a sea officer, as a lawyer he had considerable knowledge of the legal aspects of military and naval discipline, and knew something of the Admiralty law of England. He used this as his guide for the first *Rules* of our service. In some places the regulations were quoted verbatim, while in other cases slight modifications were necessary.

To augment the new *Rules and Regulations,* individual letters of instruction were issued to commanding officers, with directions such as "Use your people well, but preserve strict discipline; treat prisoners if any you make with humanity; and in all things be duly attentive to the honor and interest of America." (This passage comes from a letter of 23 August 1776, now preserved in the Library of Congress, and written to Lieutenant John Baldwin, commander of the schooner *Wasp.*)

In a letter of 1 November 1776, Captain Elisha Warren of the Continental sloop *Fly* was told: "Although we recommend your taking good care of your vessel and people, yet we should deem it more praiseworthy in an officer to lose his vessel in a bold enterprise than to lose a good prize by too timid a conduct."

The 1775 articles, or *Rules* as they were called, comprised about forty paragraphs. They sketchily defined the rights and the duties of officers, the reports required, and certain punishments for infractions of the rules. Flogging was sanctioned, and the issue of rum was authorized: one half-pint per day for each man. (The U.S. Navy was the first of the navies of the world to abolish flogging and other inhumane punishments.)

Some of the regulations in the *Rules* of 1775 were very interesting from our "modern" point of view. The third and fourth articles read:

> If any shall be heard to swear, curse, or blaspheme the name of God, the Commander is strictly enjoined to punish them for every offense by causing them to wear a wooden collar or some shameful badge, for so long a time as he shall judge proper.
>
> No commander shall inflict any punishments upon a seaman beyond twelve lashes upon his bare back with a cat-o'-nine-tails; if the fault shall deserve a greater punishment, he is to apply to the Commander-in-Chief of the Navy in order to the trying of him by a Court-Martial, and in the meantime, he may put him under confinement.

The 1775 articles had a general declaration that covered extraordinary offenses as well as those not otherwise covered. This regulation reads: "All other faults, disorders, and misdemeanors which shall be committed on any ship belonging to the thirteen United Colonies, and which are not herein mentioned shall be punished according to the laws and customs in such cases at sea."

The lawmakers of the United States were fervently occupied at this time with the codification of federal law. Penalties and offenses became definitive. British customs and usage served as a general precedent in the lawmaking of the legislative assemblies. In this connection, it is notable that in keeping with the British legal system and the fact that British common law is unwritten law, the *Queen's Regulations and Admiralty Instructions,* as well as the *Naval Discipline Acts* (corresponding to U.S. *Articles for the Government of the Navy*) referred to "customs of the sea." Section 44 of the *Naval Discipline Acts* stated that persons should be proceeded against and punished "according to the laws and customs used at sea." The *Naval Discipline Acts* also included a cover-all, known as the "Captain's Cloak": "Every person subject to the act who shall be guilty of any act, disorder, or neglect to the prejudice of good order and naval discipline not hereinbefore specified, shall be dismissed from His Majesty's Service with disgrace, or suffer such other punishment as is hereinafter mentioned."

Although section 44 was repealed by the Armed Forces Act in 1971, section 39 of the *Naval Discipline Acts* still has the cover-all governing acts "prejudicial to good order and discipline." The old form of the first of the original *Articles for the Government of the Navy* was as follows:

> The commanders of all ships and vessels belonging to the thirteen United Colonies are strictly required to shew in themselves a good example of honor and virtue to their officers and men, and to be very vigilant in inspecting the behavior of all such as are under them, and to discountenance and suppress all dissolute, immoral, and disorderly practice, and also such as are contrary to the rules of discipline and obedience, and to correct those who are guilty of the same, according to the usage of the sea.

With little change, Article 1131 of *Naval Regulations* reads:

> All commanding officers and others in authority in the naval service are required to show in themselves a good example of virtue, honor, patriotism, and subordination; to be vigilant in inspecting the conduct of all persons who are placed under their command; to guard against and suppress all dissolute and immoral practices, and to correct, according to the laws and regulations of the Navy, all persons who are guilty of them; and to take all necessary and proper measures, under the laws, regulations, and customs of the naval service, to promote and safeguard the morale, the physical well-being, and the general welfare of the officers and enlisted persons under their command or charge.

Various other British regulations were embodied in the 1798 *Naval Regulations.* The following quotations show striking similarity:

REGULATIONS AND INSTRUCTIONS
RELATING TO HIS MAJESTY'S SERVICE AT SEA
Printed in the Year 1790

The Cook

[The cook was an important warrant officer at that time. For many years the duties of the midshipmen were listed in the *Naval Regulations* after those of the cook. The "watering," or soaking, of meat was an attempt to remove the salt.]

Article I

The Cook is to have the charge of the Steep-Tub and to be answerable for the meat put therein, if any part thereof shall be lost through his want of care.

II

He is to see the meat duly watered and the provisions carefully and cleanly boiled, and issued to the men according to the practice of the Navy.

NAVAL REGULATIONS

ISSUED BY COMMAND OF THE PRESIDENT OF THE

UNITED STATES OF AMERICA

January 25, 1802

Of the Duties of a Cook

1. He is to have charge of the steep tub, and is answerable for the meat put therein.

2. He is to see the meat duly watered, and the provisions carefully boiled, and delivered to the men according to the practice of the Navy.

On reflection, it is obvious why a small, newborn navy of identical race and language should copy and adhere to many of the regulations and customs of what was then called the "English Fleet" or the British Navy. Britain claimed the mastery of the seas and was the undisputed master after crushing the French and Spanish navies at Trafalgar (1805). In 1812 the London *Times* reported that the British Navy outnumbered the U.S. Navy seven to one in armament. At the time, as Theodore Roosevelt later wrote in his *Naval War of 1812*, "there was little to choose between a Yankee and a Briton. Both were cold and hardy, cool and intelligent, quick with their hands, and showing at their best in an emergency. They looked alike and spoke alike; when they took the trouble to think, they thought alike; and when they got drunk, which was not an infrequent occurrence, they quarreled alike."

On 31 May 1951 the *Articles of War* of the Army, the *Articles for the Government of the Navy,* and the *Disciplinary Laws of the Coast Guard* were superseded by the *Uniform Code of Military Justice.* The Navy said farewell to the articles under which it had, with good discipline, high morale, and superb leadership, fought so successfully. Many of the new naval regulations and instructions conformed, in spirit if not in letter, to the venerable "constitution" of the Navy.

The Navy and flogging. Capt. Uriah P. Levy exhibits the cat-o'-nine-tails and describes its use to a group of statesmen in Washington, D.C. The abolition of corporal punishment in the U.S. Navy was largely due to his efforts. Until 1881 the cat-o'-nine-tails was used frequently for various breaches of discipline.
Puck's Pictorial History

Why the change? The short answer is that after World War II, when the Department of Defense was created, strong pressure was brought to bear that all differences in the systems of justice of the various armed services be erased. The new secretary of defense, James Forrestal, deemed it a necessary measure to effect a unification of the armed forces, and in 1948 he set up an interdepartmental committee to draft a uniform code. Their mission was: "To unify, consolidate, revise and codify, the Articles of War, the Articles for the Government of the Navy, and the disciplinary laws of the Coast Guard, and to enact and establish a Uniform Code of Military Justice."

The *Code* was sent to Congress, and after many hearings and numerous changes, Congress passed the bill, and it was signed by President Truman on 5 May 1950. One year was allowed to make the sweeping changes.

"The Uniform Code of Military Justice," wrote Hanson W. Baldwin, "was a by-product of some of the military 'reforms' that followed World War II." Most of these reforms were designed to have the overall effect of protecting to a greater degree the rights of the innocent, increasing morale, and making life in the service more pleasant. The traditional salute off posts and places of duty was waived, and other measures were taken to break down customary social distinctions of officers and enlisted personnel. It was thought at the time that this would result in increased enlistments and reenlistments. That this was not achieved is a matter of statistical fact supported by the testimony in congressional hearings of the senior officers of the armed forces. The salute was restored to its rightful place in military etiquette; dress uniforms were reapproved for evening affairs; and the Navy officer's sword was again decreed a part of uniform when appropriate. All these details give tone and cohesion to the service, continue worthwhile custom, and help to maintain tradition.

Thus have tradition, custom, usage, and experience given form to the basic laws of the Navy. It is such a source of pride that Charles R. Williams, in an article entitled "History of Discipline in the Navy," published in the March 1919 edition of the U.S. Naval Institute *Proceedings*, wrote:

> The rules of the greatest and most glorious game in the world are not a thing of yesterday or the day before. They were born of the travail and the trial of ages; they are the result of centuries of experience and experiment; heated at the forge of battle, hammered into shape on the anvil of practical knowledge; tested and approved by great heroes of the sea. Any man in the navy that has a heart to understand and appreciate the spiritual in life must breathe freer and walk with a firmer step when he recalls that he is obeying the same laws that Rodney and Nelson and Napier obeyed; that he is under the same discipline that Decatur, Macdonough, and Perry, Dahlgren and Porter, Farragut and Dewey, and a host of other patriots have honored and made illustrious.

2

SEA MANNERS AND SHORE MANNERS

4

Honors and Salutes

Salutes and salutations were, in their origin, marks of submission. We take off our hats because of old the conquered took off their helmets; we bow, because the vanquished were used to bend their necks to the conqueror; and salutes were fired shot and all, that the place or ship might be thereby without the means of present defense. Thus from the bloody forms of turbulent ages are derived the ceremonies of polished life.

The Lady's Magazine, 1821

The officer of the deck shall see that all regulations concerning salutes, honors, and ceremonies, except as modified by orders of competent authority, are carefully observed.

U.S. Navy Regulations, 1948

The naval officer, particularly when serving as officer of the deck, must understand and execute the various traditional honors, salutes, and ceremonies that must be performed aboard ship. Additionally, the general reader who has witnessed or heard of these observances may wish to become better informed regarding these time-honored procedures, closely associated with the Navy and its history.

The effect of these usages, for both the executing officer and the observing layman, derives first of all from the smartness of their execution. With this in mind, the officer of the deck should always observe these principles:

1. Keep informed and insist on a sharp lookout by signalmen and the quartermaster of the watch.
2. Make correctness, promptness, and smartness the aim in rendering honors.
3. Check and recheck honors by regulations or existing instructions where there is doubt.

4. Recognize that the promptness of a man-of-war in returning the dip of merchant ships is usually a gauge of her smartness regarding honors in general. This is an honor that is paid your flag, so be prompt to return the courtesy.

5. Ensure that ensign, flags, and pennants fly free and are hoisted to the very top of the hoist. Learn, as in the days of sail, to cast your eyes aloft.

6. When a senior ship passes, order "attention" sounded before she does, and ensure that "carry on" is given after she gives it.

7. Exercise great care that honors are never rendered of a less degree than due. In the matter of sideboys for foreign officers, if unsure, err on the high side.

8. In addition to showing correctness and smartness in the attention to honors, make sure that all persons coming alongside or visiting the ship are treated with thoughtful, dignified military courtesy.

9. Insist that the signalmen in charge of the signal watches maintain bright lookouts for boats approaching or passing with pennants and flags of senior officers flying. Inform the signal bridge when calls are expected, in order that timely information may be given the quarterdeck. Never let a VIP (very important person) get alongside or aboard without your knowledge.

10. As officer of the deck of flagships, maintain a close liaison with flag aides, and keep the admiral thoroughly informed, but remember always to make prompt reports to your commanding and executive officer.

11. Give attention to your personal appearance on watch, with particular regard to gold braid, cap, and accoutrement.

The Quarterdeck

Few modern ships have space for a quarterdeck comparable to that of the larger ships of the "Old Navy." In many ships today the "quarterdeck" is where the commanding officer says it is, because additional deck structures, weaponry, and special equipment required in modern warfare have usurped the old quarterdeck space. "The commanding officer of a ship shall establish the limits of the quarterdeck and the restrictions as to its use. The quarterdeck shall embrace so much of the main or other appropriate deck as may be necessary for the proper conduct of official and ceremonial functions" (U.S. Navy Regulations, 1948).

The quarterdeck is normally located on the main deck near the gangways, and is marked by appropriate lines, deck markings, decorative cartridge cases, or fancy work. It is always kept particularly clean and shipshape. Personnel not on duty should not be allowed on or near the quarterdeck.

Admiral Kimmel is piped aboard the quarterdeck of USS *San Francisco*.

The dignity and appearance of the quarterdeck are symbols of the professional and seamanlike attitude of a ship and her crew.

Gun Salutes

In theory, all sword or gun salutes were originally the friendly gesture by the saluter of rendering himself or his ship powerless for the moment of their rendition. Guns in old days were kept shotted, and after firing a salute, an appreciable time was required before the guns could be fired again. During Henry VII's reign, firing a gun three times or so in an hour was a good average.

The salutes to vessels flying the English flag started when the waters from the coast of Norway to Cape Finisterre were claimed as "English seas." This, of course, held particularly in the Narrow Seas, for it was asserted for a long period after Edward I that England had claim to both sides of the Channel.

One of King John's titles was duke of Normandy. The kings of England down to George II bore the title of king of France.

It is a very ancient superstition that gun salutes should be of odd number. In Boteler's *Dialogues* of 1685, published by the British Naval Records Society, the captain, referring to a very distinguished visitor aboard, says:

"Have his farewell given him with so many guns as the ship is able to give; provided that they always be of an odd number."
Admiral: "And why odd?"
Captain: "The odd number in ways of salute and ceremony is so observable at sea that, whensoever guns be given otherwise, it is taken for an expression that either the captain, or master, or master gunner is dead in the voyage."

Sir William Monson, in his *Naval Tracts* written before 1600, remarks:

The saluting of ships by another at sea is both ancient and decent, though in this latter time much abused, for whereas three, five, or seven pieces may have been the ordinary use for an admiral, and never to exceed that proportion, and an admiral not to answer with above one or three, now they strive to exceed the number, thinking that many pieces add honor to the salutation; but the owners of merchant ships would be gladden it might be done with less cost and more courtesy in another kind. But tho the admiral cannot restrain this compliment in the ship that salutes, yet he may command his gunner not to return above one or three pieces according to the old manner.

For years the British compelled weaker nations to render the first salute, but in time international practice compelled "gun for gun" response on the principle of equality of nations. In the earliest days, seven guns was the recognized British national salute. Those early regulations stated that although a ship would fire only seven guns, the forts ashore could fire three shots to each one shot afloat, or twenty-one guns. In that day, powder of sodium nitrate was easier to keep on shore than at sea. In time, when the quality of gunpowder was improved by the use of potassium nitrate, the sea salute was made equal to the shore salute as the highest national honor. Although originally monarchies received more guns than republics, eventually republics gained equality. There was much confusion because of the varying customs of maritime states, but finally the British government proposed to the United States a regulation that provided for "salutes to be returned gun for gun." At that time the British officially considered the international salute (to sovereign states) to be twenty-one guns, and the United States adopted the twenty-one guns and "gun for gun" return on 18 August 1875.

Saluting battery of USS *Iowa,* firing in recognition of Independence Day
U.S. Navy (Jeff Hilton)

Before that time our national salute had been variable—one gun for each state of the Union. This practice was partly a result of usage, for John Paul Jones saluted France with thirteen guns at Quiberon Bay in 1778. This practice was not officially authorized until 1810. By the admission of states to the Union, the salute reached twenty-one guns in 1818. In 1841 the national salute was returned to twenty-one guns. The 1875 adoption of the British proposal was a formal announcement that the United States recognized twenty-one guns as an international salute.

Upon occasion, and by presidential decree, the United States has offered a "salute to the nation," consisting of one gun for each of the fifty states. This salute is performed at noon on 4 July at American military posts, although it has been offered on a few other occasions, such as for the death of a president. The Navy full-dresses ship and fires twenty-one guns at noon on the Fourth of July. On Memorial Day, all ships and naval stations fire a salute of twenty-one guns, one every minute, and display the ensign at half-mast from 0800 until completion of the salute.

It was apparently customary at dinners on board to fire a salute when toasts were drunk to high-ranking officers, for Monson continues: "The excessive banqueting on board is a great consuming of powder, for as men's brains are heated with wine, so they heat their ordnance with ostentation and professed kindness at that instant, and many times not without danger."

(One must remember that regular shot was fired.) We are reminded of this custom in Shakespeare's *Hamlet:* "No jocund health that Denmark drinks today, / But the great cannon to the clouds shall tell."

Monson must have been a practical man, for in his command it was ordered that musketry be fired for toasts and leave-taking. He used these honors as drills and directed that the muskets always be fired at a mark in the shape of a man. The Turkish Navy fired shotted salutes until 1910. On 17 September 1781 George Washington, accompanied by Rochambeau, visited Admiral Comte de Grasse off Cape Henry in his flagship *La Ville de Paris,* then the largest ship in the world. At dinner aboard, gun salutes were rendered after each toast.

The custom of returning gun for gun is very old. In 1688 Sir Cloudesly Shovel, writing on board the *James Galley* to Sir Martin Wescomb, said: "I shall ever be careful in keeping especially my Royal orders, which positively command me to salute neither garrison nor flagg of any forrainer except I am certaine to receave gunne for gunne."

For a revolutionary or de facto government to receive a salute from a foreign state is tantamount to recognition. That is why the salute received by John Paul Jones in the *Ranger* on 13 February 1778 at Quibéron Bay, France, was so important to our fledgling nation.

The first U.S. regulations on gun salutes came in the *Rules, Regulations, and Instructions for the Naval Service of the United States* (1818):

> When a public character, high in rank, shall embark on board of any of the United States' ships of war, he may be saluted with 13 guns.
>
> When a commanding officer anchors in any foreign port, he is to inform himself what salutes have been usually given or received by officers of his rank of other nations, and he is to insist on receiving the same mark of respect. Captains may salute foreign ports with such number of guns as may have been customary, on receiving an assurance that an equal number shall be returned—but without such assurance, they are never to salute.
>
> Foreigners of distinction, on visiting the United States' ships of war, are to be saluted with such a number of guns as may suit their rank and quality.

Cheering

Manning the rail and cheering ship is a very old custom. A manuscript of Dr. Roger Marbecke dating from 1596, at the time of the English Cadiz Expedition, states:

These hailings then are in this order. When after a day's absence or more, as occasion serveth, they come near to the Lord Admiral, and yet not too near, but of such seasonable distance as they may not endanger themselves of going foul of one another; they presently man the ship and place every one of their companies both upon the upper and middle deck and also upon the waist and shrouds and elsewhere to the most advantage they can to make the bravest show and appear the greater number. Then the masters and mates of the ships immediately join upon the sounding of their whistles in a pretty loud tunable manner, all the company shaking their hands, hats and caps, give a marvelous shout, with as much mirth and rejoicing as they can, which consisting of so many loud, strong, and variable voices maketh such a sounding echo and pleasant report in the air, as delighteth very much, and this ceremony is done three times by them and three times interchangeably answered by the Lord Admiral.

U.S. Naval Instructions of 1824 stated:

In manning the rigging for cheering, the people should be chosen for their size, to stand together or on the same ratlines, observing the space of two or three ratlines between each. The men should be drest alike, the Marines at the time drawn up on the gangway without their arms. After the three cheers have been given, if the Commodore returns the same number, it must be answered by one; if he returns but one no further notice to be taken, and the people called down.

Cheering was appropriate in the nineteenth century when distinguished passengers left the ship, and for shifts of command. It has long been a maritime custom of respect. In Jones's *Sketches of Naval Life,* he describes the cheering upon Lafayette's departure from the USS *Brandywine,* as he went ashore in France after his last visit to the United States. He also describes the turning over of naval command in 1826. Jones writes in his log about "Manning the Yards and Cheering":

Tuesday, 21 [January 1826]. The Commodore visited and inspected her, on the 19th; and today Captain Read went on board to take the command. He was received by Captain Patterson; the men had been ordered to clean themselves, and all hands were piped; the officers were summoned to the quarterdeck, where the orders of the Secretary for the exchange were read by one of the lieutenants, and the two captains then saluted each other, and bowed to the officers. The shrouds were next manned, and three cheers given. The cheers were repeated when Captain Patterson left the ship; and in this manner he was also received by the *Constitution.*

When sufficient advance notice could be had of the visit of a distinguished personage who would pass close by or come aboard, all hands were ordered "to clean themselves." Then shortly afterward, at the command "Lay aloft," all hands would spring upon the rigging and cluster onto the tops around the topmost crosstrees and the topgallant masthead. The second command was "Lay out upon the yards." The men spread each way and supported themselves by means of light lifelines that were fastened to the lifts and masts. Next, when the order to cheer came from deck, the men took off their hats and waved them during the three cheers.

Herman Melville in *White Jacket* describes how Dom Pedro II, emperor of Brazil, was cheered on his official visit to the USS *United States* about 1849: "But there they stood! Commodore and emperor, lieutenants and marquises, middies and pages! The brazen band on the poop struck up; the Marine guard presented arms; and high aloft looking down on the scene, all the people vigorously hurrahed. A top-man next me on the main-royal removed his hat, and diligently manipulated his head in honor of the event; but he was so far out of sight in the clouds that the ceremony went for nothing."

Dipping the Colors

The present custom of exchanging greetings between ships at sea by dipping the colors is an outgrowth of the old indication of submission of one warship to another or of a merchantman to a warship by the act of lowering topsails.

Before Norman days, sails of foreign vessels were lowered in the "English Seas," spoken of earlier, as a mark of respect to English sovereignty—a "mark of respect" that rendered the vessel without propulsion and literally made it powerless for a time. The ship had no appreciable way on after sails were lowered, and with decks cluttered with rigging and sail, the one saluted feared no attack. From this old custom grew the more modern regulations of "tossing oars," "lying on oars," "stopping engines," and in sailboats "letting fly the sheets" to render honors to superiors.

Before international standardization, salutes were often matters of controversy. National salutes are today based upon the equality of all sovereign states. But in olden days the weak saluted the strong, and the stranger usually saluted the country that claimed jurisdiction over the waters he entered. In 1594 one of the Fugger correspondents from Rome wrote: "The disputes, which have so long prevailed among Christian powers about procedure at sea, have now been settled. Only the Pope and the King of Spain can sail their galleys with colors flying. If they meet, they must salute each other. All other nations must yield precedence to these two."

The old English Navy insisted on respect by all foreigners and English merchantmen. Captain Richard Bullen, of HMS *Nicodemus*, was severely punished in 1638 for not having forced a French ship of war to salute him. And an English merchant ship was fined 500 pounds for not lowering topsails to Charles's fleet. In 1643 instructions to the Royal Navy read: "If you chance to meet in his Majesties see any ships or fleet belonging to any foreign power or State and if they do not strike flaggs or take in topsail you are to force them thereunto."

Neither a U.S. man-of-war nor that of any other sovereign state ever dips her ensign except in return for such compliment. It is not customary today for warships of any nation to dip their colors first. All ships of the U.S. Navy, however, should be alert when passing private vessels, and if this traditional salute (usually from merchant vessels, small craft, or yachts at sea) is rendered, it must be answered, dip for dip.

The Boatswain's Pipe

The boatswain's pipe (whistle) is one of the oldest and most distinctive articles of personal nautical equipment. A pipe or flute was used in the days of antiquity, by which the galley slaves of Greece and Rome kept stroke. There is a record that the pipe was used in the Crusade of 1248 when the English crossbowmen were called on deck to attack by its signal. The pipe is mentioned by Shakespeare in *Tempest:* "Tend to the master's whistle." Pepys refers to its use in his *Naval Notes.*

In time, the pipe came to be used as a badge of office, and in some cases a badge of honor. The Lord High Admiral carried a gold pipe on a chain around his neck; a silver one was used by high commanders as a badge of office, or "whistle of command," in addition to the gold whistle of honor. The whistle was used for salutes to distinguished personages, as well as to pass orders, and the old instructions read that on most occasions it was to be blown "three several times." In the action off Brest on 25 April 1513, between Sir Edward Howard, Lord High Admiral and son of the Earl of Surrey, and the Chevalier Pregant de Bidoux, it is related that when Howard was certain that he would be captured, he threw his gold whistle into the sea. The silver whistle of command was afterward found on his body. The weight of a standard whistle of honor and names for its part were designated by Henry VIII.

Today's boatswain's mates still pipe word about the ship.
U.S. Navy (Tyler Clements)

The monarch decreed that it should weigh 12 "oons" of gold, an oon being the original ounce, as derived from the Latin *uncia*. The chain was also to be of gold and to have an equivalent in gold ducats.

Aside from the use of the pipe as a badge of office and its use by officers for piping evolutions, it was used at the reception of high personages and also at their funerals. The *New York Times* of 6 February 1952 reported: "The bells of Westminster Abbey began to toll, a bo'sun's whistle shrilled 'Admiral aboard' as the King's body was laid upon the gun carriage outside the door to Westminster Hall." Boteler in his *Dialogues* of 1645 describes the correct procedure of his day:

> In receiving, the Prince himself or his Admiral. . . . They were to be received publicly with ceremonies. . . . The ship's barge to be sent to fetch the visitor having the cockson with his silver whistle in the stern. . . . Upon the near approach of the barge the noise of the trumpets are to sound and so to hold on until the barge comes within less than musket shot, and that time the trumpets are to cease and all such as carry whistles are to whistle a welcome three several times.

Army Gen. Tommy R. Franks, commander in chief, U.S. Central Command, is piped aboard the USS *Hopper* (DDG 70).
U.S. Navy (Johnny R. Wilson)

Tending the Side

Tending the side with side boys, as we know it in modern practice, originated long ago. It was customary in the days of sail to hold conferences on the flagships both when at sea and in open roadstead; also, officers were invited to dinner on other ships while at sea, weather permitting. Sometimes the sea was such that visitors were hoisted aboard in boatswain's chairs. The pipe was used for "hoist away" and "'vast heaving." Members of the crew did the hoisting, and the aid they rendered in tending the side gave rise to the custom of having a certain number of men always in attendance. Some have reported that the higher the rank, the heavier the individual. Tending the side should not be confused with a guard of honor.

The U.S. Navy has extended piping the side to military, diplomatic, and consular officers, as well as to others of the legislative and executive departments of the government. In the Royal Navy, it is solely a nautical courtesy. By Royal Navy regulations: "No Military Officer, Consular Officer, or other civilian is entitled to this form of salute. By the Custom of the Service a corpse of any Naval Officer or man is piped over the side, if sent ashore for burial."

At the funerals of British monarchs since Queen Victoria, the venerable custom of piping is part of the ceremony. In this manner the Royal Navy, the "Senior Service," pays a seaman's tribute to the sovereigns of an empire built by sea power.

There is a tradition that the present form of the pipe (whistle) of the boatswain was adopted in commemoration of the defeat and capture of the body of the notorious Scottish pirate, Andrew Barton. Lord Edward Howard, in command of the British ships *Lion* and *Pirwin*, captured Barton after a severe battle. It is related that Howard took the whistle from the body of Barton. When Howard in time became Lord High Admiral, he caused its adoption. Whistles of other kinds had been in use prior to this date, but the design and probably the idea of a more elaborate and costly model as a badge of office sprang from this capture.

In the seventeenth century the master, the boatswain, and the coxswain, all three, rated the whistle. The coxswain had charge of the barge and the shallop, and was at all times to be in readiness to take the captain or admiral ashore. The orders were that the coxswain "is to see her [the barge] trimmed with her carpets and cushions, and to be the person himself in her stern with his silver whistle to cheer up his gang. . . . And this is the lowest officer on the ship that wears a whistle."

Cockbilling Yards: Mourning in Days of Sail

Yards were once "cockbilled," and rigging was slacked off, to show grief. The half-masting of colors is a survival of the days when a slovenly appearance characterized mourning. Even in the British Merchant Service today there are cases of trailing rope ends, "slackening off" rigging, and "scandalizing" yards to symbolize mourning. In this connection, Commander W. T. N. Beckett, RN, wrote in his book *A Few Naval Customs, Expressions, Traditions, and Superstitions:*

> I think that the last occasion that one of H.M. ships scandalized her yards as a sign of mourning, was when HMS *Exmouth* carried out the procedure in 1908 while laying off Lisbon after the murder of Don Carlos, King of Portugal. HMS *Exmouth* was commanded by Captain Arthur Henniker-Hughan and was flying the flag of Admiral the Honorable Sir Assheton George Curzon-Howe, K.C.B.

HMS *Arrogant* was also present, and for lack of known precedent, yards were cockbilled, mainstay down to starboard, foremast down to port, lower booms were dropped. *Arrogant* copied *Exmouth* and the condition prevailed from 0800 with a gun fired every fifteen minutes until sunset.

This custom was observed in the U.S. Navy, as shown by an interesting item in the journal of Mr. George Jones, a schoolmaster on board the *Constitution:*

Thursday, 25 [September 1826]. The Commodore sailed yesterday for Gibraltar and today we have been paying "honor to whom honor was due." Our flags have been at half mast all day; and at noon, twenty-one guns were fired, first by this ship, and then, by the *Porpoise.* This was the late Ex-President Jefferson. After an interval of thirty minutes, the same number were given for his compatriot, John Adams, by a singular coincidence so closely associated with him in death as well as in life. At the first gun, each ship cockbilled its yards. I will explain the term as far as I am able. On common occasions the yards are kept at right angles with the mast; and to a sailor's eye, nothing looks so slovenly as a different position; and nothing is noticed sooner, or sooner disgraces a ship. The slings, however, had now been loosed, and at the first gun, every yard was thrown into a slanting position, so as to form an angle of about 70 degrees with the horizon, the lower main yards inclining to starboard, the fore and mizen to larboard; while the upper yard of each mast took a direction contrary to that of the lower ones *passis crinibus* ["like disheveled hair"].

"Sounding Off" at Parade and Guard Mount

At parades and guard mounts in military and naval service, when the adjutant commands, "Sound off," the band plays three chords of flourishes, which are called the "Three Cheers," before marching up and then down in front of the men under arms. When the band returns to its position, "Three Cheers" is again played.

This custom originated in Crusade days. Those soldiers designated for the Crusades were set apart but formed in line with the other troops, and the music of the organization would march and then countermarch in front of those selected. This was a form of dedication ceremony. The three flourishes have remained symbolical of the applause and cheers throughout the ceremony.

**Formal dress parade at the
Naval Academy**
Naval Institute Photo Archive

The dress parade is a survival of the days when visiting celebrities in all countries were shown the king's troops in impressive parade. The original intent was to render the display formidable and to impress the visitor with the strength of the state visited, rather than the present idea of a parade as a distinctive honor rendered the visitor.

5

Naval Ceremonies

> Honors and ceremonies are based on customs and a long-established code of agreements and regulations, most of which are common to all navies. With some exceptions, honors and ceremonies take place in port, and the manner in which they are rendered or carried out under the supervision of the OOD does much to give the ship a reputation for smartness. It is important that they be conducted in a manner that also reflects credit on the U.S. Navy and the United States.
>
> *Watch Officer's Guide*, 2000*

All ceremonies should be as formal and impressive as circumstance, company, and occasion allow. The reason for ceremony is only partially for the honoree; the real purpose is for those assembled both to honor the recipient and to reinforce the concept that good deeds and service are suitably rewarded. It is selfish to shortchange the desires of a crew to recognize the deserving, simply because we have been raised in a society that eschews public indulgence.

Francis Bacon said in regard to ceremonies: "Not to use ceremonies at all is to teach others not to use them again, and so diminish the respect to himself; especially, they ought not to be omitted to strangers and formal natures; but the dwelling upon them, and exalting them above the moon, is not only tedious, but doth diminish the faith and credit of him that speaks."

The proper employment of dignified ceremony buttresses discipline and order to a degree that cannot be underestimated.

---

* Fourteenth edition revised by Capt. James Stavridis, USN. This manual, published by the Naval Institute Press, is a valuable training aid and important professional book. Recommended for the sea library of all junior officers.

Retirement ceremony of Capt. Thomas G. Kelly at the Navy Memorial Plaza in Washington, D.C.
U.S. Navy (PH3 Stover)

Preparing a Ceremonial or Formal Parade

Note that the term *parade* in this context is neither a unit marching down a street, nor a pass in review of troops, but rather the mustering of ship's company "at parade."

Many ceremonies have certain elements in common. Rather than repeat them with each discussion, we will present them first. The officer delegated responsibility for preparation of such a ceremony can then select whatever elements are applicable.

- Have a dais or platform constructed and suitably decorated with bunting or signal flags.
- Make sure that a lectern and public address system are available, and test the system to ensure that all in the audience can hear the proceedings.
- Make a seating diagram for distinguished guests and the principals on the platform.
- Consider using printed invitations and programs. These lend tone to the occasion and provide appropriate souvenirs for officers, crew, and invited guests.

- Consider providing directions and/or a simple map to the parking lot and the location of the ceremony, especially if there are many who may not be familiar with the layout of the yards or station where the ceremony is to occur.
- Make sure that the plan of the day covers all details for the crew.
- Check arrangements and allocation for guests who may be invited for refreshments in the respective messes.
- Ensure that all public media that may be interested are given sufficient advance information as to the ceremony and what facilities may be offered them.
- Prepare and distribute to the relevant parties a detailed plan, including a sketch if necessary.
- Rehearse! Rehearse! Rehearse! No effort can better keep the officers and crew from uncertainty and stress. Getting the crew expeditiously to and away from dress parade stations will make for smoothness at the ceremony.

At most ceremonies the officers of the ship stand together. A variation in this arrangement is to have visitors forward and amidships, and ship's officers and chief petty officers just abaft the visiting officers and amidships. The rule concerning "guests first" applies in this instance, and guests should be seated in such a position as to allow them the best possible view of the event. The increase in morale that this action provides can backfire, however, if the crew are relegated to a secondary role or placed in a position where they cannot observe the ceremony.

Keel-Laying Ceremonies

Tradition holds that at least four points of a ship's life be marked by appropriate ceremony. These are the laying of the keel, the christening and launching, the commissioning, and the decommissioning. While there is no rigid guidance as to what steps each must contain, they all have the basic elements listed above.

For the keel laying, the ceremony is relatively simple. Formal invitations are sent requesting the presence of those interested parties to the "laying of the keel of the *Alwaysgone*." Note that only the ship's name is used, not the designation "USS." If the ship has not yet been named, the type and hull number may be used.

At the ceremony, after the invocation, usually the president of the shipyard or company welcomes guests and introduces the guest speaker. After the

Change of command aboard the USS *Antietam*

speaker's remarks, he or she may be asked either to affix a memorial name-
plate or to weld his or her initials on the keel. The keel will then be moved
into position by the shipyard workers, and the announcement is made that
"the keel has been truly and fairly laid."

Launching Ship Ceremonies[*]

> And see! She stirs!
> She starts—she moves—she seems to feel
> The thrill of life along her keel,
> And, spurning with her foot the ground,
> With one exulting, joyous bound,
> She leaps into the ocean's arms.
>
> *Henry Wadsworth Longfellow, "The Building of the Ship"*

[*] The authors acknowledge the use of material from Robert G. Skerrett's comprehensive treatment of the subject, "The Baptism of Ships," U.S. Naval Institute *Proceedings* (June 1909).

From the earliest days of seaborne craft, launching ceremonies have had a religious significance. The custom originated as a propitiation to the gods of the elements. The Chinese have not changed in centuries their elaborate launching ceremonies, and today large junks carry a shrine honoring the Mother of the Dragon. In Tahiti it was once the custom to shed human blood at the launching ceremonies. There are records of launching ceremonies as long ago as 2100 B.C.

Wine was used in the early rituals; however, the Greeks introduced water in a ceremony of lustration. Later, the Romans used water as a token of purification in the solemn priestly blessing. Christian and pagan ceremonies have used wine as the sacrament, and water as the token of purification.

The religious zeal of the Middle Ages extended to things maritime. Ships were named after saints; shrines were placed aboard, and religious effigies found their way on figureheads and in the elaborate niches in the gilded stern galleries. The altars or shrines were placed aft in the same location as the altars of the Greeks and Romans. The name *poop deck* survives the custom. This nautical word is derived from the Latin word *puppis,* a name the ancients gave to that ceremonial, sacred, honored deck where were kept the *pupi* or doll images of the deities. Here sacrifice was offered.

In Catholic France throughout the eighteenth century and well into the nineteenth there was a launching ceremony that in most respects was analogous to the baptismal ceremony. This was performed by priests at the launching of merchant vessels and fishing craft in Brittany and Normandy. No wine was used in the ceremony of launching, but *vin d'honneur* was always served to those present.

It was only in the early part of the nineteenth century that women and those other than the clergy and high officials took any part in the ceremony of launching British ships. Queen Victoria supposedly inaugurated the religious portion of the ceremony that is now used in the launching of British warships.

The first woman to christen a U.S. Navy ship, the *Concord,* did so in 1828, but her name was not recorded. The first record found of the name of a woman sponsor is that of a "Miss Watson of Philadelphia," who used a mixture of water and wine when she christened the *Germantown,* a ship of war, on 22 October 1846. The Philadelphia *North American,* in describing the ceremony, said, "Miss Watson was attired in pure white and wore in her girdle a neat bouquet of freshly culled flowers."

The civil ceremony until recently consisted of the naming of the vessel by a sponsor, a short speech given by the sponsor, and the breaking of a bottle of

Sen. Olympia J. Snowe christens the USS *Mason* and breaks a bottle of champagne
across the ship's bow.
Bath Iron Works

wine on the bow or stem of the ship as she slipped down the ways. Because
of the "noble experiment" of Prohibition in the United States, this bottle-
breaking custom was for a time held in abeyance. Champagne has since re-
taken its place as the customary liquid for launching ceremonies. The first
time wine was used after the repeal of the Eighteenth Amendment was on
21 November 1933, at the launching of the USS *Cuttlefish*, built by the Electric
Boat Company. Mrs. B. Saunders Bullard, wife of Commander C. C. Bullard,
USN, cracked a bottle of champagne against the ship's bow as she left the
ways. In World War II days a group of ladies made strong petition to President
Roosevelt and Secretary of Navy Knox that we "cease launching and christening of our boats with liquor," and recommended that ships be launched by
chaplains with "clear water only."

The Japanese were the first to use birds in connection with launchings. In
the United States, when the *Chicago* was sponsored in 1885, Mrs. Henry W. B.
Glover released three doves from red, white, and blue ribbons. Mrs. Herbert
Hoover released a flock of white pigeons when the ill-fated airship *Akron* was
christened.

So many prominent women of the United States have launched ships that in order to preserve the records, a group of these sponsors created an organization, the Society of Sponsors of the United States Navy. They have preserved the record of the christenings of all U. S. Navy ships since 1797. As recently as 1991 the Naval Institute Press published a new edition of *Ships of the United States Navy and Their Sponsors.*

Tradition has it that water was used in the first two attempts to launch the *Constitution,* but "Old Ironsides" would not move: apparently, it took wine to launch the ship. The history of the Boston Navy Yard states: "Commodore James Sever stood at the heel of the bowsprit and according to time-honored usage baptised the ship with a bottle of choice old Madeira, from the cellar of the Honorable Thomas Russell, a leading Boston merchant."

In 1858 the USS *Hartford* was launched with three sponsors. Commodore Downes's daughter smashed a bottle of Hartford Springs water across the bows; Commodore Stringham's daughter broke a bottle of Connecticut River water across the ship's figurehead; Lieutenant Preble emptied a bottle of sea water on the bow. This was a "triple-barreled" water ceremony. Once a U.S. Army Air Corps balloon was christened with liquid air. Mrs. Franklin D. Roosevelt christened the huge flying boat *Yankee Clipper* on 3 March 1939 at the U.S. Naval Air Station, Anacostia, D.C., with a bottle of water mixed from the seven seas.

The last Navy ship to be launched down the traditional inclined track was the USS *Mason* (DDG-87) in Bath Iron Works, Maine, on 23 June 2001. The Bath plant opened a new drydock from which ships will be floated in the future.

The ceremony itself is a solemn one in which the ship is dedicated, named, and committed to the sea. The elements include an invocation, remarks by the guest speaker, and possibly remarks concerning the ship's namesake and the history of other ships of the same name, followed by the introduction of the sponsor and the actual christening. Again, the title "USS" is not used in the invitation, as the ship is not yet in commission in the naval service.

Commissioning a Naval Ship

There are two main parts to the commissioning of a naval ship. First, the ship is turned over by the builders to the Navy, in the person of a suitable area authority. The ship is his or her responsibility until it is commissioned. Therefore, no ensign, jack, or commission pennant flies before commissioning. This means that when the person who has accepted the ship comes

USS *Mason* (DDG 87) was the last ship to be launched by sliding down the building ways.
Bath Iron Works

aboard to turn over the ship, no honors other than the courtesy of meeting him at the side are rendered. Honors are given him at departure. Second, the ship is turned over to the commanding officer, who accepts her and assumes command.

Invitations reflect the host of the ceremony and may take several forms, but possibly the most important point is to include the crew among the hosts. The invitation is usually offered in the name of the "Commanding Officer and Ship's Company" or the "Commanding Officer, Officers, and Crew." Because this is a commissioning, the title "USS" (without periods) or "United States Ship" may be used. The OpNav Instruction (1710.7A) makes the point that the definite article *the* is incorrect before the ship's name as there is only one commissioned ship of a given name at a time.

The best established practice is to have the basic and official ceremony first, and after that has terminated and the ship is in commission, to continue the program with the personal remarks, official speeches, and presentations. This ensures that at all times responsibility is clearly placed; and even though very inspiring and eloquent speeches may continue for some time, officers and men are on duty at their assigned stations for port watches and should be able to cope effectively with any emergency that might arise. Furthermore, such a procedure adheres to the letter of the regulations on the subject (see U.S. Navy Regulations, art. 0881):

> (a) The formal transfer shall be effected by the supervisory authority or a designated representative.
>
> (b) As many of the officers and crew of the ship as circumstances permit, and a guard and music, shall be assembled and properly distributed on the quarterdeck or other suitable part of the ship.

Normally, officers fall in aft at dress parade stations on the quarterdeck or fantail, and the crew is marched by divisions aft to assigned stations. It is customary for officers to fall in amidships and face aft. The guard and band fall in aft at stations for colors but face the ceremony until the ensign is hoisted. Visitors should be assigned chairs or seats with an unobstructed view.

The ceremony commences with an invocation by a chaplain. In the commissioning ceremony program of USS *Forrestal,* the invocation came immediately after the commandant of the district accepted the ship from the builders. This is good practice when a new ship is taken over directly from the builders.

The executive officer should report to the prospective commanding officer that "officers and crew are up and aft, and all is ready for the commissioning ceremony." The admiral or delegated representative and the prospective commanding officer should proceed to the place of ceremony. All come to attention and "carry on" when the principals reach the platform.

Navy Regulations continue:

> (c) The officer effecting the transfer shall cause the national ensign and the proper insignia of command to be hoisted with the appropriate ceremonies, and shall turn the ship over to the prospective commanding officer.

The officer conducting the transfer reads the orders for the delivery of the ship, and orders the prospective commanding officer to "commission the USS ———." The captain, through the executive officer to the navigator (officer of the deck), relays the order. Attention is sounded on the bugle; the national anthem is played; the ensign, commission pennant, and jack are hoisted simultaneously. If an admiral effects the transfer, then his flag is hoisted and remains until he departs.

The regulations conclude as follows:

A naval vessel is commissioned. The first watch has been ordered to man their stations.

(d) The prospective commanding officer reads his or her orders, salutes the officer effecting the transfer and says, "I assume command of the USS ————." Immediately he or she orders the executive officer to "set the watch." This is most effective when the boatswain's mate commences piping to pass the word fore and aft. The officer of the deck takes his station and makes the first entry in the log. *The ship is now officially commissioned.*

The commanding officer then formally introduces the admiral or the admiral's representative, who customarily gives a short talk to the officers and men of the newly commissioned ship. This is followed by the address of the commanding officer.

Should there be a presentation of silver service or other gifts to the ship by a city, state, or organization, it is fitting that the ceremony come at this point. In this event, the commanding officer should reply to the speech of presentation by expressing the thanks of the Navy Department and the officers and crew for the gift and the motives that prompted its presentation.

The ceremony concludes with the benediction and departure of the official party, and is usually followed by a reception in an appropriate location.

Change of command at sea. Although most changes of command take place in port, this ceremony can also occur at sea. On this occasion the Seventh Fleet changed commanders just out of range of gunfire during the height of the war with North Vietnam. Within an hour, the flagship was firing again.

Change of Command

As a continuance of the line of authority established when the ship was commissioned, and because of the magnitude of responsibility of a ship's captain, changes of command must be planned with close attention to detail designed to strengthen that respect for authority vital to a military organization. Such ceremonies were once announced by engraved official invitation to the participants, but nowadays the plans are announced by naval message, with formal invitations being sent only to those whom the principals desire to attend the event.

In the days when the quarterdeck was aft, the officer to be relieved and his staff paraded on the honor side, or starboard side, of the quarterdeck. If the ceremony should take place on the forecastle or other parts of the ship, then the officer to be relieved should be to the right, the honor side of the officer relieving.

In general, the order of the ceremony is today as it has been for decades. The uniform for participants is normally full dress, in keeping with the dignity of the occasion. The officers, chief petty officers, and crew are formed in ranks so that they are not excluded from the ceremony and may observe the event that so affects their lives. Additionally, side boys, honor guard, color guard, and bands are paraded as available and appropriate. When all preparations are complete and the guests are present, the official party arrives amid the required ceremonies and salutes. After an invocation, the guest speaker (usually the next senior officer in the chain of command) makes appropriate remarks, followed by the remarks of the officer being relieved. Upon completion of those remarks, he or she and then the relief will read their orders. The ceremony then reaches its simplest and most impressive moment, with the words used traditionally at the changing of the watch: "I relieve you, sir" (or "ma'am") and "I stand relieved." The two then report the "proper" relief and assumption of command to their superior and, after the traditionally brief remarks of the new CO and a benediction, the ceremony is over.

Regulations require that the commanding officer about to be relieved inspect the command in company with the relieving officer. Usually, this is done during the change of command ceremony, since regulations also require that the crew be mustered for that event. However, there are certain drawbacks to this procedure. First, the departing captain often has words he or she would like to say to individual crew members but might refrain from doing so because of time constraints. Second, an inspection does not hold much interest for an audience and is tiring for the crew. A useful alternative is to conduct the personnel inspection at the rehearsal the day before. This takes the pressure off the inspecting officer and the crew alike, and makes the event much more enjoyable for all.

Decommissionings

Possibly the least elaborate ceremony of a ship's life is its decommissioning. It is a somber occasion by nature and generally involves short remarks, the reading of the commanding officer's orders, and the lowering of the flag and commissioning pennant. There may also be remarks by the authority that is accepting the ship.

Awards

Awards ceremonies can be large or small. They can be held before a formal parade of the unit or "in chambers," indoors or outdoors, but however they

All hands attend a special award ceremony to honor one of their own onboard USS *Bataan*.
U.S. Navy (Johnny Bivera)

are held, they must be held. To do otherwise is to dilute the award and therefore the honor which it signifies.

Regardless of the size of the event, the ceremony consists of basically the same elements: the individual is called to the front, the attendees are called to attention, the award is announced and the citation read, and the award is given to the individuals or to their families in the case of a posthumous award.

Retirements

The retirement of an officer or chief petty officer is a significant event. It is also one of those events in which the principals often are reluctant to participate. This ceremony is one of closure, held for the benefit of those left behind as much as for the retiree, and therefore should not be shortchanged.

Retirement ceremonies can be held in any suitable location, but should be arranged to honor the individual's career and accomplishments. Like

A retiring Coast Guard officer is "piped ashore."
Michael Lemke

many other ceremonies, retirement ceremonies should be opened with the parading of the national colors, which the individual has honorably served. An appropriate invocation and remarks are given, and presentations are made. The Navy provides certificates of retirement as well as certificates of appreciation to spouses for this event. Following such presentations, it is traditional for the retiree to make farewell remarks and to read his or her orders. After the benediction and retiring of the colors, the retiree is ceremonially piped over the side, often with side boys of his or her peers.

Official Visits

Occasionally, ship's captains or admirals will receive official calls from dignitaries ashore. These visits often include exchanges of gifts. As most such visits are prearranged, the nature of the gifts can often be determined by an aide, and a suitable response prepared. It is well to have a gift of similar worth if possible. Most often, ship's plaques are sufficient.

Foreign navies still lay great stress on the custom of exchanging official calls. Here the commander, Seventh Fleet, returns such a call on a fleet commander of the Japanese Maritime Self Defense Force aboard his flagship.

The visit itself often represents centuries of diplomatic contacts, and cannot be shortchanged. The details of receiving location and uniform, time of day, and refreshments are all important in these matters. Usually, there is guidance available from port directories and attachés as well as from fleet protocol officers.

Weddings

A sword should never be unsheathed in a church or sanctuary. At weddings of naval and military officers it is customary for the ushers in uniform to draw and arch swords outside the church door. After the nuptial ceremony, the bride and groom walk under the arch. This fine old English and American custom is a symbolic pledge of loyalty to the young married couple. In short, all for two. It also makes a good picture. Remember, no one but the newly married pair passes under the arch.

At the wedding reception, using the naval officer's sword to cut the cake is a nice traditional touch. While it offers a suitably ceremonial blade for the occasion, it can also lead to some spirited hijinks. Two words of caution:

first, remember that the sword was once, and still is, considered a weapon and it should not be carelessly brandished; second, never take the scabbard to the ceremony lest someone slip the "iced" blade home, thereby necessitating the expense of a replacement.

Funeral Ceremonies

Much of the ceremony at military and naval funerals is traditional. The reversal of rank at funerals is an acknowledgment that at death all are equal. Seniors take their proper precedence in the procession after burial— although, for an unknown reason, this was not done at the funeral of Adm. George Dewey. This form of "the last shall be first and the first shall be last" is carried out in the recessional and processional of churches. There was an ancient Roman custom of reversing all rank and position when celebrating the feast of Saturn.

The superstitions and significance of military funeral customs were set down by one Stephen Graham, a private in the British Guards, writing in the days before the American Revolution:

> When a soldier dies, the Union Jack is laid upon his body in token that he died in the service of the State, and that the State takes the responsibility of what it ordered him to do as a soldier.
>
> The reversed arms are an acknowledgment of the shame of killing. Death puts the rifle to shame, and the reversal of the barrel is a fitting sign of reverence.
>
> The three volleys fired into the air are fired at imaginary devils which might get into men's hearts at such a moment as the burial of a comrade-in-arms. An old superstition has it that the doors of men's hearts stand ajar at such times and devils might easily get in.
>
> The last post is the *Nunc Dimittis* of the dead soldier. It is the last bugle call . . . , but it gives promise of reveille . . . , of the greatest reveille which ultimately the Archangel Gabriel will blow.

In the early days of the U.S. Navy the colors were half-masted only for officers of the rank of captain and above. Jones, in *Sketches of Naval Life,* writing on board the frigate *Constitution* at Port Mahon, 30 October 1826, relates: "We buried one of the officers, a surgeon's mate, and a member of our mess; application was made to have him interred in the officers' burying grounds, within the walls; but his disease, the typhus fever, alarmed them, and it was refused. I expected to see our colors half-masted; but, it seems, this is an honor due only to captains, and it was not done. The funeral was attended by nearly all of the squadron."

In the seventeenth and early eighteenth centuries French men-of-war sometimes carried the remains of those who died at sea in the holds until the ships reached port. Old reports indicate that this was a very disagreeable practice and one that served solely the purpose of burying the deceased in consecrated soil. Some tall yarns are told of the British preserving bodies of senior officers in rum until they could be buried ashore, giving rise to the sobriquet "Nelson's blood" applied to rum.

The deep sentiment of sailors for their shipmates is proverbial. It is interesting, more than a hundred years later, to read the epitaphs written by messmates for their lamented shipmates. The following inscription may be found in a cemetery at Port Mahon, once the base of the old U.S. Mediterranean Squadron:

SACRED

TO

THE MEMORY

OF

ALEXANDER GRAVES

QUARTER GUNNER ON BOARD THE

U.S. FRIGATE BRANDYWINE

WHO DEPARTED THIS LIFE JAN. 17TH

AGED 44 YEARS.

HERE LIES, BENEATH THIS CONSECRATED SOD,

A MAN WHO LOVED HIS COUNTRY AND HIS GOD:

TRUE TO THEM BOTH, I'VE HEARD HIS SHIPMATES SAY;

BUT NOW HE'S GONE; AND SLUMBERS IN THE CLAY.

A BETTER MESSMATE NEVER CROSSED THE SEAS:

I HOPE HE'S GONE TO HEAVEN. GOD BE PLEASED.

FAITHFUL IN DUTY; CONTENTED WITH HIS MIND:

AND DIED LAMENTED BY THE BRANDYWINES.

Another epitaph that surely compensated in sincerity and sentiment for its deficiency in composition runs like this:

SACRED

TO

THE MEMORY

OF

JAMES SMITH

CAPTAIN OF THE MAIN TOP

ON BOARD THE U.S. FRIGATE BRANDYWINE WHO DEPARTED THIS LIFE FEB. 4TH

1826

AGED 30 YEARS

HE WHO LAYS HERE, WAS MUCH BELOVED,

BY ALL HIS SHIPMATES ROUND;

BUT HE'S NO MORE, 'TWAS ACCIDENT,

THE UNFORTUNATE MAN WAS DROWNED.

ALAS, HE'S GONE, THE DEBT IS PAID,

HE OWED FOR A SHORT TIME;

MOURN NOT FOR HIM, HE'S BETTER OFF,

HE SAILS WITH MORE DIVINE.

Burial at Sea

> Death is at all times solemn, but never so much as at sea.
>
> Charles A. Dana

Arguably the most powerful ceremony of the sea is that which consigns mortal remains to the deep. It antedates all other ceremonies. Burial rites were conducted at sea in ancient Greece and Rome; offerings were made to gain favor and forgiveness from the gods; coins were placed in the mouths of the deceased for payment of the fare to the ferryman Charon for transportation over the River Styx.

It was a time-honored custom in the British Navy that a guinea be paid from the public funds for each corpse sewn in a canvas shroud. Commander Beckett, in his *Customs and Superstitions,* reports that twenty-three guineas from government funds were paid to the rating who sewed up twenty-three bodies on a British man-of-war after the battle of Jutland. This duty was usually performed by a sailmaker or by one of his mates. According to a very old custom in preparing a body for burial at sea, the sailmaker, when sewing the canvas shroud, takes the last stitch through the nose of the deceased. Research has disclosed several instances of this custom. In *White Jacket,*

"All hands bury the dead."
"All Hands" by R. F. Zog-
baum; courtesy Harper and
Bros.

Herman Melville speaks of this custom in recounting the conversation of an old American sailmaker with a seaman concerning whether or not the stitch through the nose should be made.

Except in time of war, it is seldom necessary nowadays to bury at sea. Occasionally, officers and men who die ashore request that their ashes be spread on the deep; such requests must be submitted to the Navy Department.

If the deceased is buried at sea, the body is sewn in a canvas shroud or placed in a coffin that has been weighted to ensure sinking. The body is always carried feet first; over the coffin is draped the national flag, with the union placed at the head and over the left shoulder. A reading of Scripture, prayers, the committal, and the benediction constitute the religious rites, which may be performed by the clergy; the rest of the ceremony is usually performed by the military.

It has been customary for all officers and men not on duty to attend services when word is passed, "All hands bury the dead." The chaplain, or in his or her absence the captain or an officer detailed by the captain, reads the burial service at sea. The Protestant, Catholic, and Jewish committals differ slightly. The Protestant committal reads: "Unto Almighty God we commend the soul of our brother departed, and we commit his body to the deep; in sure and certain hope of the resurrection unto eternal life, through our Lord, Jesus Christ, Amen. (Tilt board and release body into the sea.)"*

In order to illustrate an old superstition and at the same time show how funerals were conducted under circumstances at sea that will never occur again, we present here a description written by Captain Basil Hall, RN, in 1831. The funeral was that of one of his dearest friends, a young and much beloved midshipman of his mess who was buried off the shores of the United States during the War of 1812. As Hall records it:

> The peculiar circumstances connected with the funeral, which I am about to describe, have combined to fix the whole scene in my memory. Something occurred during the day to prevent the funeral taking place at the usual hour, and the ceremony was deferred until long after sunset. The evening was extremely dark, and it was blowing a treble-reefed topsail breeze. We had just sent down the top-gallant yards, and made all safe for a boisterous winter's night. As it became necessary to have lights to see what was done, several signal lanterns were placed on the break of the quarterdeck and others along the hammock railings on the lee gangway. The whole ship's company and officers were assembled, some on the booms, others in the boats, while the main rigging was crowded halfway up to the cat harpings. Overhead, the main-sail, illuminated as high as the yard by the lamps, was bulging forwards under the gale, which was rising every minute and straining so violently at the main sheet, that there was some doubt whether it might not be necessary to interrupt the funeral in order to take sail off the ship. The lower deck ports lay completely under water, and several times the muzzles of the main deck guns were plunged into the sea; so that the end of the grating on which the remains of poor Dolly were laid once or twice nearly touched the tops of the waves as they foamed and hissed past. The rain fell fast on the bare heads of the crew, dropping also on the officers, during all the ceremony, from the foot of the mainsail, and wetting the leaves of the prayer-book. The wind sighed over us amongst the wet shrouds, with a note so mournful that there could not have been a more appropriate dirge.

* *The Ceremony of Burial of the Dead at Sea,* prescribed to be followed by all ships of the U.S. Navy where burial at sea is authorized, sets forth in detail both military procedure and the religious services of the three major faiths.

The ship, pitching violently, strained and cracked from end to end; so that what with the noise of the sea, the rattling of the ropes, and the whistling of the wind, hardly one word of the service could be distinguished. The men, however, understood, by a motion of the captain's hand, when the time came, and the body of our dear little brother was committed to the deep.

So violent a squall was sweeping past the ship at this moment, that no sound was heard of the usual splash, which made the sailors allege that their young favorite never touched the water at all, but was at once carried off in the gale to his final resting place!

Herman Melville reports a burial in 1843 in an account of his life aboard the USS *United States:*

"We commit this body to the deep!" At the word, Shenly's mess-mates tilted the board, and the dead sailor sank in the sea.

"Look aloft," whispered Jack Chase. "See that bird! It is the spirit of Shenly."

Gazing upward, all beheld a snow-white, solitary fowl, which—whence coming no one could tell—had been hovering over the main-mast during the service, and was now sailing far up into the depths of the sky. (Herman Melville, *White Jacket* [Boston: Page, 1892], p. 320)

Sailors in those days never molested sea birds, for many mariners believed them to be the spirits of dead sailors.

Firing Three Volleys at Funerals

> This the third time; I hope good luck lies in odd numbers. . . .
> There is divinity in odd numbers, either in nativity, chance, or death
> Shakespeare, *Merry Wives of Windsor,* Act V, scene 1

The superstitious custom of firing three volleys at funerals was intended to drive away evil spirits as they escaped from the hearts of the dead. In some parts of Asia, firecrackers are fired to drive away evil spirits.

The number three has long had a mystical significance. It was used in ancient Roman funeral rites: earth was cast three times into the sepulcher; friends and relatives called the dead three times by name; and then as they departed from the tomb, they pronounced the Latin word *vale,* meaning "farewell," three times.

In 1938 the Navy Department commented upon firing volleys:

The Bureau has received advice on several occasions of the undesirable and, at times, pathetic effect of the volleys fired at military funerals upon the bereaved. It is desired that this aspect of the honors rendered at the interment be considered by commanding officers when acting upon requests for funeral escorts.

The following points were ordered as a guide at funerals:

(a) That the full import of the part of the firing squad be explained to the next-of-kin or those representing the next-of-kin.

(b) That those in charge of or in command of the firing squad so place the squad that it is some distance from the grave. It is not necessary that the volleys be fired directly over the grave.

(c) That the firing squad be omitted, as a matter of expedience, in the case of funerals when the omission is expressly requested by the next-of-kin or those representing the next-of-kin.

Reverence, tact and courtesy must ever govern in carrying out the ancient and solemn ceremonies of military and naval funerals.

Although not prescribed by regulations, a short religious service is customarily held aboard for deceased officers and men when their remains are sent from ships on a foreign station for further transportation to the homeland. The crew is mustered, and a religious service is held. Volleys may be omitted, but taps should be sounded as the body is lowered to the waiting boat, and the bell tolled as customary. The flag should be half-masted in accordance with regulations.

Crossing the Line

> For you must know that any craft who'd fain
> Cross the Great Sea Lord's Special Royal Domain,
> Must pay the tribute that King Neptune wishes,
> And be received by mermaids, bears, and fishes.
> We will see you on the morn,
> And any who resist will wish he had not been born.
>> "Crossing the Line" ritual of the Royal Navy

The boisterous ceremonies of "crossing the line" are of such ancient vintage that their derivation is lost; such horseplay took place in the Middle Ages, and even before that when ships crossed the thirtieth parallel or passed through the Straits of Gibraltar. These early ceremonies were extremely rough

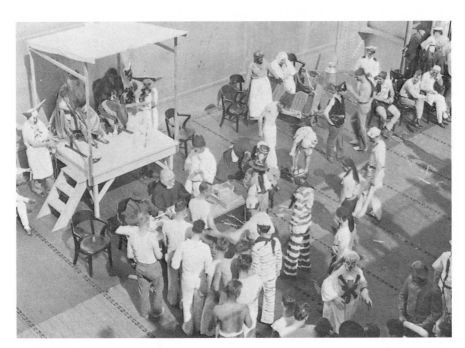

Crossing the Line ceremony with King Neptune and party

and to a large degree were supposed to test the crew to determine whether or not the novices, or "boots," on their first cruise could endure the hardships of a life at sea. Then as now, it was primarily a crew's "party." The Vikings are reported to have practiced similar ceremonies on crossing certain parallels. It is highly probable that the present-day ceremony was passed on to the Angles, Saxons, and Normans from the Vikings.

At an even earlier time there is record of ceremonies of propitiation. Seamen in the ancient world held rites to appease Neptune, the god of the seas, and marks of respect were paid those of his underwater domain. Some part of the present ceremony doubtless grew out of the superstitions of those days, even though Viking sailors had come to doubt the physical existence of Neptune. Nevertheless, Neptunus Rex is today the "majesty" who rules in the ceremonies.

Those who have "crossed the line" are called Sons of Neptune, or "shellbacks." Bonafide Sons of Neptune always compose the cast for present-day ceremonies. It is curious how people will undergo a very severe initiation in order to qualify to inflict the same on others.

Sailors treasure their Neptune certificates, issued at latitude 00°00' and a specified longitude, and usually addressed to "all Mermaids, Sea Serpents, Whales, Sharks, Porpoises, Dolphins, Skates, Eels, Suckers, Lobsters, Crabs, Pollywogs, and other living things of the sea." The certificate states that so-and-so "has been found worthy to be numbered as one of our trusty shell-backs, has been gathered to our fold and duly initiated into the solemn mysteries of the ancient order of the deep."

The crossing-the-line ceremonies of the modern Navy are most pictur-esque, with details usually left to the imaginations of those in charge of the ceremony. They may range from the discomfort of a good dousing in the tank, a slight shock of electricity from the fork of the "Devil," to the slap-happy shaving ceremony. Even today's merchant ships observe the ceremony, and it is still a rather uncomfortable procedure for those being initiated. Officers of the U.S. Navy at one time could "buy off," by giving the Neptune party a number of bottles of beer. Those days are gone, however, and it is a tradition that all officers, and younger officers in particular, undergo the initiation.

Even commanders-in-chief are not immune. Margaret Truman recounts in her biography of her father, President Harry S. Truman, that in September 1947 even the president and his family were subject to the summons of the great King Neptune. The whole family had flown to Rio de Janeiro for a meeting of the Organization of American States. They were returning on board the USS *Missouri* when, one day, strange things started occurring. Sailors were wearing clothing backward, junior officers were sitting at the wardroom table with their chairs backward, and men were singing silly songs at the table. While daughter Margaret thought it "pretty ridiculous," President Truman apparently loved every minute of the preparations and cere-mony. The whole family had to answer charges, Truman for insulting King Neptune by crossing the line southward by "a despicable and unnatural means of travel, namely by air." Despite his guilty plea and expression of facts in mitigation and extenuation—namely, that his job sometimes required such travel—he was fined autographs and cigars for the whole court. Mrs. Truman was given amnesty for the same charge, and Margaret was charged with living in a fishbowl without permission of the Lord of the Deep.

The oldest and most dignified senior "shellback" member of the crew is customarily selected as Neptunus Rex; his first assistant is Davy Jones. Other members of the court might include Her Highness Amphitrite (often a young seaman in a costume of seaweed and rope yarns), the Royal Scribe, the Royal Doctor, the Royal Dentist, the Devil, and other players that suit the fancy of the Neptune party. The Bears have the difficult task of rounding up those to be initiated, and also standing "dousing" watches in the canvas water tank.

Neptune party on USS *Enterprise*, September 1944
U.S. Navy

The night before the ship crosses the line, it is the custom that Davy Jones shall appear on board with a message to the captain from His Majesty, Neptunus Rex, stating at what time he wants the ship hove to for the reception of the Royal Party and with specific summons for certain men to appear before him. This reception of Davy Jones usually takes place after dark and may be most impressive. The ship heaves to, and amid a glare of lights and the spray of firehoses, Davy Jones emerges from the hawse or is hoisted in over the bows to deliver his message. He is always received in a dignified manner by the captain and officer of the deck. By careful planning, supervision, and timing, the commanding officer can keep within bounds the boisterous horseplay of the oldest and most interesting ceremony of the sea.

Sample Summons for a Neptune Party

USS ——— ON ENTERING
THE DOMAIN OF NEPTUNUS REX
NOTICE AND LISTEN YE LANDLUBBER

I order and command you to appear before me and my Court on the morrow to be initiated in the mysteries of my Special Royal Domain. If you fail to appear, you shall be given as food for sharks, whales, sea turtles, pollywogs, salt water frogs, and all living things of the sea, who will devour you, head, body, and soul as a warning to landlubbers entering my domain without warrant.

You are charged with the following offenses:

THEREFORE, appear and obey or suffer the penalty.

DAVY JONES
Secretary of HIS Majesty

Offenses might include too many captain's masts, excessive liberty, repeated seasickness, and so forth. Reading some of these offenses at initiation before sentence adds much to the hilarity. Decorative certificates, suitable for framing, with the traditional nautical phraseology, once furnished by the Navy Department, may now be purchased or printed by the ship. They should be presented within a few days after initiation; also, a wallet-sized card with facsimile of the certificate is often issued to the new shellback. Sailors treasure such seagoing mementoes and consider them particularly valuable when captains or executive officers of ships authenticate them with signature and title.

Nearly two hundred years ago Captain Basil Hall, RN, wrote: "Its evil is transient, if any evil there be; while it certainly affords Jack a topic for a month beforehand and fortnight afterwards; and if so ordered to keep its monstrosities within the limits of strict discipline (which is easy enough) it may even be made to add to the authority of the officers instead of weakening their influence."

Sample Ritual for a Neptune Party

This dialogue was used in the ceremony aboard the USS *Augusta,* on crossing the equator on 23 November 1936 in the Java Sea.

Davy Jones Comes Aboard

The night before crossing the line is when summonses are delivered. Shortly after dark on the night before "crossing the line," Davy Jones, the Royal Navigator, and possibly the Judge and the Undertaker of Royal Court of Neptune, come up over the bow in boatswain's chairs or come up a forward hatch amid a spray of firehoses with the scene lit by searchlights and hail the bridge.

DAVY JONES *to officer of the deck:* Ship ahoy!
OOD: Aye, aye, sir.
DAVY JONES: What ship?
OOD: USS ———.
DAVY JONES: What course?
OOD: *[State course.]*
DAVY JONES: Very well. I have been awaiting your arrival. You will notify the commanding officer that I, Davy Jones, have a message to deliver from His Royal Majesty Neptunus Rex.
OOD: Aye, aye, sir.
[Permit a half-minute or so to elapse.]
OOD: Your Honor, the commanding officer awaits and will receive you now.
DAVY JONES: Very well, sir.
[Proceeding to place designated, usually the forecastle. If the meeting takes place on the quarterdeck, word is passed for all hands to follow Davy Jones as he proceeds aft with a master-at-arms leading. A ceremony should be made out of the visit.]
CAPTAIN TO DAVY JONES: Greetings, Davy Jones. Welcome aboard.
DAVY JONES: My congratulations, Captain, on your fine command. Some years since we last met.
CAPTAIN: Yes, it was aboard the USS ——— about ——— years ago.
DAVY JONES: I have orders for you and some summonses for your pollywogs from Neptunus Rex.
CAPTAIN: I will be glad to receive them.
[Davy Jones then reads the general order from King Neptune.]
I, Davy Jones came out of the sea tonight to bring from His Oceanic Majesty, King Neptune, Ruler of the Seven Seas, all the summonses for the landlubbers, the pollywogs, the sea vermin, the crabs, and eels who have not been initiated into the Supreme Order of the Deep. We of the great Neptune's Court bring serious indictments against those who still have traces of heifer dust and cow dung on

their feet, as well as those of the big towns who think they are real city slickers. But no matter, all will be shellbacks after the rough treatment on the morrow, at which time, those summoned will appear before the Royal Judge of His August and Imperial Majesty, Neptunus Rex, and there answer for offenses committed both aboard and ashore.

Captain, a few officers and men have already requested leniency, but be it known King Neptune has no favorites. All landlubbers since men first followed the sea have endured the strict initiation required by the King of the Sea. No! There will be no leniency—all pollywogs will receive appropriate punishment on the morrow.

And remember, sorrow and woe to those who resist or talk in a light or jesting manner of the ceremony, or of His Majesty, the Ruler of the Seven Seas, or of the Queen Amphitrite, or belittle Royal Members of his Supreme Court. So—Beware! Beware!

Good-bye, Captain, I will see you with the Great Neptune on the morrow. [Leaves shouting, "Gangway for Davy Jones" as he disappears down a hatch forward or over the bow amid a firehose spray, and with appropriate lighting effects, pyrotechnics, and so on.]

Initiation in the Ancient Order of the Deep upon Crossing the Line

When all is in readiness for the reception of King Neptune and party, the ship's navigator reports the ship is on the "line." Davy Jones then appears forward and reports to the officer of the deck that the captain is to be informed that Neptunus Rex and the Royal Court have been sighted ahead. The personal flag of King Neptune, the "Jolly Roger" (skull and crossbones), is broken when King Neptune and Court appear on deck. Attention is sounded on the bugle; officers and crew fall in at quarters or where designated. If convenient, at this point there can be a very brief ceremony when Neptune encounters Davy Jones just before meeting the captain.

NEPTUNE [on meeting Davy Jones]: Well, well, what a fine ship and what a cargo of landlubbers.
[At about this time the officer of the deck should salute Neptune and with seriousness report that the captain awaits the Royal Party. Then all move to the place of ceremony, giving as many people as possible the opportunity to see King Neptune and the Royal Court before the ceremonies of initiation, for instance, by passing down one side of the ship as at personnel inspection.]
CAPTAIN [coming on deck]: A sailor's welcome to you, King Neptune. It is a great pleasure to have you with us.
NEPTUNE: The pleasure is mine. [Then brief remarks.] Allow me to present Royal Navigator Shellback who will relieve you. I am so glad to be with you, Cap-

tain, and have prepared for a busy day in order to make all your landlubbers fit subjects of my great Raging Main.

CAPTAIN: Your Majesty, may I invite your attention to the fact that I have several young officers and crew members aboard who have not been in the Navy long enough to have had the opportunity to visit your domain and become shell-backs. I beg you to be as lenient with them as possible.

NEPTUNE: Captain, I am very sorry, I must be severe, there will be no exceptions. *[The captain then introduces officers who have crossed the line before, and all converse with Neptune and his Royal Court for a minute or so.]*

CAPTAIN: Neptune, I turn over my command to you for such time as you wish.

NEPTUNE: Very well, Captain, I thank you. *[Turns to Royal Navigator.]* Royal Navigator, proceed to the bridge and direct the ship be put on the course assigned. *[The Royal Court is then escorted to the "throne." Solemnly, Neptune and Court ascend and take assigned places to witness ceremonies. On order of Neptune, initiation commences with officers first. Captain and senior officers sit behind Neptune or on another platform.]*

The *dramatis personae* can be large or small, depending on the size of the ship and space for ceremony. The traditional titles are King Neptune (Neptunus Rex) and Queen Amphitrite, sometimes a daughter (Royal Princess), the Royal Baby (often the fattest man in the crew wearing only a diaper), Davy Jones, Royal Navigator (and assistants if needed), Royal Chaplain, Royal Judge (and assistants), Neptune's Officer of the Day, Royal Chief Bear (and sufficient assistants for the tank), Barber, Jesters, Devil, and Police. Often there is a Royal Scribe to keep record of all initiations.

Crossing the International Date Line

Before World War II, when U.S. Navy transports *Henderson* and *Chaumont* made frequent cruises across the Pacific to the Far East, a ritual of initiation in some respects similar to that of "crossing the line" took place when the ships crossed the International Date Line on the westward voyages. The neophytes, both officers and men, were subpoenaed for appearance before the Court of the Grand Dragon, where sentence was pronounced and initiation took place. As in the preliminaries for the Neptune ceremonies, considerable amusement was derived from the mock charges and specifications, with humorous incidents stressed and slight personal idiosyncrasies exaggerated. Advance radio dispatches and bulletins, supposedly received from Officers of the Court of the Grand Dragon, served "to build up the act" by heightening interest and adding to the apprehension of those about to be initiated. Those who "passed the test" were given small cards attesting to that fact.

Those issued on men-of-war that crossed the 180th meridian during World War II usually stated that the ship was "on a mission of war to effect the 'Setting of the Rising Sun.'"

Golden Shellbacks

For years Navy ships crossing the 180th meridian (International Date Line) have held ceremonies that entitled initiates to become certificated as members of the Grand Dragon, often called Golden Dragon. Those who cross at the intersection of the 180th meridian and the equator are certified as Golden Shellbacks.

In 1965, while in the USS *Capitaine* (AGSS 336), Jimmie E. Brooks, YN2(SS) USN, wrote to "Shipmate" that Davy Jones, speaking to all hands, said: "To pay homage to Neptunus Rex, we are not soliciting His Majesty to come up out of the sea to greet us. Rather we are going to meet him and his royal court. To say that you have crossed the 180th meridian at the equator is one thing, but to say that you have sailed *under* that point is an honor that can be bestowed only upon submariners."

Arctic Initiations

Ships and sailors whose duties take them above the Arctic Circle are known as bluenoses. While initiation ceremonies do not generally match those for crossing the line, the bluenoses still represent a unique community. Those making their first Arctic cruise have their noses painted blue, and some ships have them wear paper sunglasses until midnight.

The USS *Nautilus* having first set the pace, the nuclear submarine *Skate* made a record trip of 3,090 miles beneath the polar ice, testing new equipment and methods of breaking holes through the polar ice cap. On 17 March 1959 the *Skate* rose to the surface of the North Pole and committed the ashes of the distinguished Arctic explorer, Sir Hubert Wilkins, to the fierce Arctic winds. But for those who had not been to the Pole before (nearly all on the *Skate*) a stiff initiation was given, beginning the day the *Skate* left the Pole. The now "old timers" were charged with various "crimes" in much the manner of "crossing the line" ceremonies, as they were brought before Borealis Rex for sentence. It was the rule that all were guilty until proven innocent, and special permission for legal counsel was given only after sentencing.

Some were charged with having "nonregulation faces" and others with being "fugitives" from other submarines. One was charged with being a "reserve officer." K.P. duty was given in most instances as sentence.

Fifty years after Adm. Robert E. Peary reached the North Pole, Cdr. James F. Calvert, USN, commanding the USS *Skate*, crunched through the ice exactly at the North Pole, where he and his officers planted a U.S. flag and stood with their men at the top of the Earth. Commander Calvert signed three certificates for all hands on the *Skate*'s first Arctic voyage: Realm of the Arctic Circle, for crossing that circle; Ancient Order of Magellan, for the round-the-world tour at the Pole; and Domain of the Royal Dragon, for crossing the 180th meridian.

Passing Washington's Tomb

When a Navy ship on the Potomac River passes George Washington's Mount Vernon tomb, it must render honors. The father of our country was a firm supporter of the Navy and insisted that victory over the British could be won only with victory by the Navy. Navy regulations specify parading the guard, half-masting the ensign, tolling the ship's bell, playing taps, and, following the raising of the colors back to the peak, playing the national anthem.

Passing Honors to the USS *Arizona*

A ship passing the USS *Arizona* Memorial in Pearl Harbor renders honors by sounding "Attention." All hands topside render a hand salute, until the ship has passed the memorial and "Carry on" is sounded.

National Holidays

Holiday routine is observed when practicable on Navy ships for all national holidays. For specific holidays, such as Presidents' Day and Independence Day, ships in port full-dress ship, and at noon all saluting ships and stations sound a national salute of twenty-one guns. On Memorial Day, the flag is lowered to half-mast at 0800, and at noon each saluting ship or station fires a salute of twenty-one minute guns. After the salute, or at 1220 if no salute is given, the ensign is raised back to the peak.

Graduates of the Naval Academy give three cheers for those they leave behind and throw their hats in the air.
Naval Institute Photo Archive

Naval Academy Graduation Caps Thrown in the Air

Many have wondered about the origin of the custom of graduating midshipmen of the Naval Academy throwing their cover in the air. Since at many colleges and universities graduating students throw their mortarboards away, and since the other service academies observe the same custom, is it simply a sign of youthful exuberance?

The tradition was started by the class of 1912 who, by an act of Congress, were the first class of midshipmen to graduate and receive their commissions at the same time. Until that time, students graduated and became "passed midshipmen" awaiting their commissions at a later date, sometimes as much as two years later. They threw their caps away, up into the air, because they no longer needed them: they were being commissioned and would no longer wear the midshipman cover.

6

Naval Social Customs

Look about you today! See the confusion and chaos that reign over all questions of doctrine, diet, hygiene, behaviour; the relations of man to man, and above all of sex to sex; and ask yourself whether everything does not already bear the indelible stamp of having been left too long without the discriminating guidance of taste. Where traditional usages are breaking down, what is rising to take their place? Where old institutions are losing their power, where are the substitutes offered by the present age?

Anthony M. Ludovici, *A Defence of Aristocracy*

Let public apathy starve our material into inaction or degenerate us into an epidemic of scraping and painting, of bright-work and holy stones, if so be it that we remain a personnel determined that the niceties of plain good manners, manners learned at home and polished up with military terms into military courtesy, shall not perish from the sea; if so be it that these manners of Paul Jones, of Lawrence, of Farragut, of Dewey; if these sea manners passed down to us by these sea-gentlemen be preserved through us of today to sea-gentlemen yet unborn; if so be it we remain determined that the heart and soul of the Navy shall not go to hell!

Adm. F. B. Upham, USN

Life is not so short, but that there is always time for courtesy.

Ralph Waldo Emerson, *Letters and Social Aims*

The traditional unwritten law of naval etiquette, sea manners, and shore manners is best learned in an officer's youth. That is why young officers are constantly reminded that they should set good examples for their crew. By the same token, as senior officers observe sound and time-honored usages, the

Often foreign port visits demand participation in foreign customs and ceremonies. Here the commander of the Seventh Fleet takes part in a rice-pounding ceremony in Japan.

junior officers learn by example and precept. If seniors give but scant attention to sea manners, why should juniors consider them worthy of adoption?

The topics discussed in this chapter were in the main prompted by observations and opinions of experienced officers of the Navy, on both the active and retired lists. The subjects range from the ordinary manners and courtesy always expected of the officer aboard ship and ashore to the amenities that constitute everywhere the savoir-faire of citizens of the world.

Details and manner of execution require the judgment and initiative of the individual officer; here, we draw attention to the custom, the principle, and in some cases the sincere gesture. It is comparatively easy to know what to do; often the real difficulty is to know what to avoid.

Old Customs on Deck

At one time it was customary to send a sideboy or messenger to the foot of the accommodation ladder when guests of flag rank came aboard. This ensured that the barge would be held snugly alongside and that parcels or luggage would be expeditiously handled. It was a courtesy that had a practical value and was a distinctive attention that was expected of the smartly run ship.

Likewise, it was once a custom that the junior officer of the deck, a junior officer, or even the officer of the deck go to the foot of the accommodation ladder and inform a visiting commanding officer when it was not convenient for the commanding officer to receive the visitor in person. The captain is often precluded from attending the side because of conferences, inspections, and so forth. This courtesy saved the visiting captain a useless trip up the ladder when he was only making a friendly and informal visit.

The "sanctity" of the quarterdeck and observation of its traditional etiquette should be ever foremost in the minds of those who respect their profession and the smartness of their ship.

In the days of sail, custom held that the starboard side aft be reserved exclusively for the admiral or captain when on deck. A captain, if on deck, would shift to the port side if the admiral came topside, particularly if he accompanied another flag officer or senior visitor; this gave the senior officer more privacy. The port side abaft the quarterdeck was for the use of the commissioned officers, and the starboard side forward was reserved on many ships for the warrant officers. The large "foc'suls" of those days gave the crew ample space for fresh air and recreation.

When at sea, admirals and captains customarily walked the weather side of the quarterdeck. This point is made by C. S. Forester in his novel *Commodore Hornblower:* "[A]nd he began to stride up and down the weather side of the quarterdeck, hands behind him, head bowed forward, in the old comfortable attitude. Enthusiasts had talked or written of pleasures innumerable, of gardens and women, wine or fishing; it was strange that no one had ever told of the pleasure of walking a quarterdeck."

Extraordinary Naval Courtesies

Oftentimes over the years, naval courtesies have been rendered, which reflect not only extraordinary honor and the dignity of the situation, but also the consideration of the extending commander. As these examples show, the issue of courtesy is not a "cookbook" affair of merely "following the rules."

For example, on 4 July 1923 all ships of the Royal Navy present in Hong Kong, by direction of the commander in chief of the British Asiatic Fleet, rendered a twenty-one-gun salute in honor of the U.S. national holiday, although the only American ship present to receive the salute was the gunboat *Pampanga,* too small to be rated as a saluting ship. Such sincere and timely gestures aid in maintaining the cordial relations existing between public officers of mutually honorable states.

Ships and squadrons once "cheered" each other as a mark of respect. On one notable occasion, the cheering was led by Admiral Beatty, RN, on 7 December 1917, when Admiral Rodman's division of U.S. battleships joined the Grand Fleet as the Sixth Battle Squadron. Admiral Beatty's waving his cap with the cheering British bluejackets was a sincere gesture at a momentous time. It was the first time since the days of John Paul Jones that the United States had joined a foreign navy as a unit.

The "Farewell" on 1 December 1918, rendered by the British Fleet commanded by Admiral Beatty, involved extraordinary honors. Francis T. Hunter, an officer who was an eyewitness aboard the flagship *New York,* reported in his book, *Beatty, Jellicoe, Sims, and Rodman:*

> The Sixth Battle Squadron weighed anchor, broke from its maintops, long streaming "homeward bound" pennants, and proceeded out of harbor (Rosyth, Scotland). Our band burst forth with "Homeward Bound" and followed it with "Good Bye-e-e." Cheers were exchanged with every vessel we passed between the columns, while their bands played our airs, and messages of comradeship and good luck floated in a score of different versions from as many yardarms. Nor was that the end. The *New York* followed by the *Texas, Nevada, Arkansas, Wyoming,* and *Florida* in column was escorted to May Island, twenty miles outside, by the ships of the Fifth Battle Squadron (British), our sister division, and the Eleventh Destroyer Flotilla. . . . There was music and cheering nearly all the way, culminating as we reached May Island. The British units turned gracefully outward swinging through 180 degrees. There was a sustained roar of cheers as the great ships parted from us. . . . From the masthead of Admiral Levenson's *Barbara* was displayed at last the plain English hoist: "G-O-O-D B-Y-E-E-E-E." Simultaneously a message was received from Lord Beatty, the Commander-in-Chief, Grand Fleet: "Your comrades in the Grand Fleet regret your departure. We trust it is only temporary and that the interchange of squadrons from the two great fleets of the Anglo-Saxon race may be repeated. We wish you good-bye, good luck, a good time; and come back soon."

Lt. (jg) E. E. Wilcox, USNR, in a personal letter to the director of naval public relations, 14 February 1943, told of one of the most dramatic occasions of cheering witnessed in the United States during World War II. It took place on a bleak November day in 1942 when the war-scarred USS *Boise* moored at the pier in the Philadelphia Navy Yard. The commandant, Rear Adm. M. F. Draemel, USN, and senior officers of the district and yard assembled with a band on the assigned pier to welcome the gallant ship and her crew who had so bravely fought the heroic night action against the Japanese off Cape Esperance on 11–12 October 1942. HMS *Royal Sovereign* was moored on the other side of the pier assigned the *Boise.* Everyone in the yard knocked off work to witness the moving ceremony. Said Lieutenant Wilcox:

> As the cruiser drew within hailing distance, the band sounded off and the music was like a tropical sunrise the way it burst out. Orders were passed and the crew of the *Royal Sovereign* manned rails. All hands on the *Boise* not required for ship's work also manned rails and there was not an inch of her [rails] topside unoccupied.
>
> Heaving lines curved ashore. Mooring hawsers were passed and as the first one was secured . . . three cheers were proposed aboard the *Royal Sovereign.* They were given lustily from more than a thousand throats, and thus did a ship of our British ally pay homage to a gallant ship.
>
> Done in a time-honored way, it was a modern enactment of the ancient evolution.

The Officers' Mess

An officers' mess should be comparable to a gentlemen's club in its efficient service, standard of behavior, and tone of conversation. The decay of that standard is attributed to many causes. Some assert that the heavy work incident to present-day fleet training and operational tasking leaves little time for the "fancy stuff." Others state that the "slackening off" is the result of an influx of officers who did not have proper junior officer training. It may be simply that the large parties of the "good old days" are never given, and with them have gone the attendant amenities of the formal dinner. Whatever may be the cause or causes, some of the sea manners and usages that were once observed and are now in many particulars disregarded deserve a word of attention.

Wardroom Customs and Etiquette

In connection with a mess, it is of great interest to read Colonel Stewart's description of Admiral Lord Nelson's routine on the *St. George:*

Wardroom of USS *Norfolk* (SSN 714)
U.S. Navy (Tina M. Ackerman)

His hour of rising was 4 or 5 o'clock, and of going to rest about 10; breakfast was never later than 6, and generally nearer to 5 o'clock. A midshipman
or two were always of the party, and I have known him to send, during the
middle watch, to invite the little fellows to breakfast with him, when relieved. At table with them, he would enter into their boyish jokes and be
the most youthful of the party. At dinner he invariably had every officer of
the ship in their turn, and was both a polite and hospitable host.

In commenting upon Nelson's courtesy to subordinates, and his desire to
teach young officers the amenities of polite society, Adm. Mark Keer, RN, in
The Sailor's Nelson, writes: "It is impossible to overestimate the value of this
[in those days] unusual procedure in forming the discipline, good feeling, and
mutual confidence of the generations who have followed him in the naval
service; it has been and still is one of the principal priceless legacies that
Nelson has bequeathed to the service, which looks up to him as a model for
all time."

Wardroom country is each officer's seagoing home, a home in which he or
she should be proud to entertain relatives and friends. It is also the officer's

club where he or she may gather with fellow officers for moments of relaxation, such as a discussion of the daily problems; a movie, radio, or TV program; or just a cup of coffee. (Previous editions of this work referred to a friendly game of Acey-Ducey, but even that seems to have fallen into the category of "ancient" tradition.) Whatever the event, it is a place where members should conduct themselves within rules of propriety, common sense, and good manners, in addition to observing the rules of etiquette founded on customs and traditions.

1. The presiding officer should be punctual for the commencement of meals. If delayed, he or she should inform the next senior whether or not to proceed with the meal.

2. Members should be prompt, so that all the mess may be seated when the presiding officer takes his or her seat. The custom of arriving three to five minutes ahead of mealtime is recommended. If an officer is late, he or she should make apologies to the senior member, and if required to leave before the termination of the meal, should ask the presiding officer, as well as those seated nearby, for permission to be excused. Never, under ordinary circumstances, should an officer leave the table precipitately.

3. A friendly, cheerful atmosphere should prevail; the wardroom is a place for pleasantries and good conversation. There were, and are still, some sensitive topics that should not be addressed at dinner. The general admonition was always to refrain from discussions of sex, religion, and politics in the mess. Instead, the goal should be, in the poet Ben Jonson's words, "[d]electable and pleasant conversation, whose property is to move a kindly delight, and sometimes not without laughter."

4. With today's stress on a healthy atmosphere, smoking has all but disappeared from the wardrooms of the fleet. Good usage and custom have never sanctioned smoking during a meal. At a formal dinner, an officer should never "light up" until the host or seniors have done so. This will generally be after coffee is served.

5. Well-regulated messes have a written policy regarding guests, with a clear-cut differentiation made between guests of the mess and those of the individual. Officers should be encouraged to bring their guests aboard ship for dinner. Every guest that enters the mess should be treated as the guest of the entire mess, and it is the duty and privilege of each member to carry out the social obligation as cohost to the best of his or her ability. All members present should be introduced to guests, and each member should come forward to meet them.

6. The criterion of a mess is that officers should be proud to bring a distinguished guest at any time, knowing that their guest will receive the same dignified hospitality that would be expected in a club or at a formal dinner. This type of mess is achieved only by the sincere cooperation of all members.

Meeting of officers in the wardroom of USS *John S. McCain* (DDG 56)
U.S. Navy (Arlo K. Abrahamson)

7. It is the duty of the commanding officer to ensure that the wardroom mess that he or she commands, generally exercising command through the president of the mess, maintains high standards in tone and behavior and reflects credit on the naval service both at home and abroad. All of this has to do with manners, and as the poet Thomas Gray said: "Manners speak the idiom of their soil." The president should privately counsel those whose deportment brings down the tone of the mess.

Uniform Regulations

The Navy Uniform Regulations prescribe the correct manner of wearing the uniform, but the purpose of its wearing goes far deeper. The uniform is primarily designed to identify the wearer as a member of the naval service; moreover, it identifies his or her rank and therefore the authority and responsibility assigned to him or her by law. The present-day uniform has evolved gradually, and the many changes embody traditions of the service.

The manner of wearing the uniform creates a lasting impression upon the observer and reflects the pride of the individual in his or her profession.

It is incumbent upon all members of the service to demand excellence in uniform appearance, for no one wishes to be associated with an organization typified by slovenly dress.

Social Club Etiquette

Naval officers may be given cards to private-membership social clubs for the short stays of the ship or the fleet in ports both at home and abroad. It is a privilege that the Navy has always enjoyed, and under no condition should it be abused. For the benefit of young officers who have never been honorary members of such clubs, a few "navigational aids" are in order.

The visitor has no special rights in the club, but is expected to conform to the club rules, like any other member. Dignified courtesy should be rendered to all members, and the officer should always remember that his or her uniform and rank permit him or her to enjoy the facilities of clubs, while often others wait many years to become members. Club members gauge the social and intellectual caliber of the Navy by the officers they meet in the club. There is an air of dignity about the best clubs, both at home and abroad. Often wealthy men, after a family has been dispersed, prefer permanent residence at clubs and, of course, expect the same atmosphere to prevail that once obtained in their homes. In no sense is a club a hotel or simply a bar.

Officers who have been extended the privilege of a temporary membership or the status of guest of a club should sign the club register. This formality has a practical reason. The staff then know who the individual is, and members are able to know what officers have visited the club. It is customary in British clubs to observe whether or not there is a card board and, if so, to leave a visiting card on the board. Leaving a card signifies that you have appreciated the invitation and have paid your respects to the members. Senior officers leave their cards in person, when convenient, or send them by a member of the staff.

It is customary for the senior officer of a division or squadron and commanding officers of ships acting singly to address a letter to the club before sailing, in which they express thanks for the kindnesses and courtesies that have been tendered the officers of their commands during the stay of the ship or ships in port. This letter is usually addressed to the secretary of the club; in some cases, it may be addressed to the president of the club.

It would be difficult to improve on Emily Post's remarks on good manners in clubs, which nowadays apply to men and women alike:

A perfect clubman is another word for the perfect gentleman. . . . Good manners in clubs are the same as good manners elsewhere—only a little more so. A club is for the pleasure and convenience of many; it is never intended as a stage setting for a "star" or "clown" or "monologist." There is no place where a person has greater need of constraint and consideration for the reserves of others than in a club. In every club there is a reading-room or library where conversation is not allowed; there are books and easy chairs and good light for reading both by day and night; and it is one of the unbreakable rules not to speak to anybody who is reading or writing.

When two people are sitting by themselves and talking, another should on no account join them unless he is an intimate friend of both. To be a mere acquaintance, or, still less, to have been introduced to one of them, gives no privilege whatever.

It is also well to remember that clubs often have customs, which one calls in the Navy "special rates": rank hath its privileges, or RHIP. That is, the oldest members have certain corners or small rooms in which they lounge, certain tables they habitually use in the dining rooms, certain desirable chairs that for years they have occupied near the windows on the street. Observation on the part of the young officer will usually disclose this deference that is paid to age and rank.

An excellent rule for a young officer to obey, in clubs or elsewhere, is George Washington's sixty-sixth "Rule of Civility": "Be not forward but friendly and courteous; the first to salute, hear, and answer, and be not pensive when it's a time to converse."

General Courtesy

It is an unwritten law that officers remove their caps when in wardroom country, and when passing through the captain's or admiral's country. This is not done when in full dress, under arms, or wearing a sword.

Those versed in the niceties of old custom *always* remove their covers when passing through the crew's quarters at mealtimes.

When officers enter the sickbay on inspection trips and otherwise, it has been customary for them to remove their caps. This custom is probably derived from the old mark of respect paid the sick and suffering. Men were about ready for "slipping the cable" when they were admitted to sickbay in the days of sail.

Strictly speaking, officers are not supposed to uncover in the open except for divine worship, funerals, and other religious ceremonies. Since standing at attention and rendering the hand salute is the highest respect that one pays the colors or the commander in chief of the Navy afloat or ashore, it should suffice for the meeting with gentlemen or ladies in the open. This, of course, does not apply to receptions and social occasions on deck.

The courtesy of passing a senior going in the same direction with a "By your leave, sir," is not to be forgotten when an officer graduates from the training commands.

In walking with a senior ashore, or acting as an aide, the position of honor is to the right. An aide should be to the left and one or two paces in the rear when approaching presentations or meetings between seniors, whether it be military, naval, or civil officers. If the aide is to make the introductions, he or she should step to the side, facing both officers who are presented. The custom of the "right hand rule" is very old. It is quaintly expressed in Washington's thirtieth "Rule of Civility": "In walking, the highest place in most countries seems to be on the right hand, therefore place yourself on the left of him whom you desire to honor; but if three walk together the middle place is the most honorable. The wall is usually given to the most worthy if two walk together."

This rule also applies to riding in automobiles with seniors. A proper "gangway" for seniors should be scrupulously observed. Again, Washington's twenty-ninth "Rule of Civility" states: "When you meet with one of greater quality than yourself, stop and retire, especially if it be at a door or any straight place to give way for him to pass."

7

Dining-In and Dining-Out

Protocol is not intended just for the benefit of senior officers. Protocol is intended for all men, officer and enlisted alike. The pride of our nation and the importance of protocol must be passed on so that our country and our tradition never dies.

Gen. George S. Patton

Formal dinners to celebrate events date back to ancient days. The Romans had great feasts, as did the Vikings, the Normans, and all the other conquering tribes of Europe, Africa, Asia, and the Americas. By the eighteenth century the British had institutionalized their military regimental dinners into formal "messes," with strict rules and procedures. Gradually these dinners became weekly affairs for the purpose of fostering fraternal bonds. The interplay between the armies and navies of the United States and Britain during the world wars fostered the idea of these formal events in our own services, and as a result they have taken on a flavor of their own among American forces.

When done properly, dinings-in (in the Marine Corps, mess nights) can be the source of much unit pride and camaraderie, and senior commanders who encourage these events can spark the continuance of a professional tradition whose sole purpose is fostering unit cohesiveness.

Perhaps the most frequently asked question about dining-in is why are the rules so formal. In these days of relaxed association, it is sometimes hard to comprehend that this rigid framework can be the basis for freedom of quite a different sort. Not only did the practice of dining-in help to educate junior officers in the arts of entertaining and diplomacy, it prepared them for public speaking and demonstrated gentlemanly behavior. Because the mess originated as the home of the military and naval officer, and because mess nights were often the "only game in town" for the officers who had to work closely with each other, the mess also became a place where, to "relieve safeties," the foibles of life became exaggerated. Practical jokes, sarcasm, jealousy, or even duels could be the result. Although dueling is no longer in vogue, remnants of the other means of entertainment have remained.

Partly because of the demise of dueling in the 1850s, the level to which such games went skyrocketed. British junior officers began engaging in all manner of horseplay, from drinking games to contests of physical and mental prowess. As a means of containing these high jinks, the various messes began to hold specific dinners just for that purpose. In an effort to save their "honor," senior officers felt compelled to join in the fun.

In spite of the apparently ribald nature of the mess night, it also featured times for formal decorum, and the demarcation between them was quite pronounced in order to give no doubt as to what actions were appropriate at what time.

We turn now to today's dining-in with a discussion of each aspect of the program. Dinings-in are at once formal and relaxed, giving opportunity for education in, and practice of, professional and personal skills. As Charles Miller wrote in his pamphlet *The Customs of the Service* for the Army Service Schools Press in 1917, they are still occasions to "promote cordiality, comradeship, and esprit de corps."

These dinners were originally "stag" affairs, for the simple reason that there were no female officers as members of the unit. Even in those early days, there were occasions when wives were invited to attend. This gave rise to the distinction between a *dining-in*, which only members of the mess (originally male only) attended, and a *dining-out*, to which spouses and other guests might be invited.* The rules were essentially the same, although the deportment at a dining-out tended to be a bit more conservative. In either case, attendance was, and still is, a "command performance." Members of the mess were expected to be there, and exemptions were allowed only by formal request to the president of the mess, and with his acquiescence.

Today the frequency of these events has dropped from the nineteenth-century British weeklies to once a year, at most. The purpose of the dinner drives some of the planning. For instance, if there are to be foreign dignitaries

---

* The Navy's use of the terms *dining-in* and *dining-out* can be confusing, and the confusion is increased by the Marine Corps' use of the term *dining-in* to mean the same as the Navy's *dining-out*—that is, an occasion at which guests are present.

The men's formal and
dinner dress uniforms for
officers and chief petty
officers
Navy Uniform Catalog

as guests, and particularly if they are to speak, it is important to attend to
such details as having their flags and appropriate music available. The choice
of a dining-in or a dining-out also makes a considerable difference as to the
set-up and order of events of the evening. In any case, planning is done by
the two primary officers of the mess, the *president of the mess* and *Mr. Vice.*
(For purposes of this discussion, and in accordance with tradition, both
officers will be referred to as "he," though today the offices may be filled by
women.) The president is normally the senior officer of the mess, most often,
the commanding officer. Mr. Vice is an officer chosen for "keen wit and skill-
ful repartee"—in other words, one who is mentally agile and able to speak
extemporaneously.

Their duties involve oversight of the planning and execution of the affair.
The president bears overall responsibility, although he often delegates specific
planning details to other members of the committee. He greets the guests
and sees to their comfort and introductions to the mess prior to entering

The women's dinner dress
uniform for officers and
chief petty officers
Navy Uniform Catalog

the dining area, and he presides over the mess during the evening. Mr. Vice acts as the second for the president. His duties include much of the legwork for the setup of the event. He is the first to arrive and the last to leave the mess, and bears the lion's share of responsibility for the conduct of the event. It is Mr. Vice who assembles the mess by signal to move to the dining area, and during the dinner regales all assembled with a choice of appropriate (and tasteful) poems, stories, and anecdotes. He is responsible for ensuring that the beef course is sampled and approved. He is the *only* member of the mess who may address the mess without the express permission of the president. And he should do so often, if for no other reason than to satisfy the "naturally inquisitive nature of seamen" by holding forth on a topic of his choosing. Usually he is seated apart from the mess, facing the president, and where he can observe the rest of the room.

The choice of venue for the event can be critical for all manner of reasons. In particular, one must give thought to the ability of the club or restaurant to support the unique requirements of a dining-in. Most military clubs are familiar enough with the program to be easily able to adapt, and they can usually handle the exclusive bookings that prevent conflicts in service and room usage. Use of a civilian site is perfectly acceptable, but it is important to take care in communicating with the staff as to the schedule of events and likely activities.

Most dining facilities have a variety of table layouts, depending on the room and number of patrons. There should always be a head table, large enough to accommodate the official party. It should be a long, straight table with seating on one side only, rather than a round or rectangular table at which individuals would be seated on both sides. The seating plan places the president at the center, with the most distinguished guest on his right, the next most distinguished guest on the president's left, and alternating right and left on down the table. Attendees are accorded seating priority by rank. In a mixed, or foreign, service atmosphere, this can be quite daunting, so a few suggestions are in order.

1. Military officers, regardless of service branch, are seated according to seniority, by rank and, if necessary, date of rank. Should there be a conflict of two officers from different services with the same date of rank, they are seated by seniority of service: Army, Marine Corps, Navy, Air Force, Coast Guard.

2. Civilian government officials are seated by rank as well. Tables of equivalent ranks are usually available from the local protocol or public affairs offices.

3. When guests with no official rank are present, they are seated generally by age, position, and general congeniality. They may be interspersed with the others as best befits the atmosphere of the dinner.

4. Should the mess consist of several units, such as an Air Wing dining-in, members of units are seated together by unit, and then by seniority within the unit. In this example, each squadron would sit separately and the wing commander would be the president of the mess, but rather than having the squadron commanders at the head table due to their seniority, they would sit at the senior positions of their individual squadrons.

5. At a dining-in, guests are usually seated separately from the members of the mess, at their own guest table(s). This includes foreign and other service guests. Should the mess include members of other services or foreign officers, they are seated with the members.

6. At a dining-out, guests are interspersed among the members, with spouses sitting, in general, to the right of their member sponsor. At the head table, the spouse of the guest of honor is to the right of the president, and the spouse of the next ranking guest to the president's left, with the president's spouse to the right of the guest of honor.

Seating charts posted near the entrance and/or in the reception area, and place cards at the tables, are a necessity at these affairs.

Decorations for the hall may include the national and unit colors, the national colors of members or guests from foreign countries, and unit trophies and mementoes pertinent to the occasion. Flags and colors are placed in order of protocol.

Since the end of the Vietnam War, with the national attention on the returning prisoners of war and the desire for an accounting for those still missing, there has been a separate table set for our missing comrades. Its setting and decoration is particular and should serve as a memorial reminder, not a shrine. Attention is usually drawn to the POW/MIA table with the toast to missing comrades during the formal toasting. It is a separate table, set with a complete place setting, usually with a Purple Heart Medal pinned to the napkin and crossed swords above the place setting. If the company is just Navy, the sword is drawn and crossed with the scabbard; if Marines are present, the Navy sword and the Marine sword are crossed. An officer's cover can also be placed on the table. In a joint setting, the table can be set for one to four settings, each one representing a service. The meanings of the items on the table can be explained as a part of the toast. They are set forth in OPNAVINST 1710.7A:

TABLE SMALLER THAN THE OTHERS symbolizing the frailty of one prisoner alone against their oppressors.

THE WHITE TABLECLOTH represents the purity of their response to our country's call to arms.

THE EMPTY CHAIR depicts an unknown face, representing no specific Soldier, Sailor, Marine, or Airman, but all who are not here with us.

THE TABLE IS ROUND to show that our concern for them is never ending.

THE BIBLE represents our faith in a higher power and the pledge to our country, founded as one nation under God.

THE BLACK NAPKIN stands for the emptiness these warriors have left in the hearts of their families and friends.

THE SINGLE RED ROSE reminds us of their families and loved ones; and THE RED RIBBON represents the love of our country, which inspired them to answer the nation's call.

THE YELLOW CANDLE AND ITS YELLOW RIBBON symbolize the everlasting hope for a joyous reunion with those yet unaccounted for.

THE SLICES OF LEMON ON THE BREAD PLATE reminds us of their bitter fate.

THE SALT UPON THE BREAD PLATE represents the tears of their families.

THE WINE GLASS TURNED UPSIDE DOWN reminds us that our distinguished comrades cannot be with us to drink a toast or join in the festivities this evening.

Preprandial Assembly

A predinner cocktail "hour" of thirty minutes or less provides time for all members and guests to arrive, mingle, and greet each other, as well as to meet briefly and welcome the guests of honor. Note that the express purpose of this time is to meet, and not to get a head start on "laying on provisions for the voyage ahead." Not only does the prudent mariner husband stores for the long passage, but departures from the mess during dinner are normally viewed as violations of the mess; thus, the immediate relief that a visit to the head might bring, might also bring a longer term discomfort of another nature. Don't use the cocktail hour to load up on liquids of any sort.

Likewise, the cocktail time is not an excuse to be "fashionably late." Members of the mess are expected to be on time, if not early, so that they can greet the guests when they arrive. It is considered poor form to arrive after the guest of honor, and this is subject to attention during the business of the mess later in the evening.

A receiving line is the most efficient means of introduction of the members and guests to the guest of honor. Other parts of the ceremony might include any unit-specific rites; installation of the unit insignia, trophies, or memorabilia; or the ritual mixing of a ceremonial punch.

When the cocktail period is over, Mr. Vice signals for the diners to enter the dining area. This can be done by means of chimes or announcement; if a band is present, it can sound attention and play appropriate music; some units have even used a lone bagpiper to lead the charge. No drinks or smoking materials may be carried into the dining room. When the members enter the dining area, they stand behind their seats and await the arrival of the head party.

The head table assembles after the crowd has departed, and enters ceremonially after the members and guests are in place, with the president escorting the distinguished guest. When all are in position, Mr. Vice announces to the president that the mess is assembled, and such opening ceremonies as the parading of the colors and the grace can start the evening's festivities.

In announcing these events, the president raps his gavel for attention and simply states: "Ladies and Gentlemen, the Colors" or "Ladies and Gentlemen, the Grace." The assumption is that, as professionals, the assembled personnel know what to do at the appropriate moment and do not need instruction as to the position of attention or supplication.

The Dinner

The dining-in is a formal, but not a stodgy, time. Many are put off by the impression that such an evening is a cold and sterile affair. On the contrary, the dinner is meant to offer the best of company and dining. The food should be the highest quality available within reasonable bounds of cost, and it should be prepared and served in the most dignified and efficient manner. The meal should consist of three to seven courses; the caterer will be able to make suggestions as to the menu. Traditionally, the Navy (and also the Army) serves roast beef as the main course. A written menu should be placed at the table, possibly as part of the event program.

A ritual parading of the beef is always a part of the ceremony. Upon signal from the president, a waiter convey a portion to Mr. Vice as the most expendable member of the mess. He then tastes the proffering and pronounces it "fit for human consumption," whereupon the dinner is served.

Wines are served with dinner as appropriate to the course; again, the caterer can advise the committee on selection. Should someone not desire wine, they may so indicate to the wine steward or put their place card over their glass. (Do not invert the glass as a signal.) At the end of a course, the wine steward or wait staff will remove that course's wine glass. Let them; it is their job to do so, and in any case, the next course will bring the appropriate wine.

Toasts normally accompany a dining-in or dining-out, as do after-dinner remarks by the guest of honor. The business of toasting is one of much tradition and formality, and is addressed later in this chapter. But there are certain general points that should be mentioned here. First, the order of formal toasts and who is to give them must be decided and published beforehand. Second, toasts are made with wine or, for those who do not drink alcohol, with some prearranged, nonalcoholic beverage or juice substitute—*never with water!* Last, toasts are never offered to an individual by name, only to an office or institution.

The Social Activity and the Business of the Mess

The events of the latter part of the evening include the serving of liqueurs, playing of games, and so forth, in keeping with good sense, and may continue for as long as members are interested and willing to participate. Usually, by this time, Mr. Vice has some business to take care of, in the form of fines and payments for violations of the mess rules. Sharing of limericks, poetry, songs, and the like by members of the mess is encouraged, especially if the selections pertain to the present company and are presented in a lighthearted spirit of fun.

One who wishes to offer a limerick or other form of fun must first ask the president for permission, by rising and addressing the president, requesting permission to address the mess. The president may or may not inquire as to the purpose but in any case either permits or turns down the request. Inside stories in which the humor is not readily discernible may need to have the stage set before proceeding, so that all may enjoy them. The target of a jibe should have time made available, before the evening's end, to riposte, lest those present be left to believe that the shot was true. Obviously, points of personal or unit sensitivity that might be found embarrassing to either the individual or the assembly are never proposed.

Games are also encouraged, but again, planning is prudent. Activities that are quite benign at normal times might become risky when conducted by those who have spent the evening imbibing. It is a good idea to have appropriate trophies or mementoes available for the winners.

Toasts

The custom of welcoming guests at a repast by offering special libations in honor of the head of the state of the visitor, or the country from which the guest hails, or the organization to which he belongs, is very ancient. In old days it was customary for the host to take a sip of the cup first to show that the beverage was not poisoned. A survival of the custom lingers in the usage that is observed when a sip of wine is poured into the glass of the host so that he may determine its quality before filling the glasses of the guests.

Although "official drinking" is of ancient vintage, the term *toast* is of Anglo-Saxon derivation. A piece of toast was at one time placed in the glass with certain wines and beverages, in the belief that this would improve the flavor of the wine. The following quotations indicate the custom of those days:

It happened that on a publick day a celebrated beauty of those times [of Charles II] was in the Cross Bath [at Bath] when one of the crowd of her admirers took a glass of water in which the fair one stood, and drank her health to the company. There was in the place a gay fellow, half-fuddled, who offered to jump in, and swore, tho' he liked not the liquor, he would have the toast. Tho' he was opposed in his resolution, this whim gave foundation to the present honour which is done to the lady we mention in our liquors, who has ever since been called a toast. (*Tatler* 24, 4 June 1709)

Go fetch me a quart of sack; put a toast in 't.
                    (Shakespeare, *Merry Wives of Windsor*)

The social education of naval officers requires them to know how toasts are given and what to do if the occasion arises. At official dinners given in honor of visiting foreign officials, toasts are made first to the head of the state, or to the country, or to the organization of the guests. For example, at an official dinner given by a British admiral for an American admiral, the routine might be as follows: the British admiral, at a point before completion of the dinner, usually at or after dessert, rises and toasts "the president of the United States"; upon completion of the toast, the orchestra plays "The Star-Spangled Banner." A minute or so after the officers are seated, the American admiral rises and toasts "the queen"; immediately thereafter the orchestra plays "God Save the Queen." Should there be other foreign dignitaries present as well, the host may either toast the heads of all the foreign nations collectively or separately, named in order of the seniority of the representatives present. (An exception is a dinner held in a foreign locale, when the local head of state is toasted first.) If they are toasted separately, the national anthem of each country should be played. After these toasts, short speeches are sometimes made, followed by subsequent toasts as the occasion demands, with the final toast to the respective services. Ceremonies differ somewhat as to the time when the first and ceremonial toasts are drunk. Officers attending such a dinner should take care to find out the local procedure.

Officers of the Royal Navy have the privilege of remaining seated when they toast the sovereign. Some authorities write that this honor was accorded the Royal Navy by William IV, while the popular service opinion is that it was Charles II who established the custom. The story goes that Charles II, when returning to England in 1660 in the *Royal Charles,* bumped his head because of the low overhead of the wardroom when replying to a toast that had been drunk to him. He made the statement forthwith that royal naval officers would never again rise to toast the British sovereign. The late marquis of Milford Haven, then admiral of the fleet and prince of Battenberg, established the custom of rising in the Royal Navy only when the toast to the king was followed by "God Save the King" (the British national anthem). In 1964, in honor of the three-hundredth birthday of the Royal Marines, Queen Elizabeth II ruled that the Marines would also make their toast to the queen sitting down.

Although the manner of toasting in military and naval messes is not in all respects uniform, some general principles may be outlined:

1. As a rule, the highest officials propose the loyalty toast to the heads of state. The host honors the guest first. Toasts to sovereigns and heads of state should be short and should not be prefaced by irrelevant remarks.

2. At smaller dinners and semiformal ones, the toast may be drunk to the navy of the visiting country, the country of the visitors, and in some cases to the senior officer and officers of the squadron or ship. These toasts may also follow the toasts to the heads of the respective states.

3. Do not drink a toast that is proposed to you or your service. All drink to the president, king, queen, or a dignitary.

4. Replies to toasts should be of similar nature and of corresponding subjects.

5. With the exception noted above, officers stand for toasts.

6. Toasts in a Navy mess are usually in the following order (in a Marine mess the order differs, and Marines traditionally drink to the Corps with a rum punch instead of wine):

    The Commander in Chief (Loyalty Toast)

    The Joint Chiefs of Staff

    The U.S. Marine Corps

    The Chief of Naval Operations

    Our Ships at Sea

    Missing Comrades

       (The preceding toasts are followed by informal toasts.)

    The United States Navy (Service Toast)

7. Since there are normally several official toasts offered in succession, officers should not drain their glass with each toast. The exception to this rule is the service toast, the last toast of the evening, when the glasses are drained before being placed back on the table.

Those who do not normally drink alcohol are not required to do so, but it is expected that they charge their glasses and raise them in honor of the toast and then return the glass to the table without bringing wine to their lips. With proper planning, these officers can easily be accommodated by having the wine steward bring out a suitable nonalcoholic substitute. In civilian circles, those who do not take wine will have their glass filled with water,

The secretary of the Navy offers the service toast at the 226th Navy Birthday Ball in Washington, D.C., 2001.
U.S. Navy (Dolores L. Parlato)

but in the Navy we never drink a toast in water, as superstition says that if we did so, the subject of our solicitude would die by drowning.

The issue of informal toasts sometimes fills officers with dread. It involves that most treacherous form of human activity, public extemporaneous speech. Nevertheless, it is a circumstance that one can survive by following a few simple guidelines. Particularly in the setting of a dining-in or dining-out, but even at a wedding reception or company dinner, it is best not to go beyond your comfort zone. If you are not naturally glib, don't attempt to be so on demand. Keep it short. Stand, make your pitch, raise your glass, and sit down. Don't prolong the agony. Many have the tendency to start strong, run out of ideas, and decide to keep talking until a suitable ending comes along. This leads to long rambling discourses, and restless and uncomfortable crowds. If you are honored by a toast, return the favor. In the end, do your homework: if you expect that you will be called upon to offer a toast, look something up in one of the myriad books on the subject or on the Internet.

After the loyalty toasts, mess rules are relaxed and the smoking lamp is lighted. (By the way, it is always "lighted," never "lit.") Cigarettes and cigars are not lit until after the president has lit his own, or has given permission for others to smoke. Pipes are not smoked without the president's permission. After the smoking lamp is lighted, anyone who wishes may leave the table except those who are in charge of the wine decanters. Officers who have "decanter custody" must first charge the officer on their left with the responsibility of the decanter. Officers leaving the decanters unattended are subject to a fine equal to the cost of the contents of the decanter.

In British messes, there is a series of toasts known as "dailies." The popular custom is for the president to call on a junior member of the mess for the toast to "——— Day," with a stiff fine to the one who doesn't jump to his feet and respond correctly and without delay. These traditional dailies are:

Monday: "Our ships"
Tuesday: "Our men"
Wednesday: "Ourselves (and may no one be like us!)"
Thursday: "A bloody war, or a sickly season"
Friday: "A willing foe and sea room"
Saturday: "Sweethearts and wives'"
Sunday: "Absent friends"

The French usually say, "I have the honor . . . [J'ai l'honneur . . .]" At a dinner for a French admiral or senior French officer, the American officer would say, "I have the honor to propose a toast to the president of the French Republic." The French officer would reply, "It is my great honor to propose a toast to the president of the United States" or simply "To the president of the United States." At regular mess dinners in the Royal Navy, the senior member of the mess proposes the toast, "The Queen," and all members in a low tone repeat, "The Queen" and drink a sip of the toast.

The last toast of the evening, the service toast, is offered, upon direction of the president, by Mr. Vice, who simply stands and states: "The United States Navy." All present immediately leap to their feet to second the toast, and after the playing of "Anchors' Aweigh," they drain their glass. At a Marine mess night, a similar procedure is followed. For the concluding toast, the president calls: "Mr. Vice, Corps and Country." All stand, "The Marines' Hymn" is played, and Mr. Vice repeats the words taken from a recruiting poster of 1 January 1776: "Long live the United States, and success to the Marines!" (The same poster is the source of the traditional use of a rum punch instead of wine for the Marine service toast.)

It is not permissible to pick up a decanter at any time to refill a glass; instead, one must wait until the decanters are passed in their normal rounds. The president may order the decanters removed at any time after the toasts are drunk, but it is usual to pass them at least once more. After the second passing, decanters are left unstoppered until removed.

Members who do not take wine when the decanters are passed for the loyalty toast are not permitted to take any at any subsequent passing. Note that this is the basis for the ceremony of the passing of the port.

Passing of the Port

The port wine is placed on the table after the table is cleared. In a small mess it is placed before the president; in larger ones Mr. Vice and possibly other officers have decanters placed in front of them as well. When the decanters are all placed on the table, the senior steward or Mr. Vice reports to the president, "The wine is ready to pass, sir." The president then unstoppers the decanter in front of him, and other officers with decanters before them follow suit. The president passes the decanters one at a time to his left, the other officers doing the same. Remember, the president and other officers in charge of decanters do not help themselves before passing the decanters. When a set of decanters arrives in front of an officer who has charge of a set, he helps himself to what he wants and keeps the new set in front of him. The stewards move the stoppers on from one officer to the other, so that they remain with their own decanters.

The decanters should be at least one place apart during their trip around the table. They should never be allowed to "pile up" beside a member. They should be "slid" from place to place, not lifted from the table.

If, due to a shortage of members, there is a gap at the end of the table, the stewards in that area should move the decanters across it.

Remember that a decanter may never be passed to the right. If you thoughtlessly do not help yourself when you desire wine, you are out of luck. Although this is not very good form, it is permissible to pass your glass down to the officer who has the decanter at the moment and ask that officer to fill it. It is not necessary to take wine if you do not want it, but if you do not take it on the first round of decanters, you may not take it subsequently.

No one may touch their wine until the loyalty toast has been proposed. When the wine has been passed and all decanters have reached their destination, the senior steward or Mr. Vice reports to the president, "The wine has been passed, sir." The president then stoppers the decanters in front of him, and the other officers follow suit.

The president raps the table for silence and begins the loyalty toast(s) by saying, for example, "Mr. Vice, the Queen." If there is a band in attendance, it then plays the national anthem, after which the vice president responds, "Gentlemen, the Queen." All members raise their glasses and repeat, "The Queen," and those with wine drink the toast.

Enforcement of the Rules of the Mess

The president of the mess will normally have a gavel to emphasize his control over the mess. Members and guests alike must be familiar with the meanings of the gavel raps. They are:

1 rap: Be seated.
2 raps: Rise.
3 raps: Attention.

Note that members standing to address the mess must do so with the permission of the president. Should the member who has taken the floor displease the president, or should the president not wish to hear the request of the member, one rap is sufficient to signal the member to sit without further argument. Likewise, approval of the president—in the case of a request to propose a toast, for instance—might well be signaled by the sounding of two raps. In the latter case, after all have stood, Mr. Vice repeats the object of the toast only (not the rationale given by the member), and after all repeat it and drink the toast, the sounding of one rap signals the mess to be seated again.

Members of the mess are expected to conduct themselves in a manner consistent with all bounds of propriety. If, during the dinner, a member observes a violation of the rules of the mess or other breach of etiquette, he or she may challenge whoever committed the breach. The proper time to do so is while Mr. Vice is conducting the business of the mess. The member stands and requests permission of Mr. Vice to address the president. The exchange might go something like this:

Member: "Mr. Vice, I request permission to address the president of the mess."
Mr. Vice: "Granted, sir. What is the nature of your inquiry?" [Or "Denied, sir."]
Member: "I wish to challenge LCDR Jones and ask that a penalty be levied against him for appearing out of uniform tonight. To wit: he is in attendance with an inverted cummerbund."
Mr. Vice: "Granted" or "Noted." Then: "LCDR Jones may stand in his defense."

With pronounced assurance, confidence, and brevity, the accused offers his or her excuse or rebuttal. The president then rules on the merits of the case, the validity of the transgression, and the ability of the defense, and assesses punishment as necessary. Punishment in some messes might be in the form of fines, and if this is the case, the attendees are well advised to carry a fold of dollar bills, for the mess does not make change for fines. However, the use of monetary fines can lead to hard feelings and does little to further the enjoyment of either the one fined or the other members. Far better to have the punishments require some lighthearted performance by the miscreant, such as having him or her hold forth on some suitable professional topic for a specific amount of time, perform some specific physical feat, or regale the members with a song or story. This will have a far better effect in deterring further violations, while contributing to the entertainment of the mess.

There may be situations in which the president either wishes to be magnanimous in his ruling or cannot come to a clear verdict. In these cases, he may wish to discern the feelings of the members by asking for any who would stand with the accused in this matter. Those who stand can be heard or simply counted, at the discretion of the president, and the charges can be dismissed or punishment levied against the entire group standing with.

It is important to note that normally only members of the mess can be assessed punishment for violations of the mess. The guest of honor is normally exempt. In the case of a dining-out, where there are guests present, each member is responsible for his or her guest's education before the dinner and actions at the event. Should a guest be charged with, and convicted of, a violation, the guest's host or sponsor is therefore liable for the punishment.

Violations of the Mess

A list of common violations might include the following:

Untimely arrival at the proceedings

Smoking at the table prior to the lighting of the smoking lamp

Haggling over date of rank

Wearing an inverted cummerbund

Not recognizing an inverted cummerbund

Making loud and obtrusive remarks in a foreign language or in English, or any other untimely or offensive emission

Not rising to speak with the president (if addressing him from the floor)

Employing improper toasting procedure

Engaging in ungentlemanly (or unladylike) conduct

Eating glass after the toast

Leaving the dining area without permission of the president

Proposing an inappropriate or inane toast such as "cheers"

Toasting with an uncharged glass

Carrying cocktails into the dining room

Wearing unauthorized insignia or uniform

Commencing a course before the president (or, in the case of a dining-out, commencing a course before the senior woman at the head table)

Attempting to toast with water

Using foul language

Wearing a clip-on bow tie at an obvious list

Being caught with an uncharged glass

Maintaining too low a profile

Behaving in such a manner as to be mistaken for a Marine

Removing articles of clothing from oneself or others

Rising to applaud particularly witty, succinct, or relevant toasts, unless following the example of the president

Lying down, closing one's eyes, and breathing in a deep and regular manner

Haggling over penalties or fines assessed

While strictly speaking not normally a violation of the mess, the throwing of rolls and other semiguided missiles at any time during the course of the meal should be frowned upon. At one dining-out, a thoughtless shipmate who failed to apply proper operational risk assessment to the situation, launched said missile in a young lieutenant's direction. The shipmate was guilty of improper targeting, and the hardtack hand grenade managed to find an errant wine glass on the table. The lieutenant's date's beautiful new white silk sheath was in the frag-pattern of the red wine secondary explosion. The lieutenant's evening and future relationship was listed as collateral damage in the after action report.

Recesses

At a dining-in, there will normally be no allowance for members to "ease springs" until the smoking lamp is lighted. At the discretion of the president during a dining-out, Mr. Vice may call for a break by suggesting that "for the benefit of the ladies, we shed a tear for Admiral, Lord Nelson." Note that this is a risky maneuver, since regaining control of the mess after such recess can be difficult.

Social Usage Prescribed and Proscribed

As you from this day start the world as a man, I trust that your future conduct in life will prove you both an officer and a gentleman. Recollect that you must be a seaman to be an officer; and also that you cannot be a good officer without being a gentleman.

> Admiral Lord Nelson, advice to a young man
> just appointed a midshipman

It is almost a definition of a gentleman to say he is one who never inflicts pain.

> Cardinal John Henry Newman, *Idea of a University*

To be a gentleman is to be one the world over, and in every relation and grade of society.

> *The Amateur Immigrant,* 1896

We all did our duty, which, in the patriot's, soldier's, and gentleman's language, is a very comprehensive word, of great honour, meaning, and import.

> Rudolf Erich Raspe, *Travels of Baron Munchausen*

"An Officer and a Gentleman"

We must, at the outset, address the words that have defined the professional naval leader: "an officer and a gentleman." The officer corps attains its highest distinction when the two nouns become synonymous. To the customs and usages of civilized countries, the gentleman will conform, for, as Cardinal Newman said in his classic definition of a gentleman: "He even supports institutions as venerable, beautiful, or useful, to which he does not assent." And an officer could also ponder what a celebrated French author had to say:

"A gentleman is one who has reflected deeply upon all the obligations which belong to his station, and who has applied himself ardently to fulfill them with grace."

Thoughtful adherence to those standards of military conduct that were of importance during the many years before the present active list entered the Navy is a worthy goal. The service has certain fine old usages that are worthy of respect, and no matter how pressing duties may become, there is always time for their observance. It is not tradition and custom alone that compel these observances; instinct also lends its voice. Some say that times have changed. Yes, they have changed in many ways, but good manners, personal dignity, punctilious courtesy without sycophancy, attention to those niceties not in the regulation book, all based on loyalty and consideration for others, still remain the hallmark of the officer and the gentleman.

One significant change is that the wardroom or ready room is no longer populated strictly by "gentlemen." Today both men and women carry out the responsibilities of naval leadership with equal ability and resolve. Nevertheless, the idea of an "officer and a gentleman" is solid, for the manners and deportment conjured up by the phrase are valid regardless of the gender of the leader. While many of the traditions of the officer corps of the Navy were generated during an all-male period of naval history, they remain perfectly good models of behavior for the leaders of today and tomorrow, both men and women. In the discussion that follows, we will use the term *gentleman* in this larger sense that includes both men and women, in keeping with the nature and spirit of today's Navy.

The term *gentleman* fits neither those who are afraid they will not be taken as such, nor those who tell the world they are. As the sixteenth-century French author Michel de Montaigne wrote: "I have often seene men proove unmanerely by too much maners, and importunate by over-much curtesie. The knowledge of entertainment is otherwise a profitable knowledge."

By all means, it is the "profitable knowledge" that should be gained. Sincerity and common sense should always govern, and nothing that makes for ease and decorum in polite society should be neglected by those in the service. The heritage of the Navy is certainly one of superior behavior and unquestioned honesty. Superior behavior comprises self-restraint, consideration for others, and a gracious conformance with the best social usage of the time. The high standards of honor and integrity in the Navy have become traditional—a fashioner of character throughout one's career.

The fundamentals of "good breeding" can be gained in childhood and early youth, but those not so fortunate can learn, by careful observation of good manners in others, a searching self-criticism, and vigilant attention to deportment and bearing, to feel at ease in any company, no matter how formal, official, or dignified the assembly. An officer should strive to possess the intellect and manners that make him or her worth meeting, at home and abroad.

A proper appreciation of social values and the exercise of superior manners requires no justification: "It is a wise thing to be polite; consequently, it is a stupid thing to be rude." Neither are good manners incompatible with the role of seamen, notwithstanding the extreme "he-man" and "hairy-chested sailor" attitudes that one may encounter. Jervis, Nelson, Perry, Lawrence, Decatur, Porter, Farragut, Dewey, Halsey, Nimitz, King, Stockdale, and Denton were gentlemen, even though some were bluff or gruff. They knew the value of tradition and dignified ceremony, and, above all, they were men of character.

As individual Americans, and as a society, we sometimes forget that foreign officials' impressions of the culture of the United States are formed to a large extent by their contact with the officers of our foreign service and the armed forces. By *Navy Regulations,* it is the duty of the naval officer to respect the customs of foreign lands. To learn something of the history, customs, modes of living, and social amenities of foreign countries is an important part of a liberal education. Naval officers do not roam the world as fact-finding politicians, freelance writers, professors, or sociologists; rather, they must keep in mind their usual status as official guests or allies, and recognize that, as such, to publicly criticize their hosts is to commit a grave breach of etiquette. We as Americans have no monopoly on civilized customs or good manners; indeed, many citizens of other countries would say that we are, as a society, crude and unmannerly. Our basic code of manners and etiquette came to us from our Old World heritage. It would be to our international benefit if we were to spend more time in mending our own fences and correcting our own shortcomings, and less time in criticizing the established customs of other people.

Religion plays a major role in the daily life of many peoples of the world. It is important that the naval officer have some basic knowledge of the world's great religions so that he or she can avoid giving unintentional offense to people of other countries and other religions.

In their international application, good manners require a reasonable conformance to the best usage of foreign states, as well as self-restraint and

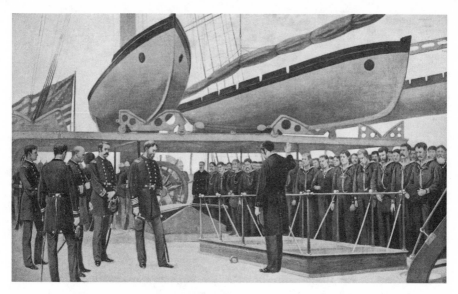

Morning Quarters—the Lord's Prayer
From "All Hands" by R. F. Zogbaum; courtesy Harper and Bros.

consideration for others. The American abroad sometimes perceives the ceremonial to be antiquated, as well as dreary forms of stilted etiquette bordering closely on servility. Some of it may even seem to be lip service, but it should be politely accepted. When in Rome, do as the Romans do—that is, if one wishes to learn something, have a good time, and be invited back.

This brings us to an important rule in official social relations: to ascertain in advance what will be expected—the ceremonies and customs that obtain on certain occasions. This policy has two practical advantages. First, all ceremonies, such as formal presentations and audiences, go more smoothly when all know the "drill." Second, although senior officers are at times invited by virtue of rank and position to attend official ceremonies, some may by advance information forgo the "pleasure," if not in official sympathy with the ceremonial or the principals.

By inquiring ahead of time, it is generally possible to learn some details in advance of official functions. Where the occasion is that of luncheon or dinner, the senior officer will often be called upon to "say a few words," whether or not he or she knows the significance of the memorial, celebration, anniversary, or feast day. As usual, preparedness should be the rule: know what is expected of you. Formal or informal inquiry through U.S. consular or diplomatic channels will generally secure the desired advance information. This is part of the business of the foreign service.

Titles

George Washington, in his thirty-ninth "Rule of Civility," wrote: "In writing or speaking, give to every person his due title according to his degree and custom of the place." This excellent rule is universal in its application. For example, it is most helpful to find out who will attend a particular ceremony, celebration, or dinner. How should they addressed? What are their official titles? How are their names pronounced? What is the correct etiquette of the occasion? The individual should be given the benefit of the doubt, but where titles are established by law, whether civilian or military, one should be precise in giving "every person his due." Official lists, rosters, registers, *Who's Who* (American and British), and, for high British titles, books such as *Burke's Peerage* will generally give all the information that is needed. Again, the foreign service and our military attachés abroad are invaluable resources.

Attention to official amenities is conducive to good morale. Senior officers' knowing what to do at the right time and the right place engenders pride in ship and service, and imbues junior officers with the desire to emulate the actions of the superior, to learn from example what to do and when to do it, when their time comes. Thus the true spirit of the gentleman aids considerably in the competent exercise of the art of command.

Captain Basil Hall, RN, who wrote a detailed and descriptive journal of his career on the sea, said in this connection over one hundred fifty years ago:

> And certainly as far as my own observation and inquiries have gone, I have found reason to believe that those officers who are the best informed and the best bred, and who possess most of the true spirit of gentlemen, are not only the safest to trust in command of others, but are always the readiest to yield that prompt and cheerful obedience to their superiors, which is the mainspring of good order. Such men respect themselves so justly and value their own true dignity of character so much and are at all times so sensitively alive to the humiliation of incurring reproach, that they are extremely cautious how they expose themselves to merited censure. From the early and constant exercise of genuine politeness, they become habitually considerate of the feelings of others; and thus, by the combined action

of these great principles of manners, officers of this stamp contrive to get through far more work, and generally do it much better, than persons of less refinement. Moreover, they consider nothing beneath their closest attention which falls within the limits of their duty; and, as a leading part of this principle, they are the most patient as well as vigilant superintendents of the labours of those placed under their authority, of any men I have ever seen.

Rules of Civility

So-called grand manners are not always good manners. Rules of civility are vested with the authority of good usage. Experience has proven their worth. Our generation did not make them, nor did our parents, but they will exist when our last cruise is over. There is a marked universality in some of them. The Chinese sage Confucius "saw the courtesies as coming from the heart," and wrote that "when they are practiced with all the heart, a moral elevation issues."

The first written collection of rules for the deportment and manners of gentlemen, called the *Bienseance de la Conversation entre les Hommes,* was composed and collated by French Jesuits in 1595. Another Jesuit, Father Perin, translated the rules into Latin, adding a chapter of his own on behavior at the table. Father Perin's edition appeared in 1617. Editions were published in Spanish, German, and Bohemian. A French edition appeared in 1640, and at the same time Francis Hawkins published an English edition in London. This book in its various translations was used as a textbook in many of the best institutions of learning responsible for the education of the young gentlemen of the day. Obadiah Walker, master of University College, Oxford, compiled a version called *Youth Behaviour,* a form of which seems to have been transcribed by George Washington in his youth.

Washington's *Rules of Civility and Decent Behaviour in Company and Conversation,* though old-fashioned and quaint, carry in essence that fundamental precept of any social code, polite deference and respect for others. It would be preposterous, however, to state that memorizing a set of rules makes a gentleman. In the last analysis, gentility is a reflection of the inner makeup of a person. The rules only give guidance to the spirit; as James I said to his old nurse: "I'll mak' your son a baronet gin ye like, Luckie, but the de'il himself couldna mak' him a gentleman."

Some Naval Social Customs

Official Calls

In a naval career, there are visits and calls that are sometimes required by regulation, by custom, and by courtesy. A personal choice or selection in the matter of visits is not the prerogative of those in official life. Good usage decrees that certain calls be scrupulously made and returned.

Many officers do not recognize the necessity for these calls and therefore despise them as junior officers and dispense with them when they reach the position where they are to be called upon. In today's Navy especially, interpersonal relationships drive an officer's employment, which affects his service reputation, and, in turn, can make or break his career. The minutes spent alone with a new junior officer allow the CO to get to know the junior officer as a person, what his or her goals are, how he or she thinks and reacts in conversation with seniors, before the junior officer is placed on the watch bill. Likewise, the new officer can find out how the skipper thinks and what he or she expects, without having to be embarrassed by guessing incorrectly in front of peers and subordinates. The bonding that can take place in such calls can prevent a multitude of problems in the future and allows both officers to get off on the right foot with each other far more quickly than would be the case if the calls were bypassed and dismissed as "relics of the days of sail."

In delivering verbal communications, it is customary for officers of the Navy to use the form, "Rear Admiral Smith presents his compliments to Captain Brown and says . . ." However, a junior never presents his compliments to a senior. Upon making a social or official call upon a senior, it is correct and customary to say, "Admiral Smith, I came to pay my respects," or to the orderly before entering the cabin, "Tell the captain (or admiral) that Lieutenant Jones would like to pay his respects."

According to *Navy Regulations,* "unless dispensed with by the senior, calls shall be made: By an officer reporting for duty, upon the commanding officer."

The courtesy call is made on the commanding officer in his cabin on board ship, or to the base or unit commander's office ashore, and should last no more than ten minutes. Naturalness in demeanor and restraint in conversation are recommended for the junior. This courtesy visit is made even though the officer may have reported to the commanding officer or commandant for duty in person. Officers report first to executive officers if afloat, and to chiefs of staff or other staff officers of the senior commands ashore, and at the same time inquire when it will be convenient to call upon the captain or the admiral. When reporting for duty, an officer always carries the orders that effected the transfer of duty. This is not required for courtesy calls.

In civilian life formal visits are seldom made, though in some neighborhoods one may still find informal calls (visits) made by neighbors on new arrivals. In the services, families moving into government housing areas will often be called upon informally by nearby service families and should return these visits within two weeks. Before World War II the calling system in the armed services was quite formal, with calling cards, strict agendas, and protocol for returning calls. For a variety of reasons, after World War II calling became very informal and much less uniform. Lack of domestic help, the difficulty of obtaining sitters for children, the uncertainty of ship schedules, and the lack of free time all contributed to the change. Often "at homes" or "hail and farewell" parties became substitutes for calls made and returned.

Should an officer receive orders to a station that requires formal calls, it is well to know what is expected. First calls generally are made within two weeks of reporting, and they are made whether the host is home or not. A formal call lasts fifteen to thirty minutes, never more; after this such meetings become "visits." Visits are paid to neighbors and friends, not to a senior upon reporting.

Card Etiquette

It used to be that calling cards were always left upon visiting with commanding officers and others on the protocol list for an officer's station. The concept of calling cards has evolved into the current usage of business cards, and the protocol for cards has changed accordingly. A calling card showed simply the name, rank, and service of the officer, with no other contact information. In the days of a predominantly male officer corps, wives' cards contained only a woman's name, in the form "Mrs. ————." In formal calls, both the officer and his wife left a card in a tray provided for such custom near the front door. In the most formal situations, the husband would leave two cards, one each for the senior being called upon and for his wife, while the officer's wife would leave only one, since the inviolable rule of polite society was that ladies did not call on gentlemen. If the senior was unmarried, only the officer himself left a card. Europeans still conform to a much more rigid etiquette than Americans, and for this reason it is important that naval officers make every effort to learn and do what is expected when abroad.

As an officer gets to a position of senior command, the term "official calls" takes on a whole new meaning. Here the fleet commander inspects the honor guard on the occasion of an official call ashore.

Upon leaving a ship or station, it was once obligatory that one call and leave cards on the commanding officer and the executive officer and their wives at their quarters about twenty-four hours before departure. If the officers were not at home, one left cards with "p.p.c." written in the lower left corner with either pen or pencil. This indicated that the callers came *pour prendre congé,* or to take leave.

One still should carry sufficient cards at all times so that when needed they are readily accessible. Specific rules for the design and usage of calling cards are included in the book *Service Etiquette,* and this work is recommended to those who require further information on the subject.

Formal Invitations at Home and Abroad

Formal invitations must always be replied to "by hand" in the third-person style and should conform to the formal invitation. The writing must be spaced with the proper indentations.

Dinner invitations must be declined or accepted as soon as possible after receipt and always within twenty-four hours. Informal dinner invitations should receive the same prompt attention as formal invitations. The hour and date of the dinner must be placed in the note of acceptance, although it is not required in notes of regret. This holds for all replies to invitations of a formal nature. "R.s.v.p." *(Répondez s'il vous plait)* invitations of all descriptions must be replied to. The custom is growing in the United States of indicating "Please reply to . . . ," or "Telephone (or e-mail) reply to . . . ," instead of "R.s.v.p."

English has become the business and scientific language of the world, but because French was for generations the diplomatic language, the tongue of *politesse,* it is well to reply to a French invitation in French. In all other cases, irrespective of the language, one may reply to the invitation in English.

When a number of officers of a ship make replies to the same shore social affair abroad, it is good practice to send all individual replies together by officer messenger to the U.S. embassy, legation, or consulate, where, if requested, they will be dispatched by messenger to the proper address.

When invitations are issued for ships' receptions, ceremonies, and formal dinner parties, it is good form and a great convenience to place in the lower corner of the invitation the name of the pier from which the boats leave. For large affairs of any description, cards should be issued to those invited that will give admittance to boats at the pier or landing designated thereon. This is most useful to civilians who know little about the piers and waterfronts of their own cities.

Formal Dinners

Formal dinners in this context are similar to official calls and visits. They are not the dinings-in or -out discussed in chapter 7. Planning for formal dinners is usually done by subordinates of the officer (usually, flag officer) giving the dinner. In this case, attention to detail is paramount. From invitations and seating arrangements to arrival plans, honors, and courtesies, the officer in charge must ensure complete coverage. One flag lieutenant noted that his credo was "micro-manage everything—trust no one." While somewhat humorous and mildly cynical, the concept is valid. These are times requiring the utmost care.

The flag lieutenant assists the admiral at all times to see that guests are comfortable and their wishes gratified. In all settings with civilians and foreign officers, conversation should be kept on a high plane. This does not bar the amusing or pointed anecdote or the inevitable discussion of the differences in language and the humorous mistakes that each country makes when employing the idiom of the other. One should refrain from a discussion of potentially sensitive topics including human rights issues, death, religion, local politics, embarrassing points of difference in foreign policies, and particularly naval shop talk, unless responding to a question from a guest. An officer should endeavor to make all guests comfortable and at ease, and should pay special attention to dividing the time in conversation with the guests on either side.

Two thoughts merit the attention of those who have the opportunity to dine with notables and senior officials, American and foreign. One is that it is impossible to receive when in the transmit mode. The other is drawn from the *Autobiography of Benjamin Franklin:* "I made it a rule to forebear all direct contradiction to the sentiments of others, and all positive assertion of my own.... I even forbid myself ... the use of every word or expression in the language that imported a fix'd opinion, such as certainly, undoubtedly, etc., and I adopted instead of them, I conceive, I apprehend, or I imagine a thing to be so and so; or it appears to me at present.... I soon found the advantage of this change in my manner; the conversations I engag'd in went more pleasantly."

Presentations and Audiences

Some of the ancient ceremonies observed by European courts, the Church, and foreign naval and military organizations are most interesting and should afford lasting memories for those who participate or observe. Here again, at any presentation an officer should learn in advance what is expected, if possible. Maintain a military bearing, but endeavor to feel at ease. Wear the prescribed uniform and arrive at the designated time, or better, a few minutes ahead of time.

On replying to a monarch, one says, "Yes, Your Majesty" or "No, Your Majesty." But "Sir" is always correct in replying to royalty, nobility, or high officials. To a queen, "Ma'am" is perfectly correct; "Sire" is also used in formal address to kings. In either formal or informal conversation, it is considered bad form to question royalty. It is never correct to turn directly away after formal presentation to commoner or king; rather, one should back away a step or so and, if necessary, to the side.

At some official receptions, particularly in European countries, guests of honor are announced individually and are expected to step forward and bow to the assembly. Consequently, an officer should be prepared to be announced and presented *tout seul* (all alone). This requires all the poise and dignity that the average person is able to muster, but as an experienced foreign service official said, "The best rule is to take it easy with a trace of smile."

One kneels during a papal audience, and should touch lips to the papal ring when personally blessed by the pope.

Letters of Appreciation and Thanks

Thank-you notes, the old "bread and butter" letters, are often the mark of the leader who truly takes care of the details. All naval officers, and particularly commanding officers, before or just after leaving port, or visiting military installations in the course of their official duties, should always observe the amenity of writing notes of appreciation and farewell to those clubs, societies, officials, and individuals who rendered courtesies and favors to them and their commands. This may be all the thanks some receive for their many courtesies and their kindness to officers of the fleet.

Social usage requires that a note of appreciation be addressed promptly to the host and hostess when one has been an overnight guest. It is also a mark of good manners to send a note of thanks when one has been a guest at a meal or other social event.

The Fighter in Gentle Company

While popular myth extols the virtues of the American tough individualist, indifference and disdain for the refined and cultured is the antithesis of poise and good manners. Rude and unpleasant strains in social intercourse are conspicuously absent in a Nelson, a Wellington, a Washington, a Farragut, and a Lee. Thackeray's social climber who "licks the boots of those above him and kicks the faces of those below him on the social ladder" is a vivid example of what a gentleman is not.

Chivalric demeanor is the hallmark of the officer corps. This means a consideration of the feelings of others rather than an aggressive or chip-on-the-shoulder attitude. Strength of character may be displayed without bombast; dignity, without frigidity; friendliness, without talkativeness. Further, an appreciation of art, music, and literature does not lessen the essentially professional character of the officer.

The officer corps should acquire the tastes of refined society, and give serious consideration to civilian points of view. Discussions pertaining to the profession of arms should not monopolize conversation with those who are not so employed. One's worth as a warrior and qualifications as an officer are not exemplified by whetting swords in society, nor by displaying indifference to the manners and tastes that mark good society. Castiglione wrote in 1528 in his *Book of the Courtier:*

> Because to such men as this, one might justly say that which a brave lady jestingly said in gentle company to one whom I will not name at present [supposed to have been a brave soldier of fortune, one Captain Fracassa] who, being invited by her out of compliment to dance, refused not only that but to listen to the music, and many other entertainments proposed to him, saying always that such silly trifles were not his business; so at last the lady said, "What is your business then?" He replied with a sour look, "to fight." Then the lady at once said, "Now, that you are in no war and out of fighting time, I should think it were a good thing to have yourself well oiled, and to stow yourself with all your battle harness in a closet until you be needed, lest you grow more rusty than you are." And so, amid much laughter from the bystanders, she left the discomfited fellow to his silly presumption.

The code of a gentleman may not be encompassed within a few written rules, or even in a volume. To some extent, it is a progressive education throughout life. There are many commendable, terse private statements of codes of conduct. We have selected one in particular, that of a naval officer and gentleman who loved the sea and who became the beloved sovereign of a vast empire and friend of the United States, King George V. We quote it here not for its royal connection, but for its universal application to all strata of the profession. The code was said to have been framed and hung in the king's bedchamber.

> Teach me to be obedient to the rules of the game.
> Teach me to distinguish between sentiment and sentimentality, admiring the one and despising the other.
> Teach me neither to proffer nor to receive cheap praise.
> If I am called upon to suffer, let me be like a well-bred beast that goes away to suffer in silence.
> Teach me to win if I may; if I may not, teach me to be a good loser.
> Teach me neither to cry for the moon nor to cry over spilt milk.

3

SYMBOLS OF A
GREAT TRADITION

★

9

The Flag of the United States

A thoughtful mind when it sees a nation's flag, sees not the flag only, but the nation itself; and whatever may be its symbols, its insignia, he reads chiefly in the flag, the government, the principles, the truths, the history which belong to the nation that sets it forth.

Henry Ward Beecher, *The American Flag*

Life on a man-of-war is well calculated to inspire love for our national flag ... the ceremony with which the colors are hoisted in the morning and lowered at night when the sunset gun is fired ... the salutes in its honor at home and abroad, the never ceasing watch for its appearance at sea or in foreign ports, the constant reference to it in nautical conversation, the carrying of it in all small boats, are only a few of the ways in which it deepens its hold upon heart and memory.

Elizabeth Douglas Van Denburg,
My Voyage in the U.S. Frigate Congress

The things that the flag stands for were created by the experiences of a great people. Everything that it stands for was written by their lives. The flag is the embodiment, not of sentiment, but of history. It represents the experiences made by men and women, the experiences of those who do and live under that flag.

Woodrow Wilson

The importance of the true meaning of the flag of our nation, its significance in the past, what it symbolizes now, and what it stands for in the future cannot be too strongly stressed.

Gen. Dwight D. Eisenhower

From time immemorial, flags, standards, and banners have been employed by kings, noblemen, knights, military and civil organizations, and religious bodies and faiths to denote by visual symbol the distinctive character of those who claimed the colors or insignia. By these devices was the presence of the supreme commander made known, the camps of military units and tribes differentiated, and enemies distinguished. Banners as distinctive tribal devices were used by the tribes of Israel. David in the Psalms wrote, "We will rejoice in thy salvation, and in the name of our God we will set up our banners." Solomon used the simile, "Terrible as an army with banners." Even the prophet Isaiah spoke of lifting up the Lord's standards and ensign on the high mountains. The units of the army of ancient Egypt had distinctive standards; the chariot of Darius, the Persian, carried his regal badge; and the eagle standards of the Caesars were recognized by tribes at the farthest reaches of the known world.

Flags and symbols have played a conspicuous part in the history of religion. Richard the Lion-Hearted bore the "Cross of Saint George" to the Crusades. The Crusades themselves are often referred to by historians as the conflict of the "Cross and the Crescent."

In the Middle Ages each nobleman, knight, and squire had his distinctive device. Many of these banners were carried to the Crusades and when brought home were honored and carefully preserved; counterparts of the insignia were in time placed on the seals, symbols, and flags of the respective countries. It is from the symbols and practices of medieval heraldry that we trace the history of flags and standards. Even in the formulation of the Flag Code of the United States, certain ancient principles of heraldry govern.

The effect of the Crusades upon European art, architecture, and letters is incalculable. After the "Holy Wars," the motif of the cross became the symbol of countries, kings, and leaders. The triple-cross flag of Great Britain and the flags of Norway, Sweden, Denmark, Iceland, and Finland to this day carry the cross, indicative of the devotion that the early Christian symbolism inspired. Robert Phillips wrote that "out of the chaos and romance of this golden epoch there emerged a universal addiction to the display of personal and family coats of arms, and of the colors of knightly and religious orders. The records of the time teem with allusions to standards, banners, banderoles, guidons, gonfalons, pennons, pennoncels."

Only in the last few hundred years have the flags in a number of countries really symbolized the land and the people. Early in the twentieth century, arms and devices on most European flags carried imperial and royal arms.

Their removal usually resulted from revolutionary changes in the respective governments.

For example, before the establishment of various democratic national flags, we have the fleur-de-lis of the Bourbons, the black eagle of the Hohenzollern, the double-headed eagles of the Hapsburgs and Romanoffs. Interestingly, long ago both the Hohenzollern and the Hapsburgs discarded their family arms and adopted the arms of their territories. In a vague, traditional way, the double-headed eagles of both imperial Austria and Russia symbolized their claim to the rule of the former Eastern and Western Roman Empires. Napoleon revived a proud Roman tradition by adopting the eagles of the Caesars. Hitler brought back the ancient symbol of the swastika that for a hectic time stood for everything free men abhor; Mussolini, in trying to echo the grandeur of imperial Rome, revived some of the ancient ceremonies and the Roman salute. Like Napoleon, Mussolini again used the eagle as a symbol for his Italian legions.

The flag of Denmark, called the Dannebrog, is the oldest national flag of a present-day state. Tradition holds that the flag was adopted in 1219 after the Danish king Waldemar beheld, at a critical point in battle, a shining cross in the sky. The second oldest flag is that of Switzerland, adopted in the seventeenth century.

The first Russian ensign before adoption of the Saint Andrew's Cross was hoisted on the *Santa Profitie* on 21 July 1694, and by a strange quirk it was the Dutch flag upside down. A. W. Meyerson, one-time lieutenant commander in the Imperial Russian Navy, writes: "When the Dutchman by name Botman completed the first Russian naval warship as such in July, 1694, he asked the Tsar Alexey Michailovich what flag he should hoist at launching. The Tsar then asked what Hollanders did. Apparently until full commission the custom was to hoist the flag of Holland upside down. This was done, and when it was explained to the Tsar that it was in practice a distress signal, he ordered the double-eagle of the Romanoffs to be placed on the middle white stripe."

The flag of Saint Andrew, the ensign of the Imperial Russian Navy until the Bolshevik Revolution in 1917, was hoisted near Bornholm for the first time on 5 August 1716, in the presence of ships from England, Holland, and Denmark, which appropriately saluted the new flag of a great power. England and Scotland had a prior claim to the Saint Andrew Cross, as it was part of the original national flag of England in 1606 before the union with Scotland in 1706–7.

The national flags of some European countries in their present form are not particularly old. The royal standard of Spain was adopted in 1785. The first well-known sea flag was that flown by the ships of Prince Henry the Navigator in the fifteenth century. The tricolor of France was born of the French Revolution and is a combination of the white of the Bourbons with blue and red, the colors of the city of Paris.

Similarly, the origin of Asian flags, banners, and devices is steeped in tradition. As far back as 1169, the emperor of Japan used the red disk of the sun as the royal emblem. In 1859, after Commodore Perry opened its ports to the Western world, Japan adopted the rising sun with diverging rays on a white field. China offers a prime example of how political changes affect national colors. In 1826 imperial China officially promulgated the design of its flag: triangular and of deep yellow color, with an "imperial dragon thereon." When the republican form of government supplanted the empire, the dragon flag gave way to a national ensign consisting of five equal horizontal stripes of colors that represented the races of China in order of their importance. Then came the "Sun Yat-Sen flag," which remains the flag of the Chinese Nationalists on Taiwan; on the mainland, the People's Republic of China adopted a flag with five gold stars on a red field.

Because of the numerous changes in the flags of many countries, the flag of the United States of America is actually among the oldest of the national standards of the world. The American flag is the symbol of the nation's progress and growth, a reminder of the ideals and aspirations of the heroic founders of the republic, and an emblem of the bond that unites every American to every other. And significantly, from the days of our first commander in chief, George Washington, until the present, the American flag stands for the sacrifices in war that men and women have made for its sake—the essence of military, naval, and air tradition.

Development of the British Flag

The Union Flag (or banner) of Great Britain was adopted in 1801 and reflects the union of England, Scotland, and Northern Ireland, by an ingenious overlay of the crosses of Saint George and Saint Patrick on the Cross of Saint Andrew. This should not be confused with the Union Jack. A "jack" is the name of the colors flown on a staff at the bow by ships or vessels not under way. It is a smaller flag than the corresponding ensign and is usually square or rectangular.

As early as the fourteenth century, the badge of Saint George was univer-

The Color Guard of the U.S. Naval Academy includes the national ensign, the Marine Corps flag, the Navy flag, and the Naval Academy flag.

sally worn by the soldiers of England as an emblazonment on the "jack," or leather surcoat (hence "jack-ette," or the modern *jacket*). This may have been the derivation of the term *jack* for a flag. More probably, the term comes from James I, who signed his name "Jacques" and under whose direction the original national flag of England was formed by the banners of Saint George and Saint Andrew conjoined. John Cabot and the early English explorers flew Saint George as the national flag of England. The realms of England and Scotland were not yet united in 1606 when James I ordered both crosses united on the same flag. He thought a common flag would help bring about a closer union; most Scots, of course, thought differently. (That union became effective in 1707.)

The Union Flag became distinctive of the Royal Navy in 1634. The land forces and the merchant ships flew either the Cross of Saint George or that of Saint Andrew. In 1649 a new Union Flag was designed for the British Navy; its design symbolized the union of England and Ireland. After the execution of Charles I in 1649, the English ships reverted to the old flag of Saint George. In 1658 the old Union Flag was reintroduced with a harp imposed, for Ireland.

The records state that in 1660 the harp was removed, "it being offensive to the King." (One may safely say that it was also perfectly agreeable to the Irish that the harp be removed from an English flag.) From all accounts the American colonists preferred the Union Flag during this period. In 1707 Queen Anne decreed that a flag of a red field with a "Union Jack" (here is where the confusion began) in the canton should be flown by all who had previously carried the flags of either Saint George or Saint Andrew. This flag today is the well-known Red Ensign of the British Merchant Service. The Blue Ensign is the distinctive ensign of the Royal Naval Reserve, and of merchant ships commanded by officers on the retired list of the Royal Navy, or officers of the Royal Naval Reserve. All British ships of war in commission wear a white ensign with the red Saint George's Cross and the Union in the upper canton.

It is reasonable to assume that the crosses of Saint George and Saint Andrew—banners flown in the New World by the earliest colonists from the British Isles—were carried by the Jamestown colonists when they landed in Virginia in 1607, and by the *Mayflower* colonists at Plymouth Rock in 1620. However, the British colonists in America at an early date secured permission to place a distinctive colonial design on the Union Flag. Up to 1776 at least four main changes had been made in the basic design. For instance, in 1737 the United Colonies of New England were authorized to use a blue flag, with the red cross of Saint George in a white canton, and in the upper corner of the canton next to the staff, a globe representing the world. Another of the popular designs of prerevolutionary days consisted of a red field with a tree instead of a globe in the canton.

Although the "Union" of Washington's Grand Union Flag of 1776 was supposed to stand for the union of the United Colonies, the traditional ties to the mother country were not overlooked, for in the canton one sees the crosses of Saint Andrew and Saint George.

Derivation of the U.S. Flag

The essence of the history of the American flag starts at least a century before the Revolutionary War. The American colonists flew the Red Ensign of Great Britain with distinctive devices for the various colonies, much as the Blue Ensign and Red Ensign of Great Britain are used today by the British Commonwealth.

We also know that the British flag of Saint George, a white field with a red upright cross on it, was in use in Massachusetts in 1635, because at that time a complaint was entered "that the ensign at Salem was defaced"—namely, one part of the red cross was taken out. This was not done in disrespect to England, but "upon the opinion that the red cross was given to the King of England by the Pope, as an ensign of victory, so a superstitious thing, and a relic of anti-Christ."

During the period of unrest surrounding the war for independence, flags of all descriptions were carried. Some of them were designed as stirring, inflammatory revolutionary banners, while others, in a more dignified way, expressed the fervor and seriousness of the patriotic colonists. The Grand Union or Cambridge Flag was never authorized by Congress and was in reality "half British." On 4 July 1776 the Declaration of Independence terminated forever the "King's Colors" and the Grand Union Flag in the United Colonies of America.

Some Early Flags Borne by Units of the Continental Army

In the interim between the stirring of flames of independence and the realization of the new country, the colonists-citizens sought a standard to rally people to the cause. In 1775 several flags made their debut. One of these, the Bedford Flag, carried at Concord, was designed originally in England for the Three County Troop in King Philip's War. It consisted of a maroon ground with mailed arm holding a short sword, on a scroll the motto *Vince aut Morire* ("Conquer or die"). Another, said to have been a present from John Hancock to General Putnam for the gallant fighting of his troops at Bunker Hill, was first unfurled at Prospect Hill, Boston. Although no illustration has been preserved, it was a red ground with the Connecticut motto *Qui Transtulit Sustinet* ("He who transplanted still sustains"), and on the reverse side a pine tree with the early motto of Massachusetts, "An Appeal to Heaven." It is almost identical with the Connecticut state flag of today. The Philadelphia Light Horse Troop Flag was of yellow silk, about 40 by 30 inches with a shield and elaborate rosette design of blue and silver. The letters "L.H." were also intertwined on the flag, and underneath the motto, "For these we strive." In the upper lefthand corner were thirteen blue and silver stripes, making this the first flag to symbolize the thirteen colonies by stripes. This flag was first carried by the Philadelphia Troop of Light Horse when it escorted Washington from Philadelphia to New York to take command of the Continental Army at Cambridge. It was probably carried at the Battle of Trenton, since the Light Horse Troop was there.

The flag of the Culpepper Minute Men, commanded by Patrick Henry, had a snake with the two mottos "Liberty or Death" and "Don't Tread on Me." Morgan's Rifles had "1776" on their flag, along with the words "XI Virginia Regiment" and "Morgan's Rifle Corps." Count Pulaski, who so gallantly cast his lot with the American colonists and lost his life for the cause, carried into his last battle at Savannah, Georgia, a crimson silk banner covered with many devices. There is still preserved the flag used by the Washington Light Infantry. The fiancée of Col. William Washington hastily made this flag out of a red curtain. This flag saw victory at Cowpens on 17 January 1781 and was carried at the Battle of Eutaw Springs, which was conceded a British victory.

The Grand Union Flag had seven red and six white stripes with the Cross of Saint Andrew and Saint George on the blue field of the canton. This flag was hoisted over the troops of George Washington about 1 or 2 January 1776 on Prospect Hill, at Charlestown on the third, and at Cambridge on the fourth. It was designed for naval use. Washington wrote on 4 August 1776, "We hoisted the Union flag in compliment to the United Colonies and saluted it with thirteen guns." Tradition relates that Commodore Esek Hopkins sailed in February 1776 from Philadelphia "amidst the acclamation of thousands assembled on the joyful occasion, with the display of a Union Flag with thirteen stripes emblematical of the thirteen Colonies."

Early Flags Flown at Sea

The Grand Union Flag was designed primarily for use at sea, but various other flags were worn by Continental ships, state ships, and privateers.

"Don't Tread on Me" Flag

A flag bearing thirteen stripes without a union, with a rattlesnake undulating across the flag, and underneath the motto, "Don't Tread on Me," was hoisted by Hopkins on 5 December 1775 at the mainmast of the *Alfred*, while Lt. John Paul Jones raised the Grand Union Flag. A portrait of Commodore Hopkins was printed in London in August 1776, and it clearly shows on his right the "Don't Tread on Me" Flag, while on his left may be observed the "Liberty Tree" Flag. As a part of the nation's bicentennial celebrations in 1976, this flag became the jack on all Navy ships. After that year, only the oldest ship in commission flew that jack until 2002, when it was again designated as the Navy's jack in response to the war on terrorism.

Washington's Navy Ensign or Pine Tree Flag

A flag bearing a green pine tree on a white field, with the inscription, "An Appeal to Heaven," was adopted in 1775 and carried by some of the first naval vessels of the United States. The pine tree was used on various New England flags, because before the Revolution it had been a symbol on banners and flags of some of the New England colonies. There were other pine tree flags used in 1775–77. This type of flag was used by the floating batteries of the Delaware. It was borne by the Massachusetts and New Hampshire regiments and was carried by many naval vessels until the adoption of the new flag in 1776.

Merchant and Privateer Ensign

A plain flag of seven red stripes and six white ones without a union, the merchant and privateer ensign was used at sea from 1775 until 1795.

Gadsden's Standard

The flag called "Gadsden's Standard" was bright yellow with a coiled rattlesnake in the center and underneath the motto, "Don't Tread on Me." This flag has a peculiar interest in that Gadsden, a member of the Naval Committee, presented it to Congress in February 1776 with the request that it be designated as the personal command flag of Commodore Hopkins, the commander in chief of the Navy. So far as can be learned, nothing was ever done about it, and the flag hung for some time in Congress. Nevertheless, a chart of early flags published in 1974 by the Washington Bi-Centennial Congressional Committee states underneath a cut of this flag that it was hoisted by Hopkins on the *Alfred*. Regrettably, no proof can be found to this effect.

John Paul Jones and the Early American Flag

John Paul Jones was so closely connected with the first American flags afloat that it is relevant to flag history to mention his association with the tradition of the first "breaking" of the flag, and the first salute to the Stars and Stripes.

Jones's commission as a first lieutenant in the first organization of the

John Paul Jones, as a young lieutenant, hoists the first flag of the colonies aboard the *Alfred*.
Naval Institute Photo Archive

American Navy was dated 22 December 1775 and was presented to him in Independence Hall by John Hancock. Immediately upon receipt of his commission, in the company of Hancock, Thomas Jefferson, and others, Jones went aboard the *Alfred*, the flagship of Commodore Hopkins. Captain Saltonstall, the flag captain, was not aboard, and for that reason Hancock directed that Lieutenant Jones take charge. He immediately hoisted to the masthead a new ensign, probably the first "flag of America" ever displayed at the mast of an American man-of-war. Admiral Preble, in his exhaustive and authoritative study of flags, was of the opinion that the flag hoisted by Jones was, in all probability, the Grand Union Flag that was hoisted two weeks later over Washington's Army at Boston. But later writers seem to agree that it was a combination of the "rattlesnake" flag and the "pine tree" flag. This flag had the rattlesnake coiled around the pine tree and the motto "Don't Tread on Me" underneath. We are certain that the snake was on the flag, for Jones wrote later in his journal: "For my own part, I could never see how or why a venomous serpent could be the combatant emblem of a brave and honest folk, fighting to be free. Of course I had no choice but to break the pennant as it was given to me. But I always abhorred the device and was glad when it was discarded for one much more symmetrical as well as appropriate a year or so later."

The Union Flag was flown when this little force that marked the beginning of the American Navy sailed from Philadelphia. The order of the day that prescribed the sailing of the fleet down the Delaware on 17 February 1776 specifically said that all vessels should fly "Saint George's ensign with stripes at the mizzen-peak." In all probability this was the Grand Union Flag at the hoist of honor, with "the standard at the main top." The standard referred to must have been the "rattlesnake" flag.

The Navy's first operation was against New Providence in the Bahamas. A writer for the London *Ladies Magazine* wrote at the time that the American ships there had colors "striped under the Union with thirteen stripes and their standard a rattlesnake." This checks closely with the order of the day.

The First Star-Spangled Banner

Unfortunately, we shall never know who stood up in the Continental Congress on Saturday, 14 June 1777, and motioned for the adoption of the resolution which read that "the Flag of the united states be 13 stripes, alternate red and white, that the union be 13 stars white in a blue field representing a new constellation."

The handwriting of the original resolution is that of Charles Thompson, secretary of the Continental Congress. Interestingly, the word *Flag* is spelled with a capital *F* but *United States* is spelled with a small *u* and *s*. Note also that it is the "Flag of the united states," not "the United States Flag."

This marks the birth of the flag in design about as we know it today. In a most curious coincidence of American naval history, at the same hour (though not in the same bill) that the new flag was adopted, the dauntless Jones was ordered to command the *Ranger*. Jones was surely cognizant of this, for afterward he wrote: "That flag and I were twins; born in the same hour from the same womb of destiny. We cannot be parted in life or death. So long as we can float, we shall float together. If we must sink, we shall go down as one."

The Official U.S. Flag's Baptism of Fire

There probably will always be a variance of opinion as to where the flag was first flown in battle. There are several claimants for the honor. Fort Stanwix (Schuyler), now Rome, New York, is the oldest contender for the honor. Col. Peter Gansevoort then in command defended the fort on 3 August 1777 against a force composed of British and Indians. Massachusetts reinforcements brought news of the adoption by Congress of an official flag. Tradition holds that the soldiers cut up their shirts to make the white stripes; scarlet material to form the red was secured from red flannel petticoats of officers' wives, while material for the blue union was secured from Capt. Abraham Swartwout's blue cloth coat. A voucher is extant that the captain was paid by Congress for the loss of his coat. But whether this flag was the Grand Union or the Stars and Stripes is still questioned by historians. Of all claims to being the first flag in battle, the claims of this flag are the most widely accepted.

After the engagement at Fort Schuyler came the Battle of Bennington. The two American flags carried in that battle are still in existence. They are curious flags in design. One of them has a blue canton with thirteen stars painted thereon. A part of a green field is attached to the canton. The other flag is now in the possession of the Bennington Battle Monument and Historical Association. It is certainly a "Stars and Stripes," though of a peculiar size and design. The flag is 10 feet long and 5½ feet wide, with seven white stripes and six red stripes. The striping makes both the bottom and top stripe white. When the original certificate of the Society of the Cincinnati was designed in Paris, the engraver used this arrangement of stripes, because it was in accordance with the rules of heraldry. The canton of the flag spanned nine stripes instead of the present seven; it was blue with thirteen white stars. Eleven stars were arranged in an arch, with one in each upper corner. All the stars are seven-pointed, with one point directed upward. The numerals "76" are under the arch. It is the oldest Stars and Stripes in existence.

Although there are no records to the effect, it is quite possible that General Gates in command of American troops flew some description of "Stars and Stripes" at the surrender of General Burgoyne in the decisive battle of Saratoga.

Another claim states that the new official flag was first flown in action at Cooch's Bridge, near Newark, Delaware, on 3 September 1777. Here Maxwell's advance corps met the British under Howe, and Washington wrote that "pretty smart skirmishing" occurred. No reference can be found in official records that the flag was flown there. This corps had been through Philadelphia on its southern march to check the advance of the British, and there is every reason to believe that an official flag was secured in Philadelphia, inasmuch as it had been adopted by Congress on 14 June, though not officially promulgated until 3 September.

In a letter to the *New York Times* dated 12 September 1932, Mr. C. W. Heathcote of West Chester, Pennsylvania, brings additional evidence as to the presence of the first official flag at the Battle of Brandywine. He writes:

> However, for the first critical battle of the Revolution, the battle of the Brandywine, the official flag floated. In carrying on research for a considerable period of time, I found a copy of a sermon preached by the Rev. Joab Trout, a chaplain near Washington's headquarters, on the eve of the battle, September 10, 1777. He said, "It is a solemn moment, Brethren, does not the solemn voice of nature seem to echo the sympathies of the hour? The flag of our country droops heavily from yonder staff; the breeze has died away along the green plains of Chadd's Ford, the plain that lies before us, glittering in the sunlight, the heights of the Brandywine arising gloomy and grand beyond the waters of yonder stream. All Nature holds a pause of solemn silence on the eve of the uproar, of the bloodshed and strife of tomorrow."

It is not likely that Washington would fly anything other than the official flag from his headquarters, and as he was ever correct in matters of military regulations, he would not fly the Stars and Stripes until he received its official promulgation. Therefore in all probability, the new U.S. flag received its baptism in the Battle of the Brandywine.

The First Salutes to the U.S. Flag

Tradition records that Capt. John Paul Jones was presented a flag for the *Ranger* that had been made from the best silk gowns of the ladies of Portsmouth, New Hampshire. Jones furnished the specifications, and as the story goes, the work was done at a quilting party, and the white stars were cut from the bridal dress of one Helen Seary. It is most probable that this is the flag that was first saluted at Quibéron Bay, France, on 14 February 1778. Jones describes this most important salute in American history as follows: "I also demanded and obtained a salute from the Flag of France both at Quibéron and at Brest, before the treaty of alliance was announced."

This official report was made to the American Board of Admiralty in March 1781, as a reply to certain questions that had been asked. Jones first saluted the French admiral La Motte Picquet with thirteen guns, while the return salute to Jones was nine guns. In the thirteen-gun salute, it was intended that there should be one gun for each state. Jones ascertained in advance that his salute to the white flag of the Bourbons would be returned, although he was disappointed that it would not be returned gun for gun. A kingdom at that time gave a republic (Holland, for example) only nine guns. This salute was rendered before the treaty of alliance with France, the first and only treaty of alliance that the U.S. government made until World War II.

While this is the first record of a salute of honor to the Stars and Stripes at sea, it was not the first salute to the fledgling nation. John Adams wrote in a letter to Josiah Quincy that the first American vessel to receive a salute from a foreign power was the *Andrew Doria,* commanded by Isaiah Robinson, on 16 November 1776, at St. Eustatius in the Dutch West Indies. The flag she carried was probably the Grand Union Flag. It was certainly not the Stars and Stripes. Cooper wrote: "For this indiscretion the Dutch governor was subsequently displaced."

The first five vessels commissioned by the Congress in December 1775 flew the first flag of the Navy. John Adams, a member of the Marine Committee, wrote:

> The first was named *Alfred,* in honor of the greatest Navy that ever existed; the second, *Columbus,* after the discoverer of this quarter of the globe; the third, *Cortez,* after the discoverer of the northern part of the continent; the fourth, *Andrew Doria,* in honor of the great Genoese admiral; and the fifth, *Providence,* the name of the town where she was purchased and the residence of Governor Hopkins and his brother Esek, whom we appointed the first captain.

The Flag in Action at Sea

Jones had the supreme honor of carrying this flag into its first action on the seas. As Buell in exuberance writes: "This was the first edition of the Stars and Stripes that Europe ever saw; the first to be saluted by the guns of a European naval power, but far beyond, and beyond anything, it was the first and last

flag that ever went down or ever will go down flying on the ship that conquered and captured the ship that sunk her."

It is a glorious tradition for a sea service to start with. Jones in his report
eloquently describes the sinking of his vessel, the *Bon Homme Richard,* after
those of his crew who were alive had been transferred to the ship of his foe,
HMS *Serapis.*

> The ensign-gaff shot away in action had been fished and put in place soon
> after firing ceased, and ours torn and tattered was left flying when we aban-
> doned her. As she plunged down by the head at last her taffrail momentarily
> rose in the air so the very last vestige mortal eye ever saw of the *Bon Homme
> Richard* was the defiant waving of her unconquered and unstrucken flag as
> she went down. And as I had given them the good old ship as their sepul-
> cher, I now bequeathed to my immortal dead the flag they had so desper-
> ately defended for their winding sheet.

The Stars and Stripes that Jones flew on the *Serapis* after taking her as
prize is preserved. It has twelve stars in the canton. It is a tradition that one
star was cut off and given to President Lincoln as a gift.

The New Flag, 1795

After Vermont and Kentucky had been admitted to the Union, they strongly
requested to be included in the symbolism of the U.S. flag. After considerable debate in the House of Representatives, a bill was passed providing that
from the first day of May 1795, the flag of the United States be fifteen stripes
of alternate red and white, and that the union be fifteen white stars in a blue
field. This bill was approved by President Washington on 13 January 1794. It
was passed by a vote of fifty to forty-two.

The Last Alteration to the Flag

For twenty-two years the flag of 1795 was hoisted ashore and afloat, over
civilian, military, and naval activities. It was truly the flag of our golden age
on the sea. It had inspired the words to "The Star-Spangled Banner." But the
epic of America was taking shape, and from the frontiers five new states
were admitted to the Union. There was again considerable congressional

Perry transfers his flag at Lake Erie. "If a victory is to be gained, I'll gain it."
By W. H. Powell; now in the Capitol Building, Washington, D.C.

debate on the change in the flag. Representative Wendover in a speech on
the floor said: "And even on those who predicted that in nine months the
striped bunting would be swept from the seas, it possessed the wonderful
charm, that before the nine months had elapsed, 'fir built frigates' and 'Yankee Cock Boats' were magnified in ships of the line; and his Majesty's faithful officers, careful for the preservation of British oak, sought protection for
their frigates under the convoy of 74-gun ships."

At that time there was no uniformity in the number of stripes of the flag.
Wendover said: "That, on the hall of Congress, whence laws emanate, has but
thirteen, and those of the navy yard and marine barracks have each eighteen.
Nor can I omit to mention the flag under which the last Congress sat during
its first session, which from some cause or other unknown had but nine
stripes."

In reality it was a hit-or-miss period of flag manufacture; there was little
uniformity. A bill was finally passed providing that from 4 July 1818: "The
flag of the United States be thirteen horizontal stripes of alternate red and
white; that the union have twenty white stars in a blue field; that one star be
added on the admission of every new state in the Union; and that the addition shall take place on the 4th of July next succeeding such admission."

Aerial view of Fort McHenry guarding the entrance to Baltimore Harbor. After a night's bombardment, the garrison raised a large American flag, and the British commander gave up and sailed off.
Marty Goppert and Don S. Montgomery

The bill passed on 31 March 1818, and was signed by President Monroe on 4 April 1818.

The signing of this bill marked the settlement of the troublesome national flag question.

"The Star-Spangled Banner"

During the War of 1812 Maryland and the Chesapeake Bay sailors were the source of much of the privateering that went on against the British. As a result, the people of Baltimore were sure that the British would soon attack their port city. They did everything they could to make preparations for that event, including commissioning a special flag to fly over Fort McHenry. The commanding officer, Maj. George Armistead, asked "to have a flag so large that the British will have no difficulty seeing it from a distance." He got his wish, and in the summer of 1813, there were two flags ordered from Mary Pickersgill, a prominent Baltimore flag maker. Delivered to Fort McHenry on 19 August 1813, one of them was 30 feet wide by 42 feet long with 2-foot-wide stripes and 24-inch stars. The other was to be the storm flag measuring "only" 17 by 25 feet.

In late 1814 Dr. William Beanes, an old and prominent resident of Upper Marlborough, Maryland, was made prisoner by General Ross of the British Army and confined on Vice Adm. Sir George Cochrane's flagship, HMS *Surprise*. Francis Scott Key, an acquaintance of Dr. Beanes, determined to request the doctor's release and for that reason repaired to the flagship, then off Baltimore. Admiral Cochrane received Key most cordially; he consented to release Dr. Beanes but informed him that, in view of important operations, it would be necessary for them to remain aboard for a few days.

On the night of 13 September 1814, the heavy shelling took place. Key, with Beanes and John Skinner of Baltimore, who had accompanied Key, were transferred to an American packet boat just before the attack. After a night of bombardment, Francis Scott Key looked out at dawn toward the fort of his homeland for signs of life. There he saw "The Star-Spangled Banner": although torn and shell-rent, it still floated over the gallant defenders of the old fort. It was then that he wrote the first draft of the song, inscribing the words on the back of an old envelope.

It is quite likely that both flags flew during the bombardment. The weather that night was terrible, with wind and rain, and the smaller storm flag was probably used for most of the night. Caroline Purdy, Mary Pickersgill's daughter, tells of her mother repairing the larger banner, so it appears to have also flown. Additionally, a letter from a British sailor reports seeing a magnificent, large ensign being raised over the fort in the morning.

After the battle and their release, Key retired to the Indian Queen Hotel in Baltimore and wrote a smooth copy of his poem. According to Judge Taney, a close personal friend, Key had music already in mind when wrote the poem. Key's brother-in-law, Judge James Nicholson of Annapolis, first printed the words and music we now know as the national anthem. There is a plaque on the grounds of the Naval Academy commemorating the first playing of "The Star-Spangled Banner" on the spot where the judge's house once stood. The first public singing of "The Star-Spangled Banner" was at the Holiday Street Theater in Baltimore on 19 October 1814. The original draft was purchased by the city of Baltimore in 1934 and is now owned by the Maryland Historical Society. The song's reference to the "foe's haughty host" alluded to the British soldiers of General Ross at North Point.

After years of inactivity, bickering, and attempts by cliques and individuals to secure recognition of other words and music, on 21 April 1930 the House adopted the words and music of "The Star-Spangled Banner" as the national anthem. President Hoover signed the act into law on 3 March 1931. Although Congress three times rejected the bill of Representative Linthicum of Maryland, he finally presented a petition that was reported to bear 5 million signatures that were obtained through the cooperation of various patriotic societies. When the argument was advanced that the song was pitched too high for popular singing, Linthicum was instrumental in bringing about a hearing before the House Judiciary Committee at which two sopranos sang and the Navy Band played the tune. The passage of the bill indicates approval.

Symbolism of the Flag

The flag of the United States means many things. It is the symbol of the most revered and reviled nation on earth. The professional soldier or sailor feels close kinship with those who have taken up arms to defend the flag in times past. Yet one sworn to defend the flag and country against all enemies, living figuratively under its folds day and night, may have no pat answer regarding its personal meaning, other than that it is a visible, external, national symbol that serves as an embodiment of patriotic faith. Some, because of strong personal feelings for its meaning, do not care to discuss or reveal to others its meaning to them. There are others who will immediately say that it means many things, but that uppermost it stands for "the land of the free and the home of the brave," and more specifically, that it is the reminder of our precious freedoms—the human and property rights embodied in the Constitution.

The flag is an undying inspiration. Its historic associations with wars and victories throughout the world provide immeasurable incentive for its defenders of the present to do as well as its defenders in the past have done. That means esprit de corps, loyalty, and devotion to cause that compel us—against all odds, if necessary—to defend it as the colorful symbol of the country we love. During the latter half of the twentieth century, the U.S. flag came under attack from within as well as from without. Protesters, both

This 48-star American flag
inspired those fighting in
World War II in the Pacific.
Naval Institute Photo
Archive

foreign and domestic, thought so much of the American flag as a symbol of
our nation that they burned it as their own symbol of destruction, never realizing that they were validating the very symbol they were attacking. For
only in the United States can such freedom be enjoyed. And while it is not
unusual for Americans to display their flag in a wide variety of ways and
places, the thrill of seeing the Stars and Stripes flying freely on a ship in a
foreign port or at an embassy, calling out for freedom and human rights in
some city overseas, is indescribable.

Charles C. Jones, a distinguished southern historian of the nineteenth
century and biographer of Commodore Josiah Tartnall, wrote:

> The allegiance of a naval officer to the flag of his country is more absolute
> than that of a soldier or civilian. In the very nature of the case that symbol
> of nationality, borne aloft upon the high seas and receiving tributes of re-
> spect wherever displayed in distant ports, comes to be regarded as the ever-
> present proof of a people's entity, as the blazon of that people's honor and
> power. To bear it nobly, and—away from government and officials—under
> sudden and trying circumstances, to maintain its dignity unsullied, is the

pride of the true sailor. To extend its protection and relief in lonely places, is his frequent duty. To uphold it manfully in the face of opposition is his special trust. Bound up in that flag are his highest and holiest hopes. It gladdens his eye in the sunshine of peace, and covers his head in the day of battle. He rejoices in the deep-toned thunders which salute its presence, and glories in the grand defiance which leaps from under its folds. His world lies within its shadow. Its service is his reward, and by this token are his companionships confirmed.

The Salute at "Colors" on Board Ship

The venerable system of saluting the quarterdeck has been recounted, but strangely, only at a comparatively recent date were naval personnel ordered to give appropriate recognition, by salute, or attention if uncovered, to the national ensign at the ceremony of colors.

The first order found on the subject is that of Rear Adm. James E. Jouett, in a squadron order dated 22 November 1884:

> The attention of the squadron is called to the fact that at colors no custom has hitherto prevailed of giving appropriate recognition, by salute or otherwise, to the flag, the emblem not only of the national authority at home, but of liberty and progress throughout the world. Under the conviction that such a recognition is fitting and desirable, and that the custom, if adopted by all, should be the spontaneous expression of a general sentiment, the commander in chief deems it only necessary to express the wish that on board the ships of the North Atlantic Squadron all officers and men who may be on deck at colors will uncover, as far as practicable without serious interruption to the occupation of the moment.

In 1884 all salutes were rendered by removing the headdress. And although there was a ceremony for the guard and others who were on duty at colors, the order clearly indicates that previously those in the vicinity had paid no attention to the ceremony. The custom of standing at attention and saluting became in time a naval regulation. Thus the "wish" of an admiral became a general custom, and afterward the order of our day.

The Flag Code

To establish a uniform set of rules for the display and use of the flag, a Flag Code was adopted at the National Flag Conference, Washington, D.C., 14–15

In December 2001, on the signal bridge of the USS *Bataan* (LHD 5), the ARG commander, the commanding officer, and the XO of the embarked Marine helicopter squadron salute the "Ground Zero" flag. This flag was raised in the midst of the rubble of the World Trade Center by New York City firefighters, and subsequently flown on U.S. Navy ships operating in support of antiterrorist operations in the Arabian Sea.
U.S. Navy (Johnny Bivera)

June 1923, and revised and endorsed at the Second National Flag Conference, Washington, D.C., 15 May 1924. The original flag conference was convened at the request of the American Legion in cooperation with sixty-eight other organizations in Memorial Constitution Hall of the National Society of the Daughters of the American Revolution. On 22 June 1942 Congress gave special recognition to the code by emphasizing its importance under Joint Resolution 623. Subsequently, the resolution was amended and became Public Law 829 on 22 December 1942. Uniformity was the aim of the law. All states have flag laws with varying penalties of fines and imprisonments for flag abuse.

There were criminal penalties that were added to the code in 1968 to protect the flag throughout the country from desecration. This law provided that a trademark cannot be registered which consists of or comprises, among other things, "the flag, coat of arms, or other insignia of the United States or any simulation thereof." The law made it a crime, punishable by a fine of one thousand dollars or one year in jail, or both, for "knowingly" casting "contempt" on the flag by "publicly mutilating, defacing, defiling, burning, or trampling upon it." Shortly thereafter, that part of the code was struck down by the Supreme Court under the auspices of the free speech rights of the First Amendment.

Destruction of the Flag

Although the Flag Code does not specify how to dispose of a flag that has reached the end of its service life, it does indicate that such a flag should be disposed of "with dignity, preferably by burning." There have been several ceremonial methods devised by various groups and individuals, but none has any more legitimacy than the others, as long as they pass the test of disposal "with dignity." The overarching principle of such a destruction should be "respect."

Destruction is only called for if the flag is no longer serviceable. There are those who maintain that the disrespect shown to a flag by allowing it to simply touch the ground should be rectified by burning. This is not the case. Indeed, the code allows for cleaning of the flag in the case of its getting dirty.

Salute to the National Anthem

When the national anthem is played and no flag is displayed, all present should stand and face toward the music. Those in uniform should salute at the first note of the anthem, retaining this position until the last note of the anthem. All others should stand at attention, men removing their headdress.

Notes on the Flag

When displayed either horizontally or vertically against a wall, in a show window, or elsewhere, the blue field is uppermost and to the flag's own right, that is, to the observer's left. According to the rules of heraldry, the blue field is the honor point and should, therefore, occupy the position of danger. But the position of danger is the position of the arm that holds the sword, that is, the right arm. Therefore, the blue field of the flag, which faces the observer, should be to its right. A simple rule of thumb that tells how to display the flag correctly in either a horizontal or vertical position is this: We always speak of the flag as the Stars and Stripes, never as the stripes and stars. Therefore, when we look at the flag it should read "stars and stripes," that is, the stars (in the blue field) should come first.

When the flag is carried in a horizontal position by a number of people, as is sometimes done in parades, the blue field is at the right (flag's own right) and front. However, it is a violation of the Flag Code to carry the flag in this manner. Everything possible should be done to discourage the practice. When carried this way, the flag is often allowed to sag in an unseemly manner, sometimes touching the ground.

Naval Funerals (NavPers 15555C) sets out the procedures for use of the flag to cover a casket. The flag should be placed so that the union is at the head of the casket and over the left shoulder of the deceased. The position of the blue field is reversed on the casket to indicate mourning. With the blue field on the right as the flag faces the coffin it may be said that the flag is embracing the deceased who in life had served the flag. The casket should be carried foot first. An exception is the funeral of a chaplain. "In accordance with an old custom based on the belief that a chaplain, even in death, should always face his/her flock, the body of a chaplain is carried head first into and out of the chapel/church and from the hearse to the grave side. Committal services for a chaplain are conducted at the foot of the grave."

Out of respect to the national ensign, articles of clothing, including ribbons, medals, covers, and swords, are not placed on top of a flag-draped casket. They may be displayed separately nearby, and the sword can be leaned against the casket's side. The flag must not be lowered into the grave or allowed to touch the ground.

To indicate mourning, when the flag is not on a staff but is displayed flat, a black crepe bowknot, either with or without streamers, is placed at the fastening points. Since the flag symbolizes the nation, it should be half-masted or dressed with crepe only in cases where it is appropriate to indicate that the nation mourns. If it is desired to show that a state, a city, a club, or a society mourns, then the state, city, club, or society flag should be half-masted or dressed in crepe. The flag should not be both half-masted and dressed with crepe, nor should it ever be tied in the middle with crepe to indicate mourning.

A multiservice honor guard salutes the flag-draped caskets of twenty-four service members whose bodies were recovered from Vietnam and Korea, during their repatriation in October 2001.
U.S. Navy (Gloria J. Barry)

Interesting Flag History and Extraordinary Salutes

The Turkish Flag Flies over Bainbridge in Command of a U.S. Frigate

In September 1800 the twenty-six-year-old Capt. William Bainbridge in the USS *George Washington,* first American man-of-war to enter the Mediterranean, delivered tribute from the U.S. government to the dey of Algiers. The dey, after much protest on Bainbridge's part, commandeered the *George Washington* for use in sending a special ambassador to the sultan of Turkey with money and rich gifts. The American consul, Gen. Richard O'Brien, went on board; the Turkish flag was hoisted at the main of the U.S. ship and saluted with seven guns. Captain Bainbridge wrote at the time to a friend:

The Dey of Algiers, soon after my arrival, made a demand that the United States' ship, *George Washington*, should carry an ambassador to Constantinople with presents to the amount of five or six hundred thousand dollars, and upwards of two hundred Turkish passengers. Every effort was made by me to evade this demand but it availed nothing. The light in which the chief of this regency looks upon the people of the United States may be inferred from his style of expression. He remarked to me, "You pay me tribute, by which you become my slaves; I have therefore a right to order you as I may think proper." The unpleasant situation in which I am placed must convince you that I have no alternative left but compliance, or a renewal of hostilities against our commerce. The loss of the frigate and the fear of slavery for myself and crew were the least circumstances to be apprehended, but I knew our valuable commerce in these seas would fall a sacrifice to the corsairs of this power, as we have here no cruisers to protect it. . . . I hope I may never again be sent to Algiers with tribute unless I am authorized to deliver it from the mouth of our cannon.

Tunis Salutes First

The first national salute by the regency of Tunis to the U.S. flag was fired to the flagship *North Carolina*, Commodore John Rodgers, in February 1827. This salute was fired at the request of Dr. S. D. Heap, U.S. consul general to Tunis. The salute was immediately returned by the *North Carolina*.

First Stars and Stripes in an English Port

Captain Bedford of Massachusetts brought the *Bedford* to London on 6 February 1783, and reported a heavy cargo of whale oil to the London Custom House. British and American peace envoys were still negotiating in London as to the terms of the peace treaty. The daring Yankee skipper was moored in sight of the Tower of London where Henry Laurens and a large number of officers and men were still prisoners of war. The ship was described as "American built, manned wholly by American seamen, wearing the Rebel colors, and belonging to Massachusetts." The *London Chronicle* of 7 February 1783 said:

There is a vessel in the harbor with a very strange flag. Thirteen is a number peculiar to rebels. A party of prisoners, lately returned from Jersey, says the rations among the rebels are thirteen dried clams a day. Sachem Schuyler has a topknot of thirteen stiff hairs which erect themselves on the crown of his head when he gets mad. It takes thirteen paper dollars to make one shilling. Every well-organized household has thirteen children, all of whom expect to be Major Generals or members of the high and mighty Congress of the thirteen United States when they attain the age of thirteen years. Mrs. Washington has a tomcat with thirteen yellow rings around its tail. His flaunting tail suggested to Congress the same number of stripes for the Rebel Flag.

Stars and Stripes Fly over British Parliament

The flag of the United States flew over the highest spire of the British Parliament Building on 20 April 1917, in celebration of the entry of the United States in World War I. It was the first foreign flag ever to fly there.

Joint Operations, American and British

Cdr. Hugh Porter, RN, wrote of the 1942 invasion of North Africa: "When two British cutters broke the boom at Oran (November 1942) with American Rangers on board, they went into action for the first time in our history wearing both the United States and White Ensigns." Of this daring exploit, Churchill wrote: "They encountered murderous fire at point blank range, and both ships were destroyed with most of those on board."

Flag Carried around the World

Capt. Robert Gray, sailing from Boston on 30 September 1787, in command of the sloop *Washington,* took command of the *Columbia* in the northwest country. Gray sailed with a cargo of guns to China and returned to Boston on 10 August 1790, "having carried the thirteen stars and thirteen stripes for the first time around the world."

Flag Hoisted over the Louisiana Purchase

The Stars and Stripes were first hoisted in Louisiana on 20 December 1803. It was not until 10 March 1804 that the formal transfer of upper Louisiana took place. St. Louis, Missouri, has the unique distinction of having been under three flags in twenty-four hours. On 9 March 1804 the Spanish flag was hauled down and that of France was hoisted. On 10 March 1804 the flag of the United States was raised for the first time over the vast territory of upper Louisiana.

The Origin of the Name "Old Glory"

The story found in various books and papers states that Capt. William Driver of Salem, Massachusetts, gave the name "Old Glory" to a flag that was presented to him by a committee of ladies in 1831. The original "Old Glory" was hoisted on his brig, the *Charles Daggett,* and afterward carried by the captain twice around the world.

When federal troops occupied Nashville, Tennessee, on 25 February 1862, a U.S. flag was first hoisted by the Sixth Ohio Volunteers, but was hauled down a few minutes later and Driver's original "Old Glory" hoisted in its place.

In an article titled "Adventures of Old Glory," William E. Beard relates that "Captain Driver, at the time of the occupation of Nashville, retired from the sea and residing in the Tennessee city, had sacredly preserved his flag during the exciting times of secession and had the distinction of raising it with his own hands over the state house. Nashville thus became the only city over which the original 'Old Glory' ever floated as an emblem of war."

Flag Hoisted over the Castle of Chapultepec, Mexico

After Mexican general Santa Anna had been forced out of Mexico City by Pillow's and Quitman's divisions, Capt. Benjamin S. Roberts of Vermont, on orders, in September 1847 planted a stand of colors on the ancient palace of the Montezumas.

Lowering and Raising the Flag at Fort Sumter

On Sunday, 14 April 1861, the U.S. flag of Fort Sumter was lowered and saluted with fifty guns, by order of Maj. Robert Anderson, U.S. Army, commanding. A premature discharge of a gun during the salute resulted in the death of a U.S. soldier, the first fatality of the Civil War.

The Confederates were not forced from Fort Sumter until 17 February 1865. To celebrate and mark the restoration, it was ordered that five days later, on George Washington's birthday, West Point and all forts, arsenals, and garrisons in the United States fire a national salute. "General Order No. 50," Adjutant General's Office, Washington, D.C., dated 27 March 1865, ordered:

> That at the hour of noon on the fourteenth day of April, 1865, Brevet Major General Anderson will raise and plant upon the ruins of Fort Sumter, in Charleston Harbor, the same U.S. flag which floated over the battlements

Retired Marine Gen. Dion
Williams with the first U.S.
flag to be flown over the
Philippines
Naval Institute Photo
Archive

of that fort during the rebel assault, and which was lowered and saluted by
him and the small force of his command when the works were evacuated
on the fourteenth day of April, 1861.

That the flag, when raised, be saluted by 100 guns from Fort Sumter,
and by a national salute from every fort and rebel battery that fired upon
Fort Sumter.

Flag Flies over Manila in the Philippines

Commodore Dewey and the American Asiatic Fleet destroyed and captured
the Spanish fleet of Admiral Montojo at Manila on 1 May 1898. It was not
until 12 August 1898 that the protocol of agreement was signed between Spain
and the United States. On 13 August Dewey sent the following dispatch to the
secretary of the Navy in Washington, D.C.:

Manila surrendered today to the American land and naval forces, after a
combined attack. A division of the squadron shelled the forts and entrench-
ments at Malate on the south side of the city, driving back the enemy, our

Army advancing from that side at the same time. City surrendered about five o'clock, the American flag being hoisted by Lieutenant Thomas M. Brumby. About 7,000 prisoners were taken. The squadron had no casualties; none of the vessels were injured.

On August 7, General Wesley Merritt and I demanded the surrender of the city, which the Spanish general refused.

The American Flag Replaces That of Spain at Santiago

Admiral Sampson and Commodore Schley defeated the Spanish fleet commanded by Adm. Pascual Cervera on 3 July 1898, after it emerged from the harbor of Santiago, Cuba. The naval action and the success of the U.S. Army in the Battle of San Juan Hill and El Caney forced the surrender of Santiago on 17 July 1898. The Spanish lieutenant Muller y Tejerio wrote on 17 July 1898, in regard to the surrender of Santiago:

> In conformity with the terms of the capitulation, the surrender of the city to the American Army took place today. At 9 P.M., the Spanish flag was hoisted on Punta Blanca Fort and saluted by twenty-one guns; shortly after, it was lowered. At 9:30 Generals Toral and Shafter, commander in chief of the Spanish and American forces, respectively, the latter accompanied by his staff and many of the commanders and officers of the American fleet, witnessed the marching by, under arms, of a company of the former, representing all the Spanish forces, as it was difficult to assemble them. The American forces presented arms and beat a march.
>
> The heights of Conosa were the theater of this sad scene. . . .
>
> The troops having evacuated the city, 1,000 men of the United States Army entered it, hoisting the flag of that nation at the Palace and the Morro.

General Castellanos formally surrendered the government to Gen. John Brooke, U.S. Army, on 1 January 1899, and the Spanish flag with the arms of Ferdinand and Isabella, the sovereigns for whom Columbus discovered the New World, was lowered at Morro Castle, Havana. By this act the last vestige of Spanish sovereignty was lost in this part of the world.

The Discovery of the North Pole by a Naval Officer

The world was excited on receipt of the following message: "Indian Head Harbor, via Cape Roy, N.F., September 6, 1909. To Associated Press, New York: 'Stars and Stripes' nailed to North Pole. Peary." After twenty years of arctic exploration Robert E. Peary, a civil engineer officer in the U.S. Navy, had on 6 April 1909 become the first person to reach the top of the Earth. The fragment of the flag he deposited there in a glass bottle was a part of the silken flag presented to him by his wife fifteen years before. Small fragments had been left by Peary at all his "farthest norths" in the years that preceded his success.

Byrd Makes First Flight over North and South Poles

On 9 May 1926 Lt. Cdr. Richard Evelyn Byrd, USN, made the first airplane flight over the North Pole. He dropped a weighted American flag on the calculated "top of the Earth." On 29 November 1929 Commander Byrd flew over the South Pole in an airplane, and from a trapdoor in the plane dropped an American flag weighted with a stone brought from the grave of his comrade, dear friend, and pilot on the North Pole flight, Floyd Bennett, former chief aviation pilot, U.S. Navy. At a later date, Byrd made another flight over the Pole and in memory of Scott and Amundsen dropped the flags of their respective countries on the "bottom of the Earth."

An Army Flag That Was Never Surrendered

After U.S. forces reoccupied Luzon in World War II, Maj. Gen. Oscar W. Griswold accepted with tear-dimmed eyes the regimental flag of the 26th Cavalry that had been preserved and treasured by American survivors of Bataan and the infamous "Death March." Lt. Henry Clay Connor Jr., who commanded this small group of Americans, said: "Take an ordinary man back in the States. . . . He doesn't know how much faith means. Those of us out here who didn't have faith these last three years in America, who didn't have something to hold like this flag, just went to pieces."

A Historic Flag of the Army Air Corps

Gen. Carl Spaatz, USAF, ordered the faded, bomb-torn flag that flew over Hickam Field when it was attacked by the Japanese on 7 December 1941 to be hoisted again at the same flagpole at 7:55 Hawaiian time, five years later. The order read: "Troops of the Seventh Air Force, with Headquarters at Hickam Field, will pass in review while an honor guard attends the raising." This same flag was first raised after the Pearl Harbor attack over the headquarters of Gen. George C. Kenney, commanding general of the Far

Eastern Forces, when he arrived in Tokyo with General MacArthur's staff and the first occupational troops.

First Official Flag of the Navy

Until 24 April 1959 the banner flown by the Navy during ceremonial and parade occasions was the U.S. Navy infantry flag. On that date President Eisenhower approved a new "blue and gold emblem" that gave the Navy an official flag for the first time in its 184 years. The infantry flag was blue with a blue fouled anchor set on a white diamond or lozenge.

Flag Procedure in Washington, D.C.

Since World War I the flag has flown night and day on both the east and west fronts of the Capitol of the United States; the flags are lowered only to be replaced with new ones.

By presidential proclamation of 1 March 1954, the General Services Administration is tasked with seeing that flags are properly handled over most official federal buildings. (Exempted from its jurisdiction are the Treasury Department and its subdivisions, the Smithsonian Institution, the Government Printing Office, and all buildings on Capitol Hill.)

On the death of a president of the United States, flags are half-masted for thirty days at all legations and military establishments abroad; also on all government buildings, grounds, and naval vessels in the District of Columbia, the United States, its territories and possessions.

First Airplane to Land at South Pole

Rear Adm. George J. Dufek, who commanded the U.S. Navy's Operation Deep Freeze (1956–59) for construction and maintenance of the South Pole Station as part of the U.S. contribution to the International Geophysical Year (IGY), in preliminary operations landed by airplane on 31 October 1956 at the South Pole. Many planes had flown across, but this was the first landing. Seven Navy men accompanied him. A hole was hacked in the ice, and a certificate of landing was deposited, on top of which an American flag was placed. The temperature was 58 degrees below zero. Admiral Dufek and his men were the first persons to set foot at the Pole since the British Expedition commanded by Robert Falcon Scott in January 1912.

U.S. Flag at South Pole

On 22 March 1957 Dr. Paul A. Siple, scientific leader of Amundsen-Scott South Pole Station (IGY project of National Academy of Science, maintained by Navy Operation Deep Freeze), stood with some colleagues and for the first time in the life of man saw the sun disappear below the horizon at the Pole. It was coincidental but fitting that the torn, wind-whipped American flag at the Pole be lowered at that time from half-mast where it was flown for ten days following the death of Adm. Richard E. Byrd.

First Ship to Reach North Pole

On 3 August 1956 the U.S. Navy's atomic submarine *Nautilus,* commanded by Cdr. William R. Anderson, reached the North Pole, cruising 1,839 nautical miles in four days, while passing from the Pacific to the Atlantic under the great ice mass of the Arctic Ocean. A few days after the cruise of the *Nautilus,* the *Skate,* the Navy's third nuclear submarine, spent ten days beneath the pack-ice making studies, frequently surfacing, and reached the Pole twice.

First Men on the Moon

At 10:56:20 EDT on 20 July 1969, astronaut Neil A. Armstrong was the first man to set foot on the moon, and as the world watched the event, he and astronaut Edwin E. Aldrin planted the Stars and Stripes on the lunar plains.

10

Naval Uniforms and Insignia

Over the history of the Navy, the uniform of the service has at once been the distinctive mark of the profession, the visual tie that binds sailors together, and the benchmark for standards of deportment and professional ability. It not only represents pride in the service, but helps generate that very pride as well. It is the sight of the uniform that sets in motion the process of unified behavior and reaction. And the uniform brings reassurance that we are all alike despite our differences, and united for the same cause. For those who have not worn the uniform of the service of their country, it may be difficult to understand the tie that the familiar cut and insignia bring, but for those who have, the visual affirmation of someone who has "been there" and "speaks the language" is palpable.

Additionally, the uniform provides instant recognition to those who can read its language. In a world-traveling service, where men and women are constantly moving from place to place and situation to situation, the uniform speaks volumes in acquainting them with their new instant comrades. Its ribbons and decorations tell where and how the individual has done his or her work, while the rank and service marks tell for how long and how successfully. While this does not provide insight to the mind and soul, it makes a start in the process.

As times and fashions have changed, so have the uniforms of the service. Practicality has helped drive the change, as has improvement in materials and even the technology of clothing. But evolution has not always been rapid, and at times there seems to have been a salute to the older styles. There is actually a slight correlation between the dress uniforms of an age and the battle or service dress of the previous war or era.

The source of the sea service uniforms resembles that of many traditions, regulations, and methods of operation. We have adapted the old to meet the needs of the new naval service, and in watching the change, one can readily see the evolution of that service as well. In the country's infancy, we wore, as the Royal Navy had before us, a variety of clothing depending on the ship and the circumstance.

For instance, it had been the custom in the Royal Navy for over one hundred fifty years that ships would carry a trunk (called a slop chest) full of coarse uniform parts, which the sailors could have issued to them to wear. The cost of the uniform would then be deducted from their pay. Since the average sailor was illiterate and innumerate, overcharging by the officer administrators was all too common. Eventually, this slop chest clothing was relegated to the standard wear for the "pressed man"; the regular sailor who had gone to sea and joined of his own volition was distinguished by being allowed to make his own choices in clothing. Since he considered himself a cut above those who were pressed into service, the volunteer tended to eschew such mass-produced garb in favor of more fashionable, civilian-looking clothing.

The officers were not much different. Often the eighteenth-century ships were clothed by the personal choice and financial ability of the captain and officers aboard. British naval officers meeting at their favorite rendezvous at Will's Coffee House, Scotland Yard, decided in 1745 that they would petition the Admiralty for an official uniform in order to standardize as was being done in other navies of the day. This was done, and the Admiralty asked certain officers to appear in what they considered a good design. Some liked gray with red facings, but Capt. Philip Saumerez is reported to have worn a blue uniform with white facings. King George II had to make the final decision. While they were deliberating, the king is said to have spied the first lord's wife, the duchess of Bedford, dressed in a blue-and-white riding outfit, and was so taken by the look that he decreed it to be the color choice for his Navy. It is said that the duchess wore the colors already selected by her husband.

In our own Navy, the regulations for a uniform came well after the Revolution. Even then, the individual captain had much leeway in how he enforced the rules. He also often prescribed modifications or additions to make his mark on his crew. In general, though, the crew dressed in white duck or blue cloth trousers with an overshirt or blouse. Some favored a straw flat-brimmed hat, while others preferred a woolen watch-cap head covering, but in any case the trend was for practicality. For instance, the square shirt flap was originally detachable and provided protection for the rest of the shirt from the long and pigtailed hair that was fashionable.

Another item of clothing for the sailor since the beginning of the country's Navy was that which gave our sailors their nickname, the American blue-jacket. It was a practical, short, double-breasted jacket that would provide protection but be out of the way when handling sails and lines. Although in use since the beginning, it was not mentioned by regulation until 1817, when the first enlisted uniforms were detailed. The bluejacket remained a standard of issue until it was replaced by the peacoat of 1886.

The issue of functionality also plays in the false, but hard to kill, legend that the black neckerchief worn first by British sailors and adopted by Americans, and likewise the three stripes on the collars of the shirt flap, were in memory of Admiral Lord Nelson, supposedly the neckerchief in mourning, and the number three commemorating his three biggest victories. This is simply not true. The neckerchief probably originated as a sweat rag, and the decorative tape was actually proposed as two rows by the 1890 committee working on uniforms. The decision to make it three was made without any mention of Nelson.

In his book, *Uniforms of the Sea Services,* Col. Robert H. Rankin, USMC, points out:

> During the latter part of the eighteenth century and until about the middle of the nineteenth century, military uniforms were brightly colored, and often highly ornamented. No attention was paid to providing a uniform designed strictly for duty in the field. Throughout the years naval uniforms, particularly those of enlisted men, have, for the most part been highly practical and comfortable in direct contrast to those of their comrades in the fighting units ashore.

Uniforms in the early American Navy were not as "uniform" as they are today. They were driven by a combination of practicality, cost, and personal taste of the wearer and the commander. Physical separation from the shore and public allowed for a more relaxed attitude toward personal presentation on a daily basis than did the life of the garrison soldier.

Officers' uniforms were somewhat more regulated. The Continental Congress Marine Committee decreed in 1776 that officers would wear a blue coat with standing collar, red lapels, flat yellow metal buttons, blue breeches, and a red waistcoat. Captains had gold lace on the waistcoat and slash sleeves, and lieutenants a plain waistcoat and round cuffs faced with red. Many of the senior officers disagreed and proposed instead a blue coat lined in white and trimmed with gold lace and gold buttons and epaulets (both bearing the "Don't tread on me" rattlesnake), white waistcoat, breeches, and stock-

Uniform of a captain in the Continental Navy
Naval Institute Photo Archive

ings. Although their preference was not acknowledged, many officers, including John Paul Jones, wore such a uniform. Congress in 1781 issued an order that no officer in the U.S. service would be allowed to wear any lace, gold, or other trappings other than prescribed by Congress or the president. They thought the practice too reminiscent of the royalty the country had just rebelled against.

The first official naval uniform regulations were issued in 1797 by the secretary of war. They included, for captains, a blue coat with buff lapels, lining, and cuffs. Lieutenants were authorized the same coat with half-lapels. Captains wore an epaulet on each shoulder, while lieutenants wore one only on the right. Surgeons were given a long, green coat with black velvet trim, over a red, double-breasted vest and dark green breeches. Other officers, sailing masters, pursers, and midshipmen wore variations of the theme, each with less ornamentation than the one before. All wore cocked hats with black cockades.

The cocked hat developed from the early, soft, wide-brimmed hat. The brim was first turned up on one side and then the other. Cocked hats were

Uniform of a captain during the
Tripolitan Wars of the early 1800s
Naval Institute Photo Archive

originally worn "athwartships" by naval officers. They were worn "fore and aft" in the British Navy by captains and below in 1795, and required as part of the uniform of all officers in 1825. Three "turn ups" were made to shape the three-cornered hats of American colonial days. Nelson's cocked hat was triangular with the back turned up. Enlisted men wore low, plain cocked hats until about 1780.

In 1802 the uniform was changed by the secretary of the Navy. Gone were the buff linings and facings, and in their place was blue with white vests and breeches. Gold lace trim and buttonholes added prestige to the look. Lieutenants still wore the single epaulet, but now on the right shoulder only when acting in command; otherwise, it was worn on the left. In 1814 the style was changed again slightly, but was still recognizable as the blue coat with gold trim. White pantaloons were authorized, held down by a strap under the instep of the foot.

The first recorded mention of the enlisted men's uniform was with the return of Commodore Stephen Decatur with the frigates *United States* and *Macedonian* in 1813. The sailors were clothed in "glazed canvas hats with stiff

Uniform of a lieutenant during the War of 1812
Naval Institute Photo Archive

brims, decked with streamers of ribbon, blue jackets buttoned loosely over waistcoats, and blue trousers with bell bottoms." The first regulations for enlisted men's uniforms were issued by Secretary of the Navy Crowninshield in September 1817. They included a blue jacket and trousers, red vest, and black hat for wear in winter. In summer, a uniform of white duck jacket, trousers, and vest was authorized. Bell-bottomed trousers were the style, but the reasoning behind the style was more for fashion than for any practical reason, such as the ability to roll them up easily or to remove them easily when a sailor found himself overboard. Both these features were pleasant by-products of the fashion. There is no basis for the story that the thirteen buttons on the old-style trousers represented the original thirteen colonies of the United States. In 1894 the trousers had only seven buttons; the thirteen were authorized later when the "broad fall" front was put on the uniform. (It was changed to pockets and regular fly in 1948.)

Over the next few years there were more evolutionary changes, including more variety of uniform for specific occasions and the introduction of the cloth cap for undress use. The 1830 regulations were particularly definitive.

Uniform of a sailor during the War of 1812
Naval Institute Photo Archive

While all officers wore cap bands of blue, senior officers were distinguished by bands of gold lace embroidered over the blue band, similar to the "scrambled eggs" type of embroidery of today. Insignia became more varied according to the growing numbers of ranks and branches in the officer corps. Some of the rank insignia was an outgrowth of practical purpose. The epaulets, for example, were held on by strips of gold lace. When the epaulets were removed for undress wear, the strips still distinguished the wearer's rank, particularly for the lieutenants who wore only one epaulet. Eventually, this led to the shoulder marks system in use during the Civil War, and it survives in the wearing of shoulder boards today.

In 1841 regulations were set for the wearing of facial hair to include a limit on whiskers (one inch below the ear and in a line extending from the mouth). These regulations also set the first marks for petty officers, consisting of a cloth device of an anchor and an eagle that was worn on the right or left sleeve, depending on the rate. Officers' gold rank stripes appeared as well, but just for surgeons. This proved embarrassing in some foreign ports, as the surgeon was rendered honors and the captain was not.

The 1840s also brought a concession to tropic wear by officially allowing the wearing of straw hats. Specifically, the brim had to be 3½ inches wide and the crown 6 inches high. Straw hats had been worn before, but with the increased service in the Mediterranean and Caribbean Seas, some form of warm-weather headgear became a necessity.

By 1852 the uniform for captains had shifted to a double-breasted coat with stand-up collar with gold lace. Lesser officers had the same uniform with less lace and trim, and with staff corps devices added as necessary. Officers' sleeve stripes were added for all officers. Blue pantaloons were authorized for

Uniform of a sailor in the Civil War
Naval Institute Photo Archive

wear above the tropics in the winter, white being for summer and tropical wear. Both civilian and military style had begun to favor a less ostentatious cover than the cocked hat, so the officers' service dress cap now shifted to a blue cloth cap with patent-leather visor with distinguishing devices based on rank.

To ensure compliance, the 1852 regulations included the requirement for each vessel departing the United States to hold a full-dress muster. Those who had failed to supply themselves with the required uniform articles were subject to court-martial. The results were to be reported to the Navy Department. Later this was changed so that only newly commissioned ships were required to report, and in 1913 it was eliminated.

With the start of the Civil War, uniforms changed dramatically. Ranks and corps were denoted only by stripes and insignia, as all officers made the transition to the sack coat and pants of the age. Epaulets started to disappear, except for full dress, and the modern cap device began to take shape. Shoulder marks also came into use, with a captain having a silver anchor and eagle; commander, a silver anchor and oak leaf; lieutenant commander, silver anchor with gold oak leaves; lieutenants, a silver anchor with two gold bars; and ensigns, a silver anchor. In 1864 the secretary of the Navy decreed that he wanted "republican simplicity" in his officers' dress and accordingly changed the uniforms once again to a simpler, more basic design and ornamentation. Full dress, epaulets, and sword knots were set aside for the duration of the war, and a cap replaced the cocked hat. The coat was a double-breasted, full-skirted frock coat faced with blue and lined with black. Also in 1864, the Revenue Cutter Service cap device consisted of an eagle on two crossed fouled anchors within a wreath. This was changed in 1873 to the current gold spread eagle holding a silver fouled anchor with a silver shield superimposed.

Corps devices were also fallout of the rapid growth of the Civil War–era Navy. With a tenfold increase in the number of officers, and the addition of the "new" engineers of the growing age of steam, instant recognition of both rank and specialty became important. The 1862 regulation eliminated the different uniforms for surgeons, pursers, and the like and made all wear the same undress uniform, with differing shoulder marks and epaulets. The device of the surgeon had changed in 1832 from the staff and serpent "Staff of Aesculapius" to an oak branch, with a brief foray during the 1850s into using the initials "M.D." In 1852 it became an olive sprig. Likewise, the symbol of the purser was originally the cornucopia, but this was changed to a strip of live oak leaves in 1841. With little change that symbol survives as the symbol of the present-day Supply Corps. The symbol of the line officer had been the fouled anchor, and in 1863 that was changed to the present inverted star.

Possibly the change with the longest term impact was the use of lithographed plates in the uniform regulations to ensure "uniformity" of the uniforms, particularly with respect to the embroidered lace and striping. While there were several differences remaining between the line and staff uniforms, and much of the civilian fashion was showing up as uniform dress, the Navy Department was trying to cut down on the personal designing and tailoring of service wear.

After the war, a rumor circulated that the Navy was going to get rid of epaulets and cocked hats for full dress. Rear Admiral Porter wrote to the secretary of the Navy on behalf of the junior officers, trying to stop the decision. In his letter he explained that when he had first heard the idea, he had been in favor of it, to save the junior officers the expense of buying these expensive items. He changed his mind when he became convinced that the junior officers would rather live on a smaller scale than give up the more elaborate dress. The secretary replied:

Our uniforms, like many other matters, spring from a desire to ape the manner, customs and dress of the courts and members of the aristocracy of Europe. Every woman in our land down to the youngest servant girl is attempting the fashion which originates in foreign courts and which is encouraged there to foster the industry of their country. It is only a few years since epaulets for younger officers were permitted. The older officers have had them and are sick of them as the younger officers will be when they see them so common. I would suggest that the younger officers be permitted to have them and the older officers not.*

The postwar 1866 regulations returned to a dress uniform coat, a double-breasted, blue coat lined with white, with a standing collar, but for service wear, a single-breasted, blue sack coat. Along with this change came an elaborate system of sleeve stripes denoting rank, with a gold star above the stripes. Interestingly, with the creation of the admiral's rank, Admiral Farragut decided that he would like a silver embroidered representation of the steam frigate *Hartford* in the center of a 2-inch star. The officers' cap device was a silver spread eagle on the shank of a gold-embroidered, fouled anchor. The present-day shield with crossed anchors was added in 1869, and at the same time, the warrant officers' crossed anchors cap device was created.

The enlisted uniforms received attention as well. For the first time specialty marks were introduced, such as a star for the master-at-arms, double marine glass (binoculars) for a quartermaster, crossed anchors for a coxswain, crossed cannon for a gunner's mate and captain of the forecastle, a broad ax for a carpenter, an open figure eight knot for a captain of the top, and a fid for a sailmaker. Enlisted personnel were also to wear the ship's name on a black ribbon cap band. Frock collars were decorated with white tape with a star in each corner. Seamen and first-class firemen and above had three rows of tape, while ordinary seamen and second-class firemen had two rows, and landsmen, coal heavers, and boys had only one.

The first working uniform for enlisted personnel came in 1869. Previously, enlisted men had worn an old and dirty uniform, but the increasing use of coal-fired steam machinery demanded something more suitable for dirty work. The answer was a pair of overalls and a white cotton jumper. The white or blue tape on the collars of the enlisted men's frock coats disappeared, only to reappear in 1876.

The sack coat was eliminated in 1877 and replaced by a service coat that

* W. M. Schoonmaker, "Naval Uniforms—Origin and Development," U.S. Naval Institute *Proceedings* 57, no. 4 (April 1932): 517–27, quoted from Col. Robert Rankin, USMC, *Uniforms of the Sea Services* (Annapolis: U.S. Naval Institute Press, 1962), p. 75.

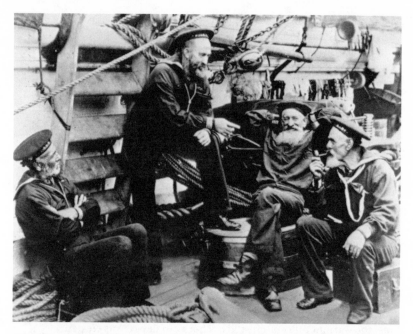

Uniforms of the "Old Navy" *(left to right):* David Ireland, age 55; Gilbert H. Purdy, age 60; John T. Griffith, age 62; and John King, age 54
Photograph by Asst. Surg. H. W. Whitaker, USN, 1888

had originated at the Naval Academy. This was a fitted, single-breasted coat with a standing collar with black braid on the collar, front, bottom, and back seams. It was originally designed as a uniform at the Academy, and officers there returning to the fleet asked to be able to continue wearing them. (In 1883 a white version was introduced, starting the two-season uniform colors we know today.) Rank devices consisted of collar devices and black sleeve striping in a pattern similar to today's rank denotation. The striping remained black until 1897, when it was replaced by gold. In his recommendation for the change, Admiral Crowninshield stated that the gold lace should never have been removed from the uniform because discipline demands instant recognition of the rank of an officer, and the black braid offered no distinguishing mark whatever.

The 1886 regulations called for the first enlisted rating badges, with a white spread eagle over a red chevron, with the specialty badge inside the angle of the chevron. At the time, masters-at-arms had three chevrons and three arcs; first class had three stripes and a lozenge; second class, three stripes; and third

Uniforms and costume for sports for midshipmen at the Naval Academy in 1888
Naval Institute Photo Archive

class, two stripes. All were worn on the sleeve according to the watch section the man was in (that is, if the man was in the starboard watch, he wore his rating badge on the right sleeve; if he was in the port section, he wore it on the left). The new regulations gave first-class petty officers a double-breasted coat with trousers similar to those of officers. In 1893 the petty officer ratings were reclassified and the chief petty officer rating established. The new chief petty officer was given the former first-class petty officer's coat, a cap device of a fouled anchor with the silver letters "USN" over it, and chevrons of the master-at-arms, with the first, second, and third class reverting to the same striping system that exists today of three, two, and one chevrons, respectively. The following year, the chiefs lost two of the arcs, and service stripes for length of enlisted service, worn on the lower left sleeve, were introduced.

The white service dress, high-collared uniform in use today made its first

Uniform of an admiral during the
Spanish American War of 1898
Naval Institute Photo Archive

appearance in 1913. Accompanying it were the white cap cover, pants, and shoes we are used to seeing in the modern-day "choker" uniform.

World War I and its introduction of modern warfare brought attention to practicality in uniforming. Aviation was not well served with the existing blues and whites, so a khaki uniform was created, consisting of a high-collared coat with outside patch pockets and trousers or breeches with high, laced brown shoes. Khaki (from the Hindu word for "dusty") was a result of the British Army's India service. The tropical white uniforms those troops wore were far too noticeable in the bright desert sun. By dyeing them to blend in with the sand-colored landscape, they achieved one of the first instances of camouflaged uniforms. The winter version of this uniform was forest green with a knee-length green overcoat. The "Wings of Gold" came into being in 1917. In 1918 the summer uniform was also made green, and the whole ensemble was referred to as an aviation uniform. In 1919 officers' pleas for a more comfortable blue service coat were recognized, and the form-fitting jacket was replaced with a double-breasted coat similar to that worn by the Royal Navy during World War I. It is this coat that survives today.

Uniform of a captain during World War I
Naval Institute Photo Archive

Submariners were recognized with their own uniforms in 1922. The gold dolphin device was created, and a single-breasted khaki coat, trousers, and shirt with black shoes and tie was authorized. The Navy's service dress khaki evolved from this uniform and lasted until the early 1970s.

Just before World War II a tropical uniform consisting of white or khaki, open-necked, short-sleeved shirt and shorts was allowed. Pearl Harbor brought a flurry of uniform experiments including a gray uniform for officers and chiefs, to help camouflage them against the sides of the gray ships. The garrison cap made its debut during the war as well. The officers' cap device, which had had the eagle facing left ("sinister," in heraldic terms) since 1869, was changed in 1941 to a right-facing ("dexter") eagle, a much stronger heraldic symbol.

Thus far we have not mentioned women's uniforms, because the history of women in the Navy begins in the twentieth century. The yeomanettes of World War I wore uniforms of basically civilian design. Modern enlisted women's dress has evolved to approach more and more the corresponding uniform of the men. Likewise, women officers' uniforms have sprung pri-

Enlisted men's uniforms of World War II, showing the "new" amphibious warfare forces insignia
Naval Institute Photo Archive

marily from the Navy Nurse Corps and have moved closer to that of male officers as women have become more closely integrated into all branches of the service.

Since World War II, there has been a recurring hue and cry to change the sailor's uniform, with specific complaints directed against the collar, neckerchief, jumper, and bell-bottom trousers. In the 1970s, then CNO Admiral Zumwalt instituted both a "salt and pepper" version of the traditional uniform (white short-sleeved shirt with black trousers) and an enlisted version of the service dress blue uniform that officers and chief petty officers wear, consisting of the same double-breasted blouse with silver buttons and a modified insignia and band around the combination cover. The foray into a suit-style uniform quickly ran afoul of issues such as stowage in shipboard berthing areas, for the combination covers and blouses wouldn't easily fit into the enlisted personnel's "Northhampton" bunk lockers, and they placed an extra load on ship's dry-cleaning plants. While the "experiment" failed, it

Female officer and chief petty
officer summer service uniforms
Navy Uniform Catalog

encouraged the Uniform Board to begin considering the look and practicality of uniforms, so that the Navy's uniforms are now moving into better
fabrics, designs, and accessories.

The uniforms of today's Navy are still evolving. Safety has driven the shipboard uniform to protective clothing. The Navy experimented with pure syn-
thetic materials and combinations of natural and synthetics, and found that
shipboard hazards, such as fire and battle damage, not to mention the threat
of chemical, biological, and radiological weapons, demand that materials be
of close weave, completely covering exposed skin as much as possible, and
yet be comfortable in all manner of climatic conditions. This is a tall order.
As a result, protective overalls developed for submarine duty have become
standard surface ship wear. Cotton, long-sleeved khakis are the working uniform for officers and chiefs, and fire-retardant suits are prescribed for aviators
and others in working conditions that require such protection. Probably the
best evidence that uniforms are still evolving is that there is a permanent
Uniform Board that constantly reviews all uniforms and is the driving force
behind change.

Shipboard working uniforms of enlisted personnel have now evolved to jumpsuit-style protective clothing. Here a divisional LPO on USS *John S. McCain* (DDG 56) conducts a morning uniform inspection before entering port in Newcastle, Australia. U.S. Navy (Andrew Meyers)

Swords

Any discussion of naval uniforms would be lacking without mention of the one item that makes the uniforms of the sea service unique—the sword. There are only rare examples of early regulations on the sword as a piece of uniform wear, probably because the sword evolved from a weapon to a ceremonial accessory. In revolutionary times and up through the Civil War, it was covered in regulations simply by stating that an officer would carry a short sword. The most that was said in the regulations up until 1841 was that the sword should have a cut-and-thrust blade.

The 1841 description was specific in that it called for a saber with slightly curved blade, an eagle pommel, and decorations on the blade and hilt of acorns, oak leaves, and a fouled anchor. In 1852 the description was changed to essentially that of today: a saber with a half-basket hilt and Phrygian helmet–shaped pommel.

Male officer and chief petty officer
service and full dress uniforms
Navy Uniform Catalog

The enlisted man's sword was a cutlass, and since it was not the property of the sailor, but of the ship, regulations did not prescribe any specific design or manner of wearing. There were ships during World War II that had cutlasses in their weapons inventory, and cutlasses were not pronounced obsolete until 1949.

Much legend surrounds the Marine Mameluke sword. It was first mentioned officially in 1825 by Commandant Lt. Col. Archibald Henderson, who called for all Marine officers to carry a plain brass scabbard sword or saber, with Mameluke hilt of white ivory. From 1859 until 1875, Marine officers carried an Army sword based on a design copied from the French Army. While this may seem curious, the economies of supply, the superiority of the model as a weapon, and the practical leather scabbard rather than the easily dented brass drove the decision. The 1875 return to the Mameluke design was applauded by much of the Marine officer corps.

The predecessor of the Coast Guard, the Revenue Marine, lacked regulation concerning swords for the same reason as the Navy. The first mention of swords was in 1834, calling for a "small sword." In 1843 the regulations specified a sword of the pattern of the Ames Manufacturing Company in Springfield, Massachusetts. That weapon had a straight, double-edged blade, straight cross quillions, and a counter guard consisting of a spread eagle clutching an American shield. During the Civil War, the design was changed to the same as the naval officer's sword. Except for a short period between the Civil War and the early 1890s, when the Revenue Marine reverted to a sword similar in design to its previous style, the Coast Guard carried the same sword as the Navy with the exception of the letters "USRM," and later "USCG," on the blade and hilt.

11

The United States Marine Corps

> Among the Americans who served on Iwo Island, uncommon valor was a common virtue.
>
> Adm. Chester W. Nimitz, USN

> They can tell it to the Marines.
>
> President Franklin D. Roosevelt

The last line of the first stanza of "The Marines' Hymn" says, "We are proud to claim the title of United States Marine." That is significant to Marine tradition. There are Army officers and soldiers, Navy officers and sailors, Air Force officers and airmen, but in the United States Marine Corps, both officers and enlisted are "Marines." Thus, it is Marine custom always to capitalize the proper noun *Marine* when referring to themselves. You will find it thus in all Marine Corps correspondence and manuals, and any work authored by a Marine.

Whence came the U.S. Marines? Seafaring nations have always had a shipboard complement who were, in the words of Rudyard Kipling, "Soldier and Sailor too." They manned some of the broadside guns, fired muskets down from "the fighting tops" as sailing ships laid themselves alongside enemy vessels, and when the cry came, "Away boarders!" they leapt over the bulwarks to an enemy vessel to put her crew to the sword, bayonet, and pike until she struck her colors. On board the enemy vessels were the enemy's marines to repel the boarders. There were other duties for these "soldiers of the sea." In the Royal Navy, when it was manned largely by crews "recruited" by the press gangs, a duty of Royal Marines aboard ship was to protect the officers from violence by the crew. A remnant of this duty is reflected in the "captain's

Marine Corps War memorial, Washington, D.C.
Naval Institute Photo Archive

orderly" duties stood proudly by the Marines of the Marine detachment (MarDet) on major ships of the line. Another duty of those early marines was to form the nucleus of a landing party and destroy or capture ports or forts. As a ship's captain, Horatio Lord Nelson lost an arm leading such a shore expedition. Among his many titles and awards, he was proud of being an honorary "Colonel of Royal Marines."

While the lineage of seagoing soldiers is long, the U.S. Marines date their origin from a resolution drafted by the Continental Congress Maritime Committee, chaired by John Adams, while they were sitting in Tun Tavern on King [Water] Street in Philadelphia after a daily debate. Thus evolved one of the first apocryphal traditions of the Marine Corps: that it was founded in a saloon. It was thus enacted on 10 November 1775:

> Resolved, That two Battalions of Marines be raised consisting of one Colonel, two lieutenant Colonels, two Majors & Officers as usual in other regiments, that they consist of an equal number of privates with other bat-

Sharpshooting Marine riflemen dominate action between *Wasp* and HMS *Reindeer,* 1814.

talions; that particular care be taken that no person be appointed to office or inlisted into said Battalions, but such are good seamen, or so acquainted with maritime affairs as to be able to serve to advantage by sea, when required. That they be inlisted and commissioned for and during the present war between Great Britain and the colonies, unless dismissed by order of Congress. That they be distinguished by the names of the first and second battalions of American Marines, and that they be considered a part of the number, which the continental Army before Boston is ordered to consist of.

Based on their date of establishment, the order of march in a multiservice parade is as follows: Corps of Cadets, Brigade of Midshipmen, Cadets U.S. Air Force Academy, Cadets U.S. Coast Guard Academy, U.S. Army, U.S. Marine Corps, U.S. Navy, U.S. Air Force, U.S. Coast Guard, all followed in the same order by reserve components. Multiservice color guards observe this same precedence for the order of flags, with the apparent exception of the Naval Academy, where the Brigade of Midshipmen colors, as the "unit colors," come between the national colors and the Marine Corps battle colors, followed by the U.S. Navy colors.

Enlisted Marine uniforms, c. 1859
Naval Institute Photo Archive

History

Foremost among Marine traditions is the role of the Corps as a professional fighting force. U.S. Marines fought in the Revolution both at sea and ashore at such battles as Princeton. They were in the "fighting tops" of the frigates in the quasi-war with France from 1798 to 1801. They fought in the war with the Barbary pirates both at sea and ashore in 1805 (hence the phrase "to the shores of Tripoli" in "The Marines' Hymn"). In the War of 1812, they fought at sea as well as ashore at Bladensburg when the militia on their flank gave way, leaving the path to Washington open and the White House burned. Marines were also at Lake Eire and Lake Champlain, and with Andrew Jackson at New Orleans, where they blunted the charge of Argyll and Sutherland Highlanders. Ships' detachments landed in Sumatra in 1832 to fight the Battle of Qualita Batto and protect the rights of American citizens. In 1835 Commandant Archibald Henderson led the Corps to join with the Army in the Florida Indian War of 1835–42. From 1846 to 1847, Marines fought against

Marine detachment, Naval Academy, after the Civil War
Naval Institute Photo Archive

the Mexicans. In that war, Marines served in California and in Mexico, where they fought in the Battle of Chapultepec, "the halls of Montezuma" before Mexico City. From 1854 through 1858, there were battles to fight in China, Shanghai (1854), Ty-ho Bay (1855), and the Barrier Forts (1856). There was a side trip to the Fiji Islands in 1856. It was Marines, this time led by Col. Robert E. Lee of the U.S. Army, who captured John Brown at Harper's Ferry in 1859.

Although a few "went south" to form a Confederate Marine Corps, U.S. Marines fought in the Civil War from the First Battle of Bull Run in 1861 to the capture of Fort Fisher in 1865. They were with Farragut at New Orleans, Vicksburg, and Mobile Bay. Even while the Civil War was raging in North America, Marines were in action afloat in both the Atlantic and Pacific. In 1863 they were in *Wyoming* when she engaged three Japanese ships and the shore batteries in the Straits of Shimonoseki, Japan. There were Marines in *Kearsarge* in the victory over *Alabama* off Cherbourg in 1864. In June 1871 Marines stormed the Salee River Forts in Korea to spike the guns and eliminate a threat to free navigation.

Headquarters flag captured at Fort McKee, Korea, June 1871
Naval Institute Photo Archive

Enlisted Marines at the Paris Exposition in 1889. Since 1875 the spiked helmet had been the standard headgear.
Naval Institute Photo Archive

Marine detachment at the U.S. consulate, Apia, Upolu (Western Samoa), 1899
Naval Institute Photo Archive

Marines went down with *Maine* in Havana Harbor in 1898. After he destroyed the Spanish fleet in Manila Bay, Admiral Dewey landed his Marines to accept the surrender and raise the American flag over Cavite. "Huntington's Battalion" secured the vital coaling anchorage for Sampson's fleet at Guantanamo Bay. During the subsequent contest for its retention at the Battle of Cuzco Well, Sgt. John Quick received a Medal of Honor for calmly standing under Spanish fire and wigwagging a signal flag directing the gunfire of the Navy offshore onto the Spanish positions. It was probably the first instance of shore-controlled naval gunfire. Marines were also in the ships of Sampson and Schley as the latter directed the destruction of Cervera's sortie from Santiago Bay. From 1898 to 1902, Marines participated in the fight to put down the Philippine insurrection. At Novaleta on Luzon the Marine column advanced under the offshore gunfire support of the Navy.

Another incident on Samar was to add a tradition to the Corps. Maj. L. W. T. Waller, USMC, led an ill-fated expedition across the island. In grueling jungle terrain, they were bushwhacked by Moros and even led into ambushes by their "friendly" native guides. The Marines reacted by giving as good as, or in some cases better than, they got. They gave no quarter, especially when they discovered many of the personal effects of soldiers of the Ninth Infantry who had been slaughtered by the Moros. Waller held summary courts and executed natives he found guilty. He burned villages and laid waste to crops. Under pressure from Washington, Army general Chaffee ordered Waller and other officers court-martialed. Fortunately, the court was headed by Brig. Gen. W. H. Bisbee, USA. He was an old Indian fighter and empathized with the situation. The Marines were acquitted. As a consequence of the double ordeal, that of the march across the island and of the questionable court-martial, it became a tradition that whenever an officer from the expedition entered a Marine mess, the first officer spotting him jumped to his feet and bellowed, "Stand, gentlemen, he served on Samar!"

The Boxer Rebellion in China in 1900 was a multinational expedition, with Marines and soldiers fighting alongside French, Russian, German, and Japanese troops, and Royal Marines and other British regiments, against the "righteous, harmonious fists," as the rebellious Chinese faction called themselves. The literal translation "Boxers" gave the name to the affair. Most of the fighting was around Tientsin as the multinational column fought its way through to relieve the legations in Peking. A Marine private, later to become a legendary gunnery sergeant, Dan Daly, won his first of two Medals of Honor defending the Tartar Wall in the legation compound. Another dual Medal of Honor winner wounded and brevetted in the actions before Tientsin was 1st Lt. Smedley D. Butler. He led a party of enlisted Marines who rescued a wounded Marine and carried him several miles under fire to safety. All the enlisted Marines were awarded the Medal of Honor, but at the time, officers of the naval service, unlike those in the Army, weren't eligible for that recognition.

Action shifted from the Western Pacific to the Caribbean and Central America. Marines were landed in Panama to shield the rebels who were breaking away from New Grenada (Colombia) in 1903. The new state of Panama was immediately recognized by the United States and signed an agreement for the canal across the isthmus. In the fall of 1912 Marines were fighting in Nicaragua in what became known as the First Nicaraguan Campaign. In April 1914, after an incident involving a naval vessel at Tampico that severely strained relations between the United States and the unrecognized Mexican government of the rebel leader Huerta, an American naval squadron was sent to intercept a German merchantman bringing a load of arms to Huerta's forces at Vera Cruz. A U.S. naval squadron, with the Second Marines embarked, was ordered to Vera Cruz and the Marines were landed. The fighting was over in two days. The commanding officer of the Second Marines, Lt. Col. W. C. Neville, and Maj. Smedley Butler were among thirty-one now eligible officers of the naval service awarded Medals of Honor. The next year began the occupation of Haiti, which was to last until 1934, and fighting on the other end of Hispanola in the Dominican Republic, whose occupation lasted from 1916 to 1924 with four battles during 1916–17. Fighting in Haiti spanned only five years of the occupation, with eight engagements classified as battles. In one of them, Maj. Smedley Butler led an assault through a culvert into a fort while under fire. For this he received his second Medal of Honor. Gy. Sgt. Dan Daly also received his second Medal of Honor in Haiti. The fighting ended with the killing by Capt. (Sgt. USMC) Herman H. Hanneken of the Haitian rebel leader Charlemagne Peralte. Hanneken received the Medal of Honor for secretly entering the rebel stronghold and personally shooting Peralte. (A word of explanation on ranks: in Haiti, Dominican Republic, and later the Second Nicaragua Campaign, it was the practice of the United States to form native government armed forces with Marines, both officers and NCOs, serving in higher commissioned ranks of the native organization, in command positions.)

When Woodrow Wilson asked for and got a declaration of war against Germany and its allies in April 1917, American troops were desperately needed in France. A U.S. army had to be raised and equipped. Secretary of the Navy Josephus Daniels, as provided for in law, offered two regiments of Marines to the secretary of the Army. Since the existing four regiments were tied up in the Caribbean and on the West Coast, two new regiments, the Fifth and Sixth Marines, were formed; with the 6th Machine Gun Battalion, they eventually formed the 4th Marine Brigade as the other infantry brigade in the 2nd Infantry Division Regular Army. They were one of the divisions in the American Expeditionary Force (AEF) commanded by Gen. John J. Pershing, USA. The AEF arrived slowly and spent almost the first year of the war training, both in the United States and France, before assuming an American sector at the front. A German drive in the spring of 1918 forced Pershing to offer a few of his trained divisions to bolster the Allied defenses and prevent the splitting of the French and British forces and the driving of the latter northwest into the sea. Thus the 2nd Infantry Division found itself passing through a fleeing French division at the Bois de Belleau (Belleau Wood) on the Paris-Metz road on 6 June 1918. It was the 4th Marine Brigade that fought the almost month-long battle, first to stop the Sturmtruppen ("Retreat hell, we just got here!" was a Marine commander's response to the advice of a

Marines fighting in the Dominican Republic, 1916
Naval Institute Photo Archive

French officer) and then to be able to proclaim, "Woods now U.S. Marine Corps entirely." The French Army commander renamed it "Bois de la Brigade de Marine," a name that did not endear Marines to Pershing who strictly controlled what units of the AEF would be identified. But Belleau Wood had more significance to the AEF than just Marine glory. A German division commander had told his men, "American success along our front, even if only temporary, may have the most unfavorable influence on the attitude of the Allies and the duration of the war. In the coming battles, therefore, it is not a question of possession or nonpossession of this or that village, or woods, insignificant in itself; it is a question of whether the Anglo-American claim that the American Army is the equal or even superior to the German Army is to be made good."*

Sustaining extremely heavy casualties, Marines had shown the mettle of the American troops and validated that claim. Arriving in France just after

* Lt. Col. Ernst Otto, German Army (Ret.), "The Battles for the Possession of Belleau Wood, June 1918," Naval Institute *Proceedings* (November 1928): 951.

Marines in France during World War I
Naval Institute Photo Archive

Belleau Wood, Brig. Gen. John A. Lejeune, USMC, took command of the 4th Marine Brigade and shortly was promoted to major general, taking command of the 2nd Infantry Division, USA. As part of the American First Army, he led the force in the Battles of Soissons and Saint-Mihiel. Then it was detached for service with the French in the Champagne Sector to reduce the German salient at Blanc Mont. A legend is that when Lejeune saw the plan the French had given him for the attack, he called for Lt. Col. E. H. "Pete" Ellis, his brilliant but sometimes wayward planner. When told that Ellis was resting, supposedly Lejeune said, "Get him! Ellis drunk is better than any one else sober." He was, and in a week the division did what the French had failed to do in four years. They broke the German line and advanced to the railroad it protected, forcing a German retreat of 40 miles. They returned to the First Army for the Meuse-Argonne campaign and crossed the Meuse the night before the Armistice ended the fighting. After a year of occupation duty, the division returned home to be disbanded. The Marine Corps was then reduced to almost its prewar size.

Marines in amphibious warfare exercise in Culebra, Puerto Rico, in 1923
Naval Institute Photo Archive

Marines were still in the Caribbean. When mail robberies became a nationwide problem, Marines were ordered to guard mail trains and some post offices. The secretary of the Navy (a World War I Marine) said that if mail was missing, he expected to see the body of a dead Marine. Their orders were to shoot to kill. They did, and the robberies stopped. A Marine Corps smaller than the police force of New York City was spread thin by commitments. Lejeune, now major general commandant (MGC), had to strip Marine barracks at Navy yards to reactivate the Sixth Marines and join it with the Fourth Marines for an expedition during internal unrest and threats to American interests in China in 1927. Before that, a civil struggle in Nicaragua called for the commitment of Marines to an occupation of the country that lasted six years. In addition to the regular formation of the Marine Brigade, as in Haiti and Santo Domingo, officers and NCOs were seconded to the native military organization. The Second Nicaragua Campaign, as it is officially termed, was a guerrilla war against bands in the jungle interior. The chief guerrilla was a bandit and killer, Augusto Sandino. (In the 1980s, a new group of simi-

Uniform inspection aboard
USS *Pennsylvania*, 1935
Naval Institute Photo Archive

lar insurgents styled themselves Sandinistas.) Their mission accomplished, Marines left Nicaragua on 3 January 1933, just three days short of six years there.

Although there were to be no Marines in actual combat for almost another nine years, until the U.S. entry into World War II, Marines were on the fringes during much of the 1930s. Pearl Harbor catapulted the nation and the Marines into another world war. After the fall of France and the subsequent air assault and U-boat siege of Great Britain, U.S. naval forces conducted the Neutrality Patrol off the Atlantic Coast of North America. There were Marine detachments in almost all the larger combatant ships. The Marine Brigade from San Diego relieved British troops occupying Iceland in 1941. They were used instead of the East Coast–based 1st Marine Division because the latter had a contingency commitment to the seizure of Martinique and/or the Azores. As a force of volunteers, Marines were used instead of Army because the Selective Service Act of 1940 forbade using draftees outside the United States or its possessions. In November 1941 the Fourth

The flag of victory.
On 23 February 1945,
five Marines and
a Navy hospital
corpsman raised
their flag on Mount
Suribachi, Iwo Jima.

Marines were withdrawn from China to the Philippines. They were there on 8 December when bombs fell on Pearl Harbor on the other side of the International Dateline. They surrendered with Lieutenant General Wainwright's Army forces on Corregidor in May 1942, with the regimental CO personally burning their battle color.

There were Marines at Pearl Harbor on 7 December 1941 as well as in Marine detachments afloat, Marine barracks at Guam, and defense battalions with air squadrons at Midway Island and Wake. Guam fell; Midway's defenders beat off the Japanese; and the Marines on Wake, in a stubborn defense against overwhelming odds, wrote a new chapter in the saga of the Corps before being overrun. Many a bet at the bar has been lost by an "expert" on military history who has risen to the bait: "During World War II, U.S. Marines were renowned for their amphibious assaults. Can you name two amphibious assaults involving U.S. Marines which were failures?" (with failure defined as being repulsed at the beach and driven back into the sea).

Marines are greeted with celebration upon their post–World War II occupation of China.
Naval Institute Photo Archive

The embarrassed loser usually pays up when informed that the correct answer is "the first and second Japanese assaults on Wake!"

There were Marine detachments in every major engagement in the Pacific, as well as on board major combatants in the Atlantic and Mediterranean, and off North Africa. In addition, there were illustrious names appended as silver bands to the Marine Corps battle color staff. These included Guadalcanal, Makin Island, Vella Lavella, Cape Gloucester, Bougainville, Green Islands, Treasury Islands, Choiseul, Tarawa, Kwajalein, Majuro, Eniwetok, Roi, Namur, Saipan, Tinian, Guam, Peleliu, Leyte, Iwo Jima, and Okinawa.

Preceding the signing of the surrender on 2 September 1945 on board *Missouri* in Tokyo Bay, Marines landed on Honshu to disarm Japanese units. Marines were involved in north China until withdrawn in 1948 as the Chinese Communists (CCF) forced the Nationalists farther south and into eventual evacuation to Taiwan. The CCF and Marines were to meet again.

In 1948, as instability reigned in southern Europe, Marines were assigned to the Sixth Fleet as Landing Force Mediterranean. Expanded to a Marine expeditionary unit (MEU), this capability exists still. In the summer of 1950, the Marine Corps was at a low almost equaling that of the days before World War II. Its size had been cut, and the recruiting posters on the sides of U.S. postal trucks proclaimed, "Only 100,000 May Serve." The two existing Marine divisions, the 1st Marine Division in Camp Pendleton, California, and the 2nd Marine Division in Camp Lejeune, North Carolina, were bobtailed. Vertical cuts—e.g., a platoon from each rifle company, a company from each battalion—had the Corps woefully under strength. Air squadrons were similarly short. Deployed units were afloat at what passed for full strength.

On 27 June 1950 tanks and infantry of the North Korean People's Army (NKPA) crossed the Thirty-eighth Parallel boundary between North and South Korea in an invasion of the South. NKPA aircraft struck Republic of Korea (ROK) airfields. Except for advisers, there was no U.S. military presence in the ROK. The U.S. Eighth Army was scattered about Japan as occupation troops. While USAF and USN carrier aircraft attempted to blunt the southward-marching NKPA, the ROKs and hastily dispatched U.S. infantry divisions were steadily pushed back to a small perimeter around Pusan in the southeast tip of the peninsula. Meanwhile, things were moving stateside. The 1st Marine Brigade (Provisional) was built around the Fifth Marines in Camp Pendleton. At Marine Corps Air Station, El Toro, California, tactical squadrons prepared to go aboard escort carriers as the "Fire Brigade" got ready to sail from San Diego. Marines never go anywhere anymore without their air support. The Fire Brigade arrived, and with the help of their own artillery and Marine close air support, stopped the NKPA cold at the two battles of the Naktong (River). The Pusan Perimeter held.

The Supreme Commander Allied Forces, Gen. Douglas MacArthur, was planning a bold stroke. It was to be an amphibious end run around the west of the peninsula to Inchon, close to the South Korean capital of Seoul. Anticipating that more Marines would be needed, the Marine Corps Reserve was activated, and with drafts from Marine barracks around the country, the 1st Marine Division was being rebuilt to strength. The anticipation was correct, and MacArthur asked for "his" 1st Marine Division. (They had fought under him at Cape Gloucester, New Britain.) Other Marines were assimilated from units in Camp Lejeune, North Carolina, and those serving with the Navy's Sixth Fleet in the Mediterranean, plus units at Pusan, to fill out the 1st Marine Division. They were embarked and led the assault on Inchon on 20 September 1950. The Marines went on to capture Seoul, reembarked, and set out to assault Wonsan on the east coast of North Korea. The surprise flanking assault on Inchon had caused the collapse of the NKPA, which fled north.

Invasion of Wonsan, Korea, 1950
Naval Institute Photo Archive

Pursuing ROK units got to Wonsan before the Marines could assault. They came ashore administratively to be greeted by a USO troupe headed by comedian Bob Hope.

But the fighting was far from over. As the Marines advanced in the cold November storms toward the Chinese border, the Chinese decided to play a hand. "Volunteers" in well-organized units sneaked across the border at night. The two antagonists met at the Chosin Reservoir. As the friendly units on either flank gave way, the CCF pushed around and behind the Marines. They were surrounded but not cut off. In addition to "The Frozen Chosin," names like Yudam-ni, Hagaru, and Koto-ri were added to the Marine saga as the 1st Marine Division made the breakout south with their equipment, and their dead and wounded, to the port of Hungnam. "Retreat, hell, we're attacking in a different direction," said it all.

The evacuated division went ashore at Masan in the south to reorganize, and while there destroyed an NKPA division fighting as guerrillas in the south. The Marines were in the summer offensive of 1951 that was blunted after the Chinese and North Koreans drew the United Nations into truce talks at Panmunjon to the west just south of the Thirty-eighth Parallel. The positions along the entire front were fixed in place. In March 1952 the 1st Marine Division was trucked west to positions guarding the gateway to Seoul. There they engaged in the "Outpost War," a series of bloody encounters with the CCF to take or hold various hills in front of the main line of resistance. It lasted until the termination of hostilities on 27 July 1953.

In California, the 3rd Marine Division was reactivated at Camp Pendleton, and in the summer of 1953 was transferred overseas to the home islands of Japan. In 1957 the 3rd Marine Division shifted the last of its units south to Okinawa, still occupied by the United States. Except for sojourning south for the Vietnam War, the division has been continuously in Okinawa since then. But the 3rd Marine Division is not the Marine unit that has been stationed overseas for the longest period of time. That distinction belongs to the 1st Marine Air Wing, whose battle colors shifted to Japan in 1950 and which, except for a similar journey south, has been in Japan ever since.

The end of combat in Korea enabled the 1st Marine Division to return to Camp Pendleton, and the three divisions and aircraft wings were able to concentrate on their mission of being a force in readiness. In the mid-1950s Fleet Marine Force (FMF) units responded to a variety of missions: assisting earthquake victims in the Ionian Islands, protecting American citizens during a coup in Guatemala, evacuating Chinese from the Tachen Islands to Taiwan, evacuating American citizens from Egypt during the Suez crisis, landing in Lebanon during a major crisis there, protecting the water supply at the Guantanamo Naval Base when Fidel Castro threatened to cut it off, deploying a Marine Aircraft Group (MAG) from Japan to Taiwan to strengthen Chinese Nationalists' air defenses when the CCF made threatening gestures in bombarding the offshore islands of Quemoy and Matsu, and providing relief to Turkish earthquake victims as well as to hurricane victims in British Honduras. Two particular examples of readiness stand out: deploying a Marine Expeditionary Brigade (MEB) to Thailand in 1962 to protect its borders from possible incursions from Laos, and deploying almost all of the Fleet Marine Force, Atlantic, for the Cuban missile crisis in the fall of 1962. The 2nd Marine Division embarked in jam-packed amphibious shipping to conduct, if necessary, a landing east of Havana and link up with the air-dropped XVIII Airborne Corps, USA. Except for the air-drop, the operation had been rehearsed off Camp Lejeune the previous spring under the watchful eye of President John F. Kennedy.

The year 1965 was to be a significant one in Marine Corps annals. In the

Marines come ashore in Vietnam.
Naval Institute Photo Archive

spring, violence in the Dominican Republic brought Marines back to a place they had left more than forty years before. Units of the 6th MEB landed to restore order and protect lives and property. At almost the same time, halfway around the world, what was to be the first of an eventual twenty-five Marine infantry battalions (with attendant support) landed at Da Nang, Republic of Vietnam. What was to be the "longest war" had begun.

Although the initial Marines were ashore at Red Beach north of Da Nang, III Marine Amphibious Forces spread out from the Demilitarized Zone (DMZ) in the north along the border between North and South Vietnam, south to Chu Lai. The latter was the site of an expeditionary short airfield for tactical support (SATS). It was another Marine innovation, with aluminum matting for runways, arresting gear, and a catapult.

Slightly less than six and a half years since the first Battalion Landing Team (BLT) had gone ashore at Da Nang, Marines began to be withdrawn in accordance with President Nixon's determination to turn the war over to the Vietnamese to fight. The Marines who died of their wounds, and all

Marines load supplies during underway replenishment aboard USS *Wisconsin*
(BB 64) in support of Desert Storm.
Naval Institute Photo Archive

those who served and survived, added a new litany of heroic names to the
Marine Corps annals. These include Da Nang, Hue City, Con Thein, A Shau
Valley, Khe Sanh, DMZ, Leatherneck Square, Arizona Territory, the Rock-
pile, Dewey Canyon, Starlight, Dai Do, "Bastards' Bridge," Quang Tri, Cam
Lo, Phu Bai, Tet, and others. They take their place alongside Brandywine,
Samar, Belleau Wood, and Guadalcanal.

One final incident in Southeast Asia stemmed from the seizure by Cam-
bodians of the American ship SS *Mayaguez* in May 1975. A Marine battalion
was flown from Okinawa to Thailand and then by USAF helicopters to Koh
Tang Island, where the ship and crew were reportedly located. Both ship and
crew were subsequently returned.

During internal troubles in Lebanon in the fall of 1983, a Marine expeditionary unit was landed in Beirut to guard the airfield. In October 1983 a
truck loaded with explosives and driven by a suicide driver smashed into

Marines moving into attack positions during Operation Desert Storm
Naval Institute Photo Archive

the barracks headquarters of the Marines. There were 238 Marines and 22 from the Navy and Army killed and 151 wounded. A replacement Marine Expeditionary Unit, while en route, was diverted to the seizure of Grenada in the Caribbean and rescue of Americans under siege there. After the rescue, the unit proceeded to the Mediterranean for its original relief mission. When U.S. forces invaded Panama in 1989 to depose President Noriega, there were Marines in the invasion. In 1990, when Iraq invaded Kuwait and the United States drew "a line in the sand," a Marine Expeditionary Unit was immediately dispatched to pose an amphibious threat, while other U.S. forces moved to Saudi Arabia to stage the liberation of Kuwait. Some units of both the 1st and 2nd Marine Divisions were able to join up with maritime prepositioning ships (MPS) with heavy combat equipment. When the Persian Gulf ground war was ready to kick off, both divisions abreast smashed though Iraqi defenses and were in Kuwait City in a few days. Almost a year later, a Marine Expeditionary Unit landed in Somalia and saw action there. Marines ended the century seeing active service in Liberia, Albania, Congo, Kosovo, and East Timor.

Marines afloat in the Indian Ocean were among the first forces ashore, seizing an airfield for the subsequent employment of U.S. Army divisions in the mountains of Afghanistan in the forefront of the war on terrorism following the September 2001 attacks on the World Trade Center and the Pentagon.

Innovation

In addition to being "first to fight," Marines have been innovators in the military art. Although their public reputation and image is that of lean, mean, and physically tough individuals, they are also among the military's intellectual elite.

When the age of sail passed into history and the need for musketry from the "fighting tops" or the cry of "Away boarders" or "Stand by to repel boarders" was overtaken by technology, the Marines faced a new era, and they were ready for it. Long-range, breech-loading naval guns on steam-driven warships opened the distance at which battles at sea were fought. It seemed that the need for Marines at sea was over. But steam-driven warships required fuel and advanced bases where they could refuel and refit. If the United States owned such bases, they had to be defended. If the United States didn't own them, they had to be seized and defended. Marines were to be the land component of a naval campaign.

At the start of the twentieth century, the first steps were taken in what was to be known as amphibious warfare. A detour to France in 1917–18 delayed development of this art of warfare, and the British debacle at Gallipoli in 1915 nearly made it stillborn. Yet visionaries of a "new Corps" led by Marine Corps commandant, Gen. John A. Lejeune, and his assistant, Lt. Col. Earl H. Ellis, were looking toward the Marine Corps of the twentieth century. On 23 June 1921, Lejeune approved Operation Plan 712, Advance Base Operations in Micronesia. The author was Ellis. It opened with these words: "In order to impose our will upon Japan, it will be necessary for us to project our fleet and land forces across the Pacific and wage war in Japanese waters." It was the basis for the thrust across the central Pacific, which was started in January 1944 and culminated in Tokyo Bay in September 1945.

Amphibious warfare involves forced entry from the sea with a rapid buildup of combat power from zero to ultimate control of the terrain dominating the landing area. The landing area was initially a beach, but in more modern scenarios it is projected beyond the shoreline to inland helicopter

Marine amphibious operations off Vietnam, 1967
Naval Institute Photo Archive

landing zones. Concomitant with amphibious operations is the offshore fire support and the means to direct it. Initially, it was naval gunfire but it now includes longer range missiles to neutralize an objective area. From the initial use by Marine pilots (all earn the wings of gold as naval aviators) in Nicaragua, dive bombing was developed into the concept of close air support of Marines on the ground in contact with the enemy. Marines flew in the face of all nautical wisdom by demanding a craft and eventually a ship that was intentionally driven onto the shore, dropped a ramp, and allowed vehicles as large as a tank to be run out onto the beach. Further, after the first use of an atomic bomb in warfare seemed to sound the death knell for concentration of amphibious ships in an objective area, the Marines countered with the superior mobility of the helicopter as a military vehicle. This was a result of applying Clausewitz's principle about the advantage of fighting on interior lines, realizing that it reduces to "distance equals rate times time." Clausewitz was dealing with infantry who moved at a rate of 2.5 miles an hour. The helicopter rate was 90 knots.

A more recent Marine innovation is the Marine Air-Ground Task Force, a combined arms command, applicable at various echelons of formations containing a command element, maneuver element, combat support element, combat service support element, and organic air, both fixed and rotary-wing. It is a potent combat package in each of its several sizes. Another concept is sea basing, projecting ground maneuver elements ashore without the requirement for a logistical buildup there. The Marines operate from the logistical support of the ships at sea off the objective area. When the mission is accomplished, Marines reembark, and the task force moves elsewhere, ready to accomplish another mission. A further innovation involves having ships preloaded with heavier combat equipment than that usually loaded in amphibious ships, and positioned where they can steam to a port captured by an amphibious operation. The heavier equipment is matched up with Marine units flown to the captured port for further combat employment. Marines have also been taking the lead in training units for urban warfare, as well as reaction to biochemical terrorist attacks.

Of course, Marine innovations don't occur in a vacuum. They are a direct result of the close association with its sister service, the Navy. There is a distinct advantage to being "Soldier and Sailor too."

Organization

Marine Corps organizations have evolved from the two battalions contemplated that day in 1775 at Tun Tavern. For most of the nineteenth century, Marine Corps units were mainly aboard ships as Marine detachments or stationed at Navy Yards as Marine barracks. The site for the first Marine barracks was chosen in 1801 by the second commandant (1798–1804), Lt. Col. William W. Burrows, and President Thomas Jefferson. It is in southeast Washington, D.C., near the Navy Yard. Now expanded to newer accommodations for the Marines, it was originally located in the city block bounded by G and I Streets and 8th and 9th Streets. It is known throughout the Corps as "Eighth and Eye," the "Home of the Commandants." After the White House, it is the oldest public building in Washington still in use.

The home, on the north side of the Marine Barracks Quadrangle, 8th and I Streets, has been the official residence of all but two of the commandants who have headed the Marine Corps. This residence was not burned when the British under Admiral Cockburn and General Ross burned the Capitol, the White House, and much of the Navy Yard in retaliation for the American raid on York (now Toronto) the previous summer. One story holds that it was earmarked as headquarters for the British; another, that it was spared because of General Ross's admiration for the determined resistance of Capt. Samuel Miller and his Marines from Washington Barracks and Capt. Joshua Barney and his sailors from the gunboat flotilla, at the battle on the Bladens-burg road. Both Barney and Miller were severely wounded and captured. Because of the heroic conduct of this small force, the British commanders, both navy and army, expressed high commendation, and immediately paroled Barney, the senior officer.

Undoubtedly one of the most colorful residents, partly by reason of his long tenure of office, was the fifth commandant, Archibald Henderson. In 1836, because of an Indian uprising, Henderson gathered all the Marines he could muster and, under orders of President Andrew Jackson, reported to the Army. On leaving Washington, Henderson tacked a message on his office door: "Gone to Florida to fight the Indians. Will be back when the war is over." When he died in 1859, General Henderson had occupied the residence for thirty-nine years, and served under eleven presidents. President Buchanan and his cabinet attended his funeral. The *Marine Corps Gazette* reported in May 1954:

> Stories of buried treasure and of ghosts add unique interest to this house of tradition. However, a true story should be recounted which shows the narrow boundary between fact and fancy. When General Thomas Holcomb, then Commandant, told some dinner guests that he had signed that day the order establishing the Women's Reserve, he added as an interesting side-remark, that, "Old Archibald would certainly turn over in his grave if he ever found out that females could become commissioned officers in his beloved Marine Corps." And just as he finished the remark, the portrait of General Henderson, which hung in the dining room, crashed to the floor.

Through the years, the commandants and their wives have added excellent period reproductions of furniture, crystal chandeliers, and valuable old prints to the residence, along with outside wrought iron work. One may see today the portraits of all commandants, less the fourth, of whom no likeness has been found.

The Quadrangle, seen from the Commandant's House, is the setting for the inspiring "sunset parade" and the "drill without orders." Starting with the seventh commandant and continuing until the present, on each New Year's Day morning the Marine Band has serenaded the head of the Corps, who invites them in for a "libation" and breakfast. A tradition of "mutual surprise" has marked this ceremony through all the years.

When expeditions had to be mounted, companies were drawn from various Marine barracks and assembled for embarkation. Often a battalion or regiment was put together at pier side. This sometimes caused confusion, as companies were lettered in the various Marine barracks. The confusion arose when, for example, the Marine barracks in Brooklyn, Philadelphia, and Annapolis all sent their Company A. To sort out this confusion, an early decision was made to assign companies numbers. These were further extended to include Marine detachments. There was no real order to the numbering. Marine barracks, Annapolis, might have 15th Co., 31st Co., and 45th Co., while a Marine detachment on a battleship might be 13th Co. This seeming disorder was less confusing than having all companies with the same letter designation together. After the war with Spain, occupations for larger Marine units increased. The Boxer Rebellion in China, insurrection in the Philippines, and the problems arising from the Roosevelt Corollary to the Monroe Doctrine in the Caribbean and Central America required large standing formations rather than ad hoc ones. This led to the organizing of regiments distinct from Marine barracks and Marine detachments. The new regiments were numbered (spelled out) as First Marine Regiment, Fourth Marine Regiment, and so forth. These were later shortened in usage to "First Marines," and so on. Just before World War II, the initial Marine Divisions (MarDiv) were formed. By 1941 there were two in existence, 1st Marine Division on the East Coast and 2nd Marine Division in San Diego. After action at Guadalcanal, which brought fame to the 1st Marine Division, the press and public used to refer to it as "the First Marines." Although the First Marines were in the 1st Marine Division, the Fifth, Seventh, and Eleventh Marines were there too. They resented one regiment getting all the public acclaim. It is lubberly to refer by number and "Marines" to anything but a regiment.

When the Fifth and Sixth Marines were formed for combat in France, companies were still designated by number (Arabic ordinals). The Fifth Marines was composed of existing companies with no numerical sequence. The Sixth Marines was composed of newly raised companies and assigned to battalions in numerical order. Later, after the war, when regiments became the standard unit and had subordinate units of battalions, company designations returned to letters. Artillery batteries also were lettered.

There is a sequence of designations of units, from the lowest, the fire team, to the highest, the Marine Expeditionary Force (MEF; formerly, the Amphibious Corps). Each fire team in a squad is numbered consecutively in that squad, as is each squad in a platoon, and the platoons in a company. At the company (and artillery battery) level, letters are used, and the lettering runs completely through the regiment. Depending on how many companies are assigned to a battalion by the table of organization (T/O) in effect (over the years it has varied from three to four companies) the 1st Battalion could have Cos. A, B, and C, or, if it was a four-company T/O, Co. D as well. In the four-company T/O, that would mean the 2nd Battalion would have Cos. E, F, G, and H, and so forth to the 3rd Battalion. Companies are sometimes referred to in speaking by phonetic alphabet (e.g., "Alpha Company"), but this is never found in official correspondence. Battalions are designated by an Arabic ordinal; the sequence within a regiment applies only to order in a parade and has no tactical significance. Regiments, as we have seen, have their numerical designation spelled out. Divisions and brigades revert to the alternating Arabic ordinals, while Amphibious Corps or Marine Expeditionary Forces use Roman numerals (e.g., III MEF). To sum up, a new second lieutenant might be assigned to lead the 1st Plt, Co. A, 1st Bn, First Marines, 1stMarDiv. By T/O, lieutenants lead platoons, captains command companies, lieutenant colonels command battalions, colonels command regiments, brigadier generals command brigades, major generals command divisions, and lieutenant generals command MEFs.

On the aviation side, a squadron is the smallest unit with a designation. It has a three-digit Arabic numeral after its tactical designation (e.g., VMFA [Marine Fighter/Attack Squadron] 311). Squadrons are commanded by lieutenant colonels. The next echelon is the Marine Air Group (MAG), commanded by a colonel. It is a varying mix of squadrons by types, such as VMF (fighter) or VMA, and numbers of squadrons. Two or more MAGs make up a Marine Air Wing (MAW), commanded by a major general. One or more Marine divisions and Marine Air Wings with an appropriate logistic command constitute a Marine Expeditionary Force.

For a time during the Vietnam War, the administration thought that the word *Expeditionary* might be offensive to other nations and some domestic entities. Thus *Amphibious* replaced it, as in III Marine Amphibious Force (III MAF).

Smaller, task-organized formations are Marine Expeditionary Brigades (MEB) and Marine Expeditionary Units (MEU, pronounced "mew"). The MEB headquarters directs a Regimental Landing Team (RLT) consisting of an infantry regiment, supporting artillery, combat support units, a MAG, and a combat service (logistics) support unit. A MEU is similarly built around a Battalion Landing Team (BLT) and a composite, fixed- and rotary-wing, squadron.

Federal law calls for no fewer than three active-duty Marine divisions and

Marine Air Wings. Appropriations don't always support complete notional divisions of three infantry regiments of three battalions each, a four-battalion artillery regiment, and supporting units. To live within appropriations and the law, cuts are made, usually vertically, for example, a battalion from a regiment or a regiment from a division. Historically, as shown during the Korean War, such cuts are quickly reconstituted and full-strength formations go into combat. Similar curtailments of active strength, without compromising safety, are made in the Marine Air Wings. Further, there is a Reserve Marine division and Marine Air Wing, with drilling reservists in cities and towns throughout the country.

During World War II, there was eventually a total of six Marine divisions and nine Marine Air Wings. There were twenty-nine regiments, eighteen of which were infantry, while six were artillery regiments, and five were engineer regiments with one of their battalions being a Navy construction battalion.

The genesis of the Marine Corps in its current role as a force ready to prosecute the land operations of a naval campaign occurred on 7 December 1933 with the formation of the Fleet Marine Force (FMF). The commandant was to provide to the commander in chief, U.S. Fleet, a commanding general with an appropriate staff to command such Marine forces as designated for operations, including training operations. The FMF, in effect, became a type-command of the U.S. Fleet, subject to further assignment in whole or in part to subordinate task-organized forces of that fleet. The FMFs, one in each ocean, endured for sixty years. They evolved into Marine Forces (MARFOR) after the Persian Gulf War in 1990–91, and this was formalized in 1994, making them components of the unified commands in the Atlantic and Pacific.

Heraldry

There is some heraldry, as would be expected, in a Corps of proud traditions. The official colors of the Marine Corps are scarlet and gold. The battle color of the Marine Corps is the color of the Corps. On a field of scarlet there is the Marine Corps emblem with a Western Hemisphere of white and silver, and a fouled anchor and eagle in gold (save for the eagle's head, which is white). A white scroll above the eagle's head has the motto "Semper Fidelis" in scarlet. Below the globe and anchor is a larger scroll, outlined in gold, with a scarlet "United States Marine Corps" on a white field. Battle honors, citations, and battle streamers for every award to the Corps are fixed to the top of the staff. Silver bands representing specific engagements, which are stars on the battle streamers, encircle the staff. As the Corps approaches its two hundred fiftieth anniversary, these bands exceed the available space on the shaft. Similar colors are authorized for every Fleet Marine Force unit. These have the designation of the particular unit in the larger scroll beneath the globe and anchor. The battle honors earned by the particular unit are attached as streamers to the top of the staff, and silver bands encircle the staff.

The scarlet and gold were officially adopted as Marine colors during the term of John A. Lejeune, thirteenth commandant; before that time, regimental battle colors had a blue field.

Before the adoption of the "emblem," various devices were worn to designate Marines from other services. After the Civil War, the current emblem was adopted, and it has been the distinguishing mark of a Marine ever since. It is a three-dimensional badge when worn on the uniform. It is half a globe depicting the Western Hemisphere with a fouled anchor to the rear with the flukes to the left as one faces it. Surmounting the globe is an American bald eagle facing toward the flukes. That is the way it is depicted in flat presentations. Since it also is worn on the uniform collars or lapel, the one on the right collar or lapel reverses the position of the anchor flukes and the head of the eagle. The flukes and the facing of the eagle are always inboard. The "Eagle, Globe and Anchor" is the distinguishing mark of a U.S. Marine worldwide.

Marine general officers (the correct reference, as opposed to the lubberly "generals") rate a personal flag with the appropriate numbers of white stars to their rank, on a scarlet field, just like Navy flag officers. (Marine general officers are not referred to as "flag officers," however.)

During World War I, when the 4th Marine Brigade was in the Army 2nd Infantry Division, Marines adopted the Army custom of wearing an embroidered division patch on the left arm of the uniform just at the shoulder. It was the Indian Head patch of the 2nd Infantry Division. When the division was disbanded, the practice was discontinued. As Marine divisions were formed before and during World War II, unit pride called for official recognition by division patches. When the 1st Marine Division came off Guadalcanal ("The Canal") to Australia, someone designed a diamond-shaped blue patch with the white stars of the Southern Cross and a red numeral one with vertical white letters spelling "Guadalcanal." The 2nd Marine Division had a scarlet arrowhead with the Southern Cross and a hand that holds high a gold torch with a scarlet numeral two. The 3rd Marine Division had a curved, three-sided scarlet patch with a gold border and inside a black and gold triad. The 4th Marine Division had a simple scarlet diamond with a large gold numeral four inside. The 5th Marine Division patch was of similar shape to that of the 3rd Marine Division, with gold letter *V* and a blue spearhead superimposed. The 6th Marine Division had a circular patch with a blue outer ring with "* Melanesia * Micronesia * Orient *" in gold; the inside circle in scarlet had a gold numeral six with a vertical gold sword through it. Each of the Marine Air Wings had similar patches. They were horizontally elongated scarlet diamonds with a gold border. Inside was a gold globe and anchor superimposed on horizontal gold wings. A Roman numeral indicated the number of the Marine Air Wing. Patches continued to be worn for a few years after World War II, but they were abolished as part of the uniform in the belief that they violated the spirit of there being just one Marine Corps. The spirit of the division insignia lingers on in the letterheads of the various division associations.

Uniforms

Marine uniforms are distinctive. They range from field uniforms to service uniforms to dress uniforms and formal dress. Uniforms have evolved over the years to be more functional and adaptive to new materials. As an example, consider Marine headgear. The tricorner hat of the early days gave way to the field hat (not campaign hat, which is an Army term), which is sometimes irreverently called the "Smokey the Bear" hat. Although it is no longer an item of general issue, it is proudly worn as a symbol of position by drill instructors and rifle range personnel. Billed caps, defined as frame caps, can be worn by all Marines, as can the garrison cap (a fore-and-aft headcover that lies flat when removed). A soft utility cap with bill matches the current version of utilities (Marine working and field uniforms, which are never referred to by the Army term of "fatigues" or "BDUs"). Of course, the ultimate field working cover is the steel helmet. Incidentally, the camouflage cover now used by all services over the helmet was a Marine innovation in World War II. Originally, it was reversible. It had a predominately green motif for jungle fighting, which reversed to a brown combination for fighting on barren coral reefs across the Central Pacific. During the Korean winter, Marines wore their speckled helmet covers "brown side out."

Footgear also has changed during the years. It has always been a Marine tradition that commanders see to the care and well-being of the Marines in their charge, especially their feet. Foot inspection after a long march is de rigueur. Feet were checked for blisters or, in extreme climates, for frostbite or "immersion foot" (a condition in which tissue turns to a spongelike consistency because of overexposure to moisture or mud). Field boots were fitted in boot camp as the recruit stood with a bucket of sand in each hand to simulate the weight on his feet while marching with a full pack. Thus, the proper fit was obtained. The footgear then was the old "boondocker," a reverse leather ankle-high boot. Today's footgear is of a smooth black leather that encourages shining, ignoring the fact that polish seals the pores of the leather causing feet to perspire. In cold weather this can lead to freezing. With the old boondockers, Marines wore a yellowish brown legging that laced up the outside. In Korea the combination of leggings and helmet covers caused Marines to be referred to by the enemy as "the yellow legs and speckled helmets." Opponents have a special way of describing Marines. In World War I, it was *Teufelhund* (devil dog).

Before World War II, enlisted Marines wore a capped-toe, ankle-high shoe, while officers wore an oxford. Both took a high gloss after hours of "spit-shining." Many officers opted for the more expensive cordovan leather. In the early 1960s, efforts to cut costs decreed that all services would wear black shoes. Along with that, all Marine leather, including Sam Browne belts, became black. The last major uniform change was the substitution of black for bronze-colored buttons and collar, lapel, and cap emblems.

The field uniform or utilities were adopted for World War II and have evolved since. The initial ones were green herringbone cotton twill. They had a tendency to fade with washing and exposure to the sun. Many thought that it was the sign of an "old salt" if his utilities were almost white. Subsequent utilities were of a darker, olive drab green and not given to fading. All versions were distinguished by the emblem emblazoned on the left breast pocket. This has been retained on the present-day "cammies," but in conformity with the practices of the other services, "U.S. Marines" has been added over that pocket. One of the drawbacks of the precamouflage utilities was the tendency to starch them for a parade-ground look. This made them retain body heat and was counterproductive in hot climates in the field. Even the pattern of the camouflage has evolved to a modern, computer-generated "pixelated" style.

Now, thanks to improvements in materials, the only color for the service uniform, both officers and enlisted, is Marine green. It can come in a winter and a summer weight. Usually, just the trousers of the latter are worn with an open-necked, short-sleeve shirt, and without field scarf (necktie).

The dress uniform or "blues" is similar for officers and enlisted. A dark blue, high-collared tunic is worn with lighter, sky-blue trousers. The buttons on the tunic are brass. The enlisted tunic has red piping on the edges and

Marines of a heavy guns platoon equipped with newly designed force protection
clothing/urban camouflage uniforms
U.S. Navy (Eric Logsdon)

epaulettes. Officers and noncommissioned officers (NCOs) wear a scarlet
stripe (wider for officers) down the outside seam of the trousers. An unsub-
stantiated but long-held tradition is that the "red" stripe represents the blood
shed by the officers and NCOs at Chapultepec in the Mexican War. There is
an exception to the nonmatching tunic and trousers. General officers wear
matching blue trousers with their dress and undress blues with a stripe of
gold braid instead of a scarlet one. Blues are either dress or undress, according to whether ribbons with shooting badges (undress) or medals without
shooting badges (dress) are worn. Other insignia, such as aviator's wings or
parachutist wings, are worn on both versions. Enlisted personnel wear a white
belt with a flat, shiny brass buckle. Officers wear either a matching cloth belt
or, depending on the occasion, a Sam Browne belt of highly polished black
leather.

The epitome of elegance in uniforms is evening dress. It consists of a
high-collared, open-front, short jacket, whose open front tapers to the sides,
revealing a boiled-front white shirt with gold studs. A high-waisted pair of
matching blue trousers is topped by a scarlet cummerbund. In lieu of the

Modern-day grenadier
Naval Institute Photo Archive

cummerbund, general officers wear a red waistcoat. The trouser has a stripe of gold braid down the outside with a smaller scarlet stripe in the middle. The sleeves have a square device on each with different designs for company grade, field grade, and general officers. The first is a gold quatrefoil (cross-shaped braid), the second contains gold-braided leaves, and the third is similar, with heavier leaves. Miniature medals are worn on the left breast of evening dress.

One further mention of headgear is in order here. The frame cap comes with two versions. The enlisted cap has a polished black leather bill and a black chin strap. It can be fitted with either a green or a white cover depending on what uniform it is worn with. Officer cap covers are likewise interchangeable. But officer cap bills vary with category of rank. Company-grade officer caps have a polished black bill and black chin strap. When the white cap cover is used, the chin strap is gold braid with red stripes across the front horizontally. Field-grade officers have gold braid on the bill, while general officers have heavier braid. Officer cap covers are distinguished by having a quatrefoil on the top. Legend has it that in the days when Marines manned the "fighting tops" on sailing ships, officers chalked a cross on the top of their headgear so marksmen aloft could identify their own officers and not fire on them. Whatever its origin, it was officially adopted in 1859.

One final word on uniforms concerns the "Mameluke sword." Its name comes from its cross-hilt and ivory grip. These are traced back to their use by Muslim fighters of Arabia and North Africa. Tradition holds that when Lt. Presley O'Bannon stormed the fort at Derna, Tripoli, in 1805, he won the sword from the commander of the fort, and this resulted in its adoption by the Marine Corps. Swords are carried in parades and other ceremonies. Traditionally, at weddings, the newlyweds exit the church under an arch of swords. Also, at the wedding reception, the groom's sword is used to cut the cake. One word of caution about this: Never bring the scabbard to the reception. Some well-meaning civilian invariably tries to be of help by returning the sword to the scabbard. It is impossible to get cake and frosting out of a scabbard once an uncleaned sword has been thrust into it.

Ranks

Marines have three categories of officers. *Company grade* are second lieutenants, first lieutenants, and captains. *Field grade* are majors, lieutenant colonels, and colonels. *General officers* are brigadier generals, major generals, lieutenant generals, and generals. Warrant officers (WO-1) and the first two grades of commissioned warrant officers (CWO-2 and CWO-3) rank with company-grade officers for privileges and housing. A CWO-4 rates the housing of a field-grade officer.

Terminology

As one of the sea services, Marines have almost all of the sea-going customs of the Navy, as well as a few of their own. Marines, too, speak the nautical language and use all the words peculiar to seafarers. The first time a recruit (boot) refers to a vertical partition as a "wall" he will find himself standing at rigid attention while the DI in a few choice words tells him that it is a "bulkhead" and that "if he draws the pay, he should speak the language." But there are some words that are peculiar to the Marines Corps. For example, *barracks cap* denotes the frame cap. The *boondocks* is any raw, uninhabited, or uncivilized place, such as forest or jungle, fit only for the training of Marines. *Boondockers* are field shoes. A recruit is a *boot* and is trained in one of two Marine Corps Recruit Depots (MCRD) or *boot camps*. A *crumb* is someone who is so slovenly that he shouldn't be a Marine. The word *dope* has nothing to do with narcotics, but has two related meanings. The first is the latest word, sometimes called the "hot, smoking dope" (misinformation is "bum dope"). The other meaning is the individualized setting of sights on a Marine's weapon. *Doc* is the word for a corpsman. It is the finest appellation that a Marine can bestow on a sailor. *Doggie,* short for *dog-face,* is a soldier. *Eight-ball* is anyone who is not completely "squared away" at all times and usually in more than his share of trouble. *Field hat* is the broad-brimmed felt hat worn by DIs and range personnel. It has a four-dent crown and is not a "campaign hat," which is the Army term. *Field music* usually refers to a bugler but can include members of a drum and bugle corps of a smaller command. A *field scarf* is a regulation Marine Corps khaki necktie. At one time, a collar bar attached to the collar points lifted the knot away from the neck and the two ends of the field scarf were free to fly in the wind (some Marines eliminated that unkemptness by fastening the field scarf to the shirt front by a hidden safety pin). The "battle bar" at the collar was dropped as part of the uniform, and a tie bar (clasp) was made part of the uniform to keep the ends of the scarf fastened to the shirt front.

A *first soldier* is the first sergeant or senior enlisted Marine in a company or battery. *Flag allowance* refers to Marines assigned duty in an admiral's headquarters or staff. *Fore-and-aft cap* is the garrison cap. *Gravel cruncher* is a term often used by aviators to describe "ground-pounding" Marines. Gunnery sergeant is contracted to *gunny* but is not to be confused with a *gunner,* who is a warrant officer. A *hard-charger* is a professionally adept, aggressive, and dynamic Marine, the epitome of the Corps. *Iron Mike* is a statue at Parris Island of a World War I Marine. A similar work, officially called *Fighting for the Right,* stands at Quantico. Tradition has it that the French had a bronze cast of an American soldier and presented it to the Army. When the Army found that the statue had a Marine Corps emblem on the front of the helmet, it was glad to turn the piece over to the Marines. *Pogey-bait* is candy or snacks. The *pogey-rope* refers to the *fourragagere* presented by the French to the 4th Marine Brigade in World War I. It is a green and red braided cord worn on the left shoulder. A Marine fires his or her individual weapon for qualification on *record day.* A unique designation is *782 gear.* This is individual combat equipment issued to Marines on Memorandum Receipt Form 782. *Shipping-over music* is any inspirational martial music invoking the glories of the Corps. A Marine on post can find a beer or other libation at the *slopchute. Semper Fidelis* is the Marine Corps motto and is the Latin for "always faithful." Marines use a contraction, *Semper Fi,* among themselves as a friendly sign of greeting or recognition. It can have an irreverent connotation as well, depending upon the inflection when uttered. A promotion calls for the new insignia of rank to be *wet down.* A traditional *wetting down party* includes all former and present seniors and juniors to the newly promoted Marine who are in the vicinity. One final admonition about "drawing the pay and speaking the language" is important. CMC has forbidden the Marine use of the Army practice in stating the time of day either orally or in writing. Both services use the 2400-hour system of time, but a

Field music (Alaska, 1943)
Naval Institute Photo Archive

Marine never says, "1200 hours." He says (or writes), "1200." Of course, the expression "eight bells" would be more nautical.

Weddings

As noted above, Marine weddings feature the sword. More must be said about such important affairs. An older tradition had the groom and his groomsmen decking themselves out in all their decorations of either ribbons and badges or, more formally, the medals themselves. This has given way to a more modern "tradition." On the premise that the wedding day belongs to the bride, it has become a custom that the bride be the groom's only "decoration" on that day. Likewise, the groomsmen are also bereft of anything above their left breast pocket.

Another "custom" that has crept into Marine weddings of late has no basis in good taste and should never be allowed to become a tradition. This is the deplorable practice when a groomsman, upon the emergence of the bridal couple from the arch of swords after the ceremony, drops his sword and flicks his wrist to bring the flat of the blade swat across the bride's derriere with the exclamation, "Welcome to the Corps!" That bit of juvenile delinquency is hardly worthy of a Corps with dignified traditions.

Conclusion

One tradition that is worthy of the Corps concerns "The Marines' Hymn." At the first note, all Marines within hearing rise to their feet, clicking their heels together and standing at attention until the last note fades away. This is practiced by everyone, whether in uniform or not, including those no longer on active duty or discharged. "Once a Marine, always a Marine." There is no such thing as an "ex-Marine."

The ultimate in Marine tradition is the Marine Corps Birthday. It is a day of pomp and ceremony. The mess hall serves a holiday meal. There are parades on post. In many commands holiday routine prevails after the ceremonies have been performed. A Marine Corps Birthday Ball is held, wherever more than a few Marines are present. Balls range from formal pageantries with present-day Marines in period uniforms to events featuring simply a cake with a Marine Corps emblem in the center being escorted by a pair of Marines in every rank to colonel. The cake is cut by Mameluke sword by the senior Marine present. The first piece goes to the oldest Marine present and the second to the youngest.

One thing is mandatory on 10 November, Article 5060.2 *Marine Corps Manual* must be published, preferably by being read, to all hands.

On November 1st, 1921, John A. Lejeune, 13th Commandant of the Marine Corps, directed that a reminder of the honorable service of the Corps be published by every command to all Marines throughout the globe, on the 10th of November, the birthday of the Corps. . . . therefore, in compliance with the will of the 13th Commandant, Article 38, U.S. Marine Corps Manual, Edition of 1921, is republished as follows:

1. On November 10, 1775, a Corps of Marines was created by a resolution of the Continental Congress. Since that date many thousand men have borne the name Marine. In memory of them it is fitting that we who are Marines should commemorate the birthday of the Corps by calling to mind the glories of its long and illustrious history.

2. The record of our Corps is one which will bear comparison with that of the most famous military organizations in the world's history. During 90 of the 146 years of its existence the Marine Corps has been in action against the nation's foes. From the Battle of Trenton to the Argonne,

Marines have won foremost honors in war, and in the long areas of military tranquility at home generation after generation of Marines have grown gray in war in both hemispheres, and in every corner of the seven seas that our country and its citizens might enjoy peace and security.

3. In every battle and skirmish since the birth of our Corps, Marines have acquitted themselves with the greatest distinction, winning new honors on each occasion until the term "Marine" has come to signify all that is highest in military tradition and soldierly virtue.

4. This high name of distinction and soldierly repute we who are Marines today have received from those who preceded us in the Corps. With it we also received the eternal spirit which has animated our Corps from generation to generation and has been the distinguishing mark of the Marines in every age. So long as that spirit continues to flourish Marines will be found equal to every emergency in the future as they have been in the past, and the men of our Nation will regard us as worthy successors to the long line of illustrious men who have served as "Soldiers of the Sea" since the founding of our Corps.

The Marine Corps holds a peculiar place in the U.S. military establishment. It is a separate service within the Department of the Navy and not one of the Navy's "communities" (aviation, surface warfare, submarine, and so on). At the same time, the CMC sits, along with the chiefs of staff of the Army and Air Force and the chief of naval operations, as a permanent member of the Joint Chiefs of Staff. There are those who, in the past, have recommended the abolition of the Corps as a cost-saving measure, but each time the public outcry has been so loud as to drown out any possibility of such action. The nation loves the Marine Corps for what it is and what it stands for. As the recruiting slogan went: "The few, the proud, the Marines!"

In 1958, a high civilian official of the Department of Defense was visiting Okinawa. At a lunch in his honor put on by the Army, Marine Corps, Navy, and Air Force, the official kept referring to the wonderful cooperation among the three services on the island. Finally, the CG 3rdMarDiv, a future CMC, stood up. "Mr. Secretary, you keep referring to the three services. As a Marine, I feel that it is incumbent upon me to invite your attention to the fact that we now have four services. Even though they are relatively new, since 1947, we have had a separate Air Force."

12

The United States Coast Guard

You have to go out, but you don't have to come back.

Surfman's unofficial motto

But the men that sail the ocean
In a wormy, rotten craft,
When the sea ahead is mountains
With a hell-blown gale abaft;
When the mainmast cracks and topples,
And she's lurching in the trough,
Them's the guys that greets the cutter
With the smiles that won't come off.

Arthur Somers Roche, "The Coast Guard Cutter"

To graduate young men and women with sound bodies, stout hearts, and alert minds, with a liking for the sea and its lore, and with that high sense of honor, loyalty and obedience which goes with trained initiative and leadership; well grounded in seamanship, the sciences and amenities, and strong in the resolve to be worthy of the traditions of the commissioned officers in the United States Coast Guard in the service of their country and humanity.

Mission of the United States Coast Guard Academy

The United States Coast Guard is unique, for no other nation has a comparable organization. The history of the Coast Guard is at once colorful and largely unknown to the general public. The precursor to the Coast Guard was created at the request of Alexander Hamilton, secretary of the treasury, to control that scourge of the new nation, smuggling. On 4 August 1790 Congress authorized the building of ten revenue cutters. The authorization was

U.S. Coast Guard barque *Eagle*. The *Eagle* carries 21,350 square feet of sail and is one of only five such training barques in the world.
U.S. Coast Guard (Telfair Brown)

for cutters, but not for a Coast Guard, therefore the name of the new organization was left to evolve. By the end of the nineteenth century habit and usage had settled on the Revenue-Marine, or Revenue Cutter Service, created by act of Congress in 1863.

The first U.S. naval commission was issued to the master of a revenue cutter, Capt. Hopley Yeaton, on 21 March 1791. The historic document bears the signatures of both Washington and Jefferson. The Coast Guard searched for years for this first commission and secured it in 1934 from Miss Mary Yeaton, great-granddaughter of Captain Yeaton. Included in the first group of commissions was David Porter, the father of Commodore David Porter and grandfather of Adm. David Dixon Porter.

Before the first cutter was even finished, the Revenue-Marine was assisted in its fight by a black woman by the name of Marie Lee. Marie was a teamster charged with delivering swivel guns from the Philadelphia foundries to the Portsmouth, New Hampshire, yards where the cutters were being built. Six smugglers got wind of the delivery and decided to divert the shipment for their own purposes. When they ambushed Marie between Philadelphia and New York, she promptly beat them all senseless and continued on to make her delivery.

The early revenue service patrolled much as today's Coast Guard does, stopping ships along the coasts, inspecting their cargoes and comparing them with their manifests to stop unauthorized goods from entering the country. By the time of the quasi-war with France, the Revenue Service made up about one-third of the American naval effort.

The spirit of the early Coast Guard was most evident in defeat. The cutter *Eagle* was intentionally grounded while being chased by the English ship *Dispatch* during the War of 1812. Her crew removed her guns and dragged them to the top of a nearby bluff where they continued the fight. Even after they ran out of their own ammunition, they collected the British shot and fired it back at them. Today, Coast Guard Academy cadets go to sea in the *Eagle*'s namesake.

In another losing engagement, the enemy provided ample comment on the fight with the revenue cutter *Surveyor* at Gloucester Point, Virginia, on 10 June 1813:

> *His Majesty's Ship Narcissus:*
> *Your gallant and desperate attempt to defend your vessel against more than double your number, on the night of the 12th inst., excited such admiration on the part of your opponents, as I have seldom witnessed, and induced me to return you the sword you had so nobly used, in testimony of mine. Our poor fellows have severely suffered occasioned chiefly, if not solely, by the precautions you had taken to prevent surprise; in short, I am at a loss which to admire most, the previous engagement on board the Surveyor, or the determined manner by which her deck was disputed, inch by inch.*
> *You have my most sincere wishes for the immediate parole and speedy exchange of yourself and brave crew; and I cannot but regret, that I myself have no influence that way, otherwise it should be forthcoming.*
> *I am, sir, with much respect,*
> *Your most obedient,*
> *John Crerie*

During the years leading up to the Civil War, the Revenue cutters were instrumental in cutting off the activities of smugglers and slavers. They built a reputation as a force to be reckoned with. In 1831 the *Gallatin* began the first lifesaving patrols, adding another dimension to the expanding mission of the service.

One of the first shots fired in the Civil War was from the cutter *Harriet*

Sandy Hook Light, New Jersey, the oldest standing lighthouse in North America

Lane standing off Charleston, South Carolina, in support of Fort Sumter. The cutter *Miami* served as President Lincoln's personal transport during a trip to view a proposed landing site at Norfolk. Both during and after the war the Revenue Service continued its work of controlling smuggling and establishing and enforcing U.S. trade regulations.

In the exploration and growth of the Alaskan territory, the cutter *Bear* was a legend. The *Bear* was a 200-foot steam barkentine that spent over forty years off the coast of Alaska, providing a federal presence and becoming one of the law enforcement agencies for the Alaskan gold rush. She protected seals and fisheries, and even brought the first reindeer to Alaska from Siberia. Her most famous exploit involved the rescue of a whaling fleet in 1897. The fleet was trapped in the ice when winter descended. The *Bear* sailed as close as she could get, then sent a party ashore with 400 reindeer to go the last 1,600 miles to deliver the herd to the isolated men. The herd sustained them until the following spring when they could be extricated. The mascot of the Coast Guard Academy is the bear, in recognition of this great ship.

Scituate Light, Massachusetts. It was here in 1814 that an "army of two" young women held off a British invasion.

The modern Coast Guard is an amalgamation of several former organizations. In addition to the Revenue Cutter Service, it includes the Lighthouse Service, the Life-Saving Service, the Steamboat Inspection Service, and the Bureau of Navigation.

The first of these, the Lighthouse Service, dates to colonial times. The first American lighthouse was Boston Light, built in 1716. It was destroyed by the British in 1776 and replaced in 1783. The oldest standing lighthouse is at Sandy Hook, New Jersey, and was built in 1764. These structures, in addition to being critical navigational aids and the saviors of countless seamen, are architecturally beautiful and have been inspirational to men and women throughout our nation's history. Due to the daily task of having to trim the wicks of the lamps to keep them burning brightly, the keepers of these lights were often called "wickies."

Keepers lived in isolation, and those whose families accompanied them were often enlisted as assistant keepers. Ada and Abigail Bates, daughters of Simon Bates, the keeper of Scituate Light, managed to convince the crew of the British ship *La Hogue* that they were a colonial army ashore. In September 1814 they were home alone when they saw the *La Hogue* anchor nearby. By playing on a fife and drum for hours, they confused the enemy and caused them to withdraw.

The lighthouses, being located near navigational hazards, became natural lifesaving stations for those who either disregarded their warnings or were unable to safely navigate the shoal water nearby. One of the most famous of the lifesaving keepers was Ida Lewis. Ida became the keeper of the Lime Rock Light at the mouth of Newport harbor after the death of her father, the former keeper. She held the post for over fifty years, and in that time performed enough rescues to make her a national celebrity, with a cover feature in *Harper's Weekly* in 1869.

The United States was only the third country to build lifesaving stations. (The Chinese and the British preceded our efforts during the mid-1700s.) At first, lifesaving stations were built by local groups and cities; then, as a need for coordination arose and the equipment technology became more sophisticated and more expensive, they started to band together. In 1847 the federal government began to build lifesaving stations, although there was no funding to staff them, which left the stations as bare equipment sheds for local groups. In 1854, when the ship *Powhatan* ran aground off Long Beach, New York, and 311 people died, the public demanded trained and paid crews, and the system began to respond.

By the 1880s the system had grown to the point where the crews not only were trained properly, but also were paid well enough for the job to attract a more professional lifesaver. Probably the most famous of these was Joshua James. He joined the Massachusetts Humane Society, a state-run lifesaving group, at the age of fifteen. He entered the U.S. Life-Saving Service at the age of sixty-two, after a career spent in the family shipping business. On 25–26 November 1888, his crew rescued twenty-nine people by breeches buoy and rowboat from at least four different wrecks, having one of their own boats smashed on the rocks and going back with a second boat to finish the job.

The Midgetts are probably the first family of the rescue service, indeed, of the Coast Guard. Hundreds of members of the family have served since L. Barrister Midgett was appointed a station keeper in 1874. Seven members of the family have earned the Gold Life-Saving Medal, and three the Silver Medal. One of these was for the daring rescue of the crew of the *Mirlo* off Chicamacomico, North Carolina, in 1918. Keeper John A. Midgett and his crew, all but one of whom were members of the Midgett family, braved

Pea Island Life Saving Station, base of the first all-black crew of surfmen, for over sixty-five years was one of the best in the service.

a heavy surf and after several hours managed to save all fifty-two crew members.

North Carolina's Outer Banks is the site of the Coast Guard's only all-black lifesaving crew. The crew was formed in 1880, in the wake of a scandal involving the previous crew who were dismissed for missing an assignment and falsifying reports about the incident. The investigating officer recommended that Richard Etheridge be the new keeper. Since he was black, no white surfmen would work for him. So he gathered an all-black crew and spent endless hours drilling them to make them the best and eliminate all possible question from their detractors about their abilities or competence. For over sixty-seven years the Pea Island station was one of the best, performing hundreds of dramatic rescues, despite harassment in the early years.

Probably the most important factor in improving marine safety was the creation of the Steamboat Inspection Service. With the advent of steam propulsion, there came a spate of tragic accidents. Most involved the design and maintenance of the steam power plant. Early boiler design and metallurgy could not withstand the pressures and saltwater environment, and therefore were prone to explosion. The 1837 explosion of the *Pulaski* caused a public outcry that led to federal money being invested in a new regulatory agency to inspect shipboard propulsion systems for safety. Over the following years regulations and technology combined to improve ship safety.

An interesting side mission was derelict destruction. Ships abandoned at sea became hazards to navigation, and the Coast Guard was given the task of destroying these hulks. This was not easy. Boarding an abandoned ship, particularly if there was any sea running, was a delicate evolution at best, and taking a hulk under tow or attaching explosives to sink it was even more risky. In 1907 the Coast Guard was authorized to build a derelict-destroyer.

The Revenue Cutter Service was graced with its own colors in 1872, about nine years after its formal organization. The secretary of the treasury decreed that the service would fly "an ensign and pennant consisting of sixteen perpendicular stripes, alternate red and white, the Union of the Ensign to be the Arms of the United States, in dark Blue on a White field." Service vessels flew this ensign instead of the national ensign in U.S. waters. The only change to this scheme was the addition of the Revenue Cutter Service seal over the stripes in 1910.

As did the Naval Academy, the Coast Guard originally educated its future officers at sea. In 1876 an act authorized the appointment of Coast Guard cadets who, after two years of training, could sit for the third lieutenant's exam. A school ship, the sail cutter *Dobbin,* was designated and homeported in New Bedford, Massachusetts, where the first nine cadet "swabs" began their schooling. She was replaced by the school ship *Chase* in 1878, but a decline in the number of cadets caused the whole endeavor to be abandoned in 1890, when new third lieutenants were selected from the Naval Academy's passed midshipmen. But the Naval Academy, then as now, served the needs of the Navy. The naval expansion in the 1890s meant that no passed midshipmen were available, and at that time the *Chase* was reactivated. Over the next few years, several ships acted as school ships, with a gradually growing enrollment and course length. At the same time, as these ships spent less and less time in New Bedford, the service acquired its first shore facility, located at Curtis Bay near Baltimore. It made sense to move the school there, and this was done in 1900. Ten years later, the school was relocated again, this time to the site of Fort Trumbull, in New London, Connecticut. Finally, in 1932, it was moved into its present quarters just a few miles up the Thames River.

Wright Brothers Flyer, as photographed by surfman John T. Daniels of the Kill Devil Hills Life-Saving Station, whose crew of five helped in the launches and recoveries of the first powered flights.

Coast Guardsmen were at the forefront of the transportation revolution. Members of the Kill Devil Hills Life-Saving Station helped the Wright brothers position and launch their airplane in 1903. One Coast Guardsman was injured during the recovery of that first flight, becoming the first man to be injured in an aircraft accident. In 1905 the lightship *Nantucket* sent the world's first radio distress signal, using the morse letters for "help." The "SOS" code was first used in 1909, when the cutter *Seneca* responded to the steamship *Republic*, saving the crew before the ship sank. The sinking of the *Titanic* in 1912, and the 1914 International Conference on the Safety of Life at Sea, caused the Revenue Cutter Service to initiate the North Atlantic iceberg patrol. Since that time no ships have been lost to icebergs in the area while patrols were being run.

In 1915 the Revenue Cutter Service and the Life-Saving Service were merged into the newly created U.S. Coast Guard. According to Oliver M. Maxam in a 1929 article in U. S. Naval Institute *Proceedings*, the Life-Saving Service brought to the Coast Guard a record of 177,286 lives saved from the perils of the sea between 1871 and 1914. During World War I, the Coast Guard served as convoy escort, having been transferred to the Department of the Navy just hours after the declaration of war, by the cryptic dispatch: "Plan 1, Acknowledge." The Coast Guard had the highest proportion of battle casualties of all the U.S. forces in that war. The lifesaving stations up and down the Atlantic coast were kept busy on the lookout for ships and survivors from attacks by the new weapon, the U-boat.

Coast Guard aviation started at about the same time. The first air wing began with the training of six Coast Guard aviators at the Naval Air Station in Pensacola. Although it failed to survive the postwar spending cuts, a Coast Guard aviator did make aviation history by being one of the first pilots to cross the Atlantic Ocean, with the N-C-4 flight. Not until the 1930s did the aviation arm again grow. Airplanes were used for flying lifeboats, smuggling patrols, and enforcing fishery laws.

It might well be said that Prohibition saved the Coast Guard. After World War I, the officer corps and many of the service and political leaders wanted the Coast Guard to remain under the Department of the Navy. Obviously, this would have meant an end to the Coast Guard's autonomy. Fortunately, there were several influential members of Congress who wanted the Coast Guard to revert to the Treasury Department, and so it did. But times were lean, and until the passage of the Eighteenth Amendment, the Coast Guard had little money to do its duty. Prohibition caused the numbers of vessels seized in 1923 to almost quadruple from the previous year, and this assured the Coast Guard's continued mission. This did not translate into popularity, however. The public, and even other governments, were not happy with the Coast Guard's growing success. After all, the more cargoes seized, the less alcohol there was in the speakeasies. The repeal of Prohibition didn't stop smuggling. It just changed the nature of the cargo, and the Coast Guard continued its efforts.

World War II brought new involvement. The cutter *Taney* was at Pearl Harbor and managed to get into the fight. Coast Guard vessels served as convoy protection, sinking eleven U-boats. A Coast Guard aircraft was the first to sink a submarine. Coast Guardsmen manned amphibious landing craft and used their surfboat handling skills to teach Navy coxswains how to deal with the vagaries of close-to-shore currents and effects. One of these, Signalman 1/c Douglas Munro, became the Coast Guard's first and only Medal of Honor recipient for saving the lives of Marines stranded in the waters off Guadalcanal. The first use of the newly developed helicopter as a rescue tool came as a result of the war. Civilian sailors were given temporary

U.S. Coast Guard cutter *Taney* (WPG 37)
Naval Institute Photo Archive

Reverse of SM1 Douglas Munro's Medal of Honor

enlistments in the Coast Guard Reserves so that they could patrol coastal waters in their own sail craft looking for U-boats. These amateur lookouts gave rise to the sobriquet "Hooligan Navy." Beach patrols using dogs, and even horses, ran on U.S. shores and on occupied islands in the Pacific. A women's auxiliary, the SPARs, was created by Navy WAVE Lt. Dorothy Stratton, to help ease the manpower load. *SPAR* was an acronym for the Coast Guard's motto, "Semper Paratus, Always Ready." The first successful military integration of blacks was in the weather patrol yacht *Sea Cloud*. Of the 173-man crew, nearly one-third were black, including four officers.

Postwar operations involving the Coast Guard included Arctic Ocean patrol and exploration, as well as the development of ice-breaking ships and techniques. The law enforcement aspect of the service mission has grown. With increases in drug smuggling and illegal immigration, the Coast Guard has done more and more border patrolling. Additionally, international fishing treaty enforcement has grown with better knowledge of the environmental impact of unrestrained harvest. Environmental impact itself has been added to the long list of concerns to watch over. Ship inspections now include all manner of environmental checks, from petroleum and other effluent discharges, to hazardous materials being dumped either intentionally or unknowingly.

Perhaps the most notorious environmental disaster occurred in 1989 with the grounding of the supertanker *Exxon Valdez* off the coast of Alaska. The Coast Guard took the lead in coordinating a huge operation. Between the off-loading of the remaining cargo and the cleanup of the surrounding water and beaches, men and women of the Coast Guard were busy for months.

In April 1967 the Coast Guard was transferred to the Department of Transportation after 177 years under the secretary of the treasury. In 1970, taking advantage of the sea change for the service, the new commandant, Adm. Chester Bender, enacted a suggestion he had made two years previously and changed the Coast Guard uniform from that of the Navy with different insignia to a wholly restyled and different color uniform. Despite some grumbling, "Bender blues" became the new uniform. Along with this, the ships were soon adorned with the now familiar orange and blue "racing stripe" at the bow. The post–September 11, 2001, war on terrorism caused the Coast Guard to again relocate to the newly created Department of Homeland Security.

The late Rear Adm. F. C. Billard, USCG, defined the Coast Guard's community of interest with the Navy and the high professional standards of his service:

Coast Guard ice breaker in the Polar Sea near McMurdo, Antarctica
U.S. Coast Guard (Rob Rothway)

Having fought as a part of the Navy in all our wars, and taking an especial pride in being fully prepared to perform creditable service in the Navy whenever called upon, the officers and men of the Coast Guard are inspired not only by the high tradition and fine history of their own service, but also by the splendid traditions, history, and indoctrination of the United States Navy. They have thus two rich heritages to be proud of and two standards of the same lofty character to live up to.

Today the Coast Guard stands proudly in the forefront of U.S. military efforts. First of the sea services, first to implement racial integration, first to admit women into the service academy, first to allow women command at sea, unique among the militaries of the nations of the world, the Coast Guard is, indeed, "Always Ready."

4

THE SEA

★

13

Some Traditions, Customs, and Usages of the Service

The worth of a sentiment lies in the sacrifices men will make for its sake. All ideals are built on the ground of solid achievement, which in a given profession creates in the course of time a certain tradition, or in other words a standard of conduct.

Joseph Conrad

I should like to emphasize the confidence that our citizens have in their first line of defense. It is a faith of free men in the defenders of the democratic tradition; it is a trust that our citizens repose in a Navy that has never failed its country.

President Franklin D. Roosevelt, Navy Day letter
to Acting Secretary of Navy, 26 October 1939

Some of our naval customs and traditions originated in antiquity, while others grew from practices in the Middle Ages and the great Age of Discovery. This chapter describes some of the best known traditions, customs, and usages of our naval service. These customs are a part of the naval profession; to overemphasize them is a mistake, but to underestimate them displays a lack of perspective.

A New Navy in a New World

From the Royal Navy came the greater share of the U.S. Navy's first usages and written regulations. In any study of American traditions and customs

John Paul Jones Crypt, located beneath the main sanctuary of the Naval Academy chapel and modeled in part on that of Napoleon, except that the visitor is not forced to "bow his head" to look at it but may meet a naval hero on eye level.
Naval Institute Photo Archive

of the sea, one must ever turn to the archives of maritime Britain for valuable source material.

Like other colonists who fought during the Revolution, "The Father of the U.S. Navy" was born a British subject. Inlaid in letters of bronze near his marble sarcophagus in the Crypt of the Naval Academy Chapel at Annapolis, Maryland, are these words: HE GAVE OUR NAVY ITS EARLIEST TRADITIONS OF HEROISM AND VICTORY.

As might be expected of the person who wrote after the Revolutionary War that "in time of peace it is necessary to prepare, and be always prepared for war by sea," John Paul Jones gave profound thought to matters affecting the defense of the country and proffered much constructive criticism when the U.S. Navy was founded. In 1776 Jones wrote: "I propose not our enemies as an example for our general imitation, yet, as their Navy is the best regulated of any in the world, we must in some degree imitate them, and aim at such further improvement as may one day make ours vie with, and exceed theirs."

Later, in 1782, Jones wrote to the U.S. minister of marine: "We are a young people, and need not be ashamed to ask advice from nations older and more experienced in Marine matters than ourselves."

The Hand Salute

The hand salute was "assumed" from the Royal Navy, which had borrowed it from the British Army. Its origin is of interest but, like the custom of saluting the quarterdeck, it has various explanations. That the hand salute represents the first part of the movement of uncovering is generally agreed; that there was nothing in the hand is a possible explanation of the British and French Army salute with the palm turned out.

From the earliest days of organized military units, the junior has uncovered in addressing or meeting the senior. Admiral the Earl of St. Vincent in 1796 promulgated an order to the effect that all officers were to take off their hats when receiving orders from superiors, "and not to touch them with an air of negligence." One finds in Jones's *Sketches of Naval Life,* written on board USS *Constitution* in 1826, an account of Sunday inspection on board and a description of the salute of the day: "The Captain and First Lieutenant, Mr. Vallette, are now on deck; they pass around and examine every part of it, each man lifting his hat as they pass or, in default of one, catching hold of a lock of hair."

There is a certain plausibility in placing the origin of the salute in the days of chivalry. It was customary for the knights in armor to raise their visors so that friends could see the face. In time, the gesture came to denote membership in the same order of knighthood, or other friendly organization. Because of the strict gradations of social class and rank in olden days, it is believed that the junior was required to make the first gesture, and therefore distinction in class and grade entered at the very beginning of the custom.

Today, the personal salute is a significant military gesture. It is the act of military and naval personnel looking into the eyes of a companion in arms and, by a proper gesture of the hand, paying due respect to the uniform of another defender of the republic. Up the scale, from the "jack of the dust" to the commander in chief, the junior salutes first. But humble and high meet on common ground when the circle is completed by the respect that all pay the flag, the highest symbol of the state.

An official visit, in the days
when the salute consisted
of holding the bill of the
cap or raising it
From "All Hands" by R. F.
Zogbaum; courtesy Harper
and Bros.

An official visit, in the days when the salute consisted of holding the bill of the cap or raising it
From "All Hands" by R. F. Zogbaum; courtesy Harper and Bros.

Salutes are always rendered with the right hand by Army and Air Force personnel. Naval personnel may use the left hand if the right hand is encumbered. A soldier or airman may salute while sitting down or while uncovered. Naval personnel do not. (They may do so, however, when failure to return a salute from a member of another service would be embarrassing.)

The salute is rendered when the person to be saluted is near enough to recognize that he is to be saluted and still has time enough to return the salute. Six to ten paces is considered normal.

Although the U.S. Army salute is the same as that of the U.S. Navy, this is not the case in the other armies of the world. A good explanation of this is made by Lieutenant Commander Lowry, RN. He sets forth the training ship regulations of 1882, in which the salute is defined as follows: "The naval salute is made by touching the hat or cap or by taking it off, always looking the person saluted in the face. By touching the hat is meant holding the edge with the forefinger and thumb."

We see that the naval salute evolved from the palm "inboard." In 1888 this British order was amended to read: "The naval salute is made by touching the hat or cap, or taking it off and looking the officer saluted in the face. Admirals, captains, officers of the same relative rank and the officers commanding the saluter's ship of whatever rank, are on all occasions saluted by the hat being taken off."

In practice, however, there was a great lack of conformity. Therefore, in January 1890 the hand salute only was decreed by Queen Victoria because of her displeasure at seeing officers and men uncovered when they appeared for royal commendation.

In the U.S. Navy, officers in the open uncover only for divine services. Enlisted uncover when at "mast" for reports and requests, at certain division inspections, and in officers' country when not under arms. Both officers and enlisted uncover when passing through compartments where naval personnel are at meals.

Nothing gives a better indication of the state of discipline of a ship or organization than prompt execution of the salute—the most common form of military courtesy.

Saluting the Quarterdeck and the Colors

The salute to the quarterdeck is derived from the very early seagoing custom of the respect that all paid to the pagan altar on board ship—and later to the crucifix and shrine. There are a few competent authorities on customs and traditions who do not fully support this belief, but instead trace the custom to the early days of the Royal Navy when all officers who were present on the quarterdeck returned the first salute of the individual by uncovering. Nevertheless, the majority opinion is that it was a salute to the seat of authority, the quarterdeck, the place nearest the colors. The flags of the suzerain or sovereign became in time symbolical of the religion of the state and emblematical of the royal or imperial house of the ruler. Subsequently, the colors had a twofold significance, religion and state. The custom of respect survived after the shrines were removed from deck. Kings once ruled by the theory of "divine right," and as eventually the "king's colors" were symbols of church and state combined, the colors became the dominant symbol to respect.

The quarterdeck has been a "sacred" area from the earliest days. Capt. Basil Hall, RN, writing in 1831 of his midshipman days, said:

Every person, not excepting the captain, when he puts his foot on this sacred spot, touches his hat; and as this salutation is supposed to be paid to the privileged region itself, all those who at the moment have the honor to be upon it are bound to acknowledge the compliment. Thus even when a midshipman comes up and takes off his hat, all the officers on deck (the admiral included, if he happens to be of the number) return the salute.

So completely does this form grow into a habit, that in the darkest night, and when there may not be a single person near the hatchway, it is invariably attended to with the same precision.

In addition to paying respect to the quarterdeck, one boarding or departing a ship should also pay respect to the flag. Upon reaching the top of the ladder or brow, military personnel in uniform should salute the flag, and civilian dignitaries on official visits and all those in civilian dress should uncover and stand at attention for a moment, facing toward the colors. At night, and any other times when the flag is not flying, a salute is no longer required. This is an old and impressive tradition—a short, dignified, personal recognition of the colors, the symbol of the state, the seat of authority.

The Sword, Symbol of Authority and Badge of Office

The ancient Hebrew prophets dreamed of a golden era when swords would be beaten into plowshares, but, alas, that vision is far from being realized. Nevertheless, although the practical value of the sword was probably last demonstrated by horse-mounted cavalrymen, it remains, even in the nuclear age, as a badge of office worn by officers of the armed services of all nations and by the diplomatic officers of many foreign powers when in full dress uniform.

Even before the days of the Roman *gladius,* the sword was a highly personal weapon and carried symbolic importance. The surrendering of officers' swords has always been a token of submission. Many Americans are justly proud to possess the swords and sabers carried by their forebears through the wars of the United States. It was sometimes the custom in olden days to take an officer's sword and break the blade if he was dismissed in disgrace. Before World War II any officer of the Navy who was placed under arrest pending court-martial was required by regulation to deliver his sword to his commanding officer until after the verdict of the court.

To leave behind a "clean sword," whether death comes in peace or in war, remains the high goal of officers of the armed forces. From their first

A naval officer's sword is a unique part of the uniform.

commissioned days, naval officers may carry their sword to inspections and ceremonies. The sword may be worn at an officer's wedding, retirement ceremony, and assumptions and reliefs of command. It may finally rest by an officer's funeral casket. All this helps explain why so much sentiment has always been attached to the sword and its symbolism.

One of the supreme honors that can be conferred upon an officer is the award by Congress or by state legislatures of a sword in recognition of services to the country. The magnificent gold sword, with the inscription "Louis XVI, the rewarder of the valiant avenger of the sea avenged," presented to John Paul Jones by the king of France, may be seen in the crypt near Jones's sarcophagus at Annapolis. The City of London, England, knew of no higher symbol of respect and gratitude to present to Gen. Dwight D. Eisenhower at the close of World War II than a reproduction of the great two-handed sword of the Crusades.

Sword Salute

Authorities differ over the derivation of the sword salute. The Royal Military Training College taught for some years that the sword salute came from the

Full dress-white uniform
James Davis

oriental custom of the junior raising the sword and shading his eyes from the magnificence of the superior. The first etiquette or "school of the sword" was most probably of Eastern origin. But the evidence seems to indicate that the salute as we know it is probably of crusader origin.

The crucifix, symbolical of the cross, was in the days of chivalry symbolized on the sword by the handle and the guard. It was customary, in that tumultuous time of religious crusades, to kiss the sword hilt before entering battle and, of course, for vows and oaths. The cross on the sword survives: on British midshipmen's dirks, on the swords of the Scottish archers, on the undress swords of the Highland regiments, and on the dress swords of diplomatic officers of several foreign countries. After Christianization, Norsemen had the name of Jesus etched on their sword hilts.

Most of the ancient history of the sword salute is displayed in the present-day salute. The sword held at arm's length was originally the hail or initial salute to the superior. The act of permitting the point to descend to the ground is the junior's acknowledgment of subservience. The start of both these movements—bringing the sword hilt to the mouth or chin—is a survival of the custom of kissing the cross on the sword.

The sword salute on the march is a survival of the fancy turns and flourishes that were made by military officers in the reviews of the seventeenth century. Halberds and short swords were used in those days, and apparently the fancier the flourishes, the better the show on parade and the more effective the salute. The fancy flourish of the drum major is a modern-day holdover.

Never draw a sword in the wardroom! Long ago this strict taboo may have been instituted to prevent serious sword play when drinking stimulated argument. The fine for so doing in the old Navy was a bottle of champagne to be paid for by him who drew.

Possession of the sword, sword knot, and belt is required of all U.S. naval officers, lieutenant commander and above (except chaplains), for wear with full dress uniforms worn for ceremonial occasions. Swords were once worn at all personnel inspections and at all ceremonies. Check the uniform regulations to ensure that the sword knot is properly dressed and the sword properly hooked on the sword belt.

The Royal Navy has an interesting sword custom. When an officer is tried by court-martial, he unhooks his sword and places it on the table just before the proceeding starts. If he is found guilty, his sword is then placed on the table with the point toward the accused; if he is found not guilty, the hilt is placed toward him. It is from this practice that we "get the point."

Coins at Step of Mast

The custom of placing coins under the step of a mast at the time the vessel is built is an old one. A Spanish wreck found in the Orkney Islands had under the mast and on the keel a coin dated 1618.

One explanation, given by Commander Beckett, RN, is that the custom possibly is a survival of the old Roman tradition of placing coins in the mouths of the dead to pay the ferryman Charon for their transportation across the River Styx; if a ship met with mishap at sea, the coins under the mast ensured that the fare of all hands was paid.

This custom tends to show that seafaring men still subscribe to outmoded superstition, and that sea services support many longstanding traditions that have no particular bearing on modern sea life. Indeed, when the island of the nuclear-powered carrier USS *Harry Truman* was stepped in the building process, the prospective commanding officer placed a set of aviator's wings beneath it in similar obeisance.

The Sounding of Tattoo and Taps

The word *tattoo* is derived from the Dutch word *taptoe*, meaning time to close up all the taps and taverns in the garrisoned towns. In a volume entitled *Military Guide for Young Officers*, by Thomas Simes, Esq., reprinted in Philadelphia in 1776, there are instructions for the officer of the guard:

> The tat-too is generally beat at nine o'clock at night in the summer and eight in the winter. It is performed by the Drum-Major, and all the drummers and fifers of that regiment which gave a captain of the main guard that day. The tat-too is the signal given for the soldiers to retire to their barracks or quarters, to put out their fire and candle, and go to bed. The public houses are at the same time, to shut their doors, and sell no more liquor that night.

Col. H. L. Scott, inspector general, USA, in the *Military Dictionary* which he published in 1861, defined *tat-too* and *taptoo* as equivalent terms meaning "drum-beat and a roll call at night."

In time, trumpets were used for tattoo. The *Century Dictionary* defines the word as a beat of drum or bugle call at night, while *taps* is defined as a signal upon a drum or trumpet at about a quarter of an hour after tattoo. The British use the term *post* for this call. Maj. Gen. G. E. Voyle, Royal Bengal Artillery, defined the term in his military dictionary, published in 1876: "the term Post is given to the bugling which precedes the tattoo. This is the first part; the last part, that which follows it, is the last Post." The last post is sounded on the trumpet or bugle at British military funerals.

There was a melody for taps as early as the American Revolution; it was probably that of the last post of the British Army, for the two have a few identical notes. The *St. Louis Globe Democrat* wrote in September 1933:

> The American Army's heart-touching salute to the dead, the "song of truce to pain," the final bugle call of the night, as soldiers in field and barracks roll into their blankets, arose anew last fall. It was announced in Paris that the French Army had adopted the bugle call for its own and that it would be used in France as it is used in America, to end the day and to mark the burial of the dead.

Taps being played at a flag-raising ceremony at the site of the former World Trade Center in commemoration of the terrorist attacks on the United States U.S. Coast Guard (Tom Sperduto)

The author of a *Century Magazine* article published in 1898 and entitled "The Trumpet in Camp and Battle" claimed that he was unable to determine the author or origin of the tune "Taps." In response, he received an angry letter from Oliver W. Norton. In July 1862 Norton had been the brigade bugler assigned to duty with the Butterfield Brigade from the Eighty-third Regiment of Pennsylvania Volunteers camped at Harrison's Landing on the lower James River in Virginia. He had been called to see Gen. Daniel A. Butterfield, the brigade commander, who had some musical notes written on an envelope, which he wanted Norton to sound out on his bugle. He did so, and after the general made a few changes, he was told to start using the tune to signal "lights out." The story was confirmed later when General Butterfield acknowledged his authorship, but maintained that he could neither read nor write music. He had hummed the tune over and over in his head until he had gotten it to sound a reflection of the melancholy he felt over the previous day's carnage and then had an aide help him to transcribe it into musical notation. The haunting tune was immediately popular and was picked up and passed along from bugler to bugler in both the northern and southern armies.

Just when the American Navy adopted the custom of sounding taps at funerals seems to be unknown. The "Dead March from Saul" was all the music rendered by the musicians on board *Constitution* at a burial at sea in 1846. Commodore Claxton was buried at Valparaiso in 1841, and at the same time mention was made of the "Dead March" and the muffled drums. Officially, the first reference comes from the Army's Infantry Drill Regulations in 1891. It was used soon after it was composed, by Capt. John C. Tidball, an artillery battery commander in the Butterfield Brigade. Tidball ordered it played at the funeral of one of his cannoneers instead of firing three volleys over the grave, since the gunfire might be mistaken by the enemy as the start of an attack.

Drawing a Dead Horse

Often, to many a young naval officer's regret, under certain conditions one may draw an advance in pay. A colorful ceremony was once connected with the time when the crew "stopped working for nothing." Particularly in the Merchant Marine, seamen were permitted to draw some money in advance; in the British Merchant Service it was approximately a month's advance when the sailor shipped. After five weeks or so at sea, or subsequent to whatever time the debt was worked off, the men made a horse out of canvas stuffed with old cordage and waste material, or out of a cask with oakum tail and mane, and then permission was requested to light "the horse" and hoist it out to the end of a boom or yard. This was done amid cheers, because it marked the time when the crew started to again work for wages "on the books," rather than for "salt horse," or food. The advance had usually been spent in riotous living in the last port, and now definite plans could be made for the port ahead. It was a joyous occasion.

When burning the "dead horse," both watches used to sing in chorus:

> Now, old horse, your time has come,
> And we say so, for we know so!
> Altho' many a race you've won,
> Oh! poor old man,
> You're going now to say good-bye

And we say so, for we know so;
Poor old horse, you're going to die.

Dueling among the Officers of the Navy

In the first half-century of our Navy there are records of numerous duels. President Andrew Jackson, a duelist, believed strongly that dueling should be forbidden to civilians but should be permitted for the officers of the Army and Navy. The practice of settling by duels "affairs of honor among gentlemen" was not confined to the senior officers, but was also a method of redress among juniors and midshipmen. The history of the early Mediterranean Squadron of the U.S. Navy discloses a tragic record of this custom. One may read today on a tombstone near Syracuse, Sicily, the following epitaph: "In memory of William R. Nicolson, a Midshipman in the Navy of the United States, who was cut off from society in the bloom of his youth and health, on the 18th day of September, A.D. 1804, aged eighteen years. His untimely death resulted from a duel fought with Midshipman Frederick C. DeKraft of the same ship."

Shelved between bulky tomes of historical reference in the Library of Congress is a thin, red-bound book, titled *The Code of Honor*. Written by "A. Southron," probably a pseudonym for a southerner, it was printed in Baltimore in 1847. There were originally but 175 copies, and the one in the Library of Congress seems to be the only one extant. There were thirty-nine articles of *The Code of Honor*, including these:

No apology can be received for a blow.
For being intentionally spit on; for having wine, snuff, etc., thrown in the face, no apology is admissible, but redress must be sought by the duel, if the party aggressing rank as a gentleman.

Such a code explains why so many men went to an early grave for alleged violations. One historian claims that more officers were killed in duels than in the naval actions of the period. The historic duels that took place at Bladensburg, Maryland, such as that when Stephen Decatur was mortally wounded, were fought under the rules of this little red book.

The Code of Honor read: "After taking your place, you will salute your antagonist with a distant but not discourteous inclination of the head." Many officers of the time so saluted their opponent.

Among the fatal duels fought by officers was that of Lt. William B. Finch,

U.S. Navy, who killed Lt. Francis B. White of the Marine Corps in a duel fought at Boston in 1819. Finch afterward changed his name to William Compton Bolton and died as a commodore in command of the Mediterranean Squadron in 1849. In another example, Commodore Oliver Hazard Perry fought a duel with Capt. John Heath of the Marine Corps with Commodore Decatur as Perry's second. In yet another case, Lt. William Bainbridge killed the secretary of the British admiral commanding at Gibraltar in a duel fought over an affair involving the "honor of the service." Stephen Decatur acted as Bainbridge's second.

The most famous duel in our naval history was that between Commodore Barron and Commodore Decatur. This duel took place after a long exchange of acrimonious correspondence. The dispute centered on Barron's restoration to duty after five years' suspension of rank and pay, in consequence of the *Chesapeake-Leopard* action off the Virginia capes on 27 June 1807.

The duel was fought on the morning of 22 March 1820, in a valley one-half mile from Bladensburg village, outside Washington, D.C. Decatur had Commodore Bainbridge as a second; Barron had Capt. Jesse D. Elliott. Just before the duel Barron expressed to Decatur the hope that "on meeting in another world they would be better friends than in this." Decatur replied, "I have never been your enemy, sir." The firing took place on the count of two. Both officers fell. Decatur was shot through the abdomen, and Barron wounded in the thigh.

The intrepid Decatur died at the age of forty-one, twelve hours after he was carried to his home in Lafayette Square, Washington. Barron was subsequently restored to the active list and lived to become the senior commodore of the Navy, but never again secured active sea service.

Raising the Right Hand When Sworn as a Witness

The custom of raising hands and eyes heavenward when taking an oath is of great antiquity, and from early days the head was bared to the particular deity or to superior authority when taking the oath. With the advent of printed and bound Bibles, the right hand was placed upon the book during the administration of the oath, and upon completion the Bible was kissed. While the Bible is no longer used in military courts-martial, the trial counsel and witnesses still raise their right hand in affirmation.

The practice of raising the right hand ungloved (always) came from the early days in England when all criminals were branded on the right hand.

The hand was bared in order to ascertain whether or not the witness to be sworn was branded.

Custom of Wearing Medals on the Left Breast

Medals and decorations are generally worn on the left breast. This custom may be traced from the practice of the crusaders in wearing the badge of honor of their order near the heart. Also, the left side was the shield side of the crusader, and the large shield carried on the left arm protected both the heart and the badge of honor. Swords were worn on the left side in order to be quickly drawn by the right hand.

Divine Service at Sea

> But our own hearts are our best prayer rooms, and the chaplains who can help us most are ourselves.
>
> Herman Melville

The following description of divine service at sea is taken from *Cruise of the Frigate "Columbia"* by William Murrell. The *Columbia* made a typical around-the-world cruise in 1838–41, visiting 18 ports, spending 459 days at sea and 313 days in port.

On Sunday mornings, immediately after quarters, should the weather permit, all hands are called to muster. The summons is instantly obeyed, by every one proceeding to the quarter-deck (the sick alone exempted) where the minister stands in readiness, arrayed in his clerical robes, and the capstan covered with the national flag to answer the purpose of a pulpit. The commodore takes his station on the weather side of the chaplain; the lieutenants, and all other commissioned and warrant officers on the weather side of the deck; the forward officers at the fife-rail, and petty officers at the fore-part of the main-mast. The blue-jackets take up their position abaft the mizzen-mast, clad in white frocks with blue collars, white trousers, and straw hats, looking the picture of cleanliness; whilst the Marines are stationed and drawn up in rank, on the lee side of the deck, headed by their commanding officer, all in blue uniform. . . . After the usual routine of divine services had been performed, every monthly Sunday the articles of war are read. Punishments are always read, that is to say, death, or *worse* punishment as the sailor says. By worse punishment, he alludes to his grog being stopped, which article constitutes his principal creed.

Constitution, **best known as**
"Old Ironsides"
Naval Institute Photo Archive

To hold divine services, chaplains today are often brought from larger vessels to smaller vessels and returned after services by helicopter. Without disrespect, this maneuver is known officially as "Operation Holy Joe," "Holy Joe" being an old sea-going name for the chaplain.

The *Constitution* ("Old Ironsides")

The U.S. Navy possesses in "Old Ironsides" the most successful and historic frigate that ever sailed the seas. She battered down enough of the stone forts of Tripoli to contribute directly to the treaty with that Barbary state. She escaped from Broke's squadron of six ships after a four-day chase. It was by the unparalleled seamanship and masterly stratagem of Captain Hull that the *Constitution* made her escape without losing a man, a gun, a boat, or an anchor. Hull's first lieutenant called it "the advantages to be expected from perseverance under the most discouraging circumstances as long as any chance of escape may remain." She defeated the *Guerriere,* a crack British frigate, dismasting her twenty-five minutes after firing the first broadside, and she shot every spar out of the British frigate *Java*. It is a tradition that the *Constitution* did not take in her royals for this fight. She captured the British *Cyane* and *Levant* at the same time. They were smaller than "Old Ironsides," with a combined armament of fifty-five guns to the *Constitution*'s fifty-two, but the more effective long twenty-fours of the American frigate and Captain Stewart's excellent maneuvers carried the day.

Moses Smith, sponger of number-one gun on the *Constitution*, in the battle with the *Guerriere*, wrote: "Several shots now entered our hull. One of the largest the enemy could command struck us, but the plank was so hard it fell out and sank in the waters. This was afterwards noticed and the cry arose: 'Huzza! Her sides are made of iron! See where the shots fell out!' From that circumstance, the name of the *Constitution* was garnished with the familiar title, 'Old Ironsides.'"

Privateers and Letters of Marque

The majority of naval historians have underemphasized the work of the U.S. privateers. The Library of Congress has compiled a list of about seventeen hundred "letters of marque" issued to the privateers of the Continental Navy. The total number of private vessels carrying arms was about two thousand, with eighteen thousand guns and seventy thousand men. Compare this number with the list of officers of the Continental Navy, which comprised about three hundred thirty names, including the officers commissioned in France. While there are no complete lists extant of the medical officers, pursers, midshipmen, and warrant officers, the number of petty officers and seamen of the Continental Navy reached an estimated total of three thousand men.

The Origin of "Checkered" Painting of Wooden Ships

The USS *Constitution*, "Old Ironsides," uses today the traditional outboard design of paint work: the white stripe with the black gunports. Lord Nelson originated this method of painting. Before Nelson attained high command, ships of the Royal Navy were painted buff, black, or buff and black. Black and white was used for side painting, but before Nelson's order the lines of the wales (strakes of thick outside planking) were painted white, and this gave a very narrow white band. Nelson ordered that the white stripes follow the lines of the deck. Black strakes between were made wider and gun lids were painted black, all of which produced the well-known checkered broadside. After Trafalgar, and probably in memory of Nelson, this method of painting became universal in the British Navy. The same design and colors were soon adopted by other navies; from that day until sails of war left the sea, it was the general practice. The inboard vertical surface was in time painted white; red was also used for many years. Tradition tells us that the red bulkheads had practical value, for they did not show blood as much as other colors.

Essex, First American Man-of-War to Double Cape of Good Hope and Cape Horn and to Fight in the Pacific

The *Essex,* built in 1799 by subscription of the people of Salem, Massachusetts, cost $154,686.77; she was the fastest sailer in the Navy for several years, and took the largest number of prizes of any vessel in the War of 1812.

In 1800 the *Essex,* under command of Capt. Edward Preble, rounded the Cape of Good Hope.

Capt. David Porter, in command of the *Essex,* rounded Cape Horn in 1813 and stood into Valparaiso for supplies. His object was to break up British navigation. He succeeded so well that it was only a short time until his major problem was to dispose of the merchant ship prizes and prisoners. Midshipman David G. Farragut, not quite twelve, was one of the youthful prize masters.

The final and fateful engagement came when *Essex* was defeated by the British ships of war *Phoebe* and *Cherub.* In that fight, some of the deeds of Porter's heroic crew were truly blood stirring. Dying men who had hardly ever attracted notice among the ship's company expressed their loyalty and patriotism by exceptional acts. To take a single example, two men, upon being told that they had each lost a leg, jumped overboard rather than burden the capacity of the medical department.

Recruiting during the Revolution

In 1771, one Sergeant Galbet was sent to raise recruits for the Marine Corps in Birmingham, England. His activities were announced in the following advertisement, 22 July 1771:

GREAT
ENCOURAGEMENT
FOR
SEAMEN.

ALL GENTLEMEN SEAMEN and able-bodied LANDSMEN who have a Mind to diſtinguiſh themſelves in the GLORIOUS CAUSE of their Country, and make their Fortunes, an Opportunity now offers on board the Ship RANGER, of Twenty Guns, (for France) now laying in Portsmouth, in the State of New-Hampshire, commanded by JOHN PAUL JONES Eſq; let them repair to the Ship's Rendezvous in Portsmouth, or at the Sign of Commodore Manley, in Salem, where they will be kindly entertained, and receive the greateſt Encouragement.---The Ship Ranger, in the Opinion of every Perſon who has ſeen her is looked upon to be one of the beſt Cruizers in America.---She will be always able to Fight her Guns under a moſt excellent Cover ; and no Veſſel yet built was ever calculated for ſailing faſter, and making good Weather.

Any Gentlemen Volunteers who have a Mind to take an agreable Voyage in this pleaſant Seaſon of the Year, may, by entering on board the above Ship Ranger, meet with every Civility they can poſſibly expect, and for a further Encouragement depend on the firſt Opportunity being embraced to reward each one agreable to his Merit.

All reaſonable Travelling Expences will be allowed, and the Advance-Money be paid on their Appearance on Board.

In CONGRESS, March 29, 1777.

RESOLVED,

THAT the Marine Committee be authorised to advance to every able Seaman, that enters into the Continental Service, any Sum not exceeding FORTY DOLLARS, and to every ordinary Seaman or Landſman, any Sum not exceeding TWENTY DOLLARS, to be deducted from their future Prize-Money.

By Order of Congress,

JOHN-HANCOCK, President.

DANVERS: Printed by E. Russell, at the Houſe late the Bell-Tavern.

Revolutionary War recruiting broadside. This is the earliest known existing American naval recruiting poster.
The Essex Institute, Salem, Massachusetts

He that Works Hard is Sure to be Poor
After six days hard labor come Sunday—you Rest
And no sooner peeps Monday but you are quite shy of cash.
Therefore to make life easy and fill your Pockets with Money
Sergeant Galbet will learn any young man a Profession (without Fee or Reward) by which the Learner will be sure to earn a Guinea and a Crown the very first Hour. He will also introduce you to His Majesty's First Division of Marines, which is always quartered at Chatham, only thirty miles from London, to which Pleasure-Boats carry Passengers for Six-pence each. When you arrive at Chatham, you are immediately provided with Cloaths, free Quarters in a Public House, where you will be sure to meet with merry Fellows, a kind Land lady, and a rousing fire do nothing but on a fine day dance to the softest Music, feed on Dainties, drink the best Liquors and play at "Why won't you" with the prettiest girls, saying "Chatham forever" and "God save the King."
N.B. He teaches no Militia or Apprentice
The Globe and Laurel

The last section of the *U.S. Naval Regulations* (1818) gives some idea of "Jack ashore" of the day and also of the system of recruiting men:

> That seamen should be rescued, as far as practicable, from the fangs of rapacious landlords and others who frequently taking advantage of their habits of intoxication, and generally unsuspicious characters swindle them of the whole amount advanced to them by the recruiting officer, and to the prejudice of the seamen and of the Service generally, leave them in a naked and destitute condition at the time of their appearance on board.

The section ends with advice to the recruiting officer to prevent the swindling of the men, by inducing them "to repair on board the receiving ship." The final words of the section are touched with a shade of irony: "and to take every means in his power to render [to the recruit] the Service as pleasing as possible."

New Year's Midwatch Log in Rhyme

> This New Year's midwatch poetry
> Comes hard to men who go to sea.

New Year's Eve watches are generally despised, since they often conflict with a sailor's desire to party. The midwatch from midnight to 0400 in the morning of that first day of the year is particularly onerous. Over time, tradition has it that the watch must strike sixteen bells at midnight, eight for the end of one year and eight for the beginning of the next. How and when the custom of writing the New Year's Day midwatch log in rhyme began, no one knows. It may have started simply as a means of passing this most undesirable of watches. Regardless of rhyme, Navy Regulations and OpNav Instructions require that certain information be reported. Those requirements, plus the awkward names of some of the ships present, the lack of euphony in many nautical expressions, and the need to comply with "the poetic form" pose challenging problems in the choice of words for the officer of the deck —the poet for a day—as evidenced by this excerpt from the log of Ens. D. Kraushaar of USS *Watts:*

> But with licence poetically I'll say here
> I'm grateful New Year's comes but once a year.

A collection of midwatch log poetry is well beyond the scope of this work, but some examples should provide a flavor of the genre.

From USS *Dale* (DLG 19) and published by *All Hands* in 1969:

> On New Year's morn, while protecting our nation,
>   We're steaming the waters of southern SAR station.
> With 806 on both her sides,
>   Higbee—our shotgun—not far from us rides.
>
> The captain of our ship is OTC,
>   And also the SOPA and CTE.
> He heads the Element, and tells what to do;
>   It's seven-seven-point-zero-point-one-point-two.
>
> We're one little unit under ComSeventhFlt
>   Who fields a team that's quite hard to beat.
> One-Bravo, Two-Alfa, are the boilers in use,
>   And the "B" generators provide us with juice.
>
> These give us the steam to proceed at ten knots,
>   While changing locations 'tween various spots
> Zero-two-five is the course that we steer,
>   With Higbee remaining two miles from here.
>
> Two-seven-zero on station she'll bear,
>   And unless she is lost, she's already there.
> We look toward her station and see not a light,
>   For both ships are darkened throughout the night.
>
> To ensure that our needs for safety are met,
>   Conditions Three and Yoke are set.
> Because of this conflict, we're victims of fate,
>   And the holiday season we can't celebrate,
> Our loved ones and friends are at home far from here,
>   But to them, and to all, a "Happy New Year"
>
>   *(Lt [jg] Elliott K. DeMatta)*

From USS *Rankin* (AKA 103), also published by *All Hands* in 1969:

> A strange relief took place last night,
> (Though it happens every year)
> It occurred on our quarterdeck;
> I was close enough to hear.
>
> The New Year showed up right on time—
> A squared-away young boot.

The old OOD heaved a sigh
And gave a tired salute.

The word passed down was not all good,
But the New Year took it well.
I could not understand it all,
But what I did, I'll tell.

"SOPA tonight is PhibGruFour
For the Little Creek retreat.
And here are resting many ships
Of the U.S. Atlantic Fleet.

"While all these ships are an able lot,
Manned by the country's best.
The Rankin, berthed at pier Fifteen,
Stands high above the rest.

"Her lines are doubled, fore and aft;
A wire leads to the shore,
But if it were left up to her and her crew,
They'd rather sail than moor.

"Her engine room is on cold iron,
Her generators still.
That steam line running from the pier
Keeps out the winter's chill.

"She also gets electric power,
And fresh water from the beach.
Her men are all turned in below.
Or within an easy reach.

"With modified Yoke below the decks
And material Condition Five,
You may think that she's sound asleep,
But she's really quite alive.

"Now I stand relieved, New Year,
I pass it all to you.
My last fine hour has slid away,
There's no more I can do.

"Except to tell you once again,
Before I cross the brow,
It makes no difference—where or when—
The Rankin's 'Ready Now.' "

(CWO Oscar M. Baker)

And finally from USS *Clark* (DD-361) on 1 January 1937, and printed in
Shipmate Magazine in 1982:

Once a year there comes a time to write the log in metric rhyme,
although a sailor finds it hard to emulate a bloomin' bard.
The O.O.D. must disregard the salty terms he's always heard
and shamefully must interlard with many an artificial word,
so reader be upon your guard. Moored at Boston Navy Yard,
dreary even at its best. Lines extend to Pier 6 West,
gangway at the starboard side. Rising with a flooding tide
our trim destroyer idly rocks, receiving service from the docks:
water, light and telephone, steam from boilers not her own.
At every mast a Christmas tree, half the crew ashore and free
and all the officers but me.

Other ships in company: MOFFETT, QUINCY (S.O.P.),
Number 19 EAGLE Boat (very few are still afloat),
WANDANK, CONYNGHAM, and CASE, with their lines of speed and grace,
LAMSON, TILLMAN and the PHELPS. Every sturdy vessel helps
to keep our flag upon sea, a national necessity
ever since the CONSTITUTION proved herself the real solution.
Topmasts housed, she's with us here, tall and strong for many a year.
Building under wintry skies, incomplete the MUGFORD lies
near another, moored in line, TALBOT (RALPH) of new design.
Soon they'll join the Fleet with pride, take their places side by side.
Coast Guard ships a few I see: CAYUGA, PEQUOT, THETIS—three.
Odds and ends of district craft, cranes and barges and a raft.

Naval treaties died tonight, expiration of the fight
by warriors of the conference table, men-o-Mars without the label,
asking much but giving less, meaning "No" but saying "Yes,"
sinking ships with ink and pen, pronouncing peace on earth to men.
War will not be stopped by phrases coined within the crafty mazes
of the human heart, perverse, coupled with a mind diverse.
In the lessons of the past one at least will likely last:

a man who won't protect his own will never reap the grain he's sown.
When greedy neighbors come along the winner is the one who's strong.

Naturally, a naval race with lesser nations losing face
is an economic blunder which can tear the world asunder.
Only one can win a race, others have to take their place.
Rivals bite their lips and glower as they strive for greater power.
Yet pacifists are like a man who tries to stop a running fixture
by a thumb against the faucet 'stead of turning off the mixture.
No effect is counteracted by a set of hopeful laws;
to eliminate an evil we must first correct the cause.
Navies needn't sail the brine when little children cease to whine
their earliest complaint, "It's mine."
When our towns need no police, then will come a lasting peace,
but long as robbers covet pelf an honest man defends himself.
So give us ships and give us men, give us guns and know that when
the nation needs to show the Stick, we'll waste no time on rhetoric.

Though New Year bells ring out tonight, I make no pious resolution,
yet I voice a fervent hope that beach-hounds all avoid pollution.
Seamen's troubles evermore have started when they neared the shore.
I would to God we were at-sea, the place a sailor ought to be.
So cheerio to '37; it may be hell, it won't be heaven.

                                                    (Lt. A. R. McCracken)

First Watch after Commissioning in Rhyme

Some ships, in respect to tradition, have had all or part of the first watch of
the new log book entered in rhyme, as with the first log of USS *Stack:*

The USS *Stack,* Monday the 20th, November, the year '39
At Portsmouth, Virginia, in the Navy Yard there, this ship was moored
     at the time,
To Pier Number 3 in Berth 24, with three-quarter-inch wire for its line.
The admiral's flag was then hauled down,
The commission pennant broke in its place,
And soon of the guests and spectators, there remained not even a trace.
But it was not the weather that caused it,
Nor was it the type of the grub
But the desire to wet their whistle,

At a party, by the ship, at the club.
Seriously—this ship commissioned,
Midst cold wind, rain, and a storm,
Though the spirit of its men and their officers
Will, to the credit of our country, perform.

(Lt. H. M. Hemhag, OOD
Lt. Cdr. Olch, Cmdg.)

An Attempt at Mutiny

In the mid–nineteenth century a midshipman, Philip Spencer, and two sea-men were hanged at the yardarm of the U.S. brig *Somers* for attempting to incite a mutiny. The hangings took place in late November 1842 while the *Somers* was en route from Liberia to New York. Spencer, who was the son of the Hon. John C. Spencer, then secretary of war under President Tyler, con-spired with seamen Cromwell and Small to kill the officers, seize the ship, and go on a pirating expedition. Cromwell protested his innocence; Small con-fessed. There was overwhelming proof of Cromwell's guilt, and both seamen were hanged at the same yardarm with Spencer.

Cdr. Alexander Slidell Mackenzie, USN, in command, was a stern, pious officer. He considered that his actions were warranted: "Safety, our lives, and the honor of the flag entrusted to our charge, require the prisoners be put to death."

The national flag was hoisted at sea, drums rolled, a gun fired, and the crew walked away at the whips, hoisting the three in the air. Captain Mackenzie then talked to his crew, asked them for three cheers, and wrote: "Three heartier cheers never went up from the deck of an American ship. In that electric moment I verily believe the purest and loftiest patriotism burst forth from the breasts of even the worst conspirators."

The captain then had the ensign half-masted, and read the service for the dead. He concluded: "Preserve us from the dangers of the seas, and the vio-lence of enemies; bless the United States, watch over all that are upon the deep, and protect the inhabitants of the land in peace and quiet, through Jesus Christ, our Lord."

In a rough sea and by lantern light, the bodies of Spencer, Cromwell, and Small were committed to the deep. The church pennant was hoisted above the ensign, and the crew was dismissed after singing the Hundredth Psalm.

Commander Mackenzie was tried by a court-martial on the charge of murder. The general court-martial was convened at the Brooklyn Navy Yard on 2 February 1843, and lasted for six weeks. Mackenzie was honorably acquitted, and the verdict was approved by President Tyler. Public feeling over the affair brought pressure to bear on Congress to approve the establishment of a Naval School ashore for midshipmen's training.

The Legend of Santa Barbara, the Patron Saint of Cannoneers and Ordnance Men

"Santa Barbara, virgin and martyr," is said to have lived at the close of the third and beginning of the fourth century. In the Roman, Greek, and Russian calendars, her feast day was celebrated on 4 December, the presumed anniversary of her martyrdom.

Barbara's legend tells how her rich father, Dioscorus, denounced his lovely and erudite daughter for becoming a Christian and beheaded her himself after she had been condemned by the governor. Dioscorus was struck by lightning and killed. Santa Barbara has from that time been considered the protector against lightning, thunder, and flame. When gunpowder was used by Europeans, she became the patron saint of cannoneers and ordnance men.

The first official recognition was by the cannoneers of Lille, France, who were commissioned in 1417 by letters patent as the "Confrères de Sainte Barbe." Other countries of Europe followed. A picture of Santa Barbara, donated by Cdr. W. F. Folger, chief of the Bureau of Ordnance, in 1890, hung in the office of that bureau's chief up until about 1993.

The regimental tie (worn with civilian clothes) of the Royal Artillery is blue with dark red zig-zags over it, symbolic of Santa Barbara's protection against flame and lightning.

Some First Events in Navy History

We may dispose of some questions of priority at the outset. John Manley, under a Massachusetts commission and under the pine tree banner, was the first to make a British naval vessel strike her flag. John Paul Jones was the first to raise the Grand Union or American flag on a ship of war. Esek Hopkins was the first commander under a commission of Congress to carry the Grand Union Flag in naval operations and to make a capture under it. John Barry was the first under a commission of the Congress and under the Grand Union Flag to fight a battle with a British warship and make her strike her colors.

The first naval officer to become a commodore was John Barry, senior officer in the Navy, appointed in 1794 after the Navy was reorganized.

The first naval officer to become an admiral was David Glasgow Farragut, so appointed on 25 July 1866.

The first shell fired by the U.S. Navy in World War I was by J. O. Sabin, a gun-pointer on the naval collier *Jupiter,* at a submarine in the Bay of Biscay, 5 June 1917. Sabin also helped sink the last German sub when he acted as gun-pointer of the crew that finished off the U-97 in Lake Michigan at a target practice in 1921.

The first naval officer to become an engineer in the U.S. Navy was Charles Haynes Haswell. He was commissioned 19 February 1836 by Secretary of the Navy Dickerson to design steam power equipment. The first appointment of an engineer in the Royal Navy came in 1837. The corps was not incorporated in the U.S. Navy *Register* or regularly organized until 1843.

The first U.S. warship to circumnavigate the world was *Vincennes,* commanded by Cdr. William Bolton Finch. She left New York 3 September 1826 and returned via the Cape of Good Hope on 8 June 1830.

The first U.S. warship to be docked in a government drydock was the *Delaware* at the Norfolk drydock, Portsmouth, Virginia, 17 June 1833.

The first warship with propelling machinery below the waterline was the screw warship *Princeton,* designed by John Ericsson in 1841.

The first paddle-wheeled steam warships were the *Mississippi* and *Missouri,* finished in 1841. The *Fulton the First* of 2,745 tons was built by Robert Fulton in 1814–15 for the Navy at a cost of $320,000.

The first American warship of iron using steam was the *Michigan,* built at Erie, Pennsylvania, under act of Congress, 9 September 1842. She was fabricated in Pittsburgh and transported in parts to Erie where she was completed and launched in 1844. On 17 June 1905 she was renamed the *Wolverine.* She was officially stricken from the naval list 12 March 1927.

The first U.S. battleship was the USS *Maine.* The keel was laid 17 October 1888, and the ship was launched in 1890. The *Maine* was destroyed by a mysterious explosion in the harbor of Havana, Cuba, 15 February 1898, leading to the declaration of war with Spain. Of a crew of 354, only 16 escaped injury or death. The *Maine* had 12-inch side armor and two 10-inch guns in each of the two turrets.

The first hospital ship definitely assigned for the purpose was the *Solace,* fitted out in 1898. The idea and general supervision of fitting out is credited

USS *Putnam* (DD 757)
Naval Institute Photo Archive

to Adm. William Knickerbocker Van Reypen. The *Navy Register* (1864) lists *Red Rover* as "Hospital Steamer."

The first electrically propelled vessel of the Navy was the *Langley* (former collier *Jupiter*). The *Langley* was commissioned 7 April 1913 and converted to an aircraft carrier 21 April 1920.

The first large, floating drydock of the Navy was the *Dewey,* at Olongapo, Philippine Islands. This dock was towed there from the Chesapeake Bay, a distance of 13,000 miles. The passage took 150 days.

The first ship (a Japanese transport) sunk by a surface ship of the U.S. Navy since the Spanish American War was sunk in World War II in 1942 in the Battle of Makassar Straits by the *John D. Ford* (DD 228).

The first U.S. ship to fly the flag of the United Nations was the USS *Putnam* (DD 757) at noon on 23 July 1948, when she was anchored in the harbor at Haifa, Israel. She was in the service of the United Nations, being assigned to

U.N. mediator Count Folke-Bernadotte, who later met his death while trying to negotiate a truce between the Arab nations and Israel.

The USS *Higbee* was the first combatant ship to commemorate the name of a woman. Mrs. Lena Sutcliffe Higbee, who died in 1941, was the second superintendent of the Navy Nurse Corps. USS *Hopper* was named for Rear Adm. Grace Hopper, computer innovator and author of the COBAL computer language.

U-505, the only German submarine ever boarded and captured by the U.S. Navy, is on display at the Museum of Science and History, Chicago. A bronze plaque tells the story: "This prize of war is dedicated to the memory of the American seamen who went down to unmarked ocean graves helping to win victory at sea." *U-505* was forced to the surface and captured by a hunter-killer task force commanded by Capt. Daniel V. Gallery on 4 June 1944 off Cape Blanco, French West Africa. It was the first man-of-war captured by the U.S. Navy since 1815. Both the Royal and Royal Canadian Navies boarded and captured German U-boats during World War II as well.

The world's first nuclear-powered submarine, the *Nautilus* (SSN-571), was commissioned in September 1954. She is approximately 320 feet in overall length, has a surface displacement of approximately 3,000 tons, and cost an estimated $55 million. Now decommissioned, she serves as a museum at Groton, Connecticut.

The Naval Academy was established at Fort Severn in Annapolis on 10 August 1845, transferred to Newport, Rhode Island, on 5 May 1861, and returned to Annapolis in September 1865. The Naval War College was established at Newport, Rhode Island, 6 October 1884. The Postgraduate School was established at Annapolis on 1 October 1909 and moved to Monterey, California, 22 December 1951.

The first surgeon and surgeon's mate were authorized by the act of 6 January 1776. The surgeon was commissioned; the mate was a warrant officer. In 1777 an examination was provided for both surgeons and surgeon's mates. The pay of the first surgeons was increased in 1789 to $50.00 per month from $21.33–$25.00 per month.

The first Naval Militia was established by the State of Massachusetts on 29 March 1890.

The nurse corps (female) was authorized by an Act of Congress in 1908.

The first dental corps was established in 1912. The original act provided for a corps that could be expanded to one dentist per fifteen hundred enlisted personnel.

WAVES, the officially recognized title for "Women Accepted for Voluntary Emergency Service," was established by an act of Congress on 31 July 1942. Recruiting ended in 1945 with a peak enrollment of eighty-six thousand. The force was greatly reduced after the war ended, and after the passage in 1948 of the Women's Armed Service Integration Act, women—both commissioned and enlisted—were taken into the regular Navy. The organization was commanded until 1946 by Mildred H. McAfee, president of Wellesley College on leave and the first WAVE to be promoted to captain (in 1945).

The first commander in chief of the Army and Navy to hold divine services for Navy personnel was President Franklin D. Roosevelt. On Easter Sunday, 1 April 1934, the president in the absence of a chaplain stood on the quarterdeck of the *Nourmahal* and read the service from the Episcopal Book of Common Prayer. The officers and men of USS *Ellis* were present.

Development of the Organization of the Navy Department

The first agency to handle naval matters was the Marine Committee, consisting of three members, established by Congress in legislation of 1775. In November 1776 a "Continental Navy Board" was established, to consist of three competent persons and to be subordinate to the Marine Committee.

In October 1779 a Board of Admiralty succeeded the Marine Committee, and its subordinate Continental Navy Board was given direct control of all naval and Marine affairs. The Board of Admiralty consisted of five commissioners—two of the board to be members of Congress and three to be appointed.

In February 1781 the Board of Admiralty was succeeded by a secretary of marine. Then, in August 1781, an agent of marine was appointed, who took over all duties of agents, boards, and committees previously established.

In August 1789, a law placed the Navy under the secretary of war, and there it remained for nine years.

On 30 April 1798 a Navy Department was established "at the Seat of Government" under the control of a "Secretary of the Navy." This marked the beginning of the present organization, the Navy Department. Government Navy yards were established in 1800 and 1801. The president directed the secretary of the Navy to purchase and establish Navy yards at Portsmouth, New Hampshire, Boston, New York, Philadelphia, and Gosport, near Norfolk, Virginia. The first yard acquired was the Portsmouth Navy Yard. The property embraced 58.18 acres and had been in use as a shipbuilding yard. The price was $5,500. These yards are today on the original sites with the exception of the yard at Philadelphia, which was moved to League Island in 1868.

In February 1815 a "Board of Commissioners" was created to supplement the Navy Department and serve under the secretary. The board was made up of captains of the Navy who received appointments from the president subject to confirmation by the Senate. This board was in existence for twenty-seven years. Matthew F. Maury, then a junior line officer, writing under the nom de plume of "Harry Bluff," did much to bring about the establishment of the bureau system by his "broadsides" on the failings of the "Navy Board." In August 1842 the board of commissioners was abolished and five bureaus were established under the secretary of the Navy:

1. Bureau of Yards and Docks
2. Bureau of Construction, Equipment, and Repair
3. Bureau of Provisions and Clothing
4. Bureau of Ordnance and Hydrography
5. Bureau of Medicine and Surgery

In July 1862 the Navy Department was reorganized and eight bureaus were provided by law:

1. Bureau of Yards and Docks
2. Bureau of Equipment and Recruiting
3. Bureau of Navigation
4. Bureau of Ordnance
5. Bureau of Construction and Repair
6. Bureau of Steam Engineering
7. Bureau of Provisions and Clothing
8. Bureau of Medicine and Surgery

Following World War II, the National Security Act (1947) and the Defense Reorganization Act (1949) placed the Army, Navy, and (newly created) Air Force under the Department of Defense. James Forrestal, then secretary of the Navy, was the first to hold the powerful office of secretary of defense.

Today, the secretary of the Navy heads administratively the commandant of the Marine Corps and the chief of naval operations. The chief of naval operations has a vice chief and various deputy chiefs.

Under the chief of naval operations fall both the operating forces of the Navy and the shore establishment. The operating forces consist of the Naval Reserve Force, the Operational Test and Evaluation Forces, Naval Special

Warfare Command, Military Sealift Command, and the Area Commanders: Naval Forces Europe, Central, Atlantic, and Pacific, with their numbered fleets, the sixth, fifth, second, and third fleets respectively. The shore establishment includes most of the functions previously administered by the various bureaus: the Bureau of Personnel, Bureau of Medicine and Surgery, Naval Sea Systems Command, Naval Computer and Telecommunications Command, Naval Air Systems Command, Naval Supply Systems Command, Office of Naval Intelligence, Naval Facilities Engineering Command, Chief of Naval Education and Training, Space and Naval Warfare Systems Command, and Naval Security Group Command.

Naval Grades and Seniority

In an article published in November 1956 in the Naval Institute *Proceedings,* entitled "From Admiral to Midshipman," Lieutenant Sprince, USN, presented the evolution of the naval grades of the line officer. Note the downgrading of the boatswain, and the changes in status of the grade of midshipman:

1775—Captain,[1] Lieutenant, Boatswain, and Master Mate

1794—Captain,[1] Lieutenant,[2] Sailing Master, Boatswain, Master Mate, and Midshipman

1806—Captain,[1] Master Commandant, Lieutenant,[2] Sailing Master, Master Mate, Boatswain, and Midshipman

1837—Captain,[1] Commander (heretofore called Master Commandant), Lieutenant,[2] Master (heretofore called Sailing Master), Passed Midshipman, Master Mate (only if warranted as such),[3] Boatswain, and Midshipman

1852—Captain, Commander, Lieutenant, Master, Passed Midshipman, Midshipman, and Boatswain

1862—Rear Admiral,[4] Commodore,[5] Captain, Commander, Lieutenant Commander (heretofore senior Lieutenants called Lieutenants Commanding), Lieutenant, Master, Ensign, Passed Midshipman, and Midshipman

1882—Admiral, Vice-Admiral, Rear Admiral, Captain, Commander, Lieutenant Commander, Lieutenant, Lieutenant Junior Grade (JG) (hereto-

1. Senior captains of a fleet or squadron were given the courtesy title "commodore."
2. Senior lieutenants who had command of ships of lesser magnitude were called "lieutenants commanding."
3. Warrant mates were not in line for promotion. Consequently this rate died out quickly.
4. The titles of admiral and vice admiral were established at this time; the grade of vice admiral was not filled until 1864 and that of admiral until 1866.
5. This title was abolished by an act of 3 March 1899.

fore called Master), Ensign, Ensign JG (heretofore called Passed Midshipman), and Naval Cadets[6] (heretofore called Midshipmen)

1902—Admiral of the Navy,[7] Admiral, Vice-Admiral, Rear Admiral, Captain, Commander, Lieutenant Commander, Lieutenant, Lieutenant (JG), Ensign, and Midshipman

1944—Fleet Admiral, Admiral, Vice-Admiral, Rear Admiral, Commodore, Captain, Commander, Lieutenant Commander, Lieutenant, Lieutenant (JG), Ensign, and Midshipman

In the 1970s Congress toyed with the concept of creating a rank of commodore-admiral to give the Navy a singular title to correspond with the other services' brigadier general. In the end the Navy's rank structure was left alone, save the addition of the postscript "lower half" and "upper half" to distinguish between one- and two-star ranks.

Miscellaneous Historical Facts

A Case of Restoration of Rank

On 22 August 1952 President Truman signed a document posthumously restoring William S. Cox to the rank of third lieutenant, a rank of the Navy of sail. The reappointment dates to 17 October 1874, when Lieutenant Cox died.

In the *Chesapeake-Shannon* fight off Boston Harbor on 1 June 1813, James Lawrence, the commanding officer, was mortally wounded. The only other surviving officer was Cox, who had been promoted in battle from midshipman to third lieutenant. Lawrence ordered, "Don't give up the ship! Fight her till she sinks!" and then asked to be taken below for medical attention. The ship was captured and Lawrence died four days later.

A court-martial found Lieutenant Cox guilty of leaving his post during the brief engagement, took away his rank, and discharged him. Rep. E. E. Cox of Georgia (no relation) sponsored the bill that restored Cox's rank. The president ordered the official rank of third lieutenant be placed in his naval record.

White Flag of Truce

The use of the white flag of truce is so old that its origin has been lost. One writer believed it was established first by the Roman Catholic Church in the Middle Ages by an agreement reached between the Church and the warring

---

6. The grade of midshipman was dropped, but it was revived in 1902.
7. Only Admiral Dewey ever held this grade.

Naval Medal of Honor

barons to suspend hostilities on certain festivals, saints' days, and Sundays. Beginning in southern France, the practice of unfolding a white cloth to put an instant stop to fighting spread throughout Europe. In 1095 Pope Urban II proclaimed it in effect for all of Christendom. Some authorities believe that the color white was chosen as an emblem of purity and may have had some connection with the white samite that was believed to cover the Holy Grail.

Medal of Honor

Although frequently miscalled the Congressional Medal of Honor, the Medal of Honor is only one of many established by Congress. It was once called the Congressional Medal of Honor, but in 1944 the secretaries of the Army and Navy and officials of the White House agreed to use the shorter title. It is presented by the president in the name of Congress. The Navy Medal of Honor was first authorized for enlisted men in 1861. In 1915 the same award was authorized for officers of the Navy and Marine Corps; the act of 7 August 1942 provided for both enlisted men and officers.

Veterans Day

In 1954 Congress passed the resolution and on 2 June 1954 President Eisenhower signed a bill proclaiming 11 November to be designated as Veterans Day, to be observed in honor of all veterans, living and dead, of all the wars. The date was based on the former Armistice Day, commemorating the end of World War I, 11 November 1918. It also brought the United States more in line with the Remembrance Day celebrations of the British Commonwealth of Nations.

14

Nautical Words and Naval Expressions

The sea language is not soon learned, much less understood, being only proper to him that has served his apprenticeship: because that, a boisterous sea and stormy weather will make a man not bred on it so sick, that it bereaves him of legs and stomach and courage, so much as to fight with his meat, And in such weather, when be hears a seaman cry starboard, or port, or to bid alooff, or flat a sheet, or haul home a cluing, he thinks he hears a barbarous speech, which he conceives not the meaning of.

Sir William Monson, *Naval Tracts*

It's very odd that sailor-men should talk so very queer.

Thomas Ingoldsby, *Ingoldsby Legends; or, Mirth and Marvels*

Those who study the derivation of English nautical words and expressions —sea terms stemming from Greek, Latin, Norse, Spanish, French, and Dutch words—are constantly reminded of their polyglot sources. Although many Anglo-Saxon and old English words are used at sea today, many other terms were given English shape and sound after being borrowed from foreign sources. Because British sailors and ships have from the birth of the nautical arts had a high incidence of contact with foreign people, and in particular with others who followed the sea, it is natural that English sea language borrowed whatever could be used effectively. One of the most interesting aspects of the unique talk of sailors is the large number of nautical idioms that have been borrowed by landsmen and used with a metaphorical significance now understood by all.

How often do we hear and use nautical terms that have passed from sea to shore? *To take someone in tow; to be in the same boat with; to show one's true colors; to take the wind out of someone's sails; to tide you over; at a low ebb; on the rocks; to jump ship; from stem to stern; when my ship comes in; left stranded; to break the ice; to be first- or second-rate; by and large; backing and filling; to pull together; to take it easy.* All these expressions and many more were originally part of the vigorous speech of the English-speaking sailor.

Logan Pearsall Smith wrote:

> Our oldest sea terms divide themselves into two main classes, and are de-rived from the two far-distant corners of Europe, where, in prehistoric times, men of European races first built themselves ships and ventured on the sea. These places were in the South among the islands and peninsulas of Greece, and in the North along the shores and shallows of the North Sea and the Baltic. From Greece the arts of navigation spread with their ap-propriate terms over the Mediterranean, while the sailors of the North car-ried their Teutonic speech along the coasts of the Atlantic. Gradually, these two vocabularies met and mingled, and the sea vocabularies of England and the other European countries are largely made up of a mixture of these North Sea and these Mediterranean terms. The most English and anciently established ones in our language are, of course, of Northern origin, and consist of those words which the Angles and Saxons brought with them to England, and which safely survived the Norman Conquest. (L. P. Smith, *Words and Idioms: Studies in the English Language* [London: Constable, 1933], p. 2)

In the glossary of the language of the sea that follows, it must be kept in mind that the great thalassocracies (sovereignties of the seas) contributed directly and indirectly to the language of the English-speaking mariner. Apart from the customary meaning of the terms for those afloat, the philologist finds in them much of interest. Usage has shaped pronunciation in many cases. The lexicographer may not agree in pronunciation with the sailor who says "starburd" for *starboard*, "focsul" for *forecastle*, "boy" for *buoy*, "tay-kel" for *tackle*, and even "starn" for *stern*, but why should not sailors "in ships" differ in speech from those who occasionally take passage "on ships"?

TO BE ABOVE BOARD. To have nothing concealed, nothing below deck; frank, honest, open-minded.

> "Now, for my part, d'ye see, I'm for carrying things above board, I'm not for keeping anything under hatches, so that if you b'ent as willing as I, say so a' God's name, there's no harm done." (William Congreve, *Love for Love*)

Shipboard activities: *top,* reefing topsails; *center,* lowering a lifeboat on the quarter; *bottom,* heaving the chip log.
Heck's Iconographic Encyclopedia

ADMIRAL. The title may be traced to the Arabic *Amir-al-Bahr,* "commander (ruler) of the seas." *Bahr* was dropped, and the Romans called the admirals *Sarraccenorum Admirati* introducing the *d* into the Latin form. It was a title of great dignity. The term was introduced into Europe during the Crusades. There is record of its use first by the Sicilians and then by the Genoese.

The first English admiral appointed was William de Leyburn with title of "Admiral of the Sea of the King of England." This appointment was made by Edward I in 1297. The wide powers of this office gradually merged into the title of "Lord High Admiral of England." In the time of Edward II, we find that the Latinized term *admiralius* had been Anglicized as *admyrall.*

The first extant royal commission to a British naval officer was dated 1302, when Gervase Aland was appointed "Captain and Admiral." Authorities are of the opinion that the title of "captain" delegated executive command, while that of "admiral" delegated legal powers.

On 28 May 1493 Columbus officially received the office and title of "Admiral of the Ocean Sea." The letters patent of Ferdinand and Isabella appointed D. Cristobal Colon "nuestro Almirante del Mar Oceano"; also, "Capitan General de la Armada."*

At the beginning of the Crusades, the Sicilians and Genoese conferred the honor of admiral on the commander of a squadron of ships.

Queen Anne acted once as lord high admiral of England upon the death of her consort who had held the title. The Earl of Berkeley was the first officer not of royal blood to win the flag of lord high admiral. At the age of twenty he had his second command, the *Litchfield;* at twenty-three he commanded the *Boyne;* at twenty-seven he was made vice admiral of the Blue, and the next year vice admiral of the Red. On 29 March 1719, at the age of thirty-eight, he hoisted his flag on the *Dorsetshire* as lord high admiral, with the title vice admiral of England and first lord of the Admiralty.

From the seventeenth century, the colors red, white, and blue were flown to distinguish the major groups or divisions in the British Fleet, which often numbered more than two hundred sail. The three seniors—usually, admiral, vice admiral, and rear admiral because of their distinctive colors (plain flags)—commanded ships that as units were known as Red, White, and Blue Squadrons. The admiral with the "red at the fore" was in the center and senior. Or one could be rear admiral of the Red and take precedence over all other rear admirals if he were senior. Red denoted position and seniority. In 1653 the seniority was made Red, Blue, and White. Because of the danger of confusion, Nelson ordered the whole British Fleet to hoist the white ensign

* Samuel Eliot Morison, *Admiral of the Ocean Sea* (Boston: Little, Brown, 1942), p. 20.

Adm. Horatio Nelson (Lord Nelson)
Naval Institute Photo Archive

at the Battle of Trafalgar. In 1864 it was ordered that all H.M. ("His/Her Majesty's") ships would in the future fly white ensigns; that British merchant ships commanded by retired officers of the Navy or officers of the Royal Naval Reserve would fly the blue ensign after obtaining Admiralty permission; and that all other ships and vessels belonging to H.M. subjects would fly the red ensign. Yachts of members of yacht clubs that have a royal warrant may fly the blue ensign. Members of the Royal Yacht Squadron fly the white ensign.

Louis IX, "Saint Louis," introduced the title of admiral to France. At that time, the rank of admiral was equivalent to a marshal of France, but prerogatives became so great that by the reign of Louis XIII, the royal adviser Richelieu assumed the title and suppressed it in others. In 1669 Louis XIV revived the ancient title but made no appointments. Napoleon, in 1805, made Murat a "grand admiral," but the appointment was honorary. The title of "grand admiral" was never revived in France until after the 1830 revolution.

From the beginning of our Navy, the need of higher naval commissions was urged. John Paul Jones wrote to Robert Morris in 1776: "I am convinced that the parity in rank between sea and land or marine officers is of more consequence to the harmony of the service than has generally been imagined."

Jones reported the British system, and then added: "Were that regulation to take place in our Navy, it would prevent numberless disputes and duellings that otherwise would be unavoidable."

The relative ranks with the Army were fixed on 15 November 1776. However, the four highest naval grades were not then established, so for nearly a hundred years, captain was the highest grade.

Secretary Upshur wrote in his annual report for 1841:

> The rank of admiral is known in all the navies of the world except our own; it has existed through a long course of past ages; and has been fully tested in the experience of all nations. It still exists and is still approved. . . . Our naval officers are often subjected to serious difficulties and embarrassments in the interchange of civilities with those of other countries or foreign stations.

Repeated attempts were made by the secretaries of the Navy and by the press, but the opinion prevailed in Congress that the title of admiral had a monarchical connotation. Congress did not create the grade until 16 July 1862 and since then has jealously guarded the authority to fix the numbers of each admiral grade. The secretaries of the Navy had repeatedly recommended the establishment of the grades vice admiral, rear admiral, and commodore. The 16 July 1862 act provided for nine grades of commissioned officers and carried the authority to appoint nine rear admirals.

In 1864 Congress authorized the appointment of a vice admiral from the rear admirals of 1862. Farragut was appointed the first vice admiral. In 1865 a bill made Farragut an admiral and permitted one vice admiral (David Dixon Porter) and ten rear admirals. With the death of Admiral Farragut in 1870, Vice Admiral Porter became admiral and Rear Admiral Rowan became vice admiral. In 1875 Congress provided that grades of admiral and vice admiral should not be filled by promotion. In other words, the grades were abolished upon the death of Porter and Rowan. As a result, Farragut and Porter were the only active officers who ever held the permanent grade of admiral in the Navy, although many have held the temporary grade.

On 2 March 1899 the president was authorized to appoint "an Admiral of the Navy." George Dewey was appointed and held the title until his death on 16 January 1917. The titles of admiral of the Navy and general of the Armies were honorary offices that were specially created for Admiral Dewey and General Pershing. Both offices were abolished upon their respective deaths and have never been revived.

On 3 March 1899 the Navy Personnel Act made provision for eighteen rear admirals. For purpose of pay, the grade was divided in halves. The upper nine received the same pay and allowances as major generals; the lower half, the pay and allowances of brigadier generals. That was changed subtly on 13 May 1908 when the 1899 Navy Personnel Act was modified with different pay rates for "rear admirals, first nine" and "rear admirals, second nine."

The Naval Appropriation Act of 3 March 1915 authorized that the commanders in chief of the Atlantic, Pacific, and Asiatic Fleets should have the rank of admiral while on that duty, and the seconds in command should hold the rank of vice admiral while on that duty. On 20 August 1916 the number of officers in the different grades was increased, and provision was made for pay and allowance of staff officers of flag rank as well as the line. And on 20 August 1916, the chief of naval operations was given the rank and pay of admiral, and took rank after the admiral of the Navy (Dewey). On 22 May 1917 the act of 3 March 1915 was repealed, and the president was authorized to make a selection of six officers for the commands of the fleets (then called Atlantic, Pacific, and Asiatic), three of which, while assigned to the duty, would have the rank and pay of admiral, and three, the rank and pay of vice admiral.

In 1944 Congress established the ranks of fleet admiral and general of the Army (five-star rank), stipulating that there is no higher rank in the respective services. Leahy, King, and Nimitz were promoted to this rank in December 1944 and Halsey in December 1945. Leahy, King, Nimitz, and Halsey were the only officers who ever held the title of fleet admiral with the provision that they would not retire, but would remain on active duty for life with full pay and allowances.

Since World War II there have been several minor adjustments in authorized strength and ranks, particularly within the ranks of rear admiral, including a brief foray into the resurrection of the rank of commodore (actually called commodore admiral) during the 1970s. Currently there are rear admirals, lower half, and rear admirals, upper half.

ADMIRAL, REAR. In order that the natural son of Charles II, Henry, Duke of Grafton, could at tender years hold the title of vice admiral of England, Admiral Arthur Herbert in c. 1683 was made the first rear admiral of England. This office was effective until 1895, but was not filled until 1901, when it was revived, as was that of vice admiral of the United Kingdom, by Edward VII. Both offices are now held but carry no emoluments. These high honorary titles brought the terms into English nautical phraseology; we mention them here for their historical interest.

ADMIRAL, VICE. This early office in the Royal Navy may be traced to the vice admiral of the United Kingdom, which was the evolution of the ancient title of lieutenant admiral or lieutenant of the Admiralty. It later became vice admiral of England in 1672, then vice admiral of Great Britain in 1707, and finally vice admiral of the United Kingdom in 1801. In 1876 the office was not held and remained vacant until 1901 when King Edward VII revived it.

AHOY. This was once the dreaded war cry of the Vikings—a distinctly nautical hail.

AIGUILLETTE. There are many amusing theories as to the origin of this term. The best known is that the aide-de-camp of a superior knight carried the rope and pegs for tethering the knight's horse, and thereby the rope became the badge of the one near the leader. Other traditions relate that it was to tie a pencil with which to write dispatches, or even to represent a hanging rope with which the general could hang the troops should they not acquit themselves favorably on the field of battle, or similarly, the rope of the provost marshal used in hanging the condemned. All are false. The term actually comes from the French referring to the lacing used to tie personal armor together, particularly that for the arms and shoulders. When so used, it often had a knot or lacing hanging down from the shoulder.

Aiguillettes first appeared in 1907 for the aides to the president and the secretary of the Navy. Later they were authorized for aides to flag officers. It is a custom that aides to the president of the United States and to sovereigns, royalty, and viceroys wear aiguillettes on the right side, and that aides to all other senior officials, officers, and dignitaries wear them on the left. Normally, the number of cords denotes the number of stars or the relative rank of the wearer's principal. Naval aiguillettes are blue and gold, while those of the Marine Corps and the Army are red and gold. Air Force aiguillettes are silver.

ALOOF. From the sailing term *a-luff*. When sailing too close to the wind, one's sails are apt to lose their aerodynamic shape and to have the windward edge luff or flap noisily in the wind. When one's head is held too far up (as with a sailing vessel's head held too far into the wind) one is said to be aloof. Likewise, to keep clear of a dangerous situation, such as grounding or collision, a sailing vessel might head up into the wind, causing his sails to luff, and thereby hold himself clear or apart.

Anchor of USS *Theodore Roosevelt* (CVN 71)
U.S. Navy (Dennis Taylor)

ANCHOR. This term is derived from a Greek word for "hook" or "crook." Sailors say today "drop the hook," or refer to the anchor as "the old mud hook." The original Greek meaning has been lost, and the word today has only one connotation—a means of holding a ship when she is not under way.

One expert on Chinese history writes that ships carrying anchors, rudders, and oars were known as early as 2000 B.C. Supposedly, Emperor Yu invented the anchor, but emperors in those days often took credit that belonged to their subjects. Emperor Yu was said to have been the first to use anchor chains. The peculiar noise of chain running out gave rise to the Chinese mariners' expression *mao,* which in Chinese signifies "cat" or "iron cat."

Bags of sand or stone were used as anchors by the early navigators. In time, stone anchors were used by the Greeks and Romans. In the book of Stephanus Byzantius, titled *De urbibus* ("On Cities"), there is the statement that the town of Ancyra in Egypt derived its name from the manufacture of anchors in its quarries.

Large lead trunks exhibited as ancient Greek anchors may be found in the archeological collections of the Boreli Museum in Marseilles, the British Museum in London, the Old Museum in Berlin, and in many smaller museums of southern Europe.

The Romans used the anchor as a symbol for wealth and commerce, while the Greeks gave to the anchor a significance of hope and steadiness, a meaning that persists in religion and heraldry today. For the early Christians the anchor symbolized steadfastness, hope, and salvation. Pictures of anchors comparable in shape to those used today may be seen in the catacombs. The drawings sometimes have an inscription, such as *Spes in Christo,* "Hope in Christ." The foul anchor with a line wound around the shank may be found on the world-renowned sculptures of the Temple of Neptune in Rome. The anchors of modern aircraft carriers weigh 60,000 pounds each. Their 1,800-foot anchor chains weigh almost 250 tons and are the longest and strongest ever forged.

ANCHOR'S AWEIGH. When the anchor is aweigh, or clear of the bottom, the ship is no longer fast to the land, but is free to sail on its own. *Aweigh* is from the old English *woeg,* meaning "to raise."

To be AT SEA. To be doubtful or hesitant. Short for being "lost at sea," or wandering without apparent direction or compass.

AYE AYE. *Aye* is Old English for "yes," probably taken from the Latin verb *aio,* "to affirm."

BACK. The wind backs when it changes counterclockwise, but VEERS when it changes clockwise. Square sails are backed or aback when the wind blows on their forward side, thrusting them against the mast and stopping the motion of the vessel. Should this occur through a shift of wind, the effect of a heavy sea, or the carelessness of the helmsman, a ship is said to be TAKEN ABACK. Similarly, when a person is stopped in his tracks by some new development, he is taken aback. To back water with oars is the opposite of a regular stroke—that is, to push instead of to pull. TO BACK a piece of gear means to rig or set up a preventer. To back an anchor refers to the practice of sending an extra anchor to the bottom or holding ground with its shank made fast on the chain of the first anchor in order to back it or assist it. It also means to shackle or otherwise secure the extra anchor to the chain near the lower anchor before letting go. "To back chain" is sometimes confused with "to veer chain," but in general usage it means easing out a few fathoms in deep water before letting go the anchor. TO BACK AND FILL, like an indecisive person, involves alternately backing (spilling the wind from the sail) and filling a sail in order to tack into the wind, albeit in a short, vacillating manner.

BARGE. The barge was the admiral's boat and was rigged for ten or twelve oars. Admirals' boats are still referred to as barges.

BATTEN DOWN THE HATCHES. A *batten* is a board used for stiffening. In today's sailing parlance, it is usually a long, thin, flat board slipped into a pocket in the luff of a sail to help preserve the sail's shape. Originally, it referred to boards that were clamped over deck hatch covers to reinforce them and keep them closed during heavy weather, when the hatches were "battened down." It still means to prepare for a heavy blow.

BEACHCOMBER. Originally this was someone who searched the beaches for material washed up from wrecked or stranded ships. Beachcombing in winter after a blow was quite a profitable business for the longshoremen of British ports and watering places in the old days. It has been stated that "in the happy pre-war era of gold, such a beach as that of Brighton, Hastings, or Ramsgate yielded up many a golden guinea after it had been bared by a winter gale." The expression today connotes tramps of the sea, unreliable drifters. It is also applied in some cases to impoverished and stranded landsmen in foreign sea ports.

BEAM ENDS. A person who has been knocked on his beam ends has been knocked flat, like a ship when wind and storm has knocked her over on her sides, on the ends of the beams (athwart ship deck members).

BECKET. An eye for securing a line to a block. Anchors on sailing ships had a becket on one fluke, which could be used to either secure the anchor while it was up, or to attach an anchor buoy to while it was out. Certain insignia, including naval aviator's wings, display this historic detail.

BERSERK. A frenzy or uncontrollable rage. The term comes from the Vikings who would allegedly work themselves up to the point that they would tear off their mail shirts and fight bare-chested or "bar-sark" (without shirt). This is also the source of the phrase, "keep your shirt on."

BETWEEN WIND AND WATER. Referring to the part just below the waterline when sailing in smooth water that becomes exposed when the ship rolls, this term describes the vulnerable part of anything.

> And just e'en as he meant, sir,
> To loggerheads they went, sir,
> And then he let fly at her
> A shot 'twixt wind and water,
> That won this fair maid's heart.

(William Congreve, *Love for Love*)

BINNACLE. Originally spelled *bittacle*. A space about the size of a large cupboard in which were placed two compasses, log board, lighted candle or lamp at night, and other navigation gear. Now only the stand used to house the compass. The **BINNACLE LIST** or daily sick list once hung on or near it.

BITTER END. The end of anchor chain secured aboard or the free end of a line or rope. "A bitter end is but the turn of a cable about the bits, and veare it out little and little, and the bitter's end is that part of the cable doth stay within board" (*Seaman's Grammar*, 1653).

BLEEDING A BUOY. To let the water out.

BLUEJACKET. The first uniform that was ever officially sanctioned for sailors in the Royal Navy was a short blue jacket open at the front. There were no definite uniform regulations for U.S. enlisted men in the War of 1812, but many wore short blue jackets. Now a term for an American sailor.

BLUENOSE. One who has entered the realm of Polaris, the God of the North. Those who cross the Arctic Circle become Bluenoses.

BLUE PETER. A signaling flag for the letter *P*, "blue pierced with white," was used in the Royal Navy from 1777 as a general recall flag and flown at the foremast preparatory to sailing. Civilians knew its significance, for merchant ships and convoys in the French wars would not sail until the escorting man-of-war hoisted the blue peter for passengers to come aboard.

There is a historic piece of doggerel, autographed "Emma," written when Nelson sailed in 1801:

> Silent grief and sad forebodings
> (Lest I ne'er should see him more)

Fill my heart when gallant Nelson
Hoists blue peter at the fore.

BOARDERS. As late as 1885 one reads of boarders: "They are men detailed to attack the enemy by boarding. They are armed with pistols and cutlasses and led by the executive officer. They are summoned by verbal order and by the springing of the rattle, and assembled in the part of the ship designated, keeping under cover as much as possible" *(U.S. Marine Encyclopedia)*. On 4 June 1944 the old battle cry of the seas, "Away all boarders!" or "Boarding parties!" was heard for the first time on loudspeakers as boats from the *Guadalcanal* (CVE 60) and *Pillsbury* (DE 133) were lowered at the commencement of their capture of the German submarine *U-505* off North Africa.

BOAT. Term derived from Anglo-Saxon *bat,* meaning "boat, small ship, vessel."

BOATSWAIN. The Saxon word *swein* meant "boy" or "servant." The "boat" referred originally to the ship and not to her boats. **COXSWAIN** has a similar derivation. *Cock* is an old word for a type of small boat. The ships were usually commanded by *batsuen* (boatswains) in the eleventh century.

> He [boatswain] is to be very particular in having ready at all times a sufficient number of mats, plats, knippers, points, and gaskets so that no delay may be experienced when they are wanted. (*Naval Regulations,* 1824)

BOATSWAIN'S PIPE. The parts of the pipe were called by old sailors the *buoy, gun, keel,* and *shackle.* Technically, the parts are the bowl, the reed, the flange, and the ring. The first reference to "call" on the whistle dates to the early sixteenth century, but the use of the whistle at sea antedates Carthaginian sea power in the ancient world. (See also chapter 4.)

BOTTOMRY BOND. A lien placed on a vessel by a master in order to obtain money to get the vessel home. The funds secured are used only for repairs. This is resorted to only when the master is out of communication with the ship's owners. Such a lien takes priority for first payment over all mortgages. A lien on cargo is a **RESPONDENTIA BOND.**

BOX THE COMPASS. To calibrate the corrections to the magnetic compass that might arise from the installation of equipment nearby, a ship must steer successively on all points of sail, and take note of the readings thereon. The term is derived from the Spanish *boxar*, "to sail around."

TO BREAK A FLAG. Normally, a signal flag or pennant is attached to a halyard and to a downhaul and hoisted to its proper place. If it is desired to have a flag or pennant at its proper place ready for instant showing, as in the case of a man overboard, or for smartness, as at a change of command ceremony, or to avoid rigging obstructions when hoisting, a different method is used. The flag or pennant is folded, and the folds secured by two or more stops made of light string; it is then attached to a halyard at its top and to a downhaul at its bottom. When so made up, it can be hoisted to its proper place and left aloft until needed. At the proper time, a sharp jerk on the downhaul will break the stops, allowing the flag or pennant to fly free instantly. This procedure is known as "breaking a flag."

BRIG. As a name for a sailing vessel the term *brig* did not come into use until the latter part of the eighteenth century. It is mentioned by Samuel Johnson in his dictionary of 1760. It is a contraction of the older word *brigantine* or *brigandine*, from *brigand* (robber). This was originally a general term for the fast sailing vessel used by pirates of the Mediterranean. Because Lord Nelson used a brig in battle for relieving his ships of prisoners, the sailors began to call a prison anywhere a "brig."

BUCCANEERS. The term was first given to early Frenchmen in Haiti, who were the original cowboys of that island. The word *boucan* was of Caribbean origin, meaning a dealer in smoked-dried meats. In the Caribbean area, the hunters placed meat to dry on wooden lattice work, known as *boucans*. The "boucaneers" eventually took to privateering and general lawlessness. After the Treaty of Ryswick, *buccaneer* became the common word for "pirate."

BUGLE. Derived from the French, *bugle* originally meant "wild ox." The bugle horn, meaning wild ox horn, was and remains in some parts of the world the true horn of the chase. Joseph Haydn, the celebrated musician, wrote the first bugle calls in about 1793. They were introduced into navies at a much later date.

BUMBOAT. A boat selling supplies, provisions, and articles to ships. The most popular derivation is from *boomboat*, signifying boats permitted to lie at booms. A British source accounts for the term as derived from *bombard*, a receptacle in which beer is carried to soldiers on duty.

BUOYS. Floating beacons, which by shape and color give the mariner valuable navigational information concerning channels, shallows, and obstructions. In coming from seaward, red buoys mark the starboard, or right, side of the channel; green buoys, the port, or left, side. A convenient way of remembering has been "red, right, returning," meaning "leave all red buoys on the right when returning from sea."

BUTTONS. As in other matters of uniform, the origin of certain insignia and distinctions of dress is not definitely recorded, but as some old stories tell it in the case of midshipmen, buttons were placed on the cuffs for a purpose. One British commentator wrote:

> In the earlier days of the last [i.e., nineteenth] century, small mites of boys eight or nine years old, and even younger, were sent to sea. When these small boys were first at sea, they were one and all so woefully homesick that they had continuous cases of sniffles, and for the first part of their term of service they were forever rubbing their poor little homesick and dripping eyes and noses on the cuffs of their coats. This was so detrimental to the appearance of their uniforms that it led to the sewing on of buttons.

Commander W. N. T. Beckett, RN, wrote: "'Snotty' is a slang term for a [British] midshipman and is derived from the allegation that these officers used to make their sleeves do duty as handkerchiefs, and that to obviate this practice, buttons were placed on the cuffs." Royal Navy midshipmen are sometimes still called "snotties" today, but as in civilian dress, the large eighteenth-century cuffs went out of fashion, and the buttons were left as a dress ornament. Midshipmen may have never had the large cuffs, and buttons were added after the shift to a plain cuff.

BY AND LARGE. A term that has come to mean "generally speaking" or "under all conditions." It is derived from the sailing terms "by the wind" (close-hauled) and "sailing large" (running free). The term AT LARGE stems also from that usage.

CAPTAIN. From Latin *capitaneus*, "the head or chief." The evolution of the post of commanding officer of a ship derives from the *batsuen* (boatswain) or the rector in the eleventh century; the rank of captain came into general use about 1300. Commander R. G. Lowry, RN, wrote that in A.D. 984, the Italians had a military rank *capitano,* which was derived from the Latin *caput,* "head." The master, although he sailed the ship, was of lower rank than the captain. In a British order in council in 1748, the relative rank was settled with the Army by dividing Navy captains into three grades. It was deemed at that time that any officer in command was entitled to the title of captain while in command, regardless of rank. All captains not eligible on the list for promotion to rear admiral were originally called "masters and commanders" and had the abbreviation "C." after their names. The rank was shortened to commander in 1794. In the Royal Navy the abbreviation "Cdr." was used after the names of commanders in 1826.

POST CAPTAIN, a term used in the Royal Navy and once used in the American Navy, distinguished captains commanding frigates from master commanders or commanders next in rank. There never was a commission of "post captain." In 1747 the rank of captain was first clearly defined in the Royal Navy. Captains who commanded post ships took rank, if of three years' standing, with colonels in the Army. Until the year 1824 the Royal Navy list classed such captains as post captains.

Until 1862 captain was the highest commissioned officer in the U.S. Navy and, according to duty, ranked with lieutenant colonel, colonel, or brigadier general.

CARGO. Comes directly from the Latin *cargo* or *carga,* "a load, freight."

To CATCH A CRAB. To fail to keep in stroke in rowing and ofttimes thereby to jam and foul other oars. The Venetians called a green hand or novice at rowing a "crab."

CATHEAD. Projections on bows for rigging tackles for purposes of hoisting anchor aboard, "to cat and fish." The term appears in English as early as 1626. A lion's face was sometimes carved on wooden timbers for good luck; hence the term, "cathead."

CHAINS. Where shrouds (mast supports) were secured to platforms on the ship's side, "chains" were used to brace the platform. This platform was used for leadsmen to stand upon when heaving the lead; today it means that platform or position from which the lead is hove.

CHANTY. Gershom Bradford, in his *Glossary of Sea Terms,* gives an excellent description of a chanty:

A song formerly always and now rarely sung aboard ship to lighten and unify labor at the capstan, sheets, and halyards. The soloist is known as the chanty-man and is usually a man of leadership in the forecastle. He is something of an improviser, for those especially successful made their verses applicable to the existing conditions in the ship, indulging in slight hits at the peculiarities of the different officers, the vociferousness of the chorus indicating the relative delight with which these squibs are received by the men. This was the only privilege allowed to pass in the old days of iron-fisted discipline. They were composed for various kinds of work such as capstan chanties, which were timed to be rhythmic with the steady tread around the capstan. They usually dwell upon the joys of being homeward-bound and farewells to the port (and ladies) when heaving up the anchor to leave. The topsail halyard chanties are the most stirring as they, at their best, are sung in a gale when the reefed topsail is being mastheaded. There are also long-pull and short-pull chanties.

As Arnold Bennett once remarked about limericks, some of the best chanties are not for general publication. They were for the most part tuneful and melodious, and smacked of the romantic age of sail. Pronounced "shanty," the probable derivation of the term is Norman French.

Capt. David W. Bone, British master mariner and author of books on life at sea, wrote in his authoritative book on chanties, *Capstan Bars,* that these songs of sailors fell under the general heads of short haul chanties, halyard chanties, debt and credit chanties, capstan chanties, windlass and pump chanties, and those "out of the blue." He believed "the chanty 'Shenandoah,' of American origin, to be the most beautiful. Always sung at weighing anchor, it is a chanty of 'haunting melody' and 'tender cadences.' "

A firsthand expert, William Applebye-Robinson, stated in a letter to the *New York Times,* 20 January 1939:

There are, or used to be, three kinds of chanteys—single-pull, double-pull, and capstan, or marching. The first, as its name implies, was used where tremendous effort was required and single pulls, with a breathing spell in between, were all that could reasonably be asked of men—hauling aft the main-sheet is an example. "Haul on the bowline" is a single-pull chantey, and the pull comes on the last word "haul"; in some ships the pull was made immediately after the word and, in my experience, it gave the best results. "Haul on the bowline" was not nearly as popular as "Haul Away,

Jo" or "Oh, Do, My Johnny Bowker," both single-pulls; "Paddy Doyle's Boots" was invariably used for bunting the sail on top of the yard, when furling any of the courses or lower square-sails.

The double-pulls were used for fairly long pulls, such as mastheading the topsails, or even to'gallant sails in vessels with single to'gallant yards. The chanteyman sang a line and the hands pulled twice on each bit of chorus; for instance, in "Blow, Boys, Blow," the chanteyman sang "A Yankee ship came down the river" (chorus) "BLOW, boys, BLOW." "And all her sails they shone like silver" (chorus) "BLOW, my bully boys, BLOW" (the pulls indicated by the upper-case).

There are dozens of double-pulls; probably the most popular was "Blow the Man Down," with "Whiskey for My Johnny" and "Reuben Ranzo" close seconds. A good chanteyman made up his lines as he went along, after the first line or two, but naturally the choruses remained the same.

Capstan chanties could be, and were, almost any song with a good rhythm and chorus: "Away for Rio" (pronounced rye-o) being perhaps the most popular; also "A- Roving"; but I've hove up the anchor many times to "Marching Through Georgia."

Incidentally, the only chanty I know of that is written in a minor key is "On the Plains of Mexico" and is of American origin.

CHAPLAIN. Chaplains have been stationed aboard warships from the earliest days. Charles I appointed a chaplain to each ship of the fleet of England. Chaplains and doctors were once paid by the seamen, the chaplain receiving from each seaman fourpence per month. The chaplains did not live in the wardroom until the end of the eighteenth century. The chaplain, purser, and doctor on almost all ships messed in their respective cabins, but some chaplains messed regularly with the captains. In the old days, the chaplain had the authority to give a midshipman sixpence for learning a psalm.

Tradition credits the title to Saint Martin, who divided his coat with a poor beggar on a cold wintry day outside of Amiens. The coat was supposedly "miraculously preserved" and thereby became a sacred banner for the kings of France. This cloak or cape (French *chape*) was preserved in an oratory that took the name of *chapelle*, while the gentleman charged with its keeping was called the *chapelain*.

A Royal Commission that in 1618 inquired into the state of the Navy set forth among other abuses that "in the narrow seas there is an allowance demanded for a preacher and his man, though no such devotion be used on board."

The practice of daily prayers on British men-of-war commenced in the days of Cromwell and the Commonwealth. At this time, Admiral Blake instituted the practice of singing hymns or psalms at eight P.M., when the watch was "set."

The second article of Navy Regulations written in 1775 states: "The commanders of the ships of the United Colonies are to take care that Divine services be performed twice a day on board and a sermon be preached on board on Sundays." Many chaplains in the early days served as secretary to the captain; often they were also instructors of midshipmen, and one chaplain served as the ship's medical officer. In 1794 provision was made for a chaplain on each of the new ships being constructed. At about that time the pay was raised from twenty dollars per month to forty.

A chaplain in the Royal Navy holds no rank. "He is considered to be of equal rank with the man he stands next to at any moment." He has a special cap badge with laurels mostly black picked out with gold. In the Royal Canadian Navy he wears officer's buttons and cap badge. Sleeve lace is never worn. Chaplains never wear side arms.

CHARLIE NOBLE. Sailor's term for the galley smokepipe. Derived from the British merchant service captain Charlie Noble, who required a high polish on the galley funnel. The funnel of his galley was of copper and its brightness became known in all ports visited. To SHOOT CHARLIE NOBLE meant to clean the galley smokepipe of soot and dirt by firing a pistol therein.

CHART. From Latin *charta*, Greek *charte*, a kind of papyrus. In Middle English, the charts or maps were known as *scacards* or "sea-cards." There are many references in the early day to "the cards," meaning the charts.

CHIT. From the Hindu word *chitti*, meaning "letter, note, bill, voucher, or receipt." The use of the term came from the old East India Company. The word has wide use in the Far East and is used throughout the British Army and Navy. The U.S. Navy on the Asiatic Station adopted it many years ago from the "pidgin" (business) English.

CLEARING THE GLASS. Reversing the sand in the hour or half-hour glass to mark the end of the watch.

CLIPPER. The term was taken from Old English *clip*, meaning "to run or fly swiftly." The fast, trim clipper ships mark the golden age of the United States in merchant ships. World-famous, record-breaking passages to San Francisco, China, and Australia placed American shipbuilders at the top of their profession for the time. McKay's *Flying Cloud* was, on long voyages, the fastest sailing vessel that ever flew the U.S. flag. This beautiful craft logged 374 miles for a day on her trials.

COCKLES OF ONE'S HEART, TO WARM (REJOICE) THE. To gladden and to cheer. Derived probably from the old English term "cockling seas," or short and quick ones; hence, applicable to that which brings short, quick heartbeats. The cockles of the heart are, of course, unknown to modern medicine.

COLORS, GUARD AND BAND FOR. Although originally a ceremony held at sunrise, Lord St. Vincent established a new regulation after the 1797 mutinies in order to make it a most impressive event. In 1844 the Royal Navy, for the sake of uniformity, set a fixed time for this ceremony.

COMMANDER. As explained under CAPTAIN, the lower grades of captains were originally styled "master and commander" and commanded small ships of war. The title was introduced in England by William III and was originally *commandeur*. The British in 1827 first appointed commanders as second in command on large ships.

The title was introduced in the pay bill approved 3 March 1837, which changed "masters commandant" to "commanders." The *Marine Encyclopedia* (1881) stated that a commander was originally supposed "to command vessels of the third and fourth classes; may be employed as chief of staff to a commodore, or duty under a bureau; or as aide to a flag officer of either grade on shore stations."

COMMISSION PENNANT. The distinctive mark, other than the national ensign, of a ship of the Navy in commission. It is a long, thin pennant flown at a masthead. In the U.S. Navy, it consists of a starred blue field with a single red-and-white stripe.

In the days of chivalry, knights rated a small pointed flag or pennon. The mark of a squire was a long pennant very similar to the "coachwhip pennant" of modern men-of-war. Bannerets ranked the knight and took precedence below a baron. They carried a knight's pennon with a slit in the end. It was customary to create barons on the battlefield by the king or general cutting off part of the fly of the pennon. This square flag was then a symbol of increased rank. Edward, the Black Prince, tore the tail off the pennon of Lord John Chandos after battle, saying, "Sir John, behold, here is your banner; God send you much joy and honor with it." One may trace directly from these customs the commission pennant, "coachwhip," broad command pennant, and burgee flags flown by commanding officers of ships and by commodores, as well as the square personal flags of the admirals of the U.S. and other navies.

Some attribute the commissioning pennant to the British response to a Dutch taunt. Adm. Maarten Harpertszoon Tromp allegedly hoisted a broom at his masthead to indicate his intention to sweep the English from the sea, and the English Admiral Blake hoisted a horsewhip, indicating his intention to chastise the insolent Dutchman. Supposedly, this was the first horsewhip pennant marking a vessel of war, adopted by all nations.*

Commander Kemp, an authority, believes both Tromp's broom and Blake's whip apocryphal. Commander R. D. Merriman, Royal Indian Navy (Ret.), wrote in 1943: "I do not think that Blake's whip 'at the fore' is the real origin of the Commissioning Pennant. It is much more likely to be an attenuated survival of the 'Pennon' used by every noble family in the Middle Ages, and on which were emblazoned the Arms of the bearer. These 'pennons' or 'streamers,' sometimes of great size and length, were flown on board ships in which the owners were embarked. The Commissioning Pennant of today is, of course, standardized, but it represents, none the less, the personal insignia of the officer appointed to command the ship."

COMMODORE. This title came from Holland. In the Dutch Wars of 1652, there were not sufficient admirals and the Dutch desired to create others without calling them admirals. The title was brought to England by William III. The broad command pennant or burgee was used by the Dutch at the same time. The rank was officially recognized by the British in 1806. The American Navy used the rank as an honorary title in the Revolution: "Commodore" John Paul Jones and "Commodore" Esek Hopkins, appointed as "commander in chief."

Until 1861 all captains in the U.S. Navy commanding or having commanded squadrons were recognized as commodores, though never commissioned as such. They flew a broad pennant distinctive of that rank. In 1862 it was established as a fixed rank; in July of that year eighteen were commissioned on the active list and seventeen on the retired list. The grade was abolished in 1899. During World War II the temporary grade of commodore was given to some officers of both the line and the staff corps. President Franklin D. Roosevelt made the original suggestion that the old title be revived.

* George Henry Preble, *History of the Flag of the United States of America* (Boston: A. Williams, 1880), p. 659.

A captain in the U.S. Navy who commands a flotilla or squadron of destroyers is called a "commodore" by courtesy. The British Ministry of Defense (Navy) continues to make appointments of a small number of commodores and, as of 2002, is introducing them as a substantive, vice honorary rank. In the 1970s, the U.S. Navy toyed with the idea of marking the distinction between rear admiral upper and lower halves by changing the name of the latter to commodore-admiral, but the change was never made.

COMPASS. Some writers hold that the Chinese made use of the compass long before European navigators, but this claim has never been conclusively established. The early Chinese records disclose that the Chinese knew of the extraordinary properties of the magnet from the third century A.D., but in all the documents relating to voyages at that earliest date no mention is made of the magnet as an aid to direction and navigation, until the Chinese water compass of the twelfth century.

The Arabs, who most probably learned of the water compass from the Chinese, were acquainted with the magnet ashore. Much earlier, the Greeks had used it for purposes of instruction. Plato wrote of the magnet in a humorous vein when he spoke of its use by jealous husbands to detect wifely virtue, but there is no record of its use at sea until much later.

The following interesting description of what may have been a compass was found in a Latin volume dealing with the art of ship handling: "Take a number of small iron bars [needles] and paint them with a mixture of cinabro and oprimento well powdered and mixed with the blood of the crest of a rooster. Heat them well and, after the Astrologer has carried them next to his skin for a period of a full lunation, lay them on straws floating on the water and they will point south."*

The water compass, first seen in Europe about 1190, was probably brought back by the crusaders after seeing those of the Arabs.

In 1248 Brunetto Latini, a Florentine, made reference in his poem "Tresor" to the instrument used on the Norman ships:

> In a tub of water placed in the center of the ship there floats the Mariniere, which is a round piece of cork with a thin hollow shaft filled with lodestone inserted through its center so that it lies parallel to the plane of the water, and the quill of a goose sealed at both ends, also inserted through the cork at right angles to the one filled with lodestone; over this there lays

---

* Capt. John M. L. Gorett, MSR, CAA, in his comprehensive compass research brought to light the Latin book, title and author unknown, with the title page missing. He places its writing in the third century A.D.

a bird's skin with the fleur-de-lis upon it, and even as our august King is our constant guide on the land, so does the fleur-de-lis upon the Mariniere guide the mariner by constantly pointing to Boreas (north) no matter how the ship may go.

The fleur-de-lis has remained, to this day on the north point of practically all compass cards.

About 1295 Flavio Gioja of Amalfi gave to the world the first practical compass. He used a large copper bowl instead of the wooden tub of the *mariniere,* in order that, when the ship's head swung in azimuth, the current of the electro-magnet induction was such as to dampen the oscillations of the compass and thereby bring the needle to rest sooner than by the old method in the wooden tub. He balanced the compass card on a vertical shaft in the bowl and placed on the card all the cardinal points of the compass. The fleur-de-lis was left for the north point.

CONN. A very old word whose exact derivation is not known. It was used first about 1520 in the present sense of controlling or directing the steering or giving orders to the helmsman, by the captain but more often by the officer of the deck.

COOK. Michael Scott in *Torn Cringle's Log* writes:

> The cook of a man-of-war is no small beer; he is his Majesty's warrant-officer, a much bigger wig than a poor little mid, with whom it is condescension on his part to jest. It seems to be a sort of rule, that no old sailor who has not lost a limb or an eye, at least, shall be eligible to the office, but as the kind of maiming is so far circumscribed that all cooks must have two arms, a laughable proportion of them have but one leg. Besides the honour, the perquisites are good.

In the seventeenth century the cook was, in most cases, an unscrupulous individual. For many years, it was the custom that the cook received his meat from the steward, and was by order to cook it and give it to "such persons as are chosen by every mess (mess cooks) for the fetching of it away from him." We learn in many cases that cooks were bribed to furnish double rations to a mess. In the time of Charles II, men who had been maimed in the Dutch Wars were given appointments as cooks in the Royal Navy. There is record of John Gamble who, although he had lost both arms "in fight the 11th of August, 1673," was recommended for cook of the navy ship *Sweepstakes,* while James Davis, "who lost all the lower part of his face in the engagement May 28, 1692," was made cook of the *Revenge.* The record reads, "that forasmuch as he is not able to eat sea biscuits or meat that he would be permitted to perform cook's duty by deputy."

To CORK (CAULK) OFF or TAKE A CAULK. To sleep or take a nap; as sailors often napped on the deck, the term is derived from the possibility of one's back becoming marked by the pitch of the seams.

CORVETTE. The word derived from Latin *corbita,* referring to a basket that was lashed to the mastheads of Egyptian grain ships to show their trade. These ships were known as the *naves onerariae,* "vessels of burden."

In the Middle Ages, the corvette was a light and fast Italian galley with one mast and propelled by either sails or oars. In the year 1687 the corvette was first seen in the French Navy as a fast, light ship used for lookout duty. In time the class ranked just after frigates. Various navies have used this title in modern times for small, fast ships.

COXSWAIN or COCKSWAIN. From *cock,* "a small boat," and *swain,* "a servant." It originally meant one who had charge of a boat and a crew in the absence of an officer.

It was once the custom that in single-banked boats the coxswain pulled the stroke oar, and the boat was generally steered by an officer; in double-banked boats the coxswain usually steered.

CRUISER. Derived from *crusal,* a fast, light vessel used by pirates in the Mediterranean. This was not essentially a fighting vessel, but was used for raiding and pillaging.

CUT OF HIS JIB. To evaluate the cut of someone's jib is to size him up, to make a personal estimate, to judge character and capabilities by appearance. In the days of sailing ships, nationality and rigs could often be distinguished by their jibs. A Spanish ship, for example, had a small jib or none at all; the large French ships often had two jibs; English ships seldom but one. From ships, the phrase was extended to people; it implies the first impression one makes on another.

> A vessel is known by the cut of her jibsail; hence the popular phrase, to know a man by the cut of his jib. (Hotten, *Dictionary of Modern Slang*)
>
> We shall be very good friends, sir, I'll answer for it, if I may judge from the cut of his jib. (F. Marryat, *Jacob Faithful*)

CUTTING A DIDO. A more recent expression commemorating HMS *Dido*, a very smart and clean ship of the Royal Navy, which often cruised around the fleet before anchoring, some said "showing off"—hence "to cut a dido."

DAGO. From Saint James, the Spanish patron saint, called Iago, Santiago, San Diego, Diego. Yankee sailors first called Spanish sailors "Diego men" or "Dagos."

DAVIT. A term dating back to 1811, referring to the tackle on main and foremost shrouds used for hoisting heavy boats and weights out and in. In more modern times the term has been applied to the swinging metal or wood fixture to which tackle is rigged. Called first "davitt," and by Capt. John Smith in 1626, "the Davids end." Derived from "Daviet," a diminutive for David, it being customary to give proper names to implements, such as billy or jack.

DAVY JONES'S LOCKER. "Possibly from the biblical Jonah, who was thrown into the sea. A familiar name among sailors for Death, formerly for the evil spirit supposed to preside over the demons of the sea. He was thought to be in all storms, and was sometimes seen of gigantic height, showing three rows of sharp teeth in his enormous mouth, opening great frightful eyes, and nostrils which emitted blue flames. The ocean is still termed by sailors Davy Jones's locker" (William A. Wheeler, *Explanatory and Pronouncing Dictionary of the Noted Names of Fiction*, c. 1889).

> As ships go to Old Davy, Lord knows how, Sirs,
> While heaven is blue enough for Dutchman's trowsers.
>
> (Thomas Hood, "Love and Lunacy")

> He dies, by not a single sigh deplor'd.
> To Davy Jones' locker, let him go.
> And with old Neptune booze below.
>
> (John Welcott, "Ode to the K . . .")

DEAD MARINE. In the old days of hard drinking at sea, this expression referred to an empty bottle. The story is told that William IV, when Duke of Clarence and lord high admiral, pointed at some empty bottles at an official dinner and said, "Take away those marines." A dignified and elderly major of marines rose from the table and said, "May I respectfully ask why your Royal Highness applies the name of the corps to which I have the honor to belong, to an empty bottle?" The duke, with that tact and characteristic grace that was his, retorted promptly, "I call them marines because they are good fellows who have done their duty and are ready to do it again." The pun also plays on the fact that in both there are no more "spirits."

DEAD RECKONING. A reckoning kept so as to give the theoretical position of a ship without the aid of objects on land, of sights, and so on. It consists of plotting on a chart the distance believed to have been covered, based on the measured speed and time elapsed, along each course steered.

In the seventeenth and early eighteenth centuries, this was always referred to as "deduced reckoning" or "deduced position." The old log books had a column for entering the "deduced position" but because of lack of space at the top of the column, it became a general custom to write "ded reckoning." Mariners referred to this by its shorter and abbreviated top-of-the-column form.

DERRICK. From the name of Thomas Derrick, a well-known hangman of the time of Queen Elizabeth. He was an ingenious fellow, who devised a spar with a topping lift and purchase for his gruesome work, instead of using the old-fashioned rope method. Derrick was the executioner of the Earl of Essex in 1601.

DEVIL TO PAY. "The devil to pay and only half a bucket of pitch" was the original expression. This is better understood when it is known that the "devil" was the longest and most difficult seam to "pay" (fill with oakum and tar) and was found near the garboard strake, accessible only by hanging from a boatswain's chair "**BETWEEN THE DEVIL AND THE DEEP BLUE SEA.**" "Pay" is from the French word *poix,* meaning "pitch": "to pay the seams" or "to pitch the seams." "The devil to pay" still means "trouble."

DINGHY or **DINGHEY.** An Indian word for a small boat, arising from the British East India Company's service. Also spelled "dinky."

DITTY BOX. The small box formerly carried by sailors, in which they kept letters, small souvenirs, toilet articles, and needles and thread. These articles were, before the use of the box, kept in a bag made of "Dittis" or "Manchester stuff"; hence a **DITTY BAG.** Possibly derived from the Saxon word *dite,* meaning "tidy."

DOCTRINE OF THE LAST FAIR CHANCE. A doctrine of the law of the sea that provides and asserts that a person in authority (senior officer) shall, when a collision is imminent, do all that is possible to avert or lessen the damage of the disaster.

DOG HOUSE, TO BE (SLEEP) IN THE. The origin of the term is nautical, albeit from a dark side of our history. In the days of the slave trade, profit was driven by the numbers of captives who could be brought onboard. As a result they were crammed into every available space below decks, including the officers' cabins. The officers were then forced to sleep on deck in small half-cylindrical boxes about 30 inches high, which gained the nickname "dog house."

DUTCH COURAGE. This derogatory term, used by the English-speaking world, is of nautical origin. It is related that when Cornelius Van Tromp and de Ruyter were in command, Dutch sailors, before going into battle, were given a drink of the well-known "square-faced gin." The English, who were their enemy at the time, called this practice "Dutch courage."

DUTCHMAN'S BREECHES. Mariners look for that small patch of blue sky that denotes the breaking up of a gale. No matter how small the patch, it has been said to be "enough to make a pair of breeches for a Dutchman."

ENSIGN. Direct from old Norman *enseigne*. Anglo-Saxon *segne* meant "flag." *Signum* in Latin meant "sign." SIGNAL and INSIGNIA come from the same root word.

The Royal Navy borrowed the word from land service in the sixteenth century when the large flag was hoisted on the poop of sea vessels. One may read in *The Theorike and Pratike of Moderne Warres* (1598): "we Englishmen do call them [ensigns] of late 'colours' by reason of the variety of colours they may be made of, whereby they may be better noted and known to the companie."

Ensign bearer, shortened to ensign, was the rank, at an early date, of a young officer in the French Army and was afterward introduced into the French Navy as a naval rank. After the British in 1861 adopted the rank of sub-lieutenant to supplant the rank of mate, the U.S. Navy in 1862 adopted the rank of ensign. The rank existed in the American Revolutionary Army and today is used in the British Army for the color bearers. It is also used by some of the old, honorary state and city military organizations in the United States.

EPAULETTES. This ornament of uniform consisted originally of bunches of ribbon worn at the shoulder. Epaulettes were common in the French service long before they were introduced in the British Army. The Royal Navy first used them as an optional part of the dress, although no uniforms were standardized. In time, British officers in France were not recognized as commissioned officers without them. When Nelson met Captains Ball and Shephard in France, he noted that "[t]hey wore fine epaulettes, for which I think them coxcombs. They have not visited me, and I shall not count their acquaintance." Epaulettes were colloquially dubbed "swabs."

In the War of 1812, American naval officers wore epaulettes. Commodores then had a uniform the same as captains, except that a silver star was worn on each epaulette. Master commandants and lieutenants wore the same dress as the captain, except that only one epaulette was worn on the right shoulder, no button on the collar, and no lace around the pocket flaps. Neither peaked hats nor fancy epaulettes have been authorized in the U.S. Navy since just before U.S. entry into World War II. Now the shoulder loops that are a part of some shirts and jackets are called epaulettes.

EXECUTIVE OFFICER. The second in command of ships of the U.S. Navy. Originally, the senior lieutenant, as the captain's next in command, was the first lieutenant. Whence comes the Royal Navy's traditional term "Number One," although even the Royal Navy is using the "XO" abbreviation more and more. Another term sometimes used, especially by RN enlisted personnel, is "Jimmy."

Capt. W. T. Truxtun in 1881 noted:

> The title of executive officer is of quite recent date and has been the cause of much discussion, bad temper, and bitter opposition. It has grown from the ashes of the old first lieutenant and finds its parallel in the Army adjutant, and in all corporations or factories employing large bodies of men, in the name of superintendent or manager. The executive officer holds by far the most onerous, most difficult, and most thankless office on board ship.... He is held responsible for the cleanliness of the ship, her good order, neat and man-of-war–like appearance, and above all, he is to do as he is told by his captain, to promulgate and execute his orders; and, last of all his duties, never to go ashore except on the sheet anchor.

EYES OF THE SHIP. Most early ships had heads of mythological monsters or patrons carved in the bow; the terms *figurehead, the head,* and *eyes of the ship* all referred to the eyes of the figures placed there. Large "eyes" are still painted on bows of Chinese junks.

Figurehead of USS *Delaware.* The statue, known as "Tecumseh," is actually Tamanend, chief of the Delaware Indians, and is a Naval Academy landmark. Naval Institute Photo Archive

FATHOM. From Anglo-Saxon *faehom,* Dutch *vadem,* Latin *patene,* referring to the act of stretching two arms wide as rough measurement of 6 feet.

FIGUREHEAD. It is not known when the custom of placing figures and images over the prow and cutwater, and between the "eyes of the ship," began. The ancient Phoenicians, Egyptians, Greeks, Carthaginians, and Romans, as well as the Norsemen, placed images of animals, renowned leaders, and deities over the prows of their war vessels with the intent to propitiate the gods of storms. The early Greeks named their vessels of war after goddesses and had an image of the goddess aboard. Spanish galleons in the sixteenth century carried images of patron saints of ships. On the sterns of ships of the Middle Ages scrolls were often carved with the words *Dieu Conduit* ("God leads").

The *Constitution,* "Old Ironsides," originally had a figurehead of Hercules. Later Andrew Jackson's figure in wood was placed there, but the head was sawed off clandestinely by a Navy yard clique of opposite politics. The *Constitution* later carried a carved scroll.

One of the most famous figureheads in America is that of the one-time

**Admiral's flag broken on board USS *Baltimore*
(SSN 704)**

chief of the Delaware Indians, Tamanend. Before it was installed at the U.S. Naval Academy, this stern image of an Indian chief once adorned the USS *Delaware.* Generations of midshipmen have referred to it as "Tecumseh." For many years it stood exposed and unprotected from the elements in front of the midshipman dormitory. In order to preserve this historic relic of sail and reminder of cherished tradition, the Naval Academy Class of 1891 donated the amount necessary to cast a duplicate in bronze and with suitable ceremony preserved the "patron saint" of midshipmen, "the god of 2.5" (then the lowest passing mark, now 2.0). The original, minus its heart and an arrow or two, which were transplanted into the replica, is now preserved by the Naval Academy museum.

Figureheads, in some cases, and shields on the majority of ships, were worn as late as 1909. They were both removed before the new instructions for painting ships, effective late in 1908. White hulls were then changed to the dove-gray color we know today.

FLAG OFFICER. A "flag officer" is an officer of the Navy above the grade of captain, so called because he or she is eligible to fly a personal flag of rank. In the U.S. Navy flag officers consist of rear admiral, vice admiral, admiral, and fleet admiral. The president of the United States appoints vice admirals and admirals by letter.

The U.S. Navy had flag officers before the square flag was flown and before the grade of admiral was created by Congress. On 16 January 1857, an act of Congress directed that "captains in command of squadrons" should be denominated "flag officers." The square flag was not prescribed at the time.

The following order is of interest in that it is a forerunner of the rank of admiral and prescribed the flag. (See also ADMIRAL.)

> Navy Department, May 18, 1858.
>
> It is hereby ordered that in lieu of the broad pennant now worn by "flag officers" in command of squadrons, they shall wear a plain blue flag of dimensions proportionate to the different classes of vessels prescribed for the jack in the table of allowances approved July 20, 1854.
>
> Flag officers whose date of commission as captain is over twenty years shall wear it at the fore; all others at the mizzen.
>
> Isaac Toucey, Secretary of the Navy

Adm. George H. Preble wrote: "This order introduced the flags of vice and rear admirals into our Navy, although the title was considered too aristocratic for republican ears at the time."

FLEET. From Anglo-Saxon *floet, floetan;* Old Spanish *flota;* hence, *flotilla.*

FLOGGING. Man's brutality for his fellow man at sea reached shocking heights in the practices of flogging and, in particular, "flogging around the fleet." A British officer in the early nineteenth century who had charge of the launch gives a long, detailed account of a "five hundred lash" sentence around the fleet:

> Two hundred lashes had now been inflicted with a cat-o'-nine-tails, or eighteen hundred strokes with a cord of the thickness of a quill. The flesh from the nape of the neck to below the shoulder blades was one deep purple mass from which the blood oozed slowly. At every stroke a low groan escaped, and the flesh quivered with a sort of convulsive twitch; the eyes were closed, and the poor man began to faint. Water was administered, and pungent salts applied to his nostrils, which presently revived him in slight degree.

Five weeks after this the man was lashed again, "then every blow brought away morsels of skin and flesh." Then there was a two years' prison term, "where he fell into consumption and ended his days" (Clark, *Battles of England*).

The last official flogging in the British Navy was in 1882, but the order in council removing authority to award corporal punishment was not made until 1949.

A flogging entry from the log of the USS *Constitution* reads:

May 10 (1834). At 6:30 P.M. punished at the gangway with one dozen of "the cats," Thomas Frazier and Thomas Webb, also Peter Hudson six, with "the cats."

The quarterly report of punishments of the USS *Columbus* reports twenty-nine men flogged from 28 May to 27 June 1846. Entries include "James Johnson . . . Ordinary Seaman . . . Knocking down master at arms . . . twelve lashes with cats" and "Thomas Childs . . . Landsman . . . Fighting . . . twelve lashes with boy's cats." (The cat-o'-nine-tails varied in size from the "king size" to "boy's cats.")

In 1850 Sen. John P. Hale of New Hampshire, a liberal and champion of the underdog, added an antiflogging clause to the Naval Appropriation Bill. Commodore Uriah P. Levy was instrumental in interesting Senator Hale in the measure.

In 1851–53, Commodore R. F. Stockton, a senator from California, further restricted flogging by legislation, and on 17 July 1862 Congress abolished the practice.

The Navy Department reported that "it would be utterly impracticable to have an efficient Navy without this form of punishment" and noted that the "colt" (a single whip) was in most instances used instead of the "cat-o'-nine-tails." Senator Hale showed where a seaman had been sentenced by court-martial "to receive 500 lashes, and actually received 400." This punishment was given in twelve-lash installments.

Many sailors as well as writers had long advocated reform in punishment. But paradoxical as it may seem, groups of sailors presented memorials to Congress requesting no change in the system, stating that without drastic punishment the good men would have to do the work of the shirkers. After the act was passed, Secretary of the Navy Gideon Welles reported on 4 December 1862 that it was impossible to reenlist the better class of seamen. The sober, hard-working men considered that they had been performing duties of the shirkers and the indolent. This led to a change in the enlistment system and the training of the Navy.

FORECASTLE, FOCSLE. In the twelfth century, castles to fight from, similar to those towers of wood used ashore, were placed forward and aft on the Norman ships. The word *forecastle* survived from this practice.

FOULED ANCHOR. An anchor that is foul of the cable or chain. The symbol is found in various Admiralty and Navy crests. This device is also on the cap badge of the American naval officer, the device of a chief petty officer, the rank of some midshipmen, and the buttons and cap badges of the British officer. Although artistic to the landsman, many sailors regard it as an emblem of careless and poor seamanship, and it was sometimes called the "sailor's disgrace." It was the badge of Lord Howard of Effingham in 1601, when he was lord high admiral, and was used first in this connection as a naval seal. As a badge, it had been in use before this time.

FRIGATE. *Frigata* originally designated a class of Mediterranean vessels that used both oars and sails. The French were the first to use frigates on the ocean for war or commerce.

Theodore Roosevelt wrote in *The Naval War of 1812*: "Towards the end of the eighteenth century the terms frigate and line-of-battle ship had crystallized. Frigate then meant a so-called single-decked ship; it in reality possessed two decks, the main, or gun-deck, and the upper one, which had no name at all until our sailors christened it spar-deck. The gun-deck presented a complete battery, and the spar-deck an interrupted one, mounting guns on the forecastle and quarterdeck." In the two victories of the *Constitution*, her broadside was fifteen long 24s on the main deck, and one long 24 on the spar deck. Also ten or eleven 32-pound carronades. The broadside was 704 or 736 pounds. A few days before her action with the *Guerriere*, the *Constitution* had a muster roll of 464 names (including 51 marines). Roosevelt wrote: "Our three 44-gun ships [*Constitution, President,* and *United States*] were the finest frigates then afloat."

FURL. Probably from the Old English *furdle,* corruption of *fardle,* meaning "to make up a bundle."

FUTTOCK SHROUDS. Lines in the rigging of square-rigged ships, which gave sailors a place to stand while working on or with the sails. Futtock is a contracted term for "foot hooks," for the toes have to be hooked or bent around the ratlines to go over them.

GALE. From Old Norse *galem,* Danish *gal,* "mad or furious." In the seventeenth century, Butler wrote: "When the wind blows not too hard, so that the ship may bear out her topsail a-trip [that is, fully hoisted, no reefs] it is called a loon gale; when it blows much wind it is called a swift and strong gale, or at least a fresh gale.

He describes the conditions when no sail could be carried, and this was considered a degree higher than a storm. The force of wind in nautical miles per hour, with equivalent designations such as "calm," "light airs," "fresh breeze," "gale," and "full gale." is employed today for logging weather. The terms were originally devised by Admiral Beaufort, RN, and are known as the Beaufort Scale or Table.

GALLEY YARN. A "scuttle-butt rumor," a rumor. In the early days the cook was often the originator of much startling news passed on to the crew.

GANGWAY. From Anglo-Saxon *gang,* "to go"; to make a passage in, or cut out, or through.

GIG. The captain's boat. It is usually a light boat of whaler build with a gilded arrow on each bow. The gig is the pride of the deck force: the general appearance of the crew and the cleanliness and neatness of the boat are usually excellent indications of the condition of the ship. The 1815 edition of Falconer's *Dictionary of the Marine* calls it "a long narrow boat . . . generally rowing six to eight oars and is mostly the private property of the captain or commander."

GIG STROKE. When ships' boats were powered by oars, this was a rhythm used by the single-banked crew of gigs, requiring a distinct pause after each stroke of the oars.

GLASS. A term employed nautically to refer to such articles of the mariner's craft as barometers, telescopes, and time glasses. HOW'S THE GLASS? means, "What is the barometer doing?" To FLOG (SWEAT) THE GLASS was a nefarious practice of olden days, whereby the time glass was agitated to make the sand flow faster, and the watch pass more quickly. To CLEAR THE GLASS was used in reference to the heaving of the chip log and signified clearing all sand out of one end of the glass before heaving the log. To COOK THE GLASS meant to heat either a time glass or a telescope in order to remove moisture.

GOB. His Excellency, Hu-Shih, Chinese ambassador to the United States, said in an interview in November 1941: "I believe that the word 'Gob,' as meaning a sailor of the United States Navy, is most probably an abbreviation of the Chinese transcription of the Spanish word 'Captain,' pronounced 'kia-pi-tan' in Pekingese ('Mandarin'), but which the people in Canton and Hong Kong pronounce 'gob-bid-dan.'" The term was applied, certainly as long ago as the early 1900s, if not before, to captains of foreign ships and, loosely, to all foreign sailors on their ships in the ports of South China or ashore. The longer word was later shortened to the first syllable. The ambassador proceeded to state his opinion that the continued use of the word *gob*, as now applied only to sailors of the U.S. Navy, was essentially complimentary rather than either "unworthy" or "undignified."

GONE WEST. An expression dating back to the Norsemen. When a Viking chief died, his body was placed in a special bier aboard a Viking war boat, the steering oar was lashed, and the sails set with the intent that the body would sail on toward the setting sun. Chiefs were occasionally buried in their boats.

GRAPE. Small iron balls an inch or so in diameter bound together in clusters and fired as antipersonnel or antirigging shot from smooth-bore cannons of old. This type of ammunition played an effective part in our early frigate actions.

GROG. A sailor's expression for watered rum. Adm. Edward Vernon, Esq., RN, vice admiral of the blue and commander in chief of H.M. ships and vessels in the West Indies, in 1740 ordered "that the rum be watered." It was Vernon's custom to wear a boat cloak of a coarse material, called "grogram." His nickname was "Old Grog," and was in turn applied to the beverage.

> Whereas it manifestly appears by the return made to my general order of 4th August, to be the unanimous opinion of both Captains and Surgeons that the pernicious custom of the seamen drinking their allowance of rum in drams, and often at once, is attended with many fatal effects on their morals as well as their health, which are visibly impaired thereby, and many of their lives shortened by it, besides the ill consequences arising from stupefying their rational qualities which makes them heedless slaves to every brutish passion, and which cannot be better remedied than by the ordering their half pint of rum to be daily mixed with a quart of water: which they that are good husbandmen may from the savings of their salt provisions and bread, purchase sugar and limes to make more palatable to them.
>
> Sailors of long ago sang:
>
>> For grog is our starboard, our larboard,
>> Our mainmast, our mizen, our log—
>> At sea, or ashore, or when harbour'd,
>> The mariner's compass is grog.

Very early the United States pursued the "Buy American" policy. The secretary of the Navy in 1806 wrote:

> Being persuaded that whiskey is a more wholesome drink as well as a much more economical one, I am anxious to introduce the use of it into our Navy generally; but this cannot be immediately effected. I have therefore made experiment to introduce it, and the result has satisfied me that in time the Sailors will become perfectly reconciled to it, and probably prefer it to Spirit [rum]. Our annual consumption of Spirit is about 45,000 gallons.

The legislation that led to the abolition of grog in the Navy is of some historic interest. The spirit ration when abolished consisted of "two dips" a day and in lieu thereof a commutation of five cents per day.

Gustavus V. Fox, assistant secretary of the Navy, in 1862 wrote to Sen. J. W. Grimes: "I beg of you for the enduring good of the service . . . to add a proviso abolishing the spirit ration." Senator Grimes championed the bill that abolished a spirit or rum ration aboard U.S. men-of-war.

> On September 1, 1862, the spirit ration shall forever cease and thereafter no distilled spirituous liquor shall be admitted on board vessels of war, except as medicine and upon the order and under the control of the medical officer of such vessel and to be used only for medical purposes. (U.S. Stat., XII, 565)

On 23 May 1872 Congress made provision for a liberal issue of coffee and prescribed its use: "an additional ration of coffee and sugar to be served at his [the seaman's] first turning out."

General Order 99, of 1 June 1914, signed by Secretary of the Navy Josephus Daniels, prohibited "the use or introduction for drinking purposes of alcoholic liquors on board any naval vessel, or within any navy yard or station." By necessity, coffee became the substitute for the daily ration of grog, and began to be referred to as JOE or A CUPPA JOE in memory of Secretary Daniels.

GUESS OR GUEST WARP ROPES. A rope carried to a distant object in order to warp a vessel toward it, or to make fast a boat. HAUL OUT also meant to haul out in its literal sense. A ship's boat would come alongside, the crew would be ordered aboard, and the boat would be made fast while alongside to a guess warp and "hauled out."*

---

* W. H. Smyth, *The Sailor's Word Book: An Alphabetical Digest of Nautical Terms* (London: Blackie and Sons, 1867), p. 354.

GUN, SON OF A. In the early days, sailors were permitted to keep their "wives" on board. Lord Exmouth, after the bombardment of Algiers in July 1816, reported that "even British women served at the same guns as their husbands, and during a contest of many hours, never shrank from danger but animated all around them."

The Admiralty issued an order in 1830 prohibiting officers' wives to be carried in men-of-war, but the order was frequently evaded. The term was actually used to refer to children born alongside the guns of the broadsides. In a larger sense, the expression questioned the legitimacy of anyone.

An old definition of a man-o'-war's man was: "Begotten in the galley and born under a gun. Every hair a rope yarn, every tooth a marline spike; every finger a fish hook and in his blood, right good Stockholm tar."

A British officer commanding a brig off the Spanish coast in 1835 wrote in his diary: "This day the surgeon informed me that a woman on board had been laboring in child for twelve hours, and if I could see my way to permit the firing of a broadside to leeward, nature would be assisted by the shock. I complied with the request and she was delivered of a fine male child. The Gunnery Department made a perfect score!"

GUNNERY. Although China had powder long before its invention in Europe, the year 1330 is given as the date of the Western discovery of gunpowder. Powder-burning guns, breech-loading and discharging a stone projectile, were reported in England in 1338. The Spaniards were armed with cannon in a sea fight against the English and the people of Poitou, off La Rochelle in 1392. This is the first naval battle wherein mention is made of artillery. In 1824 Blunt, in his *Theory and Practice of Seamanship*, writes in regard to gunnery:

> The machines, which owe their rise to the invention of gunpowder, have now totally supplanted the others; so that there is scarcely any but the sword remaining of all the weapons used by the ancients. Our naval battles are therefore almost always decided by fire arms, of which there are several kinds, known by the general name of artillery. In a ship of war, fire arms are distinguished in the cannon mounted upon carriages, swivel cannon, grenades, and musketry. Besides these machines, there are several others used in merchant ships and privateers, as cohoms, carabines, fire arrows, organs, stink-pots, etc.

In the British *Naval Regulations* (1790) the following may be found under "The Gunner":

Also every gunner ought to know that it is a wholesome thing for him to eat and drink a little meat before he doth discharge any piece of artillery, because the fume of saltpetre and brimstone will otherwise be hurtful to his brain, so it is very unwholesome to him to shoot in any piece of ordnance while his stomach is full.

Herman Melville, writing of the quarter gunners and gunners' mates, refers to them as "a class full of unaccountable whimsies. They were continually grumbling and growling about the batteries; running in and out among the guns; driving the sailors away from them, and cursing and swearing as if all their consciences had been powder singed and made callous by their calling."

GUNWALE (GUNNEL). *Wale* comes from Anglo-Saxon *wala,* "a weal, a strip, a ridge." The term is first recorded in English in 1330. It is derived from the custom of firing the top row of guns over planking which had been reinforced by "wales"; hence "gunwales."

HAMMOCKS. In 1498 in the Bahamas, Christopher Columbus found that the natives used woven cotton nets as beds, called "hammacs." The Spanish changed the word to *hamaco.* The Spanish spelling was used when the word entered the English nautical vocabulary in the Elizabethan era. In 1596 hammocks are officially mentioned as hanging "cabbons" or "beddes." After an action, as many sails as possible were expended to provide new hammocks and white trousers for the crew. Bradford writes: "Hammocks were first issued in 1629 to British ships on foreign stations. Each hammock was shared by two men; one man was always on watch."

HAND, LEND (BEAR) A. Long usage has decreed that "lend a hand" is a request for assistance, while "bear a hand" implies an order, and especially, an order to hurry.

HANDSOMELY. A term meaning "slowly and carefully," as in carrying out a command.

HARTER ACT. By this law, a ship owner is protected against claims for damage incurred through the acts of the ship's officers or crew, provided the ship was seaworthy and was fully equipped and manned on leaving port.

HARVEST MOON. Bradford writes in his *Glossary:* "The phenomenon in high latitudes of several moonlight nights at the full moon nearest the autumnal equinox in which that body rises nearly at the same time. The moon ordinarily rises later each night by an average of 51 minutes, but at this time it is coming northward very rapidly in declination, causing an earlier rising which almost overcomes the natural retardation due to its eastward movement of revolution."

HAUL. Literally "to pull or to drag." The wind "hauls" when it changes in direction with the sun. When a ship's course is so changed that her head lies nearer the wind, she is "hauled up." "To haul off" is to remove to a greater distance.

HAWSE PIPES. Hawse is an old name for "throat," and since the head was forward as well as the "eyes," the term *throat pipe* or *hawse pipe* came into being. The "pipe" is the opening through which the anchor chain runs. Enlisted men who became officers were often said to have COME THROUGH THE HAWSE, meaning that they had once worked forward or on the forecastle.

HAWSER. From French *hausser,* "to hoist." In the early eighteenth century and before, cables made of hemp, bass, or Indian grass were used for the anchors. The change from hemp to chain cables came in 1812. Hemp cables for a 1,000-ton ship were 8 inches in diameter and usually 120 fathoms long. The friction of the cable through the hawse was enormous; tar on the surface of the hemp often took fire and men stood by with buckets of water.

HEAD. A term for restrooms aboard ship. Its usage derives from the fact that in the old square-rigged sailing ships, the wind was almost always from astern, therefore in order not to relieve oneself "into the wind," a sailor needed to go to the "head."

HOLYSTONES. So named because fragments of broken monuments from Saint Nicholas Church, Great Yarmouth, England, were used at one time to scrub the wooden decks of ships of the Royal Navy. In the British service, holystones were also called "ecclesiastical bricks." The name is now used for bricks, sand stones, or medium-soft sand rock used for the scrubbing of wooden decks. They were moved fore and aft on the wet decks by means of a wooden handle placed in a depression or hole in the stone (another meaning for "holystone"). Small holystones were called "prayer books"; larger ones were called "Bibles." Holystones were of sufficient importance that the secretary of the Navy provided, in an order of 5 March 1931, that "the use of holystones for cleaning the wooden decks of naval vessels wears down the decks so rapidly that their repair or replacement has become an item of expense to the Navy Department which cannot be met under limited appropriations. . . . It is therefore directed that the use of holystones or similar material for cleaning wooden decks be restricted to the removal of stains."

HORSE LATITUDES. A belt of light and variable winds between the "westerlies" and the "trade winds" in the Northern and Southern Hemispheres where sailing vessels were often becalmed for some time. The name had its origins in the mid–nineteenth century, when numerous horses were transported from Europe to the Americas. The belt in the North Atlantic was often studded with the carcasses of horses that died during such times.

HOW'S THE ANCHOR. "How's the anchor?" (not "hawse the anchor" or "house the anchor") is a request for information from the focsle as to the direction and strain on the anchor chain.

IDLERS. Falconer's *Marine Dictionary* (1815) defines "idlers" as "all those on board a ship of war, who from being liable to constant day duty are not subjected to keep night watch, but nevertheless must go up on deck if all hands are called during the night." The term today includes sickbay attendants, cooks, yeomen, and so forth.

IT IS AN ILL WIND THAT BLOWS NO MAN GOOD. This very old expression came directly from the sea and is derived from the fact that under sail, every wind is a fair wind for some ship.

JACK OF THE DUST. A galley worker.

JAMAICA DISCIPLINE. A name for the "Articles for the Government of Pirate Ships," in the eighteenth century. The articles stipulated that the captain took two shares of all stolen booty, the officers one and one-half and one and one-quarter depending upon rank, while all the crew shared alike. In order to prevent quarrels and brawls aboard ship, gambling and the bringing of women aboard ship were prohibited. Indulgence in strong drink could take place only on deck after eight P.M.

JAVA, JAMOKE. Terms used by bluejackets of the U.S. Navy to designate coffee. The U.S. Navy uses more coffee per person than any other military or naval organization in the world. In March 1954 the Bureau of Supplies and

Keelhauling. In this most cruel punishment, a gun was fired to add to the culprit's misery before he was hauled beneath the ship and brought aboard on the port side. *Heck's Iconographic Encyclopedia*

Accounts estimated the Navy used 50,668 pounds of coffee a day. (See also GROG.)

KEELHAULING. Today, a calldown or reprimand; to be called "on the carpet." In the early days this term signified one of the most drastic and cruel forms of punishment. The victim was hoisted by a whip or light tackle to a fore yardarm and thence dropped into the sea. A weight was attached to the unfortunate to ensure that he would sink deep enough for a whip to drag him under the keel and up again to the opposite yardarm on the other side. There is record that this was originally a punishment in vogue among the pirates of the Mediterranean in the sixteenth century, and that it was afterward introduced into the English and Dutch navies.

Boteler describes this punishment in a book called *Dialogical Discourse on Marine Affairs,* written probably about 1630, but published in 1685, and dedicated to Samuel Pepys:

> The duckinge at the marine yarde arme is when a malefactor by haveing a rope fastened under his arms and about his middle and under his breech

is thus hoysted up to the end of the yarde from whence he is againe violently let fall into the sea, sometimes twice, sometimes three, severall tymes, one after the other, and if the offense be very fowle, he is also drawn under the very keele of the shippe, the which is called, keele-rakinge, and whilst he is thus under water a great gunne is given fyre unto, right over his head, ye which is done as well to astonish him the more with thunder thereof, which much troubles him, as to give warninge unto all others to looke out and beware of his harms.

Keelhauling, flogging, tongue-scraping, and gagging were common practices as early as the sixteenth century. It was in 1645 that ship court-martial was instituted and written records of all punishments kept in the Royal Navy.

TO KEEL OVER. When a vessel's keel is showing, it has been knocked well over. Therefore, someone who has keeled over has been knocked, or has fallen, down.

KNOCK OFF. As in "Knock off ship's work." From the days of slave-driven galleys whose crews could stop work only when the man who knocked the rowing tempo on a wooden block or drum stopped.

KNOTS. The maritime unit of speed. The term stems from the old method of measurement involving the use of a line run over the side with knots tied in it. It is not short for "nautical miles per hour," but its units are such. Therefore, it is correct to give a ship's speed in "knots," but absolutely not in "knots per hour." Capt. Gershom Bradford described in detail the old method of computing:

The **CHIP LOG** is a device now restricted to a few sailing vessels. It consists of a wooden quadrant about 5 inches in radius, with lead placed in the circular edge, which causes it to float upright. It is made fast to a log line by a three-part bridle. The part fitted to the upper corner has a socket and a pin which pulls out when a strain is placed upon it with the desire to haul it aboard. The chip is cast over (streamed) with the pin in position. The first 15 or 30 fathoms of line is called the stray line which is marked by a piece of red bunting. The line from this point is divided into parts of 47 feet 3 inches, each called a knot. They are marked by pieces of cord rocked through the strands with knots in their ends corresponding to the number of knots out. Each knot is subdivided into fifths and marked with a white rag. The log line is allowed to run out while a 28-second glass is emptying itself. The result is the rate of speed of the vessel. The length of the knot was derived from the proportion that one hour (3,600 sec.) is to 28 seconds as one mile (6,080 ft.) is to the length of a knot (47 ft, 3 in.). The clipper ship *Flying Cloud* off Cape Horn once ran out 18 knots and there was still a little sand in the glass.

LANGRIDGE. Knife blades, old nails, copper slugs, iron bolts, and scraps of metal in cans. Used in cannon at the time of the War of Independence and War of 1812. Bayonet blades bound with rope yarn were shot from cannon for the purpose of cutting rigging in order to effect the fall of masts. There were also shells of that time known as starshots, chain shots, "sausages," double headers, "porcupines," and "hedgehogs." (See also GRAPE.)

LARBOARD. The "load board" was the left side of the ship, in distinction to the right side of a ship where the steering gear was carried, known as "steer board." Larboard was confused with starboard, and hence the term *port* or loading entrance was adopted. The expression "steer board" may be traced to the Vikings. Viking ships have been found in a remarkable state of preservation, with the remains of chieftains buried within them. From these ships the arrangement for steering on the right or starboard quarter may be observed in detail. The Gokstadt ship, discovered in 1880, was built of oak and was 72 feet long and 15 feet, 6 inches beam, and had a displacement of about 30 tons. The quarter rudder was used by the Vikings in the ninth century, but about the twelfth century a second rudder was placed on the larboard side. Eventually the stern rudder replaced the two quarter rudders. (See also PORT.)

LASHING BROOM TO FORE TOPMAST. A broom at the masthead once indicated that a ship was for sale.

The Dutch Admiral Tromp supposedly ordered that brooms be lashed to the masts when he sailed to meet the fleet of Cromwell under Blake, signifying that he would sweep the English Channel of the English Navy. During World War II American submarines were known to return to port with a broom lashed to the periscope, indicating a "clean sweep" of the seas with their load-out of torpedoes. (See also COMMISSIONING PENNANT.)

Christmas trees have been hoisted at the trucks of U.S. ships during the holiday season, and the tips of yards have also been decorated with evergreens.

LAY TO THE . . . A command for an individual to report to a given location immediately. Generally used only in case of emergency.

LEEWAY. In modern parlance, to have room. Comes from having room to maneuver to the lee, or downwind side.

LIEUTENANT. A word derived from the French, meaning "holding in place of" or "one who replaces." The Royal Navy introduced this rank in 1580 to provide the captain with an assistant and qualified relief if necessary. The first lieutenant was for years, both in the British and American services, the executive officer of the ship. In smaller British ships particularly, the title first lieutenant still obtains, and this officer is referred to unofficially as Number One.

The following rule was in effect during the latter part of the reign of Elizabeth I: "The lieutenant must have a care that he carry not himself proudly or presumptuously, nor that his captain give him power or authority to intermeddle with the master's office; for where there is heart burning between the lieutenant and master, it will make it burst out into open discontent and then will follow mischief and factions among the company."

LIEUTENANT COMMANDER. Derived from "Lieutenant, Commanding," this title was introduced in the U.S. Navy in 1862 with the reorganization of the service. Up to this time, all lieutenants in command of smaller men-of-war had been called "lieutenants, commanding." For example, in the roster of the North Atlantic Blockading Squadron in 1862, one reads: "(USS) Valley City, Lieut. Commanding S. C. Chaplin, bearing the flag of Flag Officer Goldsborough; also (USS) Commander Perry, Lieutenant Commanding C. W. Flusser."

LIMEY. A friendly name that through the years has been used by American bluejackets in referring to British naval and merchant sailors in particular and to the British in general. It was derived from the old practice in the Royal Navy of giving lime juice to prevent scurvy. Lime or lemon juice was issued from the time of the early French wars until the twentieth century. "Lemon juice," wrote Surgeon A. Farenholt, USN, in the U.S. Naval Institute *Proceedings*, "as an antiscorbutic was first carried to sea by Captain Lancaster, in an expedition sailing from England for the East Indies in January 1600. Three ounces were given daily to each man. When Cape Town was reached, Captain Lancaster's ship, the *Dragon*, alone was free of scurvy, and his ship's crew hoisted out the boats of the entire squadron and landed the sick, 105 of whom died there."

Until 1860 this antiscorbutic was obtained from Malta and Sicily; in fact, it was the juice of the lemon, then called a lime. Medical authorities of the time considered the acid quality of citron fruit an excellent means of combating scurvy. Due to the expense and difficulty of getting lime juice from the Mediterranean area, the British authorities commenced after 1860 to secure lime juice from St. Kitts in the West Indies. Scurvy cropped up again in the Royal Navy during World War I, and a committee of experts was convened to study the question. They found that certain vitamins played the most important part and that lime juice contains a negligible percentage of those vitamins, while lemon juice had a large percentage. The acid quality had little or nothing to do with the prevention of scurvy.

Scurvy, that dread disease of sailors, has been practically eliminated by short voyages and modern refrigeration, but the old word *limey* lives on. While the Royal Navy no longer issues lime juice, in hot climates it still from time to time issues a lime-based drink called "limers." It is very refreshing, but has nothing to do with scurvy.

LISTLESS. Dull and lifeless. Comes from the days of sail when a good wind would heel the ship over as it ran. When there was no wind to give it the get up and go, the ship would ride without list, or "listless."

LOGGERHEAD. The word was derived from logger-heat, a piece of iron on a long handle used for melting pitch. The iron after heating was placed in the cold pitch. It was a deadly weapon when men "came to loggerheads."

LONGSHOREMAN. A man who works "along the shore," loading and unloading ships' cargoes.

LONG SHOT. Named from the days of muzzle-loading, nonrifled cannon that were accurate only at close range. A hit at long range was lucky at best and became known as a long shot. Similarly, a SHOT IN THE DARK was at best a guess as to target location.

LUCKY BAG. Now, a small compartment or large locker where masters-at-arms stow articles of clothing, bedding, and so forth, picked up on the decks. Originally, these articles were placed in a bag called the "lucky bag," which was in the custody of the master-at-arms. In a narrative of a cruise in the USS *Columbia* in 1838, the writer relates that the bag was brought to the mainmast once a month, and the owners of the articles "if their names are on them, get them again, with a few lashes for their carelessness in leaving them about the deck." The term *lucky* in this case is sailor's humor for "unfortunate."

MARK YOUR HELM. A command to the helmsman to call out the compass heading indicated at that moment. It can be either a request for information or, more often, a reminder to the helmsman to stay alert. A more pointed reminder would be "**MIND YOUR HELM.**"

MARTINET. A stickler for discipline, a "sundowner." The name comes from a French army officer, the Marquis de Martinet. A cat-o'-nine-tails is still called in French nautical slang a "martinet."

MASTER. Also **SAILING MASTER.** Six things required of a master in the Elizabethan age were "the cards (charts), the compass, the tides, the time, the wind, and the ship's way."

This was the title for a warrant (warranted) officer as early as 1798. In the *Regulations of the United States Navy*, issued by command of the president, 25 January 1802, some duties required of the sailing master were "[t]o inspect the provisions and stores.... To take care of the ballast.... To give directions for stowing the hold and spirit-room. Trimming the ship, and preservation of the provisions; to take special care of the rigging; to navigate the ship and see that the log and log book are duly kept."

In 1813 there were 162 sailing masters on the list of the Navy. George Farragut, father of the admiral, was on this list. The title was changed to master in 1839. In 1846 the term "masters in the line of promotion" was used to identify certain passed midshipmen to fill the vacancies by death of the old-time masters. In 1861 there were thirty-six of the grade on the active list. In 1862, on the reorganization of the Navy, they were all merged into the grades. Then master became a commissioned grade between lieutenant and ensign, with the duties of a watch officer.

MASTER-AT-ARMS. Now the Navy's shipboard police. The master-at-arms evolved from the sea corporal and was introduced into the Royal Navy during the reign of Charles I. The master-at-arms's department included all the muskets, carbines, pistols, and swords, and he exercised the ship's company, seeing that their bandoliers were filled with good powder before going into action. In the days of the *Constitution* and other early ships, there is record of drill under arms for the seamen by direction of the master-at-arms. He not only had police duties and was "chief of police," but was supposed to be qualified in close-order fighting under arms.

MATE. A rank in the old Navy. The mate, although an officer, was not in the line of promotion and held his position by appointment. He usually messed in the steerage or with the warrant officers and was ordered to duty in charge of boats, mate of the deck, or any special duty prescribed by the commanding officer. This term must not be confused with boatswain's mate, gunner's mate, and so forth. Originally, the mate was known as "master's mate," but later the rank was downgraded.

MAYDAY. The voice radio signal for distress or emergency. It stems from the French *M'aidez* or "Help Me."

MEET HER. A command to the helm meaning that the helmsman should stop the swing of the ship at the time of the command. Normally given when the ship is in a turn and the OOD wants to simply stop his turn.

MESS. Middle English *mes* meant a dish; hence the phrase "a mess of pottage." The word in English originally denoted four, and at large dinners the diners were seated in fours. Shakespeare wrote of Henry's four sons as his "mess of sons" (*Henry VI, Part II*, Act. 1). The word *mess*, meaning "confusion," is from the German *mischen*, meaning "to mix."

MESSMATES. Those eating together, comrades. "Messmate before shipmate, shipmate before stranger, stranger before a dog."*

MIDSHIPMAN. Men or boys were originally stationed amidships to carry messages, to bring up ammunition, and to relay messages from aft to the gundecks. In days of sail, midshipmen were also frequently called "reefers" because they were called upon as extra hands to reef sail in heavy weather. It was a ship's rating in the Royal Navy until the end of the Napoleonic wars. A midshipman could be disrated at any time by the captain.

In 1740 admirals and captains were permitted a certain number of followers; in some cases a flag officer was permitted fifty. They were rated midshipmen, tailors, barbers, fiddlers, footmen, and stewards. It was in 1815 that midshipmen became a naval rank in the British service. The midshipman's time on the books counted toward promotion as a lieutenant, for two years of the six years' service required at sea had to be served as a midshipman or mate. Often midshipmen were entered on the books a year or so before actual service. It was a British personnel problem in 1755 how to bring up officers

* Smyth, *The Sailor's Word-Book*, p. 478.

The midshipman's berth
Naval Records and Library, Navy Department

and gentlemen who should be able seamen, skilled to manage a ship and maintain a sea fight judiciously, of discretion and courage, and able to speak to the seamen in their own language.

Until the advent of steam, the life of the midshipman was often most disagreeable. The food was bad, the quarters cramped and located below the waterline, and the duties onerous and manifold. Without the full status of an officer and still not a member of the crew, the midshipman occupied an indefinite position aboard ship until regulations became more specific. The *United States Naval Regulations* (1818) states: "The commanding officers will consider the midshipmen as a class of officers, meriting in an especial degree their fostering care." From all accounts this "fostering care" was capable of wide interpretation.

This apprenticeship for a commission is set forth in a realistic manner by Rear Adm. Baron Jeffrey de Raigersfeld in *The Life of a Sea Officer*. He notes that "in the latter part of the eighteenth century it was not uncommon for midshipmen to be flogged, mastheaded, and disrated, if not turned before the mast." Admiral de Raigersfeld writes of his midshipman days under Capt. (later admiral) Lord Collingwood:

On board the *Mediator* all these punishments were inflicted at various times; and one morning after breakfast, while at anchor in St. John's Road, Antigua, all the midshipmen were sent for into the captain's cabin, and four of us were tied up one after the other to the breech of one of the guns, and flogged upon our bare bottoms with a cat-o'-nine-tails, by the boatswain of the ship; some received six lashes, some seven, and myself three. No doubt we all deserved it, and were thankful that we were punished in the cabin instead of upon deck, which was not uncommon in other ships of the fleet.

Being bent over the breech of a gun for caning or flogging is known in British wardrooms as "KISSING THE GUNNER'S DAUGHTER," but as one British officer wrote, "no modern gun is well adapted for this purpose."

To classify a midshipman as an officer has always been subject to qualification. In today's Navy, midshipmen rank between the senior enlisted ranks and warrant officers. Although a midshipman is an officer in a very qualified sense, it will forever stand as a record that Samuel Barron was appointed and given a midshipman's warrant on 11 April 1812, at the age of three years and four months. He was "on duty" at half pay (midshipman's pay was nineteen dollars per month) and a few cents in place of his grog ration. At the age of eight, in 1816, he reported for active duty at the Norfolk Navy Yard, and went to sea in USS *Columbus* in 1820. *All Hands Magazine*, in January 1952, points out that the Barrons left a most distinguished record as a seagoing naval family. "The family tree shows one commodore and six other officers in the Virginia Navy during the Revolution, two commodores and a captain and many other officers in the U.S. Navy, and one commodore and other officers in the Confederate Navy. Of the twenty-seven male members of the family, twenty-one followed the sea. Nine of them were lost at sea. Through seven successive generations, Barrons served as officers in the armed forces holding continuous high command for 125 years."

Farragut was a midshipman at nine and one-half years of age, and Louis M. Goldsborough, who became a distinguished Civil War officer, received his warrant at the age of seven years and ten months. In the Royal Navy there is record of babies being entered on the rolls at age one. In most cases the captain collected all pay and allowances and the original five pounds of "bounty money."

As to the many duties of the "young gentlemen" (midshipmen were so referred to even before Nelson's time), the late Vice Admiral J. K. Taussig, USN, relates that he was ordered with another midshipman to heave the lead from the chains of the *Newark* upon her departure from New York City in

1899, notwithstanding that both of the young gentlemen were in dress uniform. Vice Admiral Taussig also relates that because of a mix-up in a salute from a British captain to an American rear admiral, his senior officer ordered him as a midshipman "to go aboard that British ship and make the British captain feel sorry for his mistake." It took courage, quick wits, and above all the spirit of youth to perform creditably the duties of a midshipman at sea.

The old title "PASSED MIDSHIPMAN" in the U.S. Navy meant originally a midshipman who had passed his examination, entitling him to promotion to a lieutenant. When the title of ensign was introduced into the U.S. Navy, those awaiting promotion were called midshipmen, while undergraduates were called cadet midshipmen. In 1819 a board, of which Commander Bainbridge was senior member, met in New York to give the first examinations that had ever been given midshipmen in our Navy for promotion. This, incidentally, was the first examination of any kind instituted for officers in the U.S. Navy.

With the introduction of women into the Naval Academy in 1976, the issue arose of whether to call them midshipwomen. It was decided that the term *midshipman* referred to a rank in the Navy, and therefore, the rank of midshipman (and its plural, midshipmen) would continue to be used.

Middy is a term disliked by midshipmen and used most frequently by elderly ladies, some landlocked writers of sea stories, and a few Annapolitans.

MOOR. From the Dutch word *marten,* "to tie, to fasten."

MUFTI. Civilian dress. This is actually a term adopted from the British Army's service in India. The word stems from the Indian term for civilian or normal clothes.

NAIL ONE'S COLORS TO THE MAST. If a ship's colors are nailed to the mast, they cannot be struck, and the ship cannot surrender. A person who has taken such a stand does not look back on a decision and will press ahead regardless of the outcome.

NOT ROOM TO SWING A CAT. A very old naval expression, meaning there was not enough room, particularly overhead, to swing a cat-o'-nine-tails.

OAR. Used by mankind at the dawn of history, but our word comes from the *ayr* of the Middle Ages.

OFFICER, OFFICIALS. The following interesting history was taken from a foreign service examination pamphlet issued by the Department of State:

> Historically, the employment of the word "officer" to denote a person holding a military or naval command as representative of the State, and not as deriving his authority from his own powers or privileges, marks an entire change in the character of the armed forces of civilized nations. Originally signifying an official, one who performs an assigned duty (Latin, *officium*), an agent, and in the fifteenth century actually meaning the subordinate of such an official (even today a constable is so called), the word seems to have acquired a military significance late in the sixteenth century.
>
> It was at this time that armies, though not yet "standing," came to be constituted almost exclusively of professional soldiers in the king's pay. Mercenaries, and great numbers of mercenaries, had always existed, and their captains were not feudal magnates. But the bond between mercenaries and their captains was entirely personal, and the bond between the captain and the sovereign was of the nature of a contract. The nonmercenary portion of the older armies was feudal in character. It was the lord and not a king's officer who commanded it, and he commanded in virtue of his rights, not of a warrant or commission.

At sea the relatively clear partition of actual duties among the authorities of a ship caused the term *officer* to be adopted somewhat earlier.

PASSING TO WINDWARD. Vessels were supposed to pass to leeward of their superiors. To do otherwise would "steal" the wind from the superior's sails and cause him to luff or lose way. This was strictly observed if the inferior happened to be a merchantman. For "if the opposite procedure took place, it is accounted as unmannerly a trick as if the constable of a parish should jostle for the wall with a justice of the peace dwelling in the same country."

Whether in men-of-war or merchantmen, the weather side was the traditional side at sea for the admiral and captain, the starboard side was the "sacred ground" when the ship was at anchor or moored. The port side was to the pier; therefore the starboard side was toward the sea and was the side where "he [the captain] can feel the wind and weather upon his cheek, can sniff the land, or sight the coming squall. It was once always customary for all weather gangways to be used by superiors."

Practically speaking, this windward advantage may have stemmed from times when showering and bathing was not only difficult but feared by the crew. Their odoriferous passage to leeward would have been distinctly more pleasant to the officer on deck.

PAYING YOUR FOOTING. The following anecdote gives the meaning of this old expression. Captain's Clerk E. G. Wines, USN, who served in USS *Constellation* in 1829–31, wrote:

> On the twenty-first of August [1819] I went for the first time to the main top-gallant masthead—to me a dizzy height. . . . The old tars laughed heartily at my timidity. I asked them if they were never afraid. "Afraid!" they replied, "what good would it do to be afraid? Mr. Wines, have you never been in a top before?" . . . "No." "Then you must pay for your footing" was the next thing. Paying for your footing is treating all hands to a glass of grog on your first visit to a top. This they never fail to demand, always promising in return, to teach you all they know themselves about the rigging of the ship. At first I offered them money. "Oh," said they, "give us the grog, what good will money do us here?" I then told them I would pay my footing in their own way, if they would get permission from the first lieutenant. I thought this would stagger them, but was mistaken. "Pooh! Pooh!" they replied, "never mind the first lieutenant, send it up by a boy and call it water." More than two years afterwards, I asked the captain of the top if I didn't owe him a glass of grog. "Yes, Sir, I believe you do, Sir. Why, Sir, I believe it's to pay your footing in the main top, Sir."

PAYMASTER (PURSER). Records of the fourteenth century show "clerks" or "bursers" in English ships. In the early days their pay came from profit in the sale of supplies, which sometimes led to the purchase of assignment to lucrative positions. In 1842 the Royal Navy created the title paymaster and purser.

Melville, writing of life on the USS *United States* in 1843, says: "Of all the non-combatants of a man-of-war, the purser perhaps stands foremost in importance; though he is but a member of the gunroom mess, yet usage seems to assign him a conventional station somewhat above that of the equals in Navy rank—the chaplain, surgeon and professor."

The purser's steward in those days acted as postmaster.

The title "purser" was derived from "bursar." This was the old name for keeper of the cash, and hence the word "disburser" for one who pays out money. The term "burse magister" may be found in the English Merchant Marine in the time of Henry VI. The title "purser" was used in the U.S. Navy from its birth until 1860. The pursers were civilian appointments made only for a vessel's cruise. Their compensation was based upon a commission on expenditures. They were designated supply officers in 1917 and were authorized to be addressed by the military titles ensign, lieutenant, lieutenant commander, commander, captain, and rear admiral. This order gave military titles to all officers of the Staff Corps.

PEA-COAT. Probably from the Dutch word *pij*, a coarse, woolen cloth. For two hundred years it has been the name for the heavier topcoat worn by seafaring men in cold weather. The coat was originally made of a material called pilot cloth, which has also been viewed as a possible source of the name: pi(lot) coat.

PELORUS. Supposedly the name of Hannibal's pilot and navigator, given to the stand where we now observe the compass.

PLANK OWNER. A member of the original crew of a ship or aircraft squadron. Tradition holds that a plank owner is always welcome aboard, and when a ship is decommissioned, he or she can get a plank from the deck.

PORT. "Larboard" signified the left side on board ship in the U.S. Navy until about 1846. In that year, the following word was passed on board an American man-of-war cruising off the coast of Africa: "Do you hear there fore and aft? The word 'larboard' is to be forever dropped in the United States Navy, and the word 'port' is substituted. Any man using the word 'larboard' will be punished."

The British made the change some years before. Adm. Penrose Fitzgerald states in his memoirs that the word *port* was adopted in the Royal Navy from the orders of the Portuguese Tagus River pilots. In memory of the great navigator, Vasco da Gama, the port side is designated the "honor side" in the Portuguese Navy. In November 1497 da Gama became the first to double the Cape of Good Hope, keeping Africa at all times on the port hand. (See also **LARBOARD.**)

PORTHOLE. When King Henry VI desired heavier guns on his ships, James Baker, shipbuilder, was ordered to pierce the sides of *The Great Harry.* Baker resorted to the French method of a watertight door to close the opening when the battery was not in use. This door was called a port; hence the term *porthole,* which was originally a hole for a gun. Technically, a port is closed with a port lid. Old port lids had scuttles or bull's-eyes in them. We call the old scuttles portholes.

POSH. A term used to describe something elegant or first-rate. It was originally an acronym used by British steamship lines designating those passengers who by virtue of rank or position were to receive preferential treatment. On trips around the Horn of Africa, those un-air-conditioned ships were slightly cooler on the north side of the ship, the side away from the sun. Therefore those VIPs were to be given cabins on the port side on the outbound leg and the starboard side on the homeward trip: Port Out, Starboard Home (posh).

PRESSED INTO SERVICE. A phrase that has entered the vernacular from the days of sail and impressment of sailors, or press gangs, which did such work. Hands recruited by these means were literally "pressed" into service.

PROFESSORS OF MATHEMATICS. The first appointments of civilian teachers were made in 1831 to instruct midshipmen aboard ship. Assigned to the Naval Observatory, they were detailed to the ships throughout the fleet. Eventually, this practice was found impracticable, and after the establishment of the Naval Academy in 1846, the professors then on the list were transferred to duty at the Academy.

PULLING ONE'S WEIGHT. Or **NOT** pulling one's weight. Doing, or not doing, one's job. When a sailor has stopped pulling at his oars in a longboat or is resting on his oars, he is said to be not pulling his own weight.

QUARANTINE. Derived from the French word *quarante* or "forty." Ships entering port bearing evidence of the plague were isolated for forty days.

QUARTER, GIVING QUARTER, NO QUARTER. These expressions came from a practice that originated in the wars between the Dutch and the Spaniards, when a defeated and captured officer was given life and liberty for a ransom fee estimated at one-quarter of his yearly pay. "No quarter" thus meant that the fight was to the death.

QUARTERDECK. From the *Marine Encyclopedia* (1881): "The upper deck abaft the mainmast. Naval etiquette requires all persons to salute coming on the quarter-deck, and to conduct themselves in decorous manner while thereon." Originally the term referred to a deck that covered a quarter of the ship, a raised platform from which the ship was "conned" or controlled. Additionally, it served as a repository of the ancient shrines. Tradition thus provides a precedent for its role as an area of both temporal and religious superiority.

QUARTERMASTER. A quartermaster originally had nothing to do with the bridge or steering of a ship, but was assigned to the specific duty of looking after troop quarters. In later years these men were retained aboard after troops debarked and were assigned to other duties. The Army uses the word in its original connotation.

ROGUE'S MARCH. An old tune played when drumming bad characters out of a ship or a regiment.

ROGUE'S YARN. The yarn in rope that is either twisted the opposite way from the other yarns, or is colored. This is a means to detect the theft of government cordage.

ROPE. Today, most fiber rope is called line by sailors and the term "rope" refers to wire ropes. Old sailors assert that there are only seven ropes on a ship—the man rope, head rope, hand rope, foot rope, bell rope, buoy rope, and dip rope. Master mariners and old salts can undoubtedly come up with lists of others. When the first edition of this book was published in 1934, several more were offered by distinguished men of the sea. However, most modern sailors are not used to the subtle distinctions of what we refer to as tall ships.

The phrase "**TO KNOW THE ROPES**" comes from the days of square-masted sailing vessels, where it took a sailor a long time to get to know what specifically all of the running and standing rigging did—that is, to know the ropes.

ROUND ROBIN. "This morning we all signed a round robin, setting forth our 'willingness to return to duty on the liberation of the three men.' Our names are written in radiating lines, like the spokes of a wheel, so that there are no leading names on the list." On this point William M. Davis queries, "Is it from this custom of signing dangerous papers that the term 'ring leader' was derived?"

ROUND TURN. To take a turn around a bitt or bollard, to check the strain or weight of the load. "**TO BRING UP WITH A ROUND TURN**" is nautical phraseology for a "call-down" or reprimand.

RUDDER. Originally placed on "steer board" or starboard (right) side of Viking ships. Derived from the Anglo-Saxon *rother,* that which guides. The sternpost rudder came into use in the twelfth century. In 1262 there is record of ships paying certain dues if they had "helm-rothers," and smaller dues for "hand-rothers." This is considered as a distinction between the quarter rudder and the sternpost rudder.

RUNNING. Originally to play tricks on "greenhorns" at sea, whether the crew or midshipmen. In a description of a cruise in the *Constellation* over a hundred years ago: "The men were fond as the 'reefers' of 'running' each other, and imposing upon the credulity of landsmen." The term has also been used in the context of upper-class midshipmen's dealings with plebes at the Naval Academy.

RUNNING RIGGING. Those lines aboard ship that move, such as sheets (to control sails), halyards (from "haul-yards," to raise and lower sails), outhauls, and down-hauls (to tighten sails on a boom or mast). Running rigging is the opposite of **STANDING RIGGING,** which consists of lines designed to provide static support for ship structures, primarily masts. Stays (lines that run fore and aft) and shrouds are examples of standing rigging. When cordage was of inferior grade, so many stays of rope were used to support a mast athwartships that the mast was practically obscured, like a corpse covered by a shroud. Ratlines were placed fore and aft on shrouds to provide footing for going aloft.

SAILOR. From Middle English *saylor,* root unknown. Originally, one who has made a long sea voyage other than his first, and who is qualified to go aloft and tend the sails. A sailor is not necessarily a seaman. The term *mariner* is usually restricted to legal documents. Technically speaking, sailor means one who serves before the mast, yet no one would deny that Farragut and Nimitz were great sailors. Officer-seamen are proud to be called sailors.

SALLY SHIP. An all-hands evolution used to "rock" a ship off mud, sand, or other obstructions. On orders, men rush en masse from one side of a ship to the other in the attempt to get a roll on her. Ice breakers use the same principle to break out of ice by quickly pumping large amounts of water from tanks on one side to tanks on the other.

SALT JUNK AND HARD-TACK. Salted meat and sea biscuits, at one time the principal diet of seafaring men. This expression is seldom heard today. One who has eaten the old hard-tack fully agrees with Charles XII, who said, "It is not good but it can be eaten." In old sea narratives mention is made of "lobscouse," a delicacy in its day, although easy to prepare: it consists of potatoes and salt beef hashed together. Junk was originally a vegetable fiber from which rope was made. In time the word was used in referring to old rope. The meat, in sailing ship days, was carried in the "harness cask." Probably as a result of its resemblance to old rope, both in texture and stringiness, it was called salt horse or salt junk.

Charles Nordhoff gives this account of old-time sailors' diet: "Here the individual who was acting 'cook of the mess,' had set our supper out on a 'mess cloth' on deck. It consisted of a sea-bread, raw salt pork, cold boiled potatoes, and vinegar. We gathered around the cloth, each one bringing his tea and a seat, although some squatted right down on deck. When all was arranged an old salt said, 'Well boys here's every one for himself, and the devil for us all—Jack pass the pork.'"*

SAW AWAY THE BULWARKS. This practice was supposed to limber a ship and make her sail faster. The first record of this practice in the American Navy is found in the chase of the American cruisers *Lexington, Dolphin,* and *Reprisal* by an English ship of the line. The *Dolphin* and *Lexington,* by separating, escaped with little difficulty, but Cooper recorded in his *Naval History* that *Reprisal,* "commanded by Lambert Wickes, was so hard pressed as to be obliged to saw her bulwarks, and even to cut away some of her timbers; expedients that were then much in favor among the seamen of the day, although of questionable utility."

SCHOONER. The schooner is an American rig, and the type was originally built in Gloucester, Massachusetts, in 1713. Andrew Robinson, shipbuilder, had not decided on a name for the new rig, and tradition relates that as she left the ways a bystander sang out, "See how she scoons." Robinson heard this remark and said, "A schooner she shall be."

SCRIMSHAW. Called the "folk art of the American whaleman," scrimshaw included engravings, etchings, and carvings on sperm whale teeth, cribbage boards of walrus tusks, and scenes done on the jawbones of sperm whales— handiwork sometimes functional but usually decorative. Some work of this description was done by the naval men of the day, in particular those who were unlucky enough to be captured in the wars and placed in shore jails, where some made ship models and other small articles from the bones of animals.

SCUTTLE. This meant "hole" in Anglo-Saxon. In reality, TO SCUTTLE A SHIP means to hole her deliberately.

---

* *Man-of-War Life* (New York: Dodd, Mead, 1855), p. 30.

SCUTTLE BUTT. The sailors' source of fresh drinking water, a drinking fountain. Here men have ever gathered for exchange of gossip; hence, *scuttlebutt*, in the sense of rumors or unconfirmed information.

Melville, in *White Jacket*, describes the scuttle butt in the USS *United States* in 1843: "The scuttle butt is a goodly, round, painted cask, standing on end, and with its upper head removed showing a narrow circular shelf within where rest a number of tin cups for the accommodation of drinkers. Central within the scuttle butt itself stands an iron pump, which, connecting with the immense water tanks in the hold, furnished an unfailing supply of the much admired Pale Ale."

SEA. The sea was called *saivs* from a root *si* or *siv*, the Greek *seio*, "to shake"; it meant the tossed-about water as opposed to stagnant or running water.

SEVEN SEAS. The "seven seas" of antiquity were the Mediterranean Sea, Red Sea, Persian Gulf, Indian Ocean, China Sea, West African Sea, and East African Sea. In today's parlance: North Atlantic, South Atlantic, North Pacific, South Pacific, Indian, Arctic, and Antarctic.

SHAKEDOWN CRUISE. A cruise made in a new vessel for the purpose of testing machinery and systems, adjusting instruments, and allowing officers and men to become familiar with administration and drill aboard.

SHANGHAIED. The old city of Shanghai in China was notorious for its unscrupulous bar owners, who would drug sailors to render them unconscious and then sell them to the captains of the tea clippers, who were in need of crew. (See also **PRESSED INTO SERVICE.**)

SHE, HER. Why is a ship traditionally assigned to the feminine gender? The analogy of the sea and the ship being the sailors' mistress may play a part in the origin of this usage. The men who went to sea often ascribed gender to those objects they were close to. Thus, for example, the ship was feminine, and the sun was often masculine. Today, the custom of referring to a ship as "she" is fading, and some major commercial concerns have publicly announced that they will no longer do so.

Fleet Adm. Chester Nimitz, in a talk to the Society of Sponsors of the United States Navy, quipped that "a ship is always referred to as 'she' because it costs so much to keep one in paint and powder." In a similar vein, an article published some decades back in the Falmouth, Mass., *Enterprise* explained that

A boat is called a she because there's always a great deal of bustle around her . . . because there's usually a gang of men around . . . because she has a waist and stays . . . because she takes a lot of paint to keep her looking good . . . because it's not the initial expense that breaks you, it's the upkeep . . . because she is all decked out . . . because it takes a good man to handle her right . . . because she shows her topsides, hides her bottom and, when coming into port, always heads for the buoys.

SHIPMATE. W. H. Smyth, in his *Sailor's Word-Book,* says: "A term once dearer than brother, but the habit of short cruises is weakening it."

SHIPPING OVER. Reenlisting. Since men first followed the sea, their imagination has pictured the end of the cruise, the paying-off, the decommissioning, the shore leave, and shore work. Often the sailor exclaims, "Never again!" and that he will quit the sea, but the idle boasts come to naught, and the old-timer is back aboard, after a little hectic life ashore. In 1843 the following conversation took place after a long cruise on an American man-of-war. It is heard in substance today, but without the nautical verbiage of other days:

> "Sink the sea!" cried a forecastle man. "Once more ashore, and you'll never catch old Boom Bolt afloat. I mean to settle down in a sail loft. Shipmates, take me by the arms and swab up the lee scuppers with me, but I mean to steer a clam cart before I go again to a ship's wheel. Let the Navy go by the board, to sea again, I won't."
>
> "Start my soul-bolts, maties, if any more blue peters and sailing signals fly at my fore!" cried the captain of the head. "My wages will buy a wheelbarrow if nothing more."
>
> "I have taken my last dose of salts," cried the captain of the waist. . . . "Blast the sea shipmates!" says I.

After spending their accumulated wages, nine out of ten shipped over.

SHIPSHAPE AND BRISTOL FASHION. Neat, clean, all rigging coiled and flemished down.

SHOW A LEG. An expression used generally by boatswain's mates and masters-at-arms to rouse and turn out sleeping men. "Rouse and shine" has been corrupted to **RISE AND SHINE** in the U.S. Navy.

The call to "show a leg" is derived from the days when the "wives" of seamen were carried at sea. These women, who put out a leg for identification, were not required to turn out at first call.

The old original call, says Commander Beckett, RN, was, "Out or down

Sickbay on an American naval vessel about 1845

there, out or down there, all hands, rouse out, rouse out, rouse out. Lash and carry, lash and carry, show a leg or else a purser's stocking. Rouse and shine, rouse and shine. Lash up and stow, lash up and stow, lash up and stow, it's tomorrow morning and the sun's a-scorching your (bloody) eyes out."

SHOW ONE'S TRUE COLORS. Pirates and privateers would travel under a national flag of some nation so as not to arouse suspicion. When they would attack, they would strike their false colors and run up their own flag, thereby showing their "true colors."

SICKBAY. Originally called "sick berth." The term probably was introduced by Lord St. Vincent in 1798. After round bows were introduced about 1811, the contour of the bulkhead caused the change of name to "sickbay."

SILENCE IN A MAN-OF-WAR. The U.S. Navy has always insisted, as the British Navy did at an earlier date, that silence be observed at all drills and evolutions. When Napoleon, as prisoner, was aboard the *Bellerophon* in July 1815, he remarked as the ship was getting under way: "Your method of performing this evolution is quite different to the French. What I admire most in your ship is the extreme silence and orderly conduct of your men. On board a French ship everyone calls and gives orders and they gabble like so many geese."

SKIN OF A SHIP. The outer planking or plating of a ship is called the "skin." This usage is believed to date back centuries to those men who first sailed the seas in wicker-work coracles covered with the skins of animals. The skins were sewn together at "seams." Both "skin" and SEAM have lived in the language of seamen.

SKIPPER. Derived from the Scandinavian word *schiffe,* meaning "ship," or the Dutch word *schipper,* "captain."

SKYLARK. "To skylark" is a distinctly nautical expression. *Lark,* meaning a spree, is a corruption of the old Anglo-Saxon word *lac,* "to play or have fun." The word *skylark* was derived from the practice of young sailors laying aloft to royal yards and sliding down the backstays. *Skylarking* is used in the Navy meaning "to play" or "to cut up" when at drills or in ranks. The earliest record of the use of this term was in the early nineteenth century.

SKY PILOT. The chaplain aboard ship is called the padre or "sky pilot" by sailors. The older sailors had a religious vein that was mingled with super-stition. The bluejackets of sail seldom showed any fear of a hereafter. Their philosophy as expressed by an old "sky pilot" was that since they lived hard, worked hard, and died hard, they thought it would be hard indeed to have to go to hell.

SLIPPED HIS CABLE. Means "he died." The sailor's analogy of a ship being free from all attachments to land and able to sail as intended is very close to the soul's being free from earthly ties. A ship would not leave anchor and cable behind unless desperate to escape an enemy. It was indicative of an unplanned and hasty departure with no plan of return.

SON OF A GUN. See GUN, SON OF A.

SPLICING THE MAIN BRACE. In the days of sail, the main brace was the prin-cipal fore-and-aft support of the ship's masts. Should it part from either wear or battle damage, it would be critical to the ship's safety and the safety of all hands to splice that line immediately. Those who performed this rather important and difficult task of marlinespike seamanship received upon com-pletion of the job an extra ration of rum. Today the expression is more or less equivalent to having the "sun over the yardarm," or the Army term "to bring the flag down." meaning the business of the day is finished and it is time for the bar to open.

One may see today in the Navy Department a copy of a dispatch sent, or "signal made" as the British say, by Adm. Sir David Beatty, RN, to the Allied Fleet at Rosyth on 11 November 1918, at the end of World War I: "The Armistice commenced at 11:00 today, Monday, and the customary method in the H.M. Service of celebrating an occasion is to be carried out by the ships' companies splicing the main brace at 19:00 today. Hands are to make and mend clothes." The dispatch adds, "Negative 6 B.S.," a reference to the Sixth Battle Squadron. The Sixth was composed of U.S. ships under the command of Rear Adm. Hugh Rodman, USN, but operating under the orders of Beatty. Spirits were forbidden in the U.S. Navy. Nonetheless there were pleasant recollections by some American officers and men who visited the ships of their British allies on that memorable day.

SPRIT. From Old Saxon, meaning "to sprout." We have the bowsprit, which sprouts out from the bow. The spritsail in older ships was set under the bowsprit.

SQUARED AWAY. This term for professional competence stems from the old square-rigged ships that, when handled in that self-same professional manner, had all sails billowed, squared away before the wind.

STARBOARD. See **LARBOARD.**

STEADY AS SHE GOES. A command to the helm meaning the helmsman should steady on whatever course the compass is pointing to at the time of the command. Usually given when the ship is in a turn and the OOD wants to steady on some course short of that which he or she first indicated.

STEERAGE. A term supplanted by "junior officers' mess." In the *Marine Encyclopedia* (1881), a steerage officer was described as "an officer living or messing in the steerage. Steerage officers in the U.S. Navy are clerks, midshipmen, cadet midshipmen, mates, cadet engineers, ensigns when not in charge of a watch or division, and all officers ranking with ensign."

STRIKE. Literally "to lower," as in the expression "to strike one's colors" in surrender. Another meaning of the term is "to slow down or stop progress." In the days of sail, merchant sailors who wanted to protest working conditions or actions by the ship's officers would lower, or "strike," the ship's yards to the rails or deck, effectively stopping all progress until the grievance was settled. America's trade unions ended up appropriating the term, probably from the longshoremen. Obviously, this course of action could end up a very risky business for the crew who resorted to such measures.

SUNDOWNER. Derived from the strict captains who once required that all officers and men be aboard by sunset; later a term for any martinet or strict disciplinarian.

SUPERCARGO. Much of the early success of the British and American China and India trade was due to business diplomats who handled the sale and collection of cargo. E. Keble Chatterton wrote of such supercargoes: "He has to combine the ability of a banker and merchant, the tact of an ambassador and the loyalty and incorruptibility of an honest man. . . . His job was to sell the vessel's cargo, buy a new one, and establish relations with the highest Indian natives or with the loftiest Chinese officials."

In 1690 French priests were given free passage out to the Orient in English ships, in order that their knowledge of languages and conditions might be used in the capacity of supercargoes. An idea of the tremendous amount of business with the huge profits of those days may be seen in the investment of 430,000 pounds sterling by England's East India Company in 1674; the company's ships brought home 860,000 pounds sterling worth of commodities. In New England's early maritime development and China trade, the supercargoes were often the scions of families of shipowners, and their trade reports were some of the earliest submitted to our government.

SUPERSTITIONS, SAILORS'. Literature abounds in superstitions and explanations that the early mariners gave to phenomena actually observed at sea. From the journey of the Argonauts and the legend of floating rocks on through Flying Dutchman "appearances" to the pig tattooed on the more modern sailor's foot as a charm against drowning, some of the great superstitions of the sea arose from travelers' propensity to exaggerate in relating great adventures after long voyages to distant, strange lands.

The "Fore-Topman" of *Old Ironsides* (1839–41) wrote:

> Many clever writers have affirmed that sailors are generally the most superstitious beings in existence, and I believe with some reason, for since my sojourn on the boundless ocean, I have never seen an accident occur on shipboard but what someone would step up with prophetic countenance, and engross the attention of every bystander with a relation of some little circumstance that he had taken notice of prior to the occur-

rence, which he considered as a forewarning. . . . Sailors put great faith in the predictions of fortune tellers or persons supposed to be skilled in magic charms.

Lt. Fletcher S. Bassett, USN, wrote in 1881: "Sea shells, fish amulets, the caul, coral, amber, bunches of garlic, bits of seaweed, turf from the church yard—the belief of the sailor in these many omens, lucky signs, auguries, etc., is a survival of ancient superstitions—reminiscent of the many impositions, practiced by Chaldean magicians, and astrologers, Greek and Roman augurs, medieval sorcerers and cunning charlatans of all ages."

The phenomena, real and imagined, of the sea—waterspouts, phosphorescence, St. Elmo's fire, winds and storms, enchanted islands and rocks, mermaids, and sea monsters—all have generated among the seagoing peoples numerous legends, superstitions, and customs of propitiation with charms against dangerous effects. Many people believe in omens and prognostics; for example, the prediction of many weather phenomena by rhyming couplets, such as "Red sky at morning, sailors take warning. Red sky at night, sailor's delight."

Phantom ships and apparitions were often reported by mariners. The "Flying Dutchman" is the most famous of these legends. Some hold that the ship was attempting to round the Cape of Good Hope in a storm, and the captain cursed the Lord and swore that he would complete the passage if it took him until the "Crack of Doom." And supposedly, he is still doing just that. Others have reported seeing a full-rigged ship sailing the open ocean without sign of a crew.

F. S. Bassett in his *Legends and Superstitions of the Sea and of Sailors* relates that Columbus in his journal recorded the appearance of three mermaids. Henry Hudson reported that one of his men saw a white mermaid with "long hair hanging down behind, of color black. Seeing her go down, they saw her tail which was like that of a porpoise, speckled like a mackerel."

Smollett says that in his day Davy Jones was "the fiend who presides over all the evil spirits of the deep and is seen in various shapes. He sometimes appeared, a giant breathing flames from his wide nostrils, and having big eyes and three rows of teeth."

Lt. Cdr. A. W. Meyerson of the former Imperial Russian Navy reported on some old Russian Navy superstitions: It was bad luck to whistle aboard ship, to kill sea gulls or an albatross, to have a priest and women aboard ship together, to come on deck without a hat. Never write the port of destination in a log book until reached. Always scratch a mast to get a wind.

A nineteenth-century naval officer wrote: "Sailors always personify ships and boats. A venerable commodore in our own Navy, still living [in 1881] was one to talk to the mizzenmast of his ship. This is a common idea among old sailors, who often believe as the old captain said, 'She can do anything but talk, and sometimes she can even do that. A ship which is about to sink makes her lamentations just like any other human being.'"

SURGEONS (MEDICAL CORPS). The title "surgeon" cannot be found in any record of the Royal Navy before 1557. However, there is little doubt that some went to sea before that date. Doctors of medicine commanded regiments of cavalry and infantry in the civil wars of Charles I's time.

The term comes from French *chirurgien,* Latin *chirurgus,* originally from Greek, and means "operating with the hand." Sir William Monson says, "The surgeon is to be placed in the hold where he should be in no danger of shot; for there cannot be a greater disheartening of the company than in his miscarrying, whereby, they will be deprived of all help for hurt and wounded men."

In the Royal Navy in the eighteenth century, the pay of surgeons and chaplains came from the seamen aboard. Each sailor was required to pay to each twopence a month. In 1776, when pay for officers and men was established by Congress for the "new commissions under the free and independent states of America," surgeons on ships of twenty guns received twenty dollars per month and their mates fifteen. By 1825 the monthly pay for surgeons had increased to fifty dollars.

In 1880 the gold oak leaf with silver acorn imposed thereon became the official insignia of the Medical Corps. The oak leaf and the caduceus (staff) according to tradition became symbols of the medical profession because of their connection with the druids, legendary physician-priests of ancient England. Oak groves were their temples and their robes are said to have been embroidered with designs of oak leaves and acorns.

TAKEN ABACK. See BACK.

TAR. General name for a sailor and derived from the old custom of a sailor tarring his trousers, as well as other wearing apparel, in order to make them waterproof.

TARPAULIN MUSTER. The term comes from the hat passing of many years ago. In practice, the term is applied to a collection of money by a group of sailors. In times of need, such as a collection for the family of a deceased shipmate, a "tarpaulin" or black tarred hat was set out and, as the crew passed by, they contributed whatever they could afford.

TATTOOING. Capt. James Cook reported in his *First Voyage* that the Tahitians "have a custom . . . which they call Tattowing. They prick the skin so as just not to cause blood." The *Century Dictionary* defines *tattoo:*

> To mark, as the surface of the body, with indelible patterns produced by pricking the skin and inserting different pigments in the punctures. Sailors and others mark the skin with legends, love emblems, etc.; and some uncivilized peoples, especially the New Zealanders and the Dyaks of Borneo, cover large surfaces of the body with ornamental patterns in this way.

Human beings have from early times decorated the body with designs. Seafaring men, however, imitated, at an early date, the custom as practiced by the military.

Among Europeans, the art of tattooing originated as a mark of identification for the dead and wounded on the field of battle. It was the original identification tag of the soldier. It was by such an identification that Edith of the Swan Neck found the body of Harold on the field of Hastings. Tattooing was also once used to mark permanently a thief or a deserter.

Because of the frequent refusal of Catholics to provide burial to deceased Protestants, sailors, irrespective of creed, found a way to ensure a shore burial. Rev. Fitch W. Taylor, a chaplain of the U.S. Navy, wrote in 1838: "And so prevalent was this refusal of the rites of burial to Protestants, by Catholic communities, that there is even a custom among sailors to have a cross tattooed upon their arms, that if by chance they should die in a Roman Catholic country, their bodies might be respected, and be allowed a quiet interment on the shore."

From a means of identification, tattooing in time became the fashion of sailors of all nations. It was as much a part of the sailor's image as was nautical phraseology; it marked him as a mariner. Even now elaborate tattooing is considered by many sailors to give an added degree of "saltiness" to the one tattooed.

The practice waxes and wanes with fashion. For a great while, the social acceptance of a tattoo was dying out; now, taken up by a culture of youth, it may well be coming back with a vengeance. Some of the conventional designs of tattooing of the old school included small crests, anchors, stars, or shields, or larger designs, such as panthers and full-rigged ships. In order to express sentiment for the girls ashore, the women's initials would be tattooed

Transom of the USS *Constellation* in Baltimore Harbor
Jocs Kirby Harrison

on sailors' arms or legs. Sometimes the sailor's initials as well as those of the girl would be intertwined in a heart. Some of the more robust fellows would have a dagger that appeared to pierce the skin with a motto, "Death before dishonor." It was considered by the more superstitious that a pig tattooed on the foot was an effective means of preventing death by drowning.

Tattoo work may be surgically removed, but the process is most painful.

TO BE THREE SHEETS TO (IN) THE WIND. This expression refers to the lines used to control the sails of sailing vessels. When these sheets were cast to the wind (let go), it would cause the old sailing ships to shudder and stagger, and the resulting track would be the same as that of a drunken sailor, out of control, and "three sheets to the wind." The phrase has been taken into general usage to describe one who is very drunk.

TOM SAWYER'S TRAVERSE. An old term that meant the course and movements of a "soldiering" (no reflection on the Army) sailor to kill time, such as frequent trips to and long stays at the scuttle butt and in the head, part of the art of work dodging. An American variant of the British phrase "Tom Cox's Traverse," meaning "up one hatch and down another."

TRANSOM. In sailing ships, a transom was a horizontal timber that was a part of the stern frame and sternpost. This beam or timber was used as a seat; hence, any seat that is built in and is a permanent fixture is by usage called a transom. It has become a term for the rear end of a ship or boat.

TYPHOON. A corruption of the Chinese *t'ai-fun,* or "great wind."

WARDROOM. In the early part of the eighteenth century, there was a compartment aboard British ships below the "great cabin," called the "wardrobe." It was used for storage of valuable articles taken from prizes. The officers' staterooms were near. When the wardrobe was empty, particularly when outward bound, the lieutenants met there for lounging and for meals. In time, the compartment was used entirely as an officers' messroom, and the name was changed to wardroom.

WARRANT OFFICER. An officer who has come from the enlisted ranks and is given a warrant commission from the secretary of the Navy to provide leadership in a certain technical field. Warrants issued by a judge for search or arrest are a limited authorization for a specific task or time period. Likewise, the early Navy issued warrants for a specific task or time, such as for the duration of a cruise. These were temporary and not designed to be career appointments. In the historic sense warrants were issued by the captain of a ship to experienced sailors when there were not enough officers to cover the duties required. They might be in charge of a captured ship's prize crew, or cover a watch left empty by battle casualty.

Before the existence of standing navies, when a king needed to fight at sea, he simply commandeered a merchant ship and installed his own leaders. These leaders were usually friends of the king and often had no knowledge of the sea. To make up for this shortcoming, the king would issue "warrants" to skilled seamen to be their experts on the job.

When our own Navy came into being, Congress established two grades of officer, commissioned and warranted. The warrants were the experts in shipboard skills, such as the ship's boatswain, carpenter, and pursers. Other than a short hiatus from 1959 to 1963, the Navy has maintained the rank as the experts in the various enlisted technologies. These designations derive from their respective manner of appointment. Commissioned officers are commissioned by the president, by and with the approval of the Senate. Warrant officers are senior enlisted personnel who are given warrants by the secretary of the Navy or the president.

WATCHES. The ship's crew is divided into watches in order to keep the ship running at all times, both at sea and in port, and still allow for the crew to accomplish all ship's work and get the necessary rest and meals. Each of these watches includes enough of the various sea-going specialties to completely staff all normal operational stations. Should an emergency occur, or some unusual situation arise where more hands are needed, then special bills will be put into effect.

Normally, watches at sea are divided into four-hour periods, starting at midnight:

Mid watch, 0000–0400
Morning watch, 0400–0800
First (or forenoon) watch, 0800–1200
Afternoon watch, 1200–1600
First dog watch, 1600–1800
Second dog watch, 1800–2000
Evening watch, 2000–2400

The watches have become a familiar means of telling time at sea, in expressions such as "It happened during the first watch." Moreover, because early timepieces were not chronometers, but sand glasses, the watches were further divided into thirty-minute segments to coincide with the running of a half-hour glass. The sand glass was turned each half-hour for the "trick at the wheel." This original watch probably lasted only one-half hour, due to its strenuous nature. Lyde writes in his *Friends Adventure* that one sailor "sat down on a low stool by the helm, to look after the sandglass and to call to pump, which they had to do every half hour because the ship leaked so much."

In those days, in order that all hands should be aware of the passage of time, a bell was struck on the turning of the glass. One bell for each half-hour since the beginning of the watch. Thus, one bell would indicate the completion of the first half-hour; two bells, the first hour; three bells, the first hour and a half, and so forth, up until the sounding of eight bells at the end of the watch. For example, seven bells during the morning watch would be struck at 0730, and eight bells in the afternoon watch would be at 1600. The first report of this that can be found is from an unknown author of a book of travel and adventure. He wrote in the mid–seventeenth century and describes a Dutch ship he boarded in Leghorn, Italy: "Every half hour the steersman . . . at the ringing of a bell, is changed. The bell is rung also every time they change the watch and for prayers, breakfast, and dinner."

An old custom, once strictly observed, was that of having the oldest man in the ship, whether admiral or jack-of-the-dust, strike eight bells at midnight on 31 December. This was immediately followed by eight bells for the New Year, always struck by the youngest boy on board. It was, of course, the only time of the year when sixteen bells were struck.

Early records document a division of the sea day into watches. Pigafetta, in his detailed account of Magellan's ill-fated voyage, relates that Magellan "ordered that three watches should be set at night. The first was at the beginning of the night, the second at midnight, and the third towards break of day, which is commonly called la diane, otherwise the star of the break of day."

Sir Henry Mainwaring explains the early watches in his *Seaman's Dictionary:* "at sea the ship's company is divided into two parts, the one called the starboard watch, the other the larboard watch. The master is the chief of the starboard and his right-hand mate, of the larboard. These are in their turns to watch, trim sails, pump, and do all duties for four hours; and then the other watch is to relieve them. Four hours they call a whole watch."

Herman Melville, in *White Jacket,* describes watches and details on the USS *United States* in 1843:

> Now the fore, main, and mizen topmen of each watch, starboard and larboard, are, at sea, respectively, subdivided into quarter watches. . . . Besides these topmen who are always made up of active sailors, there are sheet-anchor men, old veterans, all whose place is on the fore-castle; the fore yards and anchors, and all the sails on the bowsprit being under their care. . . . These are the fellows, that it does your soul good to look at; hearty members of the old guard; grim sea grenadiers. . . . Then there is the after guard stationed on the quarter-deck, who under the quartermaster and the quarter gunners attend to the mainsail and spanker, and help haul the main brace, and other ropes. . . . They acquire the name of "sea dandies" and silk socks gentry. . . . Then there the waisters, always stationed on the gundeck. These haul aft the fore and main sheets, besides being subject to ignoble duties, attending to the draining and sewerage below hatches. . . . They are the tag-rag and bobtail of the crew and he who is good for nothing else is good enough for a waister.

"DOG WATCHES" were an effort to rotate the watch, so that the same section did not have to stand the same watch every day, and to allow the evening watches time to eat dinner. Several possible origins of the name are given. It may have come from "docked" or short watch or from "dodged," as the same rotation of watch was "dodged." Admiral Cradock, in his *Whispers from the Fleet,* called the dog watch a watch "curtailed."

WAY. Movement of the ship. Often used with modifiers such as "steerage way" (having enough movement for the rudder to have effect), being under way (not being attached to the ground or pier), or having "way on" (being under power or sail propulsion). Note that it is possible to be under way and not have way on.

WEIGH. From Anglo-Saxon *woeg*. To lift the anchor from the ground. This term must not be confused with *way*. "To weigh anchor" is to raise the anchor clear of the ground.

WHISTLE FOR A WIND. A very old expression of sailing-ship days. It is derived from the expression "you can whistle for it if you want it," and came from the custom of supplying a certain number of drinkers in English taverns and alehouses with whistles in order to summon the drawer for refills of tankards.

WIDE BERTH, GIVE SOMEONE A. To allow enough room around an anchored vessel to allow her to swing in all directions.

WINDFALL. The word *windfall* reflects an old custom of landholding in Britain. Some of the nobility held lands on condition that no timber would be cut except for the Royal Navy; however, those trees blown down by wind were exempt. It was therefore considered a godsend and good luck when gales effected windfalls.

WOMEN AT SEA. Despite men's former protestations about women on warships being bad luck, women were carried on many British men-of-war until after the beginning of the nineteenth century. There is record of Mary Ann Talbot, who received a pension of 20 pounds a year "for wounds received in action when she was before the mast in the Navy." Rebecca Anne Johnson served on a Whitby collier for seven years until 1808 when her sex was discovered. It is related that her mother served at sea and fell at the Battle of Copenhagen as a member of a gun's crew.

The marriage of two sailors, as reported in a London journal, is of interest:

At St. Dunstane's in the East, in May 1802, David Jones was married to Anne Robinson. They had been old shipmates on board *Le Seine,* frigate on the West Indian Station, during most part of the war, where the lady bore a most conspicuous part in the different actions in which the frigate was engaged. She was always an attendant in the surgeon's department and waited upon Jones in his wounded state. An attachment took place which ended in their union.

WRECK. From old English *wrack* or "seaweed"; a term meaning "cast ashore; drifted or driven ashore."

WRITE IN WATER. "Men's evil manners live in brass; their virtues / We write in water" (Shakespeare, *Henry VIII*).

On John Keats's tombstone in Rome, one may read: "This grave contains all that was mortal of a young English poet, who on his deathbed, in the bitterness of his heart at the malicious power of his enemies, desired these words to be engraved on his tombstone: 'Here lies one whose name was writ in water.' "

Wooden Ships and Iron Men

The following excerpts are taken from a scurrilous but entertaining work, called *The Wooden World*, first published in 1707 by Edward Ward, one-time British seaman. "Plain Ned" Ward, as he was known, ran an inn after retiring from the sea. He had a decided talent for writing and, with engaging frankness and wit, wrote various compositions, coarse, racy, but always descriptive. Some of the bawdier extracts of the old sailor's philosophy and observations would not be appropriate in a work of this kind. We here give grateful acknowledgment to Sir Geoffrey Callender for the extracts from his publication of *Wooden World*.

> *Sea captain.* Upon his first popping up, the lieutenants sheer off to the other side, as if he was a ghost indeed; for 'tis impudence for any to approach him within the length of a boat hook.
>
> *A sea lieutenant* is a gentleman, he'll tell you, by his commission, and hence it is he always carries it about with him to give you demonstration proof, in case you call it in question: He lays it out as often as he does his watch, and believes both together convincing proofs of his gentility.
>
> *A sea chaplain* is one that in his junior days was brought up in the fear of the Lord; but the university reasoned him out of it at last, and he has oftimes thanked his good stars for it.
>
> *The master of a ship of war.* His language is all heathen Greek to a cobbler; and he cannot have so much as a tooth drawn ashore without carrying his interpreter. It is the aftmost grinders aloft, on the starboard quarter, will he cry to the all-wondering operator.
>
> *The purser* is a kind of Pythagorean philosopher, not because of his pocket holes, for his breeches are commonly well lined, but for his many transmigrations, having lived in various regions, and rubbed through many callings, before he came to be a purser in the Navy.

The surgeon. He adjusts his prescriptions, as a country shoemaker does his lasts; he makes one and the same recipe serve to a hundred various tempers and circumstances. For there's no standing upon niceties, he cries, with fellows that have the constitution of a horse.

The gunner. As heavy as his guns are, they are certainly more active than he is, and do the King fifty times more service, for his grand amusement is eating and drinking; his sleeps are moderate enough, just to suffice nature, and make him ready for a fresh attack: Were it not for these, he would be a list man, for his mates do all his other business for him.

The carpenter. Tho' he is generally but a rough-hewn fellow, yet he values himself upon a well-built hull; and as for his intellects, they are much about the same model with the master's, for he has little more of the mathematicks than the boatswain.

The boatswain. It is not so much his fine silver-coil, as the illustrious chain that it hangs by, that is the distinguishing badge of his post, and which he's as proud of as my Lord Mayor is of his and prouder. He has a thousand pretty phrases and expressions pickt up at Billingsgate and elsewhere, which he never sends abroad without bedecking them with all the embroider'd oaths and curses that can be had for love or money. He has wit in his liquor, that's certain, for though he's often tipsy, it's at other men's cost.

A sea cook. The captain's cook and he are opposites as well in their practice as in their habitations, and seldom or never make incursions into each other's provinces. He cooks by the hour glass as the parsons preach sermons.

A midshipman. He's elevated as high as Flamsteed, in his own conceit, and is often times shewing you a sample of his ingenuity. He can prove the purser a rogue by Gunter's scale, and compose a bowl of punch by the rules of trigonometry . . . He's one that sometimes passes under the discipline of the cane or fist; that is when he is guilty of that great sin of omission of not giving timely notice of the captain's going from or coming into the ship.

The captain's steward. But he's too staunch a knave to trust to vain hopes and fair promises; so he takes care to make hay while the sun shines; and shuffles and cuts with everyone that has to do with him.

A sailor. He's one that is the greatest prisoner, and the greatest rambler in Christendom; there is not a corner of the world but he visits . . . but when he does get ashore he pays it off with a vengeance; for knowing his time to be but short, he crowds much in a little room and lives as fast as possible.

Appendix A: Some Makers of Tradition

Every drop of blood of me holds a heritage of patriotism.

Elias Lieberman

I drew my sword [for the American Colonies] in support of the violated dignity and rights of human nature.

John Paul Jones to the King of France

God give us men! a time like this demands
Men whom the spoils of office cannot buy
Men who have honor; men who will not lie

Josiah Gilbert Holland

From time to time, there is considerable discussion by the press, the services, and the Congress on whether military-naval careers may be made sufficiently attractive to secure a high percentage of superior individuals as professional commissioned and noncommissioned officers. For this reason, and at a time when the country more than ever requires the most intelligent and competent young men and women for its defense, we present here the records of some of the outstanding tradition makers of our Navy, from John Paul Jones to officers of our times.

Who are the outstanding leaders in the history of the Navy? That is an extremely difficult question, and here we will simply point out the desirable qualities that officers of this generation should endeavor to develop and emulate—in a word, we will emphasize characteristics of military leadership that are immutable. This helps sharpen our awareness of the importance of high personal esprit in striving to be a competent leader. Trying to live up to the best traditions of the naval service will show us what we might become if we are given the opportunity.

"Each man has his special gift," said Mahan, "and to succeed must act in accordance with it." The names of some who did may now be seen carved high in the marble amphitheater at Arlington Cemetery: John Paul Jones, Thomas Truxtun, Edward Preble, Isaac Hull, Stephen Decatur, Oliver Hazard

Bust of John Paul Jones. Executed from life by Jean Antoine Houdon, it stands in a niche in Jones's crypt at the U.S. Naval Academy. It was commissioned by the Lodge of the Nine Sisters in Paris, and was bequeathed to the Naval Academy Museum by Marshall Field of Chicago in 1958.
U.S. Naval Academy Museum

Perry, Thomas Macdonough, Charles Stewart, David Glasgow Farragut, David Dixon Porter, Andrew Hull Foote, John Lorimer Worden, George Dewey, and William Thomas Sampson. Others do not appear, but are just as deserving.

The Revolutionary War

John Paul Jones

> I have not yet begun to fight.
>
> John Paul Jones

John Paul Jones took part in several gallant actions in the early stages of the Revolutionary War off the North American coast. He was ordered to his first command, the *Providence*, on 10 May 1777. Later he commanded a squadron with his flag in the *Alfred*. On 14 June 1777 Congress appointed Jones to command the *Ranger*, and he sailed her for France late the same year. It was on this voyage that the first recognition of the American flag by a foreign government occurred, when Vice Admiral La Motte Picquet, commander of the French fleet, returned the *Ranger*'s salute of thirteen guns with nine.

In an effort to divert the British naval forces and relieve the pressure on General Washington's sea supply lines, Jones planned raids on the coasts of England proper. The *Ranger* sailed from Brest on 11 April 1778 and boldly headed for the Irish Sea, taking prizes en route. On 22 April Jones landed at Whitehaven, spiked the guns at the fort, and set fire to the shipping in the harbor. The following day he made another surprise landing, at St. Mary's Isle, and planned to seize the Earl of Selkirk as hostage for American seamen imprisoned in England—but the Earl was absent.

One day later, the *Ranger* encountered the British warship *Drake,* and in a bloody one-hour fight defeated and captured her. The *Drake* was the first man-of-war to surrender to a Continental Navy ship flying the Stars and Stripes. The *Ranger* returned to Brest with her prizes, and Jones became a hero to the French as well as the Americans.

Jones next outfitted a small squadron and put to sea with his flag in the *Bon Homme Richard* to intercept a fleet of British merchantmen. By the time he had sailed around the British Isles, circling Ireland to the west and around Scotland to the north, all but two of his ships had deserted him. He was to rendezvous with these two ships off Flamborough Head, a promontory on the east coast of England near the Scottish border. He arrived there on 3 September 1779, and there before him was a fleet of some forty-odd British merchantmen, escorted by the superior British frigate *Serapis.* Jones headed straight for the frigate and engaged her.

The battle, which began at sunset and lasted for four hours, was not only the most brilliant sea fight of the war, but one of the most remarkable single-ship actions in history. The superior guns of the *Serapis* began taking their toll almost immediately, and it was all Jones could do to bring the battered *Bon Homme Richard* alongside the frigate, where a rather one-sided slugging match began. Finally, with the *Richard*'s hold filled with four to five feet of water and in a sinking condition, with all her guns out of action except three nine-pounders, with half her crew killed or wounded, with rudder and rigging shot away and fires fast approaching the magazines, Captain Pearson of the *Serapis* hailed Jones, asking him if he surrendered. In response, Jones and his men boarded the *Serapis* as he shouted his challenging answer: "I have not yet begun to fight!" Jones captured and took command of the *Serapis.* He had to, for despite the use of pumps and every effort to save her, the *Bon Homme Richard* sank the following day from the severe damage to her hull.

Jones was given a vote of thanks by the Congress and was authorized to receive the first medal ever awarded to an American naval officer by Congress —the only officer of the Continental Navy to be so honored.

John Paul Jones's victory was a naval milestone: a fine new frigate of the then "Invincible Royal Navy" had been defeated and captured by an American captain. This action gave hope to the American cause and inspired the infant Navy by showing how it could give substantial aid to the struggling colonies.

Jones also inspired another tradition, one to which historians seldom refer: namely, that of magnanimity to a defeated foe. After the action involving the *Bon Homme Richard* and the *Serapis,* when the gallant Pearson presented his sword to Jones, tradition relates that the Royal Navy captain said: "I cannot, sir, but feel much mortification at the idea of surrendering my sword to a man who fought me with a rope around his neck." The reference was to the English allegation that Jones was a pirate.

Jones received his sword, but returned it at once, saying: "You have fought gallantly, sir, and I hope your king will give you a better ship."

Thus an American naval tradition was born. For example, in the War of 1812, after the Battle of Lake Erie, Perry returned the swords of the British captains as a mark of recognition of their stubborn resistance.

This tradition was continued when Capt. "Fighting Bob" Evans took the surrender of Captain Eulate, Spanish commander of the *Viscaya:*

> The captain [Eulate] [was] covered with blood from three wounds, with a bloodstained handkerchief about his bare head. Around him sat or lay a dozen or more wounded men. . . . The captain was tenderly placed in a chair and then hoisted to the deck, where he was received with the honors due his rank. As the chair was placed on the quarter-deck he slowly raised himself to his feet, unbuckled his sword belt, kissed the hilt of his sword and bowing low, gracefully presented it to me as a token of surrender. I never felt so sorry for a man in all my life. Of course I declined to receive the sword, or rather I hastily handed it back to Captain Eulate, but accepted the surrender of his officers and men in the name of Admiral Sampson, our commander in chief. My men were all crowded aft about the deck and superstructure, and when I declined the sword the brave hearts under the blue shirts appreciated my feelings and they cheered until I felt ashamed of myself.[*]

[*] Robley D. Evans, *A Sailor's Log* (New York: D. Appleton, 1908), p. 451.

The Quasi-War with France and the Tripolitan War

The small Navy of the Revolutionary War was finally disbanded, with nothing left behind except "the recollection of its service and sufferings," but traditions lived on. Some splendid naval leaders and seamen had been developed in a rugged school that fully qualified them to take command of the new American-built ships—all constructed under the act of 27 March 1794 and superior to any of their class in Europe.

When the famous frigates *Constitution, President, United States, Chesapeake, Constellation,* and *Congress* were completed, heroes of the Revolution —Barry, Nicholson, Barney, Dale, and Truxtun—were chosen to command the vessels. Truxtun gave a glorious account of himself in the *Constellation* when he captured the *Insurgente* and crippled the *Vengeance* in the short maritime war with France.

American naval activities then turned to another part of the world. Preble attacked the forts of Tripoli. Captains Somers, Wadsworth, and Israel went to their deaths in the daring explosive-boat attack. Before Preble's attack on Tripoli the *Philadelphia,* commanded by Bainbridge, was lost to the Tripolitan pirates. The ship went aground in shoal water before the surrender. The resistance, to say the least, was faint-hearted. Frost writes:

> It is true that then we had no naval tradition—but Germans also had none when they entered the World War. Yet they knew how to die! True, for Bainbridge there are many good excuses. But how we wish that he had stood forth there and spoken to his comrades, in the words of Beowulf:
>
>> Each of us must his end abide
>> in the ways of the world; so win who may glory ere death! When his
>>   days are told,
>> that is the warrior's worthiest doom.

Stephen Decatur afterward attacked and burned the captured *Philadelphia* that his father had once commanded. It inspired an undying tradition of naval enterprise. With few exceptions, the war with Tripoli was a brilliant naval campaign. It resulted in the elimination of payment of tribute to the Barbary Coast "racketeers" and added to the prestige of the Republic.

Stephen Decatur at Tripoli. Oil painting by William A. K. Martin.
U.S. Naval Academy Museum

The War of 1812

Next came the "second war for independence," the War of 1812. Hull's victory in the *Constitution* against the *Guerriere* astonished the public on both sides of the Atlantic. Congress thanked Hull in the name of the nation and gave his officers and crew fifty thousand dollars in prize money. This victory strengthened morale as it gave our new Navy confidence, and dispelled the prevailing idea that the British Navy was omnipotent.

Great Britain's attention was now directed, with some degree of alarm, to the daring exploits of the "Yankee sailors" and their frigates. The London *Times* wrote:

> It is more than merely that an English frigate has been taken, after what, we are free to confess, may be called a brave resistance, but that it has been taken by a new enemy, an enemy unaccustomed to such triumphs, and likely to be rendered insolent and confident by them. . . . Never before in the history of the world did an English frigate strike to an American; and though we cannot say that Captain Dacres, under all circumstances, is punishable for this act, yet we do say that there are commanders in the English Navy who would a thousand times rather have gone down with their colors flying than have set their brother officers so fatal an example.

The London *Times* was correct as to the confidence engendered, because the American Navy had achieved the first of the long list of impressive victories that astounded our own people. Decatur in the *United States* captured the *Macedonian*, while the *Constitution* shot every spar out of the frigate *Java*, and shortly afterward captured both the *Cyane* and *Levant* in the same action.

It was an era when fighting slogans were coined, such as Lawrence's dying words in the *Chesapeake:* "Fight her till she sinks and don't give up the ship." Perry carried the watchword on to Lake Erie, thus demonstrating the continuity of tradition, when he hoisted at the main royal masthead of the *Lawrence* a flag upon which were sewn Lawrence's last words: "Don't give up the ship." Then after the battle came Perry's dispatch, which has been so often quoted: "We have met the enemy and they are ours, two ships, two brigs, one schooner, and one sloop." American shipbuilders and seamen "delivered the goods" in practically all of these actions.

In the 1812–15 naval war, the Yankee sailors demonstrated their native coolness and a daring that derived from the pioneer spirit. Because of the constant gun drills, American marksmanship was unexcelled. Dashing American seamen dealt some powerful blows in this second war of independence.

Joshua Barney

For high adventure of the Captain Hornblower school, possibly none could exceed Joshua Barney of Baltimore, who left a comfortable farm to seek adventure. Barney was a master seaman and an officer who feared nothing. He had the distinction of serving in two wars, as well as in the Navy of France. He was perhaps at his best as a privateer, for once in eleven days he captured twelve ships.

At the age of sixteen he commanded a merchantman in the Mediterranean, at which time a Spanish admiral forced him to join in an attack on Algiers. He served in the state navies of Maryland and Pennsylvania, and in the Federal Navy. Not only did he command many private ships, but at the time of the French Revolution he accepted a commission in the French Navy as *chef de division des armées navales,* and for this received severe censure in the United States.

Benjamin Franklin was extremely fond of Barney, and presented him at the court of Versailles, where he kissed the cheek of Marie Antoinette and dined with Louis XVI. At another time he had a private audience with Napoleon and "saluted the hand of the Empress Josephine." Always a close friend of John Paul Jones, the intrepid Barney once accompanied him across the Atlantic for a landing in Plymouth, England. As a commodore in the French Navy in 1798, he became the friend and adviser of Toussaint L'Ouverture, the celebrated black dictator of Haiti. After visiting the Washingtons at Mount Vernon, he accompanied General and Mrs. Washington to the inaugural ceremonies in New York City, a duty that gave him the honor of being the first naval aide to a president of the United States.

Barney was a successful privateer during the War of 1812, but was captured three times by the British. Twice he was exchanged and returned to the fight. The third time he was sent to Old Mill Prison in Plymouth, England. He made a spectacular escape, commandeered a merchant, the 16-gun *Hyder Ally*, and eventually captured the 20-gun British brig *General Monk* off Cape May, New Jersey.

The remarkable Barney fought in seventeen battles in the Revolution, and in nine in the War of 1812, with a score of twenty-five victories. He was successful in all but the last battle, the so-called Battle of Bladensburg, Maryland —a fight to defend Washington, D.C. In 1814, with the American army massed in the north, the Chesapeake Bay and the cities of Washington, Baltimore, and Annapolis were left virtually undefended. Barney submitted a plan for the defense of the Chesapeake to President Madison, calling for the building of numerous gunboats. With these small, shallow-draft vessels, he was able to hold off the invaders for a time. However, the British were eventually too much, so he landed his crews, left the boats on the Patuxent River, and marched to Bladensburg to help the American militia intercept the British army. There, with a small detachment of bluejackets and marines, the doughty commodore "held his ground against a rush of British troops which scattered General Winder and his militia like chaff before the wind." He was captured once again, and was congratulated by the British commander for his gallantry. Later, he commanded a small force of naval militia that held off elements of the British land forces during the attack on Fort McHenry. As much at ease on a horse as on the quarterdeck, Barney had a mount shot out from under him at Bladensburg, where he also was wounded by being shot in the thigh.

Thomas MacDonough

Thomas MacDonough achieved a notable victory at Lake Champlain. After this action, Sir George Prevost hastily returned to Canada, and the northern frontier was never again seriously menaced. There is little doubt that MacDonough's decisive victory strongly affected the peace negotiations.

Thomas MacDonough
Naval Institute Photo Archive

After a detailed and comprehensive study of MacDonough in the *Naval War of 1812,* Theodore Roosevelt said:

> But MacDonough in this battle won a higher fame than any other commander of the war, British or American. He had a decidedly superior force to contend against, the officers and men of the two sides being about on a par in every respect; and it was solely owing to his foresight and resource that he won the victory. He forced the British to engage at a disadvantage by his excellent choice of position; and he prepared beforehand for every possible contingency. His personal prowess had already been shown at the cost of the rovers of Tripoli. . . . His skill, seamanship, quick eye, readiness of resource, and indomitable pluck are beyond all praise. Down to the time of the Civil War, his is the greatest figure in our naval history. A thoroughly religious man, he was as generous and humane as he was skillful and brave; one of the greatest of our sea captains, he has left a stainless name behind him.

The Civil War

Adm. David Glasgow Farragut

The continuity of this splendid sea tradition is illustrated by the career of Adm. David Glasgow Farragut. Trained by David Porter, Farragut was appointed prize master of the *Barclay* at the age of twelve. Half a century after assuming his first command, he won the Battle of New Orleans and became the first admiral of the U.S. Navy.

A masterful ship and fleet handler, the loyal and audacious Farragut was born near Knoxville, Tennessee, and spent his earliest years on the rugged East Tennessee frontier. As a child, on a flatboat trip down the Mississippi,

David Glasgow Farragut.
Farragut was the first officer in
the U.S. Navy to hold the rank
of admiral.
Photograph by Mathew B.
Brady; U.S. Naval Academy
Museum

he remembered the river pirates on the way, and at New Orleans he first saw
the men-of-war on which he later won imperishable fame. At the age of eight,
Farragut was adopted by Commodore David Porter; at the age of nine years
and five months, he received a midshipman's warrant; and at ten, he went to
sea under Porter in the *Essex*. At the age of twelve, he was given his first
command, the captured *Barclay*.

Farragut's career for many years was unspectacular. When the Civil War
began, he was hard put to prove his value to the Navy because of his southern birth and connections, even though he had remained loyal to the Union
cause and had moved from Virginia to New York. The chance to prove himself finally came in 1862 when Farragut, now over sixty, was given command
of the West Gulf Blockading Squadron. His heroic role as a maker of tradition evolved from this assignment that led to critical and decisive victories
at New Orleans and Mobile Bay. It was in the latter campaign that he made
his famous decision in stirring words that have become an American by-
word for courage and determination.

The scene was Mobile Bay in 1864. Farragut, lashed in the rigging of the
Hartford, noted that one ship had stopped after reports of "torpedoes ahead,"
that another had been sunk, and that the line of battle seemed hopelessly

Rear Adm. David Dixon Porter

tangled up directly under the guns of Fort Morgan. In response he made an immediate and inspiring decision: "Damn the torpedoes! Four bells! Captain Drayton, go ahead—Jouett, full speed." This order led to the capture of Mobile Bay, hastened the end of the Civil War, and gave the American Navy a new tradition for ships propelled by steam. Farragut became the epitome of the all-out offensive attack, most evident in his order for the attack on New Orleans when he noted that "the best protection against the enemy's fire is a well-directed fire from our own guns." Farragut had written to his wife before the battle: "As to being prepared for defeat, I certainly am not. Any man who is prepared for defeat would be half-defeated before he commenced. I hope for success; shall do all in my power to secure it and trust to God for the rest."

Growth as a World Power

Rear Adm. David Dixon Porter

David Dixon Porter's family was one of unsurpassed American naval tradition. His grandfather and granduncle had commanded ships in the American Revolution. His father, Commodore David Porter, who adopted Farragut, served in the French and Tripolitan wars, and in the War of 1812. David Dixon Porter, who had more continuous fighting time from 1861 to 1864 than any other "officer of distinction," rose from lieutenant to rear admiral in the Civil War and became the second American officer to attain the grade of full admiral (his adopted brother, Farragut, was the first).

At the age of ten Porter made his first cruise. He fought the Spaniards as a midshipman in the Mexican Navy at the age of fifteen. In this baptism of fire, his cousin, the commanding officer, was killed, Midshipman Porter was taken prisoner, and over one-third of the crew were killed or wounded. He became a midshipman in the U.S. Navy at the age of sixteen. After some daring exploits in the Mexican War, Porter had his great opportunity. While on monotonous blockade duty off the Southwest Pass of the Mississippi in 1861, Porter evolved a plan for the capture of New Orleans. He made a trip to Washington, D.C., and received the general approval of two senators and the secretary of the Navy. The secretary took him to see President Lincoln, who commented: "This should have been done sooner. The Mississippi is the key to the whole situation." The plan was adopted, and Porter recommended his adopted brother, Farragut, to command the operation.

After Farragut's fleet was assembled in the lower reaches of the Mississippi, Porter, with small vessels often under heavy fire, made a survey of the channel; this hydrographic reconnaissance made safe navigation possible. He was then ordered to command gunboats on the upper Mississippi, after completing a short command of a mortar flotilla on the James River in Virginia. The Mississippi command, which included all forces from St. Louis to Vicksburg, was of invaluable assistance to Gen. U. S. Grant in the capture of Vicksburg. Porter distinguished himself as a brilliant commander of gunboats.

Porter's Civil War career was climaxed with the bombardment, siege, and capture of Fort Fisher and Wilmington, North Carolina. At this time he commanded sixty vessels, of which five were ironclad—the largest force that had ever been brought together under the U.S. flag. Throughout, he impressed President Lincoln by his original ideas, his quick grasp of situations, and his superb leadership.

A vice admiral at fifty-three, Porter was ordered to the Naval Academy as superintendent. From 1865 to 1869 he made enormous strides in rebuilding the academy. Because he introduced baseball, rowing, and boxing there, some have called him "the father of Navy athletics." He certainly knew from experience what the Navy required in stamina and endurance, and few senior naval officers ever surpassed him in these qualities.

Adm. Stephen B. Luce

Adm. Stephen B. Luce

As commandant of midshipmen at the Naval Academy, father of standardized enlisted training, and founder of the Naval War College, Stephen B. Luce
led the rebirth of professional education in the Navy in the late 1800s. Luce
was a superb seaman and an equally good strategist. During the Civil War,
he came to the attention of the Navy Department for his superior work in
training midshipmen in seamanship at the Naval Academy. His textbook on
this subject was used throughout the Navy for years. In 1875 he established
the first station ship training for enlisted men, the precursor of the modern
boot camp. For years he fought the civilian bureaucracy in an effort to establish a Naval War College at Newport, Rhode Island, where naval strategy
would be taught to naval officers. The school was at last established in 1884,
and Admiral Luce continued to lecture there until he was eighty years of age.
He brought Commander (later Admiral) Mahan to the War College as one
of its first department heads. Luce insisted that naval officers should master
international law, history, the latest naval technology, and naval strategy in
a formal intellectual atmosphere.

Alfred Thayer Mahan
Naval Institute Photo Archive

Adm. Alfred Thayer Mahan

Alfred Thayer Mahan entered the Naval
Academy in 1856 as a third-class midshipman, the only person ever permitted to skip the fourth class year. After
graduation, he rose through the ranks,
carrying out the usual assignments of
the period, until 1885, when he was
assigned to the Naval War College as
a lecturer and as department head of
Naval Tactics and History. This began a long association with the War College during which Mahan served as president, lecturer, and writer even after
his retirement. In 1890 Mahan collected several of his lectures in a book, *The
Influence of Sea Power on History, 1660–1783,* the first of twenty books and
many essays on this subject. His influential book was translated into several
languages and made the required reading lists of several countries, notably
Germany and Japan. And his thinking influenced world events through the
middle of the twentieth century. Mahan's major contribution to naval tradition was his codification of the elements of sea power in such a fashion that
they could be grasped by naval students of our own Navy and of the world.

The Spanish-American War

Admiral of the Navy George Dewey

George Dewey, hero of the Battle of Manila Bay during the war with Spain
and our first and only "Admiral of the Navy," was an officer supremely con-
scious of American naval tradition. President Theodore Roosevelt wrote to
Dewey on May Day 1908, the tenth anniversary of the battle of Manila Bay:
"Surely no man in any country could hope for a higher reward than as yours,
for no other man living stands to his countrymen in quite the same position
that you do." Admiral Dewey recognized the tremendous but imponderable
effect of lofty tradition: "I have often asked myself, 'What would Farragut
do?' In the course of preparations for Manila Bay I often asked myself this

Admiral of the Navy George Dewey
Naval Institute Photo Archive

question, and I confess that I was thinking of him the night that we entered the Bay, and with the conviction that I was doing precisely what he would have done." Thus, he looked back thirty-six years to the time when he was a lieutenant with Farragut when he commanded the Union fleet and ran the gauntlet of the forts below Mobile.

After Dewey's fleet steamed at night past the island defenses of Manila Bay, he waited for first light to attack, at which time he gave the classic order, the casualness of which caught the American imagination: "You may fire when ready, Gridley." Dewey gave another order that "contributed to his subsequent reputation for laconic imperturbability, that is, the order to 'draw off for breakfast.'" Dewey afterward said that this was done to check remaining ammunition, and also because smoke was so heavy that it was impossible to fire accurately.

Although the news was seven days late arriving in the United States, never had a U.S. naval victory so caught the admiration of the American people. It inspired speeches, editorials, a congressional memorial, a "Hymn to Dewey," dozens of songs, and the manufacture of souvenirs of all descriptions.

Amid the unprecedented national adulation not many Americans sensed the long-range historic significance of the Battle of Manila Bay, since at the time there still remained a military campaign to quell the insurrection and make victory complete. This defeat of the Spanish Navy at Manila, together with the defeat of the Spanish Home Fleet at Santiago de Cuba, marked the emergence of the United States as a world power. Dewey's victory was "one of those feats," wrote Theodore Roosevelt. "which mark the beginning of new epochs." The sailor, author, and inventor, Adm. Bradley A. Fiske, believed that "the battle of Manila Bay was one of the most important ever fought. It decided that the United States should start in a direction in which it had never traveled before. It placed the United States in the family of great nations, and it put Spain into outer darkness. Before the battle, British Navy officers treated the United States Navy officers with condescension. In fact Europeans as a body treated all Americans so. They have never done so since."

Dewey's life (1837–1917) spanned the period from sailing frigates and wooden ships of the line, through the days of the steam frigates and armored vessels, to the battleship and the birth of the aircraft carrier. Four battleships that were at Pearl Harbor on that fateful day in 1941 were launched while Dewey was alive. Dewey, who knew Farragut and Porter, veterans of the War of 1812, also knew King, Halsey, and Nimitz of World War II.

In his message to Congress the day after Dewey's death, President Woodrow Wilson summed up his outstanding characteristics:

> It is pleasant to recall what qualities gave him his well-deserved fame; his practical directness; his courage without self-consciousness; his efficient capacity in matters of administration; the readiness to fight without asking any questions or hesitancy about any details. It was by such qualities that he continued and added lustre to the best traditions of our Navy. He had the stuff in him which all true men admire, and upon which all statesmen must depend in hour of peril.

World War I

Adm. William Sowden Sims

As an officer in World War I, by virtue of his attention to detail and his organization of the convoy system, William Sowden Sims will live in naval history as a symbol of U.S. Atlantic operations in that war.

Sims is credited with the doctrine and organization of the convoy system. His idea of the planned escort of merchant ships by naval vessels, with relentless war against submarines by all conceivable weapons and devices, permitted the United States to place 2,086,000 soldiers in Europe, half of whom were carried in British ships. This is remarkable considering that German submarines destroyed 6,618,623 tons of ships in 1917, while the shipbuilding of the whole world (less Germany and Austria) in that corresponding time was but 2,703,345 tons. The efficiency of Sims's plan speaks for itself in that these troops were delivered with no ships sunk en route.

The situation was critical when the United States entered the war in April 1917. Just before that, Admiral Sims was sent to confer with the British Admiralty and report on general conditions in the war area, with special attention

Adm. William Sowden Sims, commander, Naval Forces Europe

to methods used by the British to counter the submarine menace. He found that the situation was so serious that unless a more successful system for merchant ships were devised, Great Britain might have to sue for peace.

Although there was a great shortage of escort vessels, Admiral Sims strongly advocated the convoy system from the start. The British Admiralty admitted the failure of the existing antisubmarine measures, and with the support of Prime Minister Lloyd George and some progressive British naval officers, the British Cabinet ordered a trial of the escort-convoy system in May 1917.

These figures tell the story: From 1 February 1917 to 1 August 1917 the Germans destroyed an average 640,000 tons of Allied shipping per month; from 1 August 1917 to 1 February 1918, 300,000 tons a month; and from 1 February 1918 to the Armistice, 200,000 tons a month.

A British naval officer once said that the outstanding characteristic of an American naval officer is "his open-mindedness," whereas "we [British] cling too much at times to the practices of Lord Nelson." Sims's professional life epitomized the quality of "open-mindedness." In his specialty of gunnery he was one of the most progressive and best-informed officers of his time. Despite considerable Navy Department resistance, Sims, with the backing of Theodore Roosevelt, revolutionized gunnery practices and greatly improved the efficiency of the fleet in target practice. Always an indefatigable worker and a profound student of war, he also took great interest in his men. His tireless quest for new ideas inspired his subordinates and made him a shaper of tradition.

Sims set high standards for conduct of personnel and for battle readiness. In particular, he took great pride in the condition of readiness of U.S. ships of the Sixth Battle Squadron under Adm. Hugh Rodman at Scapa Flow, Scotland. When accompanying George V, the sailor king, on an inspection

Secretary of the Navy
Josephus Daniels, with the
Prince of Wales, later King
Edward VIII

of the *New York,* Sims must have been proud to hear His Majesty remark: "In the American Navy, the precept of cleanliness being next to godliness has been effectively adopted."

Sims inspired more than the respect of the enlisted men who served with him. A young officer serving in the *New York* wrote: "Each time when the sailors learned that Sims was to come, they were overjoyed and seemed to take particular interest in having the ships in the very pink of condition. Perhaps this is because a number of our chief petty officers at one time or another during their careers had served directly under Sims. The verdict of such men is perhaps, after all, the greatest test of a good commander. They loved him."

Secretary of the Navy Josephus Daniels

Most secretaries of the Navy serve briefly and do not change the nature of the service much. Secretary of the Navy Josephus Daniels was an exception. He served for eight years (1913–21), including all of World War I. He is best known for banning alcoholic beverages from Navy ships, but this is a social injustice, for he is really the "father of the modern U.S. Navy" as far as enlisted personnel are concerned. Daniels established a recruiting system that remains virtually unchanged to this day. By various general orders he set up

Fleet Adm. William D. Leahy

the service school system, the recruit training center system, and the Navy rate training courses, and he made it possible for enlisted personnel to enter the Naval Academy via the Preparatory School. He also superintended the entrance of women into the Navy in World War I. He originated the unsatisfactory discharge to rid the Navy of those who were damaging its ability and efficiency and converted the naval prison system from a holding institution to a rehabilitation organization. All these changes were made over the objection of the uniformed leaders of the Navy, and the wisdom of Daniels's actions has been proven by their lasting nature.

World War II

Fleet Adm. William D. Leahy, USN

William D. Leahy graduated from the Naval Academy in 1897 and retired as an admiral in 1939. He was then appointed governor of Puerto Rico. After approximately a year he was appointed ambassador to France, and in July 1942 was recalled to active duty as chief of staff to the president. In 1944 he was made a fleet admiral and appointed as the president's representative on the newly created National Intelligence Authority. He retired again in 1949. Admiral Leahy fulfilled to the highest degree the tradition that U.S. naval officers can serve with distinction in high government positions.

Fleet Adm. Ernest J. King, USN

> It is the particular business of the Navy to gain and keep control of the seas for the support and execution of our national policies. To accomplish this duty, we of the Navy must be prepared to defeat the enemy wherever be may be found on the seas or on the coasts bordering them.
>
> Adm. E. J. King, *Air Power*

Ernest J. King was graduated from the Naval Academy in 1901 and served in a variety of surface ships and submarine units before taking flight training in 1927. After Pearl Harbor he was appointed commander in chief of the U.S. fleet. In March 1942 the office of chief of naval operations was reestablished and was assumed by Admiral King. In 1944 he was made a fleet admiral.

For distinguished service concurrently as commander in chief of the U.S. fleet and chief of naval operations during the World War II period, Fleet Admiral King was awarded a Gold Star in lieu of the third Distinguished Service Medal with citation, in part, as follows:

> In his dual capacity [he] exercised complete military control of the Naval Forces of the United States Navy, Marine Corps, and Coast Guard and directed all activities of these forces in conjunction with the U.S. Army and our Allies to bring victory to the United States. As the United States Naval Member of the Joint Chiefs of Staff and the Combined Chiefs of Staff, he coordinated the naval strength of this country with all agencies of the United States and of the Allied Nations, and with exceptional vision, driving energy, and uncompromising devotion to duty, he fulfilled his tremendous responsibility of command and direction of the greatest naval force the world has ever seen and the simultaneous expansion of all naval facilities in the prosecution of the war.

On news of the death of Fleet Admiral King on 25 June 1956, President Eisenhower said: "The Nation has lost a great American and an outstanding naval officer. . . . Admiral King carried heavy responsibility with courage, brilliance and continued devotion to duty."

Fleet Adm. Ernest J. King

Fleet Adm. Chester W. Nimitz, USN

> The Lord gave us two ends to use: one to think with and one to sit with. The war depends on which we choose—heads, we win; tails, we lose.
>
> Admiral Nimitz's motto, as sent to Admiral Halsey

Chester W. Nimitz was graduated from the Naval Academy in 1905 and served in surface ships until entering the submarine service in 1908. Shortly after the attack on Pearl Harbor he was appointed commander in chief of the Pacific fleet and retained that command throughout World War II. Later he served as chief of naval operations and was appointed a fleet admiral. He was best known for his ability to exercise effective command over a large variety of forces and areas, thus contributing to the Navy tradition of command ability.

On 1 September 1945 (U.S. time), Fleet Admiral Nimitz was one of the signers for the United States when Japan formally accepted the surrender terms aboard the battleship *Missouri* in Tokyo Bay.

On 5 October 1945 Fleet Admiral Nimitz was presented a Gold Star in lieu of the third Distinguished Service Medal by the president of the United States personally, who cited him as follows:

> For exceptionally meritorious service . . . from June 1944 to August 1945. Initiating the final phase in the battle for victory in the Pacific, [he] attacked the Marianas, invading Saipan, inflicting a decisive defeat on the Japanese Fleet in the First Battle of the Philippines and capturing Guam and Tinian. In vital continuing operations, his Fleet Forces isolated the enemy-held bastions of the Central and Eastern Carolines and secured in quick succes-

> sion Peleliu, Angaur and Ulithi. With reconnaissance of the main beaches on Leyte effected, approach channels cleared and opposition neutralized in joint operations to reoccupy the Philippines, the challenge by powerful task forces of the Japanese Fleet resulted in a historic victory in the three-phased Battle for Leyte Gulf, October 24 to 26, 1944. Accelerating the intensity of aerial offensive by pressure exerted at every

Fleet Adm. Chester W. Nimitz

Fleet Adm. William F. Halsey Jr.
with President Harry S. Truman

hostile strong point, Fleet Admiral Nimitz culminated long-range strategy by successful amphibious assault on Iwo Jima and Okinawa . . . [and] finally placed representative forces of the United States Navy in the harbor of Tokyo for the formal capitulation of the Japanese Empire. . . . He demonstrated the highest qualities of a naval officer and rendered services of the greatest distinction to his country.

Nimitz, last of the fleet admirals, died 20 February 1966. President Johnson in tribute said: "Admiral Nimitz loved the country and the sea. His devotion to one inspired his mastery of the other, earning for his quiet courage and resolute leadership the undying gratitude of his countrymen and an enduring chapter in the annals of naval history."

Fleet Adm. William F. Halsey Jr., USN

William F. Halsey Jr. was graduated from the Naval Academy in 1904 and spent the majority of his early years at sea in destroyers. In 1935 he completed flight training and was designated a naval aviator at the age of fifty-two. When World War II began, he was commander of Carrier Division II with his flag in the *Enterprise*. After some early raids on Japanese-held islands, Admiral Halsey commanded the ships that took part in the Doolittle raid on Tokyo. He was then placed in command of the South Pacific Force in an effort to restore its morale and effectiveness. He did so, beginning his reputation for attacking whenever possible. He is best known for his forceful tactical command, a tradition he continued later when in command of the Third Fleet at the time of carrier raids on the Philippines and Japan. His pugnacity and aggressiveness earned him a place in history and promotion to the rank of fleet admiral.

Adm. Raymond A. Spruance

Adm. Raymond A. Spruance

Raymond A. Spruance was graduated from the Naval Academy in 1907 and served in surface ships throughout his career. Unlike Admiral Halsey, he did not qualify as a naval aviator. He was a quiet, studious officer and through his studies at the Naval War College was firmly grounded in naval strategy. At the outbreak of World War II he was a rear admiral in command of a cruiser division. Shortly before the Battle of Midway Admiral Halsey became ill and recommended that Admiral Spruance be placed in command of the U.S. Task Force that was being assembled to confront the Japanese at Midway. Spruance's knowledge of tactical aviation was limited, but his strategic knowledge carried the day at Midway. Later, in command of the Fifth Fleet, he demonstrated superior strategic judgment numerous times in the best traditions of the U.S. Navy.

Adm. Arleigh A. Burke

> He was not named "31-Knot Burke" for nothing. He had made it his way of life and his way of meeting the enemy. To go into action at the best speed possible, to concentrate on the job to be done, to take no half measures when an all-out effort would win. These are qualities we need in our public life and in our armed forces establishment.
>
> The *New York Times*, 27 May 1955, editorial concerning Adm. Arleigh Burke's selection as CNO

Arleigh A. Burke was graduated from the Naval Academy in 1923. He served in surface ships, but at the beginning of World War II found himself on shore duty. His repeated attempts to go to sea were rewarded with orders to command two destroyer divisions and two destroyer squadrons. He served in the South Pacific at the height of the operations in that area. Destroyer Squadron 23, known as the "Little Beaver" squadron, participated in twenty-two engagements. Admiral Burke went on to higher commands in World War II and eventually became chief of naval operations, a post he held for

Adm. Arleigh A. Burke

an unprecedented six years. He was best known as "31-Knot Burke," and he forged a new tradition for the destroyer as a versatile, fast, aggressive, hard-hitting ship always at the forefront of the toughest fighting.

The Cold War

Adm. Hyman G. Rickover

Hyman G. Rickover was graduated from the Naval Academy in 1922. He served in surface ships and submarines until 1937 and was then designated for engineering duty. In 1947 he began duty in the Bureau of Ships and with the Atomic Energy Commission. Admiral Rickover is generally credited with

Adm. Hyman G. Rickover welds his initials to a steel beam of Rickover Hall, the Naval Academy science and engineering building.

being the driving force behind the development of nuclear power for submarines and surface ships. The first such ship, USS *Nautilus*, was launched in 1953, and twenty-five years later there were 125 nuclear-powered vessels. Admiral Rickover set up a system of extreme thoroughness in the selection and training of personnel and in construction methods. As a result, there were no nuclear accidents in the program, and a new Navy tradition of safety, reliability, and performance was established.

Vice Adm. William F. "Red" Raborn Jr.

William F. Raborn Jr. was graduated from the Naval Academy in 1928. He was designated as a naval aviator and saw combat in World War II. After the war he entered the field of guided missiles. When the Navy decided to construct guided-missile-bearing submarines in 1955, the program was given the name Polaris and Admiral Raborn was designated head of the Special Projects Office that was to produce it. He was responsible for the entire system less the nuclear propulsion system of the submarine and was given top priority in personnel, money, and material. Only five years after the start of the project and without delay or accident, the USS *George Washington* went on its first deterrent patrol. Admiral Raborn had brought into being the most important weapon system ever produced by the Navy or the country. The Polaris system was followed by the improved Poseidon and Trident systems. Together they provided the United States with an invulnerable, reliable, and powerful deterrent system that prevented the Soviet Union from attacking and materially contributed to its eventual fall. Admiral Raborn was awarded the Collier Trophy and the Distinguished Service Medal, but never received adequate credit from press or public. History will record his accomplishments as being in the finest tradition of our Navy.

Vice Adm. William F. Raborn Jr.

Vice Adm. James B. Stockdale

The Vietnam War

Vice Adm. James B. Stockdale (MH)

James B. Stockdale was graduated from the Naval Academy in 1946. He served as a naval aviator in the Vietnam War before being shot down over that country. He was a prisoner of war for approximately seven years. As the senior prisoner of war in his camp, and second senior overall, he exercised strong control over his fellow prisoners in spite of torture, isolation, and brutal treatment. His personal conduct was an example to all and was instrumental in his being awarded the Medal of Honor. After release he resumed his naval career, rising to the rank of vice admiral, serving as the president of the Naval War College and, after retirement, as the president of the Military College of South Carolina, the Citadel. Together with other senior prisoners of war, he established a new tradition of outstanding conduct while a prisoner of war.

Appendix B: "The Laws of the Navy"

The first public appearance of Capt. R. A. Hopwood's poem came in the *Army and Navy Gazette* of 23 July 1898. There have been many printings since, with some minor differences in wording and number and order of stanzas. (Recent generations of Naval Academy graduates might object to the omissions below.) In the original article, Captain Hopwood acknowledges Rudyard Kipling's poem on the "Law of the Jungle." The text printed here is from the original publication. The notes indicate changes that have appeared in various publications, including the Naval Academy's Reef Points and previous versions of this book. Minor changes in spelling and punctuation are not noted.[*]

> Now these are laws of the Navy,
> Unwritten and varied they be;
> And he that is wise will observe them,
> Going down in his ship to the sea;
>
> As naught may outrun the destroyer,
> Even so with the law and its grip,
> For the strength of a Ship is the Service,
> And the strength of the Service, the Ship.
>
> Take heed what ye say of your rulers,[1]
> Be your words spoken softly or plain,
> Lest a bird of the air tell the matter,
> And so ye shall hear it again.
>
> If ye labour from morn until even'
> And meet with reproof for your toil,
> It is well; that the gun may be humbled,
> The compressor must check the recoil.

---

[*] We are indebted to Capt. Joseph J. Schweighofer, USN-Ret., for his research on the original poem.
[1] "Take heed what ye say of your *seniors*,"

On the strength of one link in the cable,
Dependeth the might of the chain.
Who knows when *thou* mayst be tested?
So live that thou bearest the strain!

When the ship that is tired returneth,
With the signs of the sea showing plain,
Men place her in dock for a season,
And her speed she reneweth again.

So shall thou, lest perchance thou grow weary
In the uttermost parts of the sea,
Pray for leave, for the good of the Service,
As much and as oft as may be.

Count not upon certain promotion,
But rather to gain it aspire;
Though the sight-line shall end on the target,
There cometh, perchance, a miss-fire.

Canst follow the track of the dolphin
Or tell where the sea swallows roam;
Where leviathan taketh his pastime;
What ocean he calleth his home?

Even so with the words of thy rulers,[2]
And the orders those words shall convey.
Every law is as naught beside this one:
"Thou shalt *not* criticise, but obey."

Saith the wise, "How may I know their purpose,"
Then acts without wherefore or why.
Stays the fool but one moment to question,
And the chance of his life passeth by.

If[3] ye win through an African jungle,[4]
Unmentioned at home in the Press,
Heed it not, no man seeth the piston,
But it driveth the ship none the less.

---

[2] "Even so with the words of thy *seniors*,"
[3] Stanza 12 in the original was moved to ninth.
[4] "If ye win through an *Arctic ice floe*,"

Do they growl? It is well; be thou silent,
So that work goeth forward amain;
Lo! The gun throws her shot to a hair's breadth,
And shouteth, yet none shall complain.

Do they growl and the work be retarded?
It is ill, speak, whatever their rank;
The half-loaded gun also shouteth,
But can she pierce armor with blank?

Doth the paintwork make war with the funnels?
Do the decks to the cannon complain?
Nay, they know that some soap or a scraper
Unites them as brothers again.

So ye, being Heads of Departments,
Do your growl with a smile on your lip,
Lest ye strive and in anger be parted,
And lessen the might of your ship.

Dost deem that thy vessel needs gilding,
And the dockyard forbear to supply;
Place thy hand in thy pocket and gild her;
There be those who have risen thereby.

Dost[5] think, in a moment of anger,
'Tis well with thy seniors to fight?
They prosper, who burn in the morning,
The letters they wrote overnight;

For some there be, shelved and forgotten,
With nothing to thank for their fate,
Save that (on a half-sheet of foolscap),
Which a fool "Had the honor to state—."

 If the fairway be crowded with shipping,
Beating homeward the harbour to win,
It is meet that, lest any should suffer,
The steamers pass cautiously in;

So thou, when thou nearest promotion,
And the peak that is gilded is nigh,

[5] Stanzas 18 and 19 were moved to seventeenth and eighteenth, respectively.

Give heed to thy words and thine actions,
Lest others be wearied thereby.

It is ill for the winners to worry,
Take thy fate as it comes with a smile,
And when thou art safe in the harbour
They will envy, but may not revile.

Uncharted the rocks that surround thee,
Take heed that the channels thou learn,
Lest thy name serve to buoy for another
That shoal, the Courts-Martial Return.

Though a Harveyized belt may protect her,[6]
The ship bears the scar on her side;
It is well if the court shall acquit thee;
'Twere best hadst thou never been tried.[7]

As the wave rises clear to the hawse pipe,
Washes aft, and is lost in the wake,
So shall ye drop astern, all unheeded,
Such time as the law ye forsake.[8]

(Capt. Roland A. Hopwood, RN)

---

[6] "Though *Armour, the belt* that protects her,"
[7] The first stanza was repeated as the twenty-fifth:

> Now these are laws of the Navy,
> Unwritten and varied they be;
> And he that is wise will observe them,
> Going down in his ship to the sea.

[8] The following stanza was added as the last:

> Now these are the Laws of the Navy
> And many and mighty are they.
> But the hull and the deck and the keel
> And the truck of the law is—OBEY.

Appendix C: "The Navy Hymn"

"Eternal Father Strong to Save"

In 1860 the Reverend William Whiting, a clergyman of the Church of England, after passing safely through a violent gale in the Mediterranean, composed what is popularly called "The Navy Hymn." John Bacchus Dykes of England wrote the music. This beautiful hymn, "Eternal Father Strong to Save," was printed in the United States in 1870, and in 1879 a young officer, Charles J. Train, in charge of the midshipman choir, initiated the singing of the hymn in the Chapel of the Naval Academy. The first stanza is always sung at the close of each chapel service.

MELITA
In moderate time
JOHN B. DYKES, 1861

1 E - ter - nal Fa - ther, strong to save, Whose arm hath bound the
2 O Christ, whose voice the wa - ters heard And hushed their ra - ging

rest - less wave, Who bidd'st the migh - ty o - cean deep Its
at thy word, Who walk - edst on the foam - ing deep, And

own ap - point - ed lim - its keep: O hear us when we
calm a - mid its rage didst sleep: O hear us when we

cry to thee For those in per - il on the sea.
cry to thee For those in per - il on the sea. A - men.

3

Most Holy Spirit, who didst brood
Upon the chaos dark and rude,
And bid its angry tumult cease,
And give, for wild confusion, peace;
    O hear us when we cry to thee
    For those in peril on the sea.

4

Lord, guard and guide the men who fly
Through the great spaces in the sky.
Be with them always in the air,
In darkening storms or sunlight fair.
    O hear us when we lift our prayer
    For those in peril in the air.

(Mary C. D. Hamilton)

5

Eternal Father, grant we pray,
To all Marines, both night and day,
The courage, honor, strength, and skill
Their land to serve, thy law fulfill;
    Be thou the shield forevermore
    From every peril to the Corps.

(J. E. Seim, 1966)

6

Lord, stand beside the men who build,
And give them courage, strength and skill,
O grant them peace of heart and mind,
And comfort loved ones left behind.
    Lord hear our prayer for all Seabees,
    Where'er they be on land or sea.

(R. J. Dietrich, 1960)

7

Lord, God, our power evermore,
Whose arm doth reach the ocean floor,
Dive with our men beneath the sea;
Traverse the depths protectively.
    O hear us when we pray, and keep
    Them safe from peril in the deep.

(David B. Miller, 1965)

8

O, God, protect the women who,
In service, faith in thee renew;
O guide devoted hands of skill
And bless their work within thy will;
    Inspire their lives that they may be
    Examples fair on land and sea.

(Lines 1–4, Merle E. Strickland, 1972, and adapted by
James D. Shannon, 1973; lines 5–6, Beatrice M. Truitt, 1948)

9

Creator, Father, who dost show
Thy splendor in the ice and snow,
Bless those who toil in summer light
And through the cold Antarctic night,
    As they, thy frozen wonders learn,
    Bless those who wait for their return.

(L. E. Vogel, 1965)

10

Eternal Father, Lord of hosts,
Watch o'er the men who guard our coasts.
Protect them from the raging seas
And give them light and life and peace.
    Grant them from thy great throne above
    The shield and shelter of thy love.

(Author and date unknown)

11

Eternal Father, King of birth,
Who didst create the heaven and earth,
And bid the planets and the sun
Their own appointed orbits run;
    O hear us when we seek thy grace
    For those who soar through outer space.

(J. E. Volante, 1961)

12

Creator, Father, who first breathed
In us the life that we received,
By power of thy breath restore
The ill, and men with wounds of war.
    Bless those who give their healing care,
    That life and laughter all may share.

(Galen H. Meyer, 1969)

13

God, who dost still the restless foam,
Protect the ones we love at home.
Provide that they should always be
By thine own grace both safe and free.
    O Father, hear us when we pray
    For those we love so far away.

(Hugh Taylor, date unknown)

14

Lord, guard and guide the men who fly
And those who on the ocean ply;
Be with our troops upon the land,
And all who for their country stand;
    Be with these guardians day and night
    And may their trust be in thy sight.

(Author unknown, c. 1955)

15

O Father, King of earth and sea,
We dedicate this ship to thee.
In faith we send her on her way;
In faith to thee we humbly pray;
    O hear from heaven our sailor's cry
    And watch and guard her from on high.

16

And when at length her course is run
Her work for home and country done,
Of all the souls that in her sailed
Let not one life in thee have failed;
    But hear from heaven our sailor's cry,
    And grant eternal life on high.

(Stanzas 15–16, author and date unknown)

"Anchors Aweigh"

Many Americans, including practically all Navy officers and enlisted personnel, have been stirred by the strains of "Anchors Aweigh." The music for this remarkable composition was written by Lt. Charles Adam Zimmerman, member of the Naval Academy band, which he had joined when he was twenty-one years of age. The band was then a civilian contract organization. Zimmerman was still with the band when its status was changed to Regular Navy on 21 April 1910, at which time he was appointed band leader and given the pay and allowances of a second lieutenant in the Marine Corps.

Lieutenant Zimmerman composed the music of "Anchors Aweigh" in 1906, with dedication to the Class of '07. It was first played publicly at the Army/Navy football game in the autumn of 1906 and, of course, ever thereafter.

Zimmerman became a highly valued institution in his capacity as leader of the Naval Academy band for more than thirty years. In 1916 a memorial monument was erected on his grave in the Naval Academy cemetery by "his midshipmen friends."

"The Navy Hymn" is played only at religious services. "Anchors Aweigh" is a football song and is played at athletic events, parades, and other similar events. Unlike the practice for "The Marines' Hymn," it is not customary for naval personnel or Naval Academy graduates to stand when "Anchors Aweigh" is played. While there was an effort to institute such a practice, the directive was never signed. Naval Academy graduates do stand when their alma mater "Navy Blue and Gold" is played.

Appendix D: "The Marines' Hymn"

1. From the Halls of Mon-te - zu - ma To the shores of Trip-o - li We fight our coun-try's bat - tles On the land as on the sea . . . First to fight for right and free - dom And to keep our hon-or clean . . We are proud to claim the ti - - tle Of U - nit - ed States Ma - rine. . .

From the Halls of Montezuma
To the shores of Tripoli;
We fight our country's battles
On the land as on the sea;
First to fight for right and freedom

And to keep our honor clean;
We are proud to claim the title
Of United States Marine.

Our flag's unfurl'd to ev'ry breeze
From dawn to setting sun;
We have fought in ev'ry clime and place
Where we could take a gun;
In the snow of far off Northern lands
And in sunny tropic scenes;
You will find us always on the job:
The United States Marines.

Here's health to you and to our Corps
Which we are proud to serve;
In many a strife we've fought for life
And never lost our nerve;
If the Army and the Navy
Ever look on Heaven's scenes;
They will find the streets are guarded
By United States Marines.

The "hymn" of the Marines is not religious in nature. It is a stirring martial piece of music designed, when heard, to quicken the blood of every Marine and every American. It is one of the most recognizable pieces of military music in the world, and many stories and legends are associated with it and its origins. The 16 August 1918 edition of the *Stars and Stripes* newspaper included this one:

> A wounded officer from among the gallant French lancers had just been carried into a Yankee field hospital to have his dressing changed. He was full of compliments and curiosity about the dashing contingent that fought at his regiment's left. "A lot of them are mounted troops by this time," he explained, "for when our men would be shot from their horses, these youngsters would give one running jump and gallop ahead as cavalry. I believe they are soldiers from Montezuma. At least, when they advanced this morning, they were all singing: From the Halls of Montezuma to the Shores of Tripoli.

The source of the song is clouded, but the music is generally attributed to the composer Jacques Offenbach, from a minor work entitled "Genevieve de Brabant," first produced in 1859 and expanded in 1867 to include a duet from which, allegedly, comes the tune. The words are even more difficult to attribute. Legend has it that they were first written by an anonymous Marine during the Mexican War. This would make the words predate the music by about twenty years. This legend solves the discrepancy by noting that Offenbach used the tune of an earlier popular Spanish folksong as his inspiration.

Whatever the source, "The Marines' Hymn" first appeared in print in 1918. And while there have been several unofficial stanzas written, since their approval in 1929 the stanzas printed above represent the Marine Corps official version. The words for the fourth line in the first stanza were changed in 1942 to: "In the air, on land, and sea." The commandant of the Marine Corps approved them after a suggestion by former GySgt H. L. Tallman, who had fought with the Marine Corps Aviation Force in World War I.

Another tradition born of Marine music concerns the U.S. Marine Band. Known as "The President's Own," for playing for every president since Thomas Jefferson, the band has played for every important occasion at the White House. In 1908 the band began the custom of standing at attention throughout the playing of the "Star-Spangled Banner." Audiences soon followed suit.

Appendix E: A Note on the Much-Quoted Letter of John Paul Jones

The letter so frequently quoted and ascribed to John Paul Jones is given below. Research has disclosed that this letter, as commonly printed, was not written by Jones, but was a composite of Jones's sayings, published for the first time by Augustus C. Buell in his work, *John Paul Jones, Founder of the American Navy.*

Without entering into details of the literary argument, the facts of which have been adequately and conclusively covered by the late professor L. H. Bolander, for many years librarian at the Naval Academy, we set forth here the first paragraph of Jones's letter and Buell's version of it.

The following quotation is from a letter, a copy of which was made by Jones's secretary and may be found in the Library of Congress. It is part of an open letter to the Marine Committee, dated 21 January 1777.

> None other than a Gentleman, as well as a Seaman, both in theory and practice is qualified to support the character of a Commissioned Officer in the Navy, nor is any man fit to command a Ship of War who is not also capable of communicating his Ideas on Paper in Language that becomes his Rank.

Please note the first two paragraphs of the letter as interpreted by Buell (see below). There is no proof that John Paul Jones ever wrote the letter; but as Bolander states in his Naval Institute *Proceedings* article "Two Notes on John Paul Jones" (July 1928), "that he truly was the author of such phrases is beyond doubt."

In short, Buell drafted a letter that covered many of Jones's suggestions and opinions; although this literary practice is not condoned, portions of the Buell letter of Jones are presented here as the essence of that brave, dashing officer's code. Of the variety of influences that have shaped our naval tradition, none has had a greater impact than the deeds and writings of the "founder of the American Navy."

Qualifications of the Naval Officer: A Collection from Jones's Reports and Letters in Modern Version as Arranged by A. C. Buell

It is by no means enough that an officer of the navy should be a capable mariner. He must be that, of course, but also a great deal more. He should be as well a gentleman of liberal education, refined manners, punctilious courtesy, and the nicest sense of personal honour.

He should not only be able to express himself clearly and with force in his own language both with tongue and pen, but he should also be versed in French and Spanish—for an American officer particularly the former— for our relations with France must necessarily soon become exceedingly close in view of the mutual hostility of the two countries towards Great Britain.

The naval officer should be familiar with the principles of International Law, and the general practice of Admiralty Jurisprudence, because such knowledge may often, when cruising at a distance from home, be neces- sary to protect his flag from insult or his crew from imposition or injury in foreign ports.

He should also be conversant with the usages of diplomacy, and capable of maintaining, if called upon, a dignified and judicious diplomatic corre- spondence; because it often happens that sudden emergencies in foreign waters make him the diplomatic as well as the military representative of his country, and in such cases he may have to act without opportunity of consulting his civic or ministerial superiors at home, and such action may easily involve the portentous issue of peace or war between great powers. These are general qualifications, and the nearer the officer approaches the full possession of them the more likely he will be to serve his country well and win fame and honours for himself.

Coming now to view the naval officer aboard ship and in relation to those under his command, he should be the soul of tact, patience, justice, firmness, and charity. No meritorious act of a subordinate should escape his attention or be left to pass without its reward, even if the reward be only one word of approval. Conversely, he should not be blind to a single fault in any subordinate, though, at the same time, he should be quick and unfailing to distinguish error from malice, thoughtlessness from incompe- tency, and well-meant shortcoming from heedless or stupid blunder. As he should be universal and impartial in his rewards and approval of merit, so should he be judicial and unbending in his punishment or reproof of mis- conduct.

In his intercourse with subordinates he should ever maintain the atti- tude of the Commander, but that need by no means prevent him from the amenities of cordiality or the cultivation of good cheer within proper limits. Every Commanding Officer should hold with his subordinates such relations as will make them constantly anxious to receive invitations to sit at his mess-table, and his bearing towards them should be such as to encourage them to express their feelings to him with freedom and to ask his views without reserve.

It is always for the best interests of the Service that a cordial interchange of sentiments and civilities should subsist between superior and subordinate officers aboard ship. Therefore, it is the worst of policy in superiors to behave towards their subordinates with indiscriminate hauteur, as if the latter were of a lower species. Men of liberal minds, themselves accustomed to command, can ill brook being thus set at naught by others who, from temporary authority, may claim a monopoly of time and sense for the time being. If such men experience rude, ungentle treatment from their superiors, it will create such heartburnings and resentments as are nowise consonant with that cheerful ardour and ambitious spirit that ought ever to be characteristic of officers of all grades. In one word, every Commander should keep constantly before him the great truth, that to be well obeyed he must be perfectly esteemed.

But it is not alone with subordinate officers that a Commander has to deal. Behind them, and the foundation of all, is the crew. To his men, the Commanding Officer should be Prophet, Priest, and King. His authority when off shore being necessarily absolute, the crew should be as one man impressed that the Captain, like the Sovereign, "can do no wrong."

This is the most delicate of all the Commanding Officer's obligations. No rule can be set for meeting it. It must ever be a question of tact and perception of human nature on the spot and to suit the occasion. If an officer fails in this, he cannot make up for such failure by severity, austerity, or cruelty. Use force and apply restraint or punishment as he may, he will always have a sullen crew and an unhappy ship. But force must be used sometimes for the ends of discipline. On such occasions the quality of the Commander will be most sorely tried. . . .

When a Commander has, by tact, patience, justice, and firmness, each exercised in its proper turn, produced such an impression upon those under his orders in a ship of war, he has only to await the appearance of his enemy's top-sails upon the horizon. He can never tell when that moment may come. But when it does come, he may be sure of victory over an equal or somewhat superior force, or honourable defeat by one greatly superior. Or, in rare cases, sometimes justifiable, he may challenge the devotion of his followers to sink with him alongside the more powerful foe, and all go down together with the unstricken flag of their country still waving defiantly over them in their ocean sepulchre.

No such achievements are possible to an unhappy ship with a sullen crew.

All these considerations pertain to the naval officer afloat. But part, and often an important part, of his career must be in port or on duty ashore. Here he must be of affable temper and a master of civilities. He must meet and mix with his inferiors of rank in society ashore, and on such occasions he must have tact to be easy and gracious with them, particularly when ladies are present; at the same time without the least air of patronage or affected condescension, though constantly preserving the distinction of rank.

Appendix F: Homeward Bound Pennant

Navy Department Bulletin of 31 August 1947

1. The Chief of Naval Operations has received many inquiries requesting information concerning the "homeward bound" pennant. The following codifies all known authentic information.

2. The use of the "homeward bound" pennant is traditional. The specifications of the design and rules for display apparently have never been adequately set forth; however, the following usage is believed to conform with tradition:

(a) A vessel which has been on duty in foreign waters outside the continental limits of the United States continuously for a period of nine months (270 days) or more flies the "homeward bound" pennant upon getting under way to proceed to a port of the United States.

(b) The "homeward bound" pennant is divided vertically into two parts: that portion next to the hoist is blue and the fly is divided horizontally into halves, the upper red and the lower white. In the blue portion is placed one white star for the first nine months that the ship has been continuously on duty in foreign waters outside the continental limits of the United States, plus one additional white star for each additional six months. The over-all length of the pennant was normally one foot for each officer and man on the ship who has been on duty outside the United States for nine months or more. Where this produces a pennant excessively long, its length is restricted to the length of the ship.

(c) The relative proportions of the pennant shall be as follows:

Length of pennant: 1

Width

at hoist: .005

at fly: .0015

Distance between centers of stars and from centers of end stars to ends of blue portion: .004

(Hence, the length of the blue portion is derived by multiplying the number of stars, plus one, by .004)

Diameter of stars: .003

(d) Upon arrival in a port of the United States, the blue portion containing the star or stars is presented to the commanding officer. The remainder of the pennant is divided equally among the officers and men of the ship's company.

Appendix G: Swallowing the Anchor
(A Note on Retirement)

[T]hereafter go thy way, taking with thee a shapen oar, till thou shalt come to such men as know not the sea, neither eat meat savoured with salt; yea, nor have they knowledge of ships of purple cheek, nor shapen oars which serve for wings to ships. And I will give thee a most manifest token, which cannot escape thee. In a day when another wayfarer shall meet thee and say that thou hast a winnowing fan on thy stout shoulder, even then make fast thy shapen oar in the earth and do goodly sacrifice to the lord Poseidon, even with a ram and a bull and a boar, the mate of swine, and depart for home and offer holy hecatombs to the deathless gods that keep the wide heaven, to each in order due. And from the sea shall thine own death come, the gentlest death that may be, which shall end thee foredone with smooth old age, and the folk shall dwell happily around thee. This that I say is sooth.

The Odyssey, Book XI, trans. S. H. Butcher and A. Lang

Bibliography

Many things contained in this book are no other than collections of other authors, and my labor is no more therein than theirs who gather a variety of flowers out of several gardens to compose one sightly garland.

Sir William Monson (1703)

Sociological and Psychological Consideration of Customs, Traditions, and Usage

Ellis, Havelock. *The Dance of Life*. Boston: Houghton Mifflin, 1924.

Ludovici, Anthony M. *A Defence of Aristocracy*. London: Constable and Co., Ltd., 1933.

Rapport, Dr. Angelo S. *Superstitions of Sailors*. London: Stanley Paul Co., Ltd., 1928.

Spencer, Herbert. *Principles of Sociology*. 3 vols. Part 4: "Ceremonial Institutions." New York, 1880.

Veblen, Thorstein. *The Theory of the Leisure Class*. New York, 1899.

Sea Lore, Customs, Traditions, Usage, Memoirs, and Naval History

Alden, Carroll Storrs, and Capt. Ralph Earle, USN. *Makers of Naval Tradition*. Boston: Ginn and Co., 1925.

Allen, G. W. *Our Naval War with France*. Boston: Houghton Mifflin, 1909.

Ammen, Daniel, Rear Adm., USN. *Old Navy and the New*. Philadelphia: Lippincott, 1891.

Arnold-Forster, D., Rear Adm., RN. *The Ways of the Navy*. London: Ward, Loch and Co., 1932.

Barney, Mary. *A Biographical Memoir of the Late Commodore Barney*. Boston, 1832.

Beckett, W. N. T., Cdr., RN. *A Few Naval Customs, Expressions, Traditions, and Superstitions*. 2d ed. Portsmouth, England: Gieves, Ltd., 1932.

Chatterton, E. Keble. *Sailing the Seas*. London: Chapman and Hall, 1931.

Clark, George R., Rear Adm., USN (Ret.), W. O. Stevens, Carroll S. Alden, and Herman F. Krafft. *A Short History of the United States Navy*. Rev. ed. Philadelphia: Lippincott, 1927.

Coggeshall, George. *History of American Privateers and Letters of Marque*. New York, n.d.

Conrad, Joseph. *The Mirror of the Sea: Memories and Impressions.* Garden City, N.Y.: Doubleday, Page, 1921.

Cooper, James Fenimore. *The History of the Navy of the United States.* 2 vols. Philadelphia: Lea and Blanchard, 1839.

DeKoven, Mrs. Reginald. *Life and Letters of John Paul Jones.* 2 vols. New York: Charles Scribner's Sons, 1913.

Duncan, Robert B. *Brave Deeds of American Sailors.* Philadelphia: George W. Jacobs, 1912.

Field, C., Col., RMLI. *Old Times Afloat: A Naval Anthology.* London: Andrew Melrose, Ltd., 1932.

Gleaves, Albert, Lt. Cdr., USN. *James Lawrence, Captain, United States Navy, Commander of the "Chesapeake."* New York: G. P. Putnam's Sons, 1904.

Green, Fitzhugh, Lt. Cdr., USN. *Our Naval Heritage.* New York: Century, 1925.

Hall, Basil, Capt., RN. *Fragments of Voyages and Travels.* London: Edward Mixon, 1846.

Hunter, Francis T. *Beatty, Jellicoe, Sims, and Rodman.* New York: Doubleday, Page, 1919.

Jones, George. *Sketches of Naval Life: A Series of Letters from the "Brandywine" and "Constitution" Frigates.* New Haven, 1829.

Kimball, H. *The Naval Temple: Complete History of the Battles Fought by the Navy of the United States.* Boston, 1816.

Lowry, R. G., Lt. Cdr., RN. *The Origin of Some Naval Terms and Customs.* London: Sampson Low, Marston, 1930.

Mackenzie, A. S. *Life of Stephen Decatur.* Boston: Chas. C. Little and Jas. Brown, 1846.

Mahan, A. T., Capt., USN. *Types of Naval Officers: Drawn from History of the British Navy.* Boston: Little, Brown, 1918.

Masefield, John. *Sea Life in Nelson's Time.* New York: Macmillan, 1925.

Melville, Herman. *White Jacket.* Boston: Page, 1892.

Monson, Sir William. *Naval Tracts in Six Books.* London: Printed for Awnsham and John Churchill, 1704.

Montgomery, James Eglington, of the Admiral's Staff. *Our Admiral's Flag Abroad: The Cruise of Admiral D. G. Farragut.* New York: G. P. Putnam's Sons, 1869.

Morgan, William James, ed. *Naval Documents of the American Revolution.* Washington, D.C.: Naval History Division, Department of the Navy, 1976.

Morris, Charles, Commodore, USN. *The Autobiography of Commodore Morris.* U.S. Naval Institute *Proceedings,* vol. 6, 1880.

Porter, D. D. *Memoirs of Commodore David Porter.* Albany: J. Munsell, 1875.

Puckle, Bertram S. *Funeral Customs: Their Origin and Development.* New York: Frederick A. Stokes, 1926.

Robinson, Charles N., Cdr., RN. *The British Tar in Fact and Fiction.* New York: Harper and Bros., 1909.

Robinson, William Morrison. *The Confederate Privateers.* New Haven: Yale University Press, 1928.

Rogers, Stanley. *Sea Lore.* New York: Thomas Y. Crowell, 1929.

Russell, Phillip. *John Paul Jones, Man of Action.* New York: Brentano's, 1927.

Sayer, Edmund S. *Ships of Other Days.* Nice, France: Imprimerie Gastaud, 1930.

Sherburne, J. H. *Life and Character of the Chevalier John Paul Jones.* Washington, D.C., 1825.

Snow, Elliot, Rear Adm. (C.C.), USN (Ret.). *Life in a Man-of-War: or Scenes in "Old Ironsides" during Her Cruise in the Pacific.* Boston: Houghton Mifflin; Cambridge: Riverside Press, 1929.

Snow, Elliot, Rear Adm. (C.C.), USN (Ret.), and Lt. Cdr. A. H. Gosnell, USNR. *On the Decks of "Old Ironsides."* New York: Macmillan, 1932.

Stewart, C. W., ed. *John Paul Jones Commemoration at Annapolis . . . 1906.* Washington, D.C.: Government Printing Office, 1907.

Swan, Oliver G., ed. *Deep Water Days.* Philadelphia: McCrae, Smith, 1929.

Ward, Edward W. *The Wooden World Dissected in the Character of a Ship of War.* London: Edwin Chappell, 1929. First published 1707; reprinted from the Fifth Edition, 1751.

Wells, Gerard, Rear Adm., RN. *Naval Customs and Traditions.* London: Philip Alan, 1930.

Wilcox, E. E., Lt. (jg) USNR. Letter to the Director of Naval Public Relations, 14 February 1943.

Yexley, Lionel. *Our Fighting Sea Men.* London: Stanley Paul, 1911.

Marine Encyclopedias; Nautical Dictionaries of Words, Phrases, and Expressions; Routine Books, Order Books, and Naval Regulations

Ansted, A. *A Dictionary of Sea Terms.* Glasgow: Brown, Son and Ferguson, 1933.

Belknap, Reginald R., Capt., USN. *Routine Book.* Annapolis: U.S. Naval Institute, 1918.

Blunt, Edmund H. *Theory and Practice of Seamanship . . . with Rules, Regulations, and Instructions for the Naval Service.* New York, 1824.

Bradford, Gershom. *A Glossary of Sea Terms.* New York: Yachting, Inc., 1927.

Cowan, Frank. *A Dictionary of the Proverbs and Proverbial Phrases of the English Language Relating to the Sea.* Greensburgh, Pa.: Olivier Publishing House, 1894.

Falconer's Marine Dictionary. Revised by Dr. Wm. Burney. London, 1815.

Heinl, R. D., Jr. *Dictionary of Military and Naval Quotations.* Annapolis: Naval Institute Press, 1966.

A Naval Encyclopedia: A Dictionary of Nautical Words and Phrases, Biographical Notices, and Records of Naval Officers. Prepared by officers of the Navy. Philadelphia: L. R. Hammersly, 1881.

Neeser, Robert Wilden. *Statistical and Chronological History of the United States Navy.* 2 vols. New York: Macmillan, 1909.

Noel, John V., Jr., and Edward L. Beach. *Naval Terms Dictionary.* Annapolis: Naval Institute Press, 1978.

Plunkett, R., Cdr., RN. *Modern Officer of the Watch.* 5th ed. London: John Hogg, 1913.

Smith, Logan Pearsall. *Words and Idioms: Studies in the English Language.* 4th ed. London: Constable, 1933.

Smyth, W., II, Vice Adm., RN. *Sailor's Word Book: An Alphabetical Digest of Nautical Terms.* London: Blackie and Sons, 1867.

Stavridis, James, Capt., USN. *Watch Officers Guide.* 14th ed. Annapolis: Naval Institute Press, 2000.

Regulations of the Colonial and United States Navy

1. *Rules for the Regulation of the Navy of the United Colonies; Pay Tables; Articles of Enlistment and Distribution of Prize Money.* Philadelphia, 23 November 1775. Text appears in Way and Gideon editions of Journals of American Congress, vol. 1, pp. 185–391 (Library of Congress book no. Z2:7:1), and in Journals of Continental Congress, edited from original records.

2. *Naval Regulations* (1802, reprint 1809). These are entitled *Naval Regulations Issued by Command of the President of the United States of America,* and are signed "by command, Rt. Smith, secretary" and dated 25 January 1802.

3. *Naval Regulations* (1814).

4. American State Papers. *Naval Affairs.* Vol. 1, 1794–1825, p. 512. *Rules, Regulations, and Instructions for the Naval Service.* President Monroe to the House of Representatives, 20 April 1818. Prepared by Board of Navy Commissioners in obedience to act of Congress 7 February 1815 entitled "An Act to Alter and Amend the Several Acts for Establishing a Navy Department, by Adding Thereto a Board of Commissioners." Called the "Blue Book."

5. *Report on the Rules for the Naval Service.* Sec't. Smith Thompson. 29 December 1819. Senate document no. 15, 16th Cong., 1st sess., vol. 1, "showing wherein the rules, regulations, and instructions adopted by the naval service are at variance with the existing laws, and suggesting amendment of the laws so as to make them conform."

6. *Rules and Regulations of the Naval Service.* Sec't. Smith Thompson. 11 January 1821. Senate document no. 65, 16th Cong., 2d sess., vol. 2, "the rules and regulations for the naval service prepared and reported under the authority of an act of Congress of 7 February 1815, with a schedule of alterations and additions as have been deemed necessary."

7. *The Rules of the Navy Department Regulating the Civil Administration of the Navy.* City of Washington: printed at the Globe office, by F. P. Blair, 1832. This was called the "Red Book"; the *Rules, Regulations . . .* of 1818, called the "Blue Book," was effective in 1832 for the military administration as distinguished from the civil.

8. *Rules and Regulations Prepared by the Board of Revision for the Government of the Navy.* 23 December 1833. House of Representatives executive document no. 20 and 375, 23d Cong., 1st sess., serial no. 254 and 258.

9. *Book of Regulations for Use of Commanders, Pursers, and Recruiting Officers* (1838).

10. *Financial Regulations for Naval Officers* (1838).

11. *General Regulations for Navy and Marine Corps.* Washington, D.C.: J. and G. S. Gideon, 1841. These regulations were prepared in obedience to a joint resolution of Congress, 24 May 1842, 72 Cong., 3d sess., House document no. 148, serial no. 421. Poore's reference on this is "Jan. 13, 1843, copy of proposed new regulations," Sec't. A. P. Upshur, in response to House of Representatives resolution.

12. *Regulations, Circulars, Orders and Decisions for Guide of Officers of Navy* (1851). In 1853 the *Orders and Instructions* for the Navy were declared not legal by the attorney general and were withdrawn. Poore refers to 1851 amendments necessary due to abolition of flogging in the Navy.

13. *Regulations of Navy* (1863).

14. *Regulations for Government of Navy* (1865).

15. *Regulations for Government of Navy* (1869). Various amendments and additions were issued.

16. *Regulations for Government of Navy* (1870). Various amendments and additions were issued.

17. *Regulations for Government of Navy* (1876). Various amendments and additions were issued.

18. *Regulations for Government of Navy* (1893). Various amendments and additions were issued.

19. *Regulations for Government of Navy* (1896). Various amendments and additions were issued.

20. *Regulations for Government of Navy* (1900). Various amendments and additions were issued.

21. *Regulations for Government of Navy* (1909). Various amendments and additions were issued.

The above references are listed in *Checklist of U.S. Public Documents, 1789–1909,* and *Poore's Index to U.S. Publications,* as well as appearing in original and state papers indicated.

22. *U.S. Navy Regulations* (1913). Various amendments and additions.

23. *U.S. Navy Regulations* (1973) with amendments.

24. *U.S. Navy Regulations* (1990) with amendments, which is effective at this writing.

War of 1812

Abbot, Willis J. *Blue Jackets of 1812: A History of the Naval Battles of the Second War with Great Britain.* New York: Dodd, Mead, 1887.

James, Wm. *Naval Occurrences of the Late War between Great Britain and the United States of America.* London, 1817.

Roosevelt, Theodore. *Naval War of 1812.* New York: G. P. Putnam's Sons, 1882.

Flags, Heraldry, and Arms

Book of Knowledge of All Kingdoms, Lands, and Lordships That Are in the World, and the Arms and Devices of Each Land. By a Spanish Franciscan. London: printed for the Hakluyt Society, 1912.

Boutell. *Manual of Heraldry.* London: Frederick Warne, 1931.

The Flag Code. Adopted at the National Flag Conference, 14–15 June 1923, as revised and endorsed at the Second National Flag Conference, 15 May 1924.

Johnson, Willis F. *The National Flag: A History.* Cambridge, Mass.: Houghton Mifflin, 1930.

Preble, George Henry, Rear Adm., USN. *History of the Flag of the United States of America: Symbols, Standards, Banners, and Flags of Ancient and Modern Nations.* Boston: H. Williams, 1880.

Preble, George Henry, Rear Adm., USN. *Origin and History of the American Flag.* 2 vols. Philadelphia: Nicholas L. Brown, 1907.

Rankin, Robert H. *Uniforms of the Sea Services.* Annapolis: U.S. Naval Institute, 1962.

Smith, Col. Nicholas. *Our Nation's Flag: In History and Incident.* Milwaukee: Young Churchman, 1908.

Tily, James C. *The Uniforms of the United States Navy.* New York: A. S. Barnes and Thomas Yoseloff, 1964.

United States Coast Guard

Annual Report on the Coast Guard, 1915. Washington, D.C.: U.S. Government Printing Office.

Bloomfield, Howard V. L. *The Compact History of the United States Coast Guard.* New York: Hawthorn Books, 1966.

Brown, Riley. *Men, Wind, and Sea: The Story of the Coast Guard.* New York: Carlyle House, 1939.

Commandant Instruction M5750.3. Coast Guard History, 17 June 1982.

Cross, Dale E., JOC, USCG. "In Service of Their Country and Humanity." *World Wars Officer Review,* January–February 1970.

Evans, Stephen H., Capt., USCG. *The United States Coast Guard, 1790–1915: A Definitive History.* Annapolis: Naval Institute Press, 1949.

Gurney, Gene. *The United States Coast Guard, a Pictorial History.* New York: Crown, 1973.

Johnson, Robert Erwin. *Guardians of the Seas: History of the United States Coast Guard 1915 to the Present.* Annapolis: Naval Institute Press, 1987.

King, Irving H. *George Washington's Coast Guard.* Annapolis: Naval Institute Press, 1978.

Shanks, Ralph, Lisa Woo Shanks, and Wick York. *The U.S. Life Saving Service.* Petaluma, Calif.: Costaño Books, 1996.

They That Go Down to the Sea: A Bicentennial History of the United States Coast Guard. Washington, D.C.: USCG Chief Petty Officers Association, 1990.

Social Customs, Conventions, Precedence, Etiquette, and Social Correspondence

Ageton, Arthur A., Rear Adm., USN (Ret.), and Vice Adm. William P. Mack, USN (Ret.). *The Naval Officer's Guide.* Annapolis: Naval Institute Press, 1970.

"Armiger." *Titles: Being A Guide to the Right Use of British Titles and Honours.* London: A. and C. Black, Ltd., 1918.

Burke's Genealogical and Heraldic History of Peerage, Baronetage, and Knightage. London: Burke's Peerage Ltd., 1921(?).

Castiglione, Count Baldesar. *The Book of the Courtier.* New York: Charles Scribner's Sons, 1903.

Ebbert, Jean. *Welcome Aboard.* Annapolis: Naval Institute Press, 1974.

Florio, John. *Translations of the Essayes of Michael Lord of Montaigne.* New York: AMS Press, 1967.

Jacobsen, K. C., Cdr., USN. *The Watch Officer's Guide.* Annapolis: Naval Institute Press, 1979.

Kornitzer, Bela. *The Great American Heritage: The Story of the Five Eisenhower Brothers.* New York: Farrar, Straus and Cudahy, 1955.

Meyers, Elizabeth. *The Social Letter.* New York: Brentano's, 1918.

Military Discipline, Courtesies, and Customs of the Service. West Point Monograph. West Point, 1930.

Post, Emily. *Etiquette.* New York: Funk and Wagnalls, 1959.

Regulations of the Navy, Army, and Foreign Service

Satow, Sir Ernest Mason. *A Guide to Diplomatic Practices.* New York: Longmans, Green, 1917.

Skerrett, Robert G. "The Baptism of Ships." U.S. Naval Institute *Proceedings,* June 1909.

Swartz, Oretha D. *Service Etiquette.* 3d rev. ed. Annapolis: Naval Institute Press, 1977.

Wedertz, Bill, and Bill Bearden. *Bluejacket's Manual.* 20th rev. ed. Annapolis: Naval Institute Press, 1978.

Welfare, Recreation and Morale, Dining-In. Department of the Army, U.S. Army Command and General Staff College, Fort Leavenworth, Kans., Pamphlet 28-1, 15 March 1985.

Whitaker's Peerage, Baronetage, Knightage, and Companionage. 1933.

Ships and Naval Prints, Sea Paintings, Etc.

Chatterton, E. Keble. *Old Sea Paintings.* New York: Dodd Mead, 1928.

Chatterton, E. Keble. *Old Ship Prints.* New York: Dodd Mead and Co., 1927.

Colasanti, J. M. *Our Navy and Defenders.* Portsmouth, Va., 1905–6.

Culver, Henry B., with drawings by Gordon Grant. *The Book of Old Ships.* Garden City, N.Y.: Doubleday, Page, 1924.

Laughton, L. G. Carr. *Old Ship Figure-Heads and Sterns.* New York: Minton Balch, 1925.

Walton, William, and others. *The Army and Navy of the United States 1776–1890.* Philadelphia: George Barrie, 1890.

Zogbaum, Rufus Fairchild. *All Hands.* New York: Harper and Bros., 1897.

Miscellaneous

Bone, David W., Capt. *Capstan Bars.* Edinburgh: Porpoise Press, 1931.

Freuchen, Peter. *Book of the Seven Seas.* New York: Julian Messner, 1957.

Paullin, C. O. *Paullin's History of Naval Administration.* Annapolis: Naval Institute Press, 1968.

Richmond, Sir Herbert, Vice Adm., RN. *Command and Discipline.* London: John Murray, 1927.

Shuon, K. *U.S. Marine Corps Biographical Dictionary.* New York: Franklin Watts, 1963.

Shuon, K. *U.S. Navy Biographical Dictionary.* New York: Franklin Watts, 1964.

Van Denburgh, Elizabeth Douglas. *My Voyage in the United States Frigate "Congress."* New York: Desmond Fitzgerald, 1913.

Index

About the Authors

Cdr. Royal W. Connell Jr., USN (Ret.), graduated from the Naval Academy in 1970 and was designated a surface warfare officer in 1971 while serving as the damage control assistant aboard USS *Vreeland* (DE 1068). In 1972 he reported for flight training in Pensacola, Florida, receiving his naval flight officer wings at NAS Glenco, Georgia, in December 1973. He was a plank owner in Carrier Airborne Early Warning Squadron One Hundred Seventeen (VAW 117) in San Diego and following an instructor tour at the Naval Academy flew as a mission commander in the E-2C with Carrier Airborne Early Warning Squadron One Hundred Twenty Six (VAW 126). He then was assigned as chief staff officer for Carrier Airborne Early Warning Wing Twelve at NAS Norfolk. In 1986 he received orders to Washington, D.C., as the deputy for career progressions at the Bureau of Naval Personnel. In 1989 Commander Connell reported to the staff of the Naval Academy as the administrative and personnel officer where he also performed duties as the officer representative for the Naval Academy Drum and Bugle Corps. Upon retirement in 1993, he became the first senior naval science instructor for the Naval Junior ROTC Unit, Annapolis Senior High School. His lifelong interest in ceremonies, customs, and traditions began as a youth when he accompanied his father to Tel Aviv, Israel, where the latter was serving as the U.S. Air Attaché.

Vice Adm. William P. Mack, USN (Ret.), served in the U.S. Navy during World War II and the Korean and Vietnam wars, commanding the Seventh Fleet during the mining of Haiphong Harbor. He began his naval career as a midshipman at the Naval Academy, class of 1937, and ended it as vice admiral and academy superintendent in 1975. He served in battleships, destroyers, and amphibious forces. His many assignments included chief of information, chief of legislative affairs, and deputy assistant secretary of defense.

Among Admiral Mack's many books are a Book-of-the-Month Club award winner titled *South to Java*, which he wrote with his son. He is also the recipient of the Navy League's Alfred Thayer Mahan Award, among other literary awards. Admiral Mack passed away in January 2003.